Legal Editing *and* Proofreading

Applying Critical Thinking and Language Skills

Lynda D. Ernst
South Central College
Mankato, Minnesota

Susan M. Kolbinger
Farrish Johnson Law Office, Chtd.
Mankato, Minnesota

St. Paul • Indianapolis

Editorial Director:	Sonja Brown
Managing Editor:	Christine Hurney
Developmental Editors:	Carley Bomstad, Brenda Owens
Copy Editor:	Heidi Thaens
Production Editor:	Bob Dreas
Proofreader:	Judy M. Peterson
Cover Designer:	Leslie Anderson
Text Designer:	Jaana Bykonich
Indexer:	Ina Gravitz

Care has been taken to verify the accuracy of information presented in this book. However, the authors, editors, and publisher cannot accept responsibility for Web, email, newsgroup, or chat room subject matter or content, or for consequences from application of the information in this book, and make no warranty, expressed or implied, with respect to its content.

Trademarks: Some of the product names and company names included in this book have been used for identification purposes only and may be trademarks or registered trade names of their respective manufacturers and sellers. The authors, editors, and publisher disclaim any affiliation, association, or connection with, or sponsorship or endorsement by, such owners.

We have made every effort to trace the ownership of all copyrighted material and to secure permission from copyright holders. In the event of any question arising as to the use of any material, we will be pleased to make the necessary corrections in future printings. Thanks are due to the aforementioned authors, publishers, and agents for permission to use the materials indicated.

ISBN 978-0-76384-411-0 (Textbook, CD, and DVD)
ISBN 978-0-76384-208-6 (Textbook)

© 2012 by Paradigm Publishing, Inc.
875 Montreal Way
St. Paul, MN 55102
Email: educate@emcp.com
Website: www.emcp.com

Printed in the United States of America

20 19 18 17 16 15 14 13 12 11   1 2 3 4 5 6 7 8 9 10

Table of Contents

Legal Editing and Proofreading: Applying Critical Thinking and Language Skills is intended to be used as an advanced review and intense practice in proofreading, editing, and critical thinking to prepare for work in the legal office. The book uses true-to-life scenarios and projects from the major areas of law to help students produce accurate, error-free documents that also may require making judgments and decisions during the editing process.

Chapter work is based upon the major areas of law practice: civil litigation; family and domestic relations; criminal law; appeals; real estate; business, corporate, and employment; estate planning and probate; and bankruptcy. The chapter projects are supported with detailed instructions for completing the procedures. Although students should follow these instructions when completing the projects, the procedures may not be exactly as they are in your jurisdiction, and students are encouraged to research differences between the procedures outlined in the textbook and their local jurisdiction's procedures and format requirements.

Students who complete this course of study should be job-ready to work in a variety of law office settings. By working through the textbook's exercises and projects, students are encouraged to reflect on their career goals and to develop a portfolio designed to highlight their legal editing and proofreading skills.

Chapter Features

The chapter features are designed to engage students and to provide the study tools they will need to succeed in this course.

Overview of Area of Law

The chapters that focus on an area of law practice begin with an overview of that area of law. This overview reinforces legal terminology and aspects of practice that provide an important context for the exercises and projects that follow.

Language Focus

All of the chapters, except the capstone chapter, include a Language Focus section. The focus of these valuable sections begins in Chapter 1 with parts of speech, continues with spelling in Chapter 2, and progresses through reviews and reminders of such topics as possessives; pronoun choices; subject, verb, and pronoun agreement; to punctuation. The Language Focus sections include exercises allowing the students to practice their editing skills in the context of the area of law for the chapter.

Editing

The textbook guides the study and development of editing skills in the Editing section of the chapters. Editing topics include understanding the document's audience, effective formatting, effective use of transitions, application of house styles, and appropriate use of active and passive voice. Editing work is done in the legal context appropriate for the chapter.

Proofreading

The Proofreading sections include discussions about the difference between editing and proofreading, methods of proofreading, double and triple checking numbers, and fact checking. Each section includes exercises to allow practice of these important skills.

How-To Guides

In addition to detailed instructions for all of the chapter exercises and projects, the text has a section called the How-To Guide for each area of law. The How-To

Guides include additional detail about the documents for a particular area of law and examples of how to complete the projects in the chapter.

Portfolio Approach

Students are encouraged to develop a portfolio of the work completed throughout the course, and portfolio icons in the margins identify the exercises, projects, and reference materials that could be included in a portfolio. The students can use the portfolio as a demonstration of their skills when looking for a position in a law office or as a reference tool once they obtain their first positions in a legal office.

Local Focus Exercises

Each legal jurisdiction has specific procedural and formatting requirements. Because it would be impossible to cover them all in the textbook, the chapters include Local Focus exercises, which guide student research about applicable local jurisdiction's procedures and format requirements. The goal of these research activities is to help the students develop their problem-solving and research skills. Local Focus icons highlight places where the discussion is specific to the state used in the textbook's project. The icon reminds students that they will be asked later to research and find how their own state handles the situation. To aid student Local Focus research, the textbook's Internet Resource center at www.paradigmcollege.net/lep provides links to several helpful online resources.

Critical Thinking Focus

Employers want to hire prospective employees who can think for themselves. This textbook is intended to take the student beyond the basic learning and skill development provided in the earlier semesters or quarters of their education. Included in each chapter are prompts for students to think deeper about the concept and to visualize what would actually need to be done in a given situation. Exercises are included in each critical thinking section to allow the students practice in thinking beyond the instructions given. Following the end-of-chapter projects is a section asking students to reflect on the projects they have just completed. These questions are ideal for class discussion.

Best Practice Tips

The Best Practice Tips feature is intended to offer students insight into their prospective careers and provide suggestions on how to effectively manage their work and responsibilities. Because of the complexity of the law, students will benefit from the advice given in these tips from experienced office professionals. These tips focus on advanced skills to give students a head start in their new jobs.

End-of-Chapter Practice and Projects

Along with a review of the law, each chapter includes practice exercises and projects in which students can apply their proofreading, editing, and critical thinking skills. The length of the projects is intended to give students a preview of the true workload in an office setting. Students will be expected to accumulate their knowledge as they progress through this book, and thus projects become more complicated in the later chapters.

Capstone Projects

The capstone projects in the last chapter of the text are designed to test students' knowledge from previous chapters and to apply critical thinking skills as well as editing and proofreading skills to a variety of legal documents. Projects based on the companion *Court Is In Session* DVD are included.

Resource Section

The appendix includes a style guide that students will need to reference in order to complete projects correctly. Students are to assume that they work for the law firm of Jordan, Leone, & Sanchez. The style guide includes law office details, such as names, addresses, phone numbers, letter and document formatting, signature block formatting, and a section on how to handle dates in exercises and projects in this book. A glossary of terms and definitions is included at the back of the text to reinforce key legal terminology.

Student Resources

Students will find additional content to support the textbook in the following components.

Student Resources CD

A Student Resources disc is provided with every copy of the textbook and contains resources needed to complete exercises and projects found in the textbook. Students will need to create chapter folders on their own storage medium and save their corrected and revised files in these folders.

Court Is In Session DVD

Also provided with the textbook, the *Court Is In Session* DVD consists of a reenactment of an appeal in the case of *State of Minnesota v. Sara Peck* presided over by a group of Minnesota Appellate Court judges. The textbook's capstone chapter includes projects based upon the *Court Is In Session* case.

Internet Resource Center

Students will find additional learning tools and reference materials posted on the course-specific Internet Resource Center at www.paradigmcollege.net/lep. Students can access the data files provided on the Student Resources CD along with study aids and web links.

Instructor Resources

Instructor resources are available in the printed *Instructor's Guide*, on the Instructor's Resources disc, and on the password-protected instructor area of the Internet Resource Center at www.paradigmcollege.net/lep. These materials include:
- Syllabus suggestions and course planning resources
- Teaching tips for each chapter
- Answer keys for chapter exercises and projects

Also Available

Paradigm's popular *Legal Transcription, Third Edition*, by Linda R. Lyle and G. Howard Doty, teaches the most current practices for transcribing and revising legal documents with correct formatting, punctuation, and spelling.

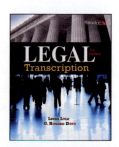

Acknowledgments

The authors would like to thank the following contributors, reviewers, and many others who have provided their ideas and support throughout the development of this textbook and ancillary materials. In addition, the authors thank the publishing and editing staff at EMC Paradigm Publishing for their professionalism, creative insight, and encouragement.

Contributors

Farrish Johnson Law Office, Chtd.
    Aaron J. Glade, Attorney
    Ashlie Byron, Legal Assistant
    Connie Froehlich, Legal Assistant
    Daniel Bellig, Attorney
    David A. Salsbery, Attorney
    Ginny Mosher, Legal Assistant
    Howard F. Haugh, Attorney
    Joanna Pell, Paralegal
    Kay L. Wallerich, Attorney
    Mary Anne Wray, Attorney
    Matthew Lutz, Attorney
    Monique Koomen, Legal Assistant
    Nancy Dorn, Receptionist and Legal Support
    Norma Heckman, Legal Assistant
    Patrick J. Casey, Attorney
    Randall J. Knutson, Attorney
    Scott V. Kelly, Attorney
    Steven H. Fink, Attorney
    William S. Partridge, Attorney
    Wyatt Partridge, Attorney
    Jay Ramos, Attorney
    Cathy Sargent, Legal Assistant

South Central College, North Mankato and Faribault, Minnesota

Colleagues in the Administrative Office and Technology Department at South Central College

Ignition Media, Andy Lundquist, Owner

Andrew Tatge, Attorney, Gislason & Hunter

Minnesota Court of Appeals
    Chief Judge Edward Toussaint
    Judge Terri Stoneburner
    Judge Jill Halbrooks
    Judge Natalie Hudson

American Way Realty
    Karla VanEman, Realtor
    Gail Stelter, Administrative Assistant
    Mary Caven, Administrative Assistant

Cynthia Brouwer, Legal Assistant, Lamm, Nelson & Cich

Melissa Stafford, Minnesota Valley Federal Credit Union

Rosengren & Kohlmeyer
    Diana Brauch, Legal Assistant
    Jason Kohlmeyer, Attorney

Lori Anderson, Legal Assistant, Patton, Hoversten & Berg

Tina Johnson, Paralegal, Gray, Plant, Mooty, Law Firm

Chesley, Kroon, Harvey & Carpenter—Lawyers
    Amanda Lokken, Legal Assistant
    Carla Ulrich, Office Manager
    Marlys Wolfgram, Legal Assistant

Kathy Conlon, Nicollet (Minn.) County Recorder

Denise Drill, Court Reporter

Lori Meixell, Court Reporter

Sharon Monshaugen, Minnesota State Patrol

Benjamin Bejar, Assistant Faribault County Attorney

Allen Eskens, Attorney, Eskens, Gibson & Behm, Law Firm, Chtd.

Bradford Delapena, Public Defender

Kenneth R. White, Attorney

Carrie Marsh Leone, Public Defender

Cora Hamann, Legal Assistant, Calvin Johnson Law Office

Toronto Globe and Mail

Bachman Legal Printing, Minneapolis, Minnesota

Paul Grabitske, Attorney, Kakeldey & Koberoski

Joseph M. Barnett, Attorney, Foley & Mansfield

Peggy Armstrong

Kathy Morrison, Halverson Law Office

Reviewers

Tammie Bolling
  Tennessee Technology Center at Jacksboro
  Jacksboro, Tennessee

Shawn Friend
  Daytona State College
  Daytona Beach, Florida

Jennifer Gornicki
  Macomb Community College
  Warren, Michigan

Cathy Kennedy
  MSB-GU and Kaplan University
  Brooklyn Center, Minnesota

Susan McCabe
  Kellogg Community College
  Battle Creek, Michigan

Elizabeth L. Nobis
  Lansing Community College
  Lansing, Michigan

Joy O'Donnell
  Pima Community College
  Tucson, Arizona

The authors and editorial staff look forward to hearing from students and educators with questions, suggestions, or comments about the text, supplements, and instructor's materials. You may contact us at educate@emcp.com.

Dedication

To our husbands, Bo and Mike. Thank you both for your constant encouragement, ideas, feedback, and patience.

To our families, friends, coworkers, and employers for their enthusiasm and moral support.

About the Authors

Lynda Ernst holds a bachelor's degree from St. Cloud State University and a master's degree in education, business, from the University of Minnesota. She has worked as an instructor at South Central College in North Mankato, Minnesota, since 1984 and designed and teaches the Legal Administrative Assistant program in the Department of Administrative Office and Technology. In addition, she teaches face-to-face and online classes in business English, business communications, and Microsoft office applications. Lynda served for 15 years as a student advisor involved in the Business Professionals of America and for three years as chair of the board of directors of the Minnesota Associate of Business Professionals of America, College Division. Lynda's dedication to teaching earned her the teacher of the year award at South Central College and the Minnesota state advisor of the year in Business Professionals of America.

Susan Kolbinger has worked as a litigation legal assistant since 1978 in the areas of personal injury, insurance defense, contract litigation, multi-district class actions, employment litigation, complex bankruptcy and construction litigation, and federal court litigation. Susan is currently a legal assistant at Farrish Johnson Law Office, Chtd., in Mankato, Minnesota. In addition to co-authoring this book, she has served on the Administrative and Office Technology Department Advisory Committee at South Central College since 1998. Susan is a mentoring advocate and frequently mentors recently graduated lawyers and legal support staff, and she volunteers as an e-mentor to students in the legal administrative assistant program at South Central College.

Legal Editing and Proofreading

Chapter Objectives

- Locate helpful resources for grammar and spelling questions
- Understand the importance of editing, proofreading, and critical thinking in the legal office
- Identify the difference between editing and proofreading skills
- Identify common editing and proofreading marks

How often have you encountered misspellings and grammatical errors in letters and emails from your friends and family? How often do you find errors in books, magazine articles, and advertisements? There is a reason why you are less likely to find errors in published and printed material, and that is because nearly all companies hire editors and proofreaders to review written matter that will be distributed to consumers. Most companies succeed when consumers seek out their products and services. A law firm is no different. In order to be successful, a legal office must provide quality services, and this includes ensuring that documents are accurate and timely. In most legal offices, the legal support staff serve as editors and proofreaders. They are expected to assist the office in creating error-free documents.

Editing, proofreading, and critical thinking are three of the most important skills that you can have as an employee of any office. Your employer will have hired you because of your specialized skills, including your knowledge of legal procedures, your ability to find and correct overlooked errors in a legal document, and your ability to plan ahead. Working to make a legal document or communication complete and understandable—as well as working efficiently with clients and your co-workers—is what makes a career in a legal office challenging and interesting.

Detail-based skills and a firm understanding of grammar and spelling are just as important as how fast you type and whether you can use your computer efficiently.

Throughout this course, you will review and practice key concepts of the English language, editing, proofreading, and critical thinking. Applying these skills to your work will make you indispensable in the office.

Language Focus: The Importance of Grammar

Although many people may feel confident in their understanding of the English language, others may feel less so in applying grammatical rules to their work. Legal writing is expected to conform to the highest standards of the English language. Poorly written documents and correspondence reflect badly on a law office and its employees. A member of the legal support staff who consistently overlooks or introduces errors in legal documents will find it difficult to stay employed.

The Sentence and Parts of Speech

For many people, grammar instruction ended in grade school and the knowledge that they retained was developed and maintained in their everyday speech and writing. Although many grammatical errors can be caught because they do not sound right, a legal support person should understand the rules behind any grammatical corrections he or she makes within a legal document. To understand English grammar and common language rules, it is important to be familiar with the parts of speech (such as nouns and verbs). Use Table 1.1 to quickly review the most basic parts of speech. You will need to fully understand these definitions as you review and practice other grammatical rules.

Note that a **sentence** is a group of words that expresses a complete thought. Every sentence must contain a **subject**, which tells whom or what the sentence is about, and a **predicate**, which indicates information about the subject—what the subject is, what the subject does, and/or what happens to the subject.

> The attorney | hired a new employee.
>   subject | predicate

A **phrase** is a word group that does not have both a subject and a verb. A **clause** is a group of words that contains a subject and a verb; clauses can be either dependent or independent. A **dependent clause** (or subordinate clause) cannot stand on its own as a complete sentence, but an **independent clause** can stand alone.

> **Phrase:** In the morning, the judge will request our testimony.
>
> **Dependent clause:** We will be able to finish the project on time if you review the details.
>
> **Independent clause:** We will call the client after you have finalized the document.

A sentence can be declarative, exclamatory, imperative, or interrogative. A **declarative sentence** makes a statement and ends in a period. An **exclamatory sentence** expresses strong feeling and typically ends in an exclamation point. An **imperative sentence** makes a request or gives an order. An imperative sentence has an understood subject (often *you*) and ends in either a period or a question mark. An **interrogative sentence** asks a question and ends in a question mark.

Table 1.1 Parts of Speech

Part of Speech	Definition	Example
Noun	A **noun** names a person, place, thing, or idea.	Our **client** met **Attorney Marks** at the **courthouse** to discuss the **lawsuit**.
Pronoun	A **pronoun** is used in place of a noun.	As our client told **her** side of the story, the jury leaned forward in **their** chairs.
Verb	A **verb** expresses action or a state of being.	In our office, the attorneys usually **arrive** before 8 a.m. and **are** pleased when the legal assistants **do** so as well.
Adjective	An **adjective** modifies a noun or pronoun.	A **fine** worker, Clark understood that **worried** clients were likely to make mistakes when they answered the most **difficult** questions.
Article	An **article** precedes a noun. The most common articles are *a*, *an*, and *the*.	**The** letters arrived in **a** box holding eight envelopes tied with **an** aquamarine ribbon.
Adverb	An **adverb** modifies a verb, an adjective, or another adverb.	We **carefully** noted the court instructions and contacted the **already** nervous client.
Preposition	A **preposition** shows the relationship between its object—a noun or a pronoun—and another word in a sentence. Common prepositions include *after, around, at, behind, beside, off, through, until, upon*, and *with*.	Many workers **within** a legal office will not be satisfied **until** they receive a glowing review from their supervisor.
Conjunction	A **conjunction** joins words or groups of words. Common conjunctions are *and, but, for, nor, or, so*, and *yet*.	I wanted to meet with my supervisor before noon today, **but** she was occupied with our client all morning.
Interjection	An **interjection** is a word used to express emotion. Common interjections are *oh, ah, well, hey*, and *wow*.	**Well**, I think the attorney's letter is incomplete and misleading.

Helpful Resources

Print and online references will be a valuable part of your office setup. An office worker must be an investigator. If you do not know the answers to specific grammar or style questions, you will need to locate resources to answer these questions. If you can find such information quickly and efficiently, your employer will appreciate it. Consider the following list of possible types of resources to which you can turn to when you have a particular question on grammar, style, or spelling.

County websites

Court websites

Regular and legal dictionaries
 (print and online)

Federal and state rules of court

State websites and search engines

Style manuals and guides

Telephone books

Thesauruses

You will benefit from applying your skills of critical thinking when you select resources, especially those online. Consider the type of website you are visiting. Ask yourself, is this a legitimate resource? Is there another, more appropriate resource? Who created this website and is it a source I can trust? Always make certain that you are visiting official government websites when you are searching for court rules and deadlines.

You may find that your office has an in-house style guide. If it does, you will have to follow the style specifications listed there. If no guide exists, you will probably be instructed to follow a well-known style manual such as *The Chicago Manual of Style*, 16th ed.; *The Elements of Style*, 4th ed., by William Strunk, Jr., and E. B. White; or *The Redbook: A Manual on Legal Style*, 2nd ed., by Bryan A. Garner, Jeff Newman, and Tiger Jackson.

In-House Style Guides

An in-house style guide is the best resource for style questions and typically trumps all other available style manuals. Any employee will benefit from committing the in-house style to memory and following the expected formatting set forth by the office.

Language Focus Exercises

Reviewing and applying the information from the Language Focus Exercises will help you to become more confident in your work. Apply what you have learned to the following exercises.

Exercise 1.1 Read through the following sentences. Draw a vertical line between the subject and the predicate and identify the sentence type (declarative, exclamatory, imperative, or interrogative) in the space provided.

Example:　Our legal office / is hiring a new legal support person.

declarative

1. The client information form has to go out tonight!

2. You need to proofread this letter before you leave today.

_____

3. Is our client aware that the court date has changed?

_____

4. I would like you to call the courthouse.

_____

5. The document was served prior to the court deadline.

_____

Exercise 1.2 Consider the list of possible grammar and style resources discussed previously in this section. Go to your web browser and locate examples of each of the listed resources on the Internet. After reviewing what is available, determine which websites would be the most helpful in a legal office and bookmark the identified websites in your browser. List these websites in the space provided and include a brief description of each. Discuss with your class the websites you visited and which you believe will be the most useful.

_____

_____

_____

_____

_____

_____

_____

_____

Exercise 1.3 Legal support staff should try to schedule about 30 minutes once a month to review the rules of grammar and punctuation. The following links are possible sites to visit when you schedule this time. Review each of these websites and create a bookmark so that you can find them quickly in the future. After you have reviewed these sites, discuss with your class which one you believe is the most useful.

http://grammar.ccc.commnet.edu/grammar/
http://www.grammarbook.com/
http://grammar.quickanddirtytips.com/
www.lep.emcp.net/

Editing: What Is Editing?

Legal support staff will be required to both edit and proofread legal materials. These materials will have been created by the attorney(s), other legal support staff, or you. Attorneys who create the written work are thinking about how to solve a legal problem. Once they draft the document, they may do a cursory edit. However, they typically pass the document to a member of the legal support staff for final editing and proofreading.

Editing a document means preparing it for publication or presentation by correcting, revising, or adapting its contents. A document is **proofread** when it is considered final; this is done to detect and correct original or introduced errors. People sometimes use the two terms interchangeably; however, it is important to note that editing is *not* the same as proofreading. Although both processes require close attention to detail, they serve different purposes and focus on different types of errors.

After writing the first draft, a writer begins the revision stage. This means going back over the document and deciding if it is organized correctly and if it was written concisely and accurately. Editing can be done by the original author or by someone else. In either instance, the editor needs to focus on a number of issues within the document. Table 1.2 indicates four common writing problems and the questions that an editor should ask to resolve them.

Table 1.2 Issues to Consider While Editing a Document

Issue	Questions to Consider
Clarity	Is the writing clear and concise? Are the ideas presented in a logical manner?
Consistency	Are elements treated consistently throughout? Are the tone and tense consistent and appropriate?
Content	Is the content of the document complete and accurate?
Style	Does the document adhere to the in-house style rules?

Editing Electronic Files

Editing can be done either electronically or on hard copy. Each office will have its own process or procedure for editing documents. In most cases, your work will be done directly in the main file and saved as the newest version. You may be required to track your edits using the track-changes feature offered in most word processing programs. By tracking changes electronically, you can allow others to accept or reject the changes you make to the file. Comment features allow you to query the original writer if you have questions or suggestions, although you may be instructed to type these notations directly into the file.

Depending on the input method (attorney dictating, attorney drafting at the computer, or attorney drafting on paper), you may need to revise documents containing handwritten notes and changes as well as to respond to dictated instructions.

Figure 1.1 shows a short excerpt of an electronic file that has been edited using a track-changes feature. The inserted text is underlined and deleted text is marked as strike-through. In this file, multiple editors have made changes, so each editor's corrections are identified in a different color.

Figure 1.1 **Electronic Editing Sample**

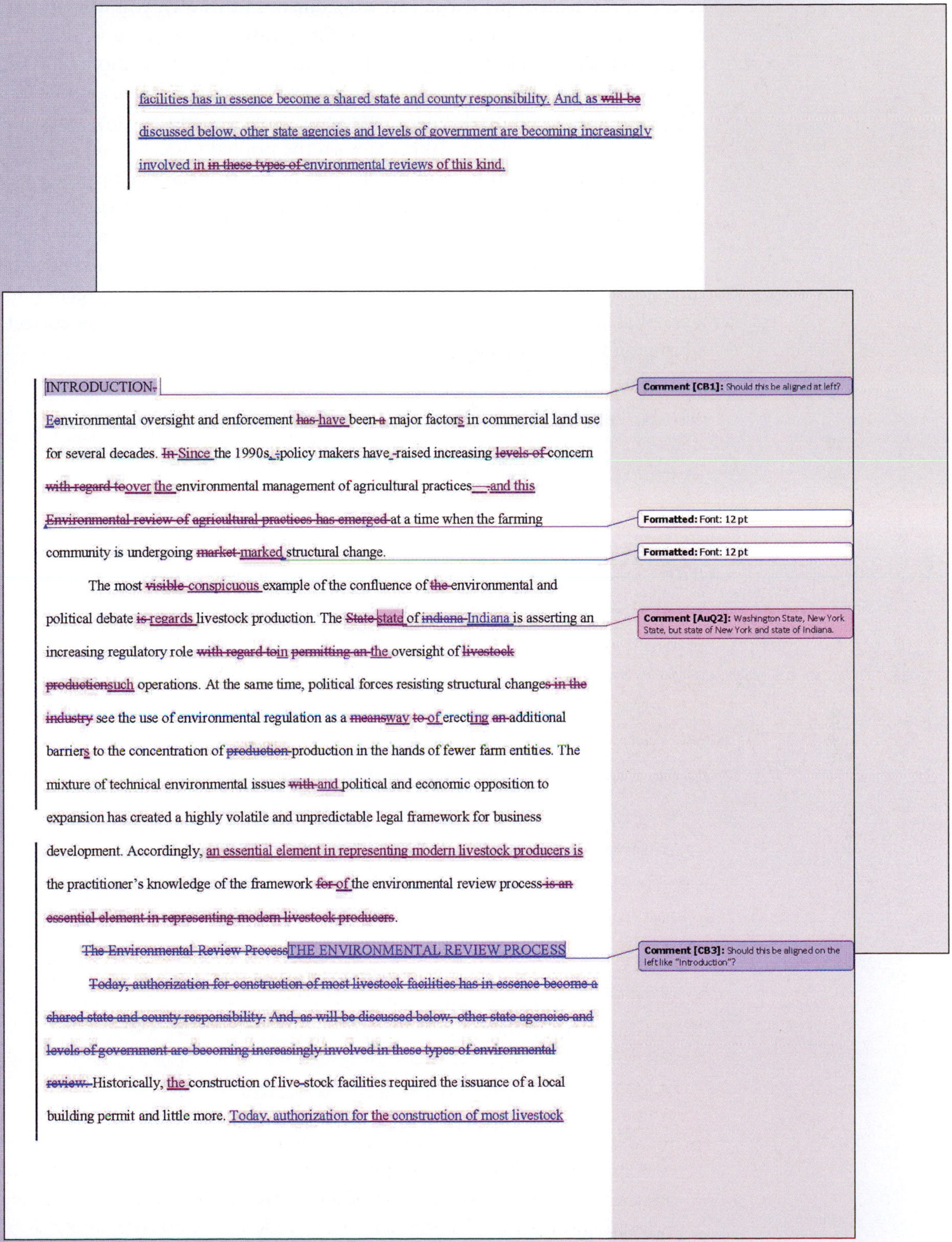

facilities has in essence become a shared state and county responsibility. And, as will be discussed below, other state agencies and levels of government are becoming increasingly involved in in these types of environmental reviews of this kind.

INTRODUCTION.

Comment [CB1]: Should this be aligned at left?

Eenvironmental oversight and enforcement has have been a major factors in commercial land use for several decades. In Since the 1990s, :policy makers have -raised increasing levels of concern with regard to over the environmental management of agricultural practices—-and this Environmental review of agricultural practices has emerged at a time when the farming community is undergoing market marked structural change.

Formatted: Font: 12 pt

Formatted: Font: 12 pt

The most visible conspicuous example of the confluence of the environmental and political debate is regards livestock production. The State state of indiana Indiana is asserting an increasing regulatory role with regard to in permitting an the oversight of livestock production such operations. At the same time, political forces resisting structural changes in the industry see the use of environmental regulation as a means way to of erecting an additional barriers to the concentration of production production in the hands of fewer farm entities. The mixture of technical environmental issues with and political and economic opposition to expansion has created a highly volatile and unpredictable legal framework for business development. Accordingly, an essential element in representing modern livestock producers is the practitioner's knowledge of the framework for of the environmental review process is an essential element in representing modern livestock producers.

Comment [AuQ2]: Washington State, New York State, but state of New York and state of Indiana.

The Environmental Review Process THE ENVIRONMENTAL REVIEW PROCESS

Comment [CB3]: Should this be aligned on the left like "Introduction"?

Today, authorization for construction of most livestock facilities has in essence become a shared state and county responsibility. And, as will be discussed below, other state agencies and levels of government are becoming increasingly involved in these types of environmental review. Historically, the construction of live-stock facilities required the issuance of a local building permit and little more. Today, authorization for the construction of most livestock

Editing Hard Copy

Although less common than working with electronic files, you may be asked to edit a document in hard copy. If you edit a document in this way, you will either turn your changes over to the document's creator for approval and/or you will transfer your corrections into an electronic file. Editing in hard copy can be more tedious than editing in electronic documents as the edits will need to be legible and complete. Notes or queries will need to be written in the margin and any major reworking might be difficult in the available space on the printed page.

Figure 1.2 is a short excerpt of a hard-copy file that has been edited by hand. Note that because of the lack of space and the need for both clarity and speed, shortcuts are used by editors and proofreaders to demonstrate changes quickly. Table 1.3 provides a list of these marks, typically called proofreader's marks. Since neither time nor space allows the proofreader or editor to explain each correction in detail, a set of standard marks was developed to indicate the most common corrections in editing and proofreading.

Figure 1.2 **Excerpt of a hand-edited document**

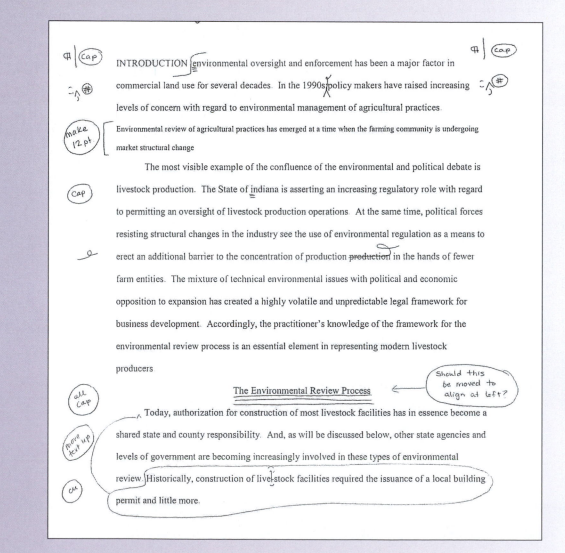

Table 1.3 Proofreader's Marks

Symbol	Definition
Operational Signs	
ℓ̲	Delete
◯	Close up; delete space
ℓ̲	Delete and close up
#	Insert space
(eq.#)	Make space between words equal; make leading between lines equal
¶	Begin new paragraph
(No ¶)	Run paragraphs together
▱	Em space
⊐	Move right
⊏	Move left
] [	Center
⊓	Move up
⊔	Move down
≈	Straighten type; align horizontally
‖	Aligh vertically
tr	Transpose
(Sp)	Spell out
(stet)	Let it stand
Typographical Signs	
lc	Lowercase capital letter
cap	Capitalize lowercase letter
sc	Set in small capitals
ital	Set in italic type
∧	Omission, insert
rom	Set in roman type
bf	Set in boldface type
wf	Wrong font; set in correct type
x	Reset broken letter
Punctuation Marks	
⌄	Insert comma
⋁	Insert apostrophe (or single quotation mark)
(set)?	Insert question mark
;	Insert semicolon
:	Insert colon
‐	Insert hyphen
$\frac{1}{N}$	Insert em dash
$\frac{1}{M}$	Insert en dash

Either the original writer or another person may edit a document. It is often more efficient for a person other than the original writer to edit a document, as the original writer may not recognize his or her own errors.

Editing Exercises

Use the information you have learned to complete the following exercise.

Exercise 1.4 Read through the paragraphs below and answer the questions that follow. Explain your reasoning for each question and offer suggestions on how the work could be improved.

> THE STATE OF MINNESOTA TO JOSEPH JOHN WALKER, THE ABOVE-NAMED RESPONDENT, 1824 ROSE, MANKATO, MN 56001:
>
> YOU ARE HEREBY SUMMONED and required to serve upon Petitioner's attorneys within thirty (30) days after service of this Summons upon you, exclusive of the day of service, an Answer to the Petition for Dissolution of Marriage which is herewith served upon you.
>
> So, if you fail to do so, Judgment by Default will be taken against you for the relief demanded in the petition for dissolution of marriage. This proceeding Involves, affects or brings in question real property situated in the City of Mankato, County of Blue Earth, State of Minnesota, legally described as follows:
>
> Lot Seven (7), Block Three (5) of the Kenwood Subdivision, City of , County of Blue Earth, State of NewYorkMinnesota

1. Is the writing clear and concise?

_____

_____

_____

_____

2. Are elements treated consistently throughout?

_____

_____

_____

_____

3. Is the content of the document complete and accurate?

_____

_____

_____

_____

4. What questions would you ask to confirm that the elements in the example conform to the formatting used in your office?

_____

_____

_____

_____

Proofreading: What Is Proofreading?

Editing and proofreading are separate and unique steps in the revision process. Proofreading should not occur until after all editing revisions have been made and the document is in its final form. Although rare, it is possible that errors could have been introduced during the editing process, so proofreading serves as the office's last line of defense against mistakes. A proofreader checks for misspelled words, grammatical errors, and punctuation.

If it is your responsibility to edit a document, do not proofread at the same time. If you proofread while you edit, you may focus on one type of mistake over another. When you are required to do both steps, retrain your brain to edit first and proofread the document after you have accepted your editing changes. You must recognize that you will proofread after editing and allow your mind to consider the larger issues of formatting and content during the editing process.

The remaining chapters in this text will introduce you to tips, tricks, and methods for proofreading. Try the different methods until you have a system that allows you to find as many errors as possible in the shortest period of time.

Best Practice Tip

HOW NECESSARY IS PROOFREADING?

Does it matter whether you proofread or not? Do not fall into the trap of thinking that proofreading is someone else's responsibility. Others may judge you and your employer based on how well the office's documents and correspondence are written. You are the one who must verify that any given document is making the best impression.

Proofreading Exercise

Complete the following exercise using the tips described previously.

Exercise 1.5 Practice using proofreader's marks by proofreading the following excerpt. Try to familiarize yourself with the marks in Table 1.3, as you may find them helpful in your future career.

Figure 1.3 **Exercise**

STATE OF MINNESOTA   IN DISTRICT COURT

COUNTY OF RENVILLE   EIGHTH JUDICIAL DISTRICT

                                                    CASE TYPE: DISSOLUTION WITH CHILDREN

                                                                        COURT FILE NO. F9-21-753

In Re the Marriage of:

Elizabeth M. Sampson,

                              petitioner,

and

David W. Sampson,

                              Respondent.

   1. The petitioner and respondent and respondent were duly married on February 19, 2001, in Fairfax, Minnesota.

   2. The parties' marriage was terminated with the entry of a Judgment and Decree of Dissolution on September 1, 2003.

   3. Petitioner, Elizabeth M. Simpson, was represented in these proceedings by Peter A. Clark of Clark & Clark Law, 91 South Main Street, Olivia, MN 56911; respondant, David W. Sampson was represented by Francesca Leone of Jordan, Leone & Sanchez, PLLP, 14937 Fairway Drive, Mankato, MN 56001

   4. The Order for Judgment and Decree was signed by the Honorable Terri j. Stoneburner.

   5. The Judgment and Decree resulted from a Stipulation.

      6.   The Judgment and Decree did not change the name of either party.

   7. The legal description of the real estate affected by the Judgment and Decree is as follows:

continues

Figure 1.3 **Exercise** *continued*

South 89 feet of West 142 feet of Southeast Quarter of Northwest Quarter of South west Quarter (SE1/4 of NW1/4 of SW1/4) of Section 22, Township 31, Range 14, Renville County, Minnesota.

8.　　　　　　　Names of persons awarded an interest in each parcel of real estate is as follows:

Interest Awarded To   Description of Interest

David W. Sampson   All right, title and interest in the real
                                       estate described at paragraph 7 above
                                       in fee simple

9.　The above-described real estate is subject to a mortgage as follows:

Mortgage in favor of Sears Mort. Corporation with a principle balance due and knowing in the approximate amount of $58,000.00.

Approved by the Court:

Dated:＿＿＿＿＿＿＿＿＿＿　　＿＿＿＿＿＿＿＿＿＿＿＿

Critical Thinking and the Legal Office

In an ideal world, daily work would progress smoothly and efficiently. However, in any actual office as opposed to an ideal one, even the most organized legal support person may encounter a variety of unexpected problems. Employers expect their employees to do everything they can to keep projects on schedule and to keep the office running as efficiently as possible. This requires that all employees keep their minds engaged and focused on what needs to be done at any given moment while also anticipating possible problems before they occur.

Planning and problem-solving abilities are known as critical thinking skills. Effective critical thinkers employ the following skills in their everyday work:

- Apply knowledge of the subject matter to the thinking process
- Consider why particular conclusions were drawn and whether they will lead to the appropriate solution or goal
- Strive to improve their own thinking process, ask for, and use feedback from others
- Review their own work, analyze current processes, and revise procedures for better performance in the future

Most employers would agree that they value employees who make few mistakes and good decisions. Employers in a legal office are no different. When an attorney gives a document to a legal support person, the attorney expects that person to focus on the purpose of the document and consider to whom it is being sent, what needs to be included, and when it is expected to be delivered.

Understanding and applying the following skills effectively will make you a better and more efficient employee:

- Knowing the background and details of the case at hand
- Questioning details that conflict or do not seem to make sense
- Taking the initiative to obtain missing details
- Asking questions of others who have the information you need
- Anticipating future needs
- Following directions carefully

Critical thinking includes working on a team. In an office, you may work independently or you may work as a member of a team. In working with a team, knowing your role on the team and having a mutual understanding of the goals for a project will help to ensure a successful outcome. For critical thinking to flourish in the work setting, there must be an environment of trust and respect. You must trust that your ideas will be respected, and you must respect the ideas of others. You must also understand that your own ideas may not work in every situation and may be changed or not used at all.

Critical Thinking Exercises

Apply what you have learned to the following exercises.

Exercise 1.6 In the space provided, explain in your own words what critical thinking is and why it is important in the workplace. Offer two or three examples of how you have used critical thinking in your own life.

_____

_____

_____

_____

_____

_____

_____

_____

_____

_____

Exercise 1.7 Locate two to three people (i.e. instructor, parent, friend, or relative) who are currently employed anywhere and ask what critical thinking means in their workplace. Summarize each response you receive and share the results with your class.

Chapter Summary and Projects

Summary

You have now read an overview of basic grammar, editing, and proofreading skills that you will apply to your role as a legal support person. Remember that as a legal support person, it will be your responsibility to complete the following tasks:

- Understand and edit legal documents for spelling, grammatical, and formatting errors.
- Edit legal documents and correspondence in both electronic and hard-copy format.
- Proofread documents and correspondence in both electronic and hard-copy format.
- Use print and online resources to answer questions regarding grammar, style, or spelling.
- Critically think about details that apply to the case at hand.
- Ask questions of the appropriate people when necessary.
- Anticipate future needs.
- Follow directions.

Key Terms

adjective, 3
adverb, 3
article, 3
clause, 2
conjunction, 3
declarative sentence, 2
dependent clause, 2
editing, 6
exclamatory sentence, 2
imperative sentence, 2
independent clause, 2

interjection, 3
interrogative sentence, 2
noun, 3
phrase, 2
predicate, 2
preposition, 3
pronoun, 3
proofreading, 6
sentence, 2
subject, 2
verb, 3

Project 1   Create a Portfolio and Establish Career Goals

When you apply for jobs, you will want to present your work to a potential employer in a manner that is helpful and professional. Portfolios are used to accomplish this goal. For this ongoing project, you will create a portfolio using the final drafts of work you created from the projects in this book, your resumé, and any additional information a potential employer would find helpful.

As you work your way through each chapter, you will create a variety of documents and search a variety of Internet resources. Portfolio icons have been inserted throughout the book to indicate suggested items to include. Best practice tips and Local Focus exercises have been provided for you throughout the textbook and are available in a file on the student data disc. Divide the portfolio into chapter sections. To assist you in describing a document to a prospective employer in the future, you may want to photocopy or retype and include instructions from the text. It may also be helpful to print and include files provided in the instructions that have information and instruction to clarify the purpose and learning objectives of the project.

Continue to update the portfolio as you progress through the chapter. It will be a complement to your resume when you interview for a position.

In Chapter 11, Project 15, you will be asked to write an essay expressing your career goals. After completing this project, print and include it in your portfolio.

Instructions

1. Print exercises and projects tagged with the Portfolio icon.

2. Include any other projects that you feel exemplify your learning. Decide which documents you would like to present to a prospective employer during an interview. If there are some on which you had errors, correct those errors and include the document in the portfolio.

3. You will want to include your resumé (if you have one prepared), a sample job application cover letter, list of personal references, as well as recommendation letters, if you have them.

4. Purchase a three-ring binder large enough to accommodate your projects, as well as a set of section dividers. Name the dividers according to the topics or chapters you are including in the portfolio. Insert examples behind these dividers.

5. Three-hole punch your projects and place them in the binder by area of law and chapter.

6. Create an index to make documents easier to find. Place this near the front of your portfolio.

7. As you progress through the textbook, add to the binder additional items that you may find helpful in future positions.

8. Make revisions after documents have been scored and insert correct documents into the portfolio.

9. Each assignment example should include a typed summary or photocopy of the original instructions so that the prospective employer will have an idea of what was required.

Civil Litigation

Chapter Objectives

- Review litigation procedures and terminology
- Practice thinking analytically
- Consider tone and audience while editing materials
- Review common spelling rules
- Practice time-management skills using a calendar
- Cross-check details

Before beginning computer exercises for this chapter, copy to your storage medium the Chapter 02 folder from the Student Resources disc that accompanies this textbook. Do this for each chapter before starting the chapter's exercises.

Attorney Perry, of the law office of Henderson, Kyle, and Perry, was contacted by Anthony Thomas, a young man seeking legal advice. Mr. Thomas explained that his roommate had moved out of their apartment with three full months remaining on their lease. Both Mr. Thomas and his roommate are listed on the lease agreement. Mr. Thomas had attempted to secure the roommate's share of the final three-month's rent, only to be told not to expect any payment. Attorney Perry invited Mr. Thomas to meet with him at the office, where the two determined that they would pursue legal action against the former roommate.

Litigation is the process of bringing and pursuing a lawsuit to enforce a right. A **lawsuit** is defined as a legal action brought between two or more private parties in a court of law, although the terms *litigation* and *lawsuit* are often used interchangeably.

For a lawsuit to begin, a perceived injury must occur. The injury can be physical or financial or involve damage to property or reputation. The injured party then seeks legal advice at an attorney's office. At the attorney's office, the legal support staff must gather information to assist the attorney in determining whether he or she will continue with the case. If the attorney accepts the case, a client information form is prepared. A **client information form** is a fact-finding document used to gather personal information about the client and the case. The attorney will use these details to prepare legal documents for the client, such as the summons and complaint, to start the action. It is important to understand that not all of the information may be available at the time that this form is provided, so it may be necessary for the legal support person to obtain the missing information and add it to the form as the case proceeds.

A firm understanding of the terms and processes of civil litigation is essential for any legal support person who is required to edit, proofread, or apply critical thinking skills in a law office. This overview is intended to remind you of the terminology and processes of litigation. Along with reviewing civil litigation procedures, you will also review spelling rules, consider tone in legal documents, analyze proofreading methods, and practice time-management skills.

The Lawsuit

A lawsuit comes about because of a controversy or disagreement. It is authorized by law to enforce the rights of the participants. A participant in a lawsuit is known as a **litigant**. There are two sides to a lawsuit: that of the **plaintiff** (also known as the *claimant* or *petitioner*), the person who starts the lawsuit and brings a complaint against the other party; and that of **defendant** (or *respondent*), against whom the lawsuit is filed and the complaint is made. Legal claims in the lawsuit are called **causes of action**. **Entity** is a general term for organizations, to distinguish them from individuals in a lawsuit.

Types of Lawsuits

There are two types of lawsuits—civil and criminal. A **civil lawsuit** or civil action is one dealing with issues that are not criminal in nature yet arise between people in the areas of business, contracts, insurance, legal and professional malpractice, estate planning and probate, domestic relations (family), personal accidents, and negligence. Sometimes the areas of civil and criminal law overlap. For example, a driver might be involved in a civil lawsuit for being negligent in causing an automobile accident that has killed or injured another person. That same driver might also be charged with a crime stemming from reckless driving or driving under the influence of alcohol or drugs. In another example, a person may be physically assaulted and bring a civil lawsuit for the injuries he or she suffered as a result of the assault (personal injury). The person who committed the assault would be sued in that civil action, and that same person could also be charged with the criminal act of assault.

A **criminal lawsuit** is a lawsuit dealing with crimes against members of the public; it includes all procedures through charging, trial, and sentencing of the convicted person. Types of criminal acts are felonies and misdemeanors. A **felony** is a crime serious enough to be punishable by death or incarceration in a county jail or state or federal prison. Examples of felonies include, among others, murder, burglary, rape, and the possession or sale of certain drugs. A **misdemeanor** is a less serious crime punishable by a fine or county jail time. Examples of misdemeanors include petty thefts, disturbing the peace, traffic violations, and public drunkenness.

Parties to a Lawsuit

Each side of a lawsuit usually has its own attorney, although parties may choose to represent themselves. The plaintiff/claimant/petitioner's attorney is known as the **plaintiff's attorney** in a civil action or the **prosecutor** in a criminal action. The defendant/respondent's attorney is known as the **defense attorney** in both civil and criminal actions. An insurance defense attorney is an attorney hired by an insurance company to defend an action brought against the company (or against the person insured by the company). When a lawsuit has more than one defendant, the individual defendants are called **codefendants**. A party who chooses to self-represent is said to be appearing **pro se**.

When a lawsuit is initiated, a location must be determined. In the legal system, the **venue** is the geographic location for the trial of a case and is the proper or most convenient location for all parties. Normally, the venue in a criminal case is the judicial district or county where the crime was committed. For civil cases, the venue is usually the district or county where the principal defendant resides, where a contract is signed or is to be performed, or where an accident took place. The parties may agree to a different venue for convenience—for example, the place where most of the witnesses are located.

In addition to determining the appropriate venue, the attorney must consider the jurisdiction that applies to the lawsuit. **Jurisdiction** is the authority given by law to a court to try cases and rule on legal matters within a particular geographic area and/or over certain types of legal cases. For example, a criminal case must be heard in a court that has jurisdiction over criminal matters.

Resources

Many resources can be used throughout the preparation of a lawsuit. The rules of practice (sometimes called **rules of court**) are the litigation guidelines set forth by the state and local courts. These rules maintain fairness in the administration of cases and control expenses; they also regulate the timing of the proceedings to avoid unnecessary delays. Rules of civil and criminal procedure as well as rules of appellate procedure govern the proceedings in civil, criminal, and appellate courts. These rules vary from state to state. Minnesota is an example of a state that has written common rules, and all courts in the state follow the same rules. Individual courts do have certain rules specific to them, but overall the rules of court are the same throughout the state of Minnesota. Other states may use rules specific to each individual court. The legal support staff or attorney in any state must look at the rules to determine specific guidelines of how to complete a procedure.

Best Practice Tip

LITIGATION PREPARATION RESOURCES

The rules of practice can generally be found on the specific court's website. For example, Minnesota's rules of court can be found at http://www.mncourts.gov/?page=511. Most states publish the rules of practice, which are made available in a formal, printed book.

The Civil Litigation Process

The plaintiff's attorney starts a lawsuit by preparing a summons and a complaint (also known as initial pleadings or first pleadings). **Initial** or **first pleadings** are the documents that are created first, and served on the defendant in the legal process, and are the first documents to be filed with the court. A **process server**, who is either a law enforcement officer or private party at least 18 years of age who is not involved in the lawsuit, will personally serve or deliver the first pleadings to the defendant. In some instances, substitute service on the defendant is allowed. To deliver a **substitute service**, the process server leaves the documents with an adult resident of the defendant's home or with a designated agent or person authorized to accept service on a business. In other cases, such as evictions, the process server may post the documents on the door or other prominent place, after which the attorney sends copies of the documents by certified mail to the defendant. In matters where the defendant is unknown or not found, the court will allow service by publication of the summons in a local newspaper for a number of times as prescribed by law.

After the defendant has been served and has answered the complaint (usually through his or her own attorney), the plaintiff's and defendant's attorneys may serve further documents on each other by mail and sometimes by fax.

Complaint

A **complaint** is a legal document that requests damages and/or performance by the opposing party. **Performance** means specific actions to be taken by a party, such as completing items required in a contract. The complaint is the first document to be filed with the court, along with the summons. It states the factual and legal bases for the claims, and its form must follow statutory requirements. Some states require the complaint to be filed with the court, which will then issue the summons and return both documents to the plaintiff's attorney for service on the defendant. Other states allow the plaintiff's attorney to prepare the summons and complaint, serve it on the defendant, and then file it with the court. A fee is usually required when a lawsuit is being filed with the court. Under certain circumstances, such as poverty, the court will waive the fee. Some courts do not require filing fees for criminal matters.

The **summons** notifies the defendant of a lawsuit and includes instructions about the length of time within which the defendant must respond; in some cases, the back of the summons will contain a form that the person serving the documents will complete. The process server or law enforcement officer, whoever officially serves or delivers legal documents, will indicate the date and time of service and the name and address of the person served. This individual or his or her attorney will then return the form to the plaintiff's attorney, who will file the form with the court at the appropriate time. A subpoena is not the same as a summons. While a summons notifies the defendant of a lawsuit, a **subpoena** orders a person to appear as a witness.

When someone is served with a summons or a complaint, he or she has a specified amount of time within which to submit an answer to the plaintiff's attorney. The **answer** is a responsive legal document prepared by the defendant or defendant's attorney that admits or denies each allegation or claim made in the complaint and sets out the defenses to be made by the defendant. In some cases, this document may also be called a *response*.

Another initial pleading similar to a complaint is a **petition**, or a written request asking for an order of the court. Petitions include writs, orders to show cause, modifications of previous orders, continuances, requests to dismiss a case, requests for the reduction of **bail** in **criminal** matters, decrees for distribution of an estate, and appointments of guardians. An **order** is a command of a court or judge, normally made or entered in writing, which determines some point or directs some step in the proceedings.

All legal pleadings related to the case will have the same caption. The **caption** is the standardized heading of a legal document, such as a motion or a complaint, which includes the names of the plaintiff and defendant, the state and county that has jurisdiction over the matter, and the court file number.

Cross-Complaint

A **cross-complaint**, or cross-claim, is a claim made by an answering party against a codefendant by which the answering party states his or her own claim against the other party related to the original complaint. For example, as illustrated in Figure 2.1, if Party A is suing Parties B and C, a cross-complaint would be made by Party B against Party C for contribution in paying plaintiff's damages. Both Parties B and C are being sued by Party A; however, B feels that C may be partly or entirely at fault and wants to settle that dispute.

Figure 2.1 Cross-complaint/cross-claim

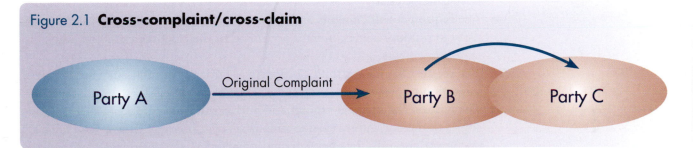

A **counterclaim**, or cross-action, is a claim made by the defendant against the plaintiff related to the original complaint. For example, in Figure 2.2, Party A is suing Party B. However, Party B feels that he is really the injured party and is counterclaiming that A is really at fault. Thus, Party B seeks relief from A for B's damages.

The defendant's attorney decides when a cross-complaint or counterclaim is appropriate. This can be done when an answer is being prepared, or the attorney can amend the answer and add a cross-complaint or counterclaim at a later time.

Figure 2.2 Counterclaim/cross-action

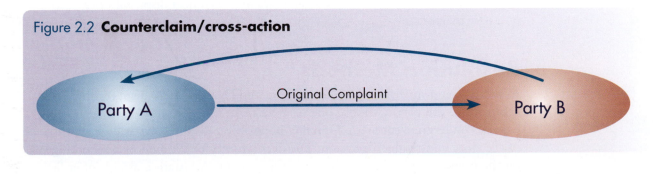

Discovery

After the defendant has answered the initial pleadings, both sides will participate in **discovery**. **Discovery** is a fact-finding process that narrows the issues of a lawsuit by discovering information that is not privileged and is relevant to the claim or defense of the parties. Discovery methods include the following:

- **Interrogatories** are written questions from one party to the other; they are used to obtain more information about the positions or claims of the parties to a lawsuit.
- A **deposition** is an oral examination before trial in which a witness is placed under oath and asked to answer questions relating to the case at hand. The questions and answers are put into printed form for the witness to read and sign in order to verify that the testimony is true and correct. Both witnesses and parties may be asked to give a deposition. Deposition testimony may be used to impeach, or discredit, a witness at trial.
- The **request for admission** is a document that relates to the pending action only and asks the opposing party to either admit or deny the truth of certain matters regarding statements, opinions of fact, or the genuineness of documents. If a party does not answer the requests for admission within the prescribed deadline, the request is deemed to be admitted. Matters admitted do not need to again be proven at trial. An admission admits only certain facts, not blame or guilt.
- The **request for documents and things** is a document requesting the other party to produce copies of items pertaining to the case, such as photographs, maps, statements, and so on.
- The **request for inspection of property** is a document requesting an inspection of property to verify certain claims.
- The **request for medical reports and authorizations** is a document requesting copies of medical information to support a claim of injury or lost wages. This document also calls for signed permission allowing the defendant's attorney to request medical information from the plaintiff's medical providers. A **medical provider** is an institution or individual who has rendered health care of any type to persons involved in litigation.

If a party fails to respond to discovery requests, the party seeking information may ask the court to compel answers and may be awarded sanctions against the nonresponsive party. A **sanction** is a penalty or punishment attached to a court order or law, intended to ensure that it will be followed. A sanction may require the offending party to pay the requesting party's attorney's fees incurred in asking the court to compel answers and in certain cases may include a dismissal of the action or a part thereof.

Resolution Methods

Arbitration and mediation are alternative methods of resolving disputes. In **arbitration**, the parties choose one or more neutral people (usually an attorney who has undergone specialized training in resolving disputes) to listen to both sides of the story and render a decision. The decision may be binding or nonbinding on the parties, depending on their prior agreement. Arbitration awards offer little option for appeal.

In **mediation**, the parties agree on one neutral person to facilitate discussions between the parties in an attempt to settle the matter outside of court. Mediation does not always result in settlement. Most court systems are overloaded with cases, so many require all matters to be arbitrated or mediated before a trial is requested.

Matters that cannot be settled are submitted to trial by either the court or a jury. In a **court trial**, a judge hears all testimony and makes a final ruling that is binding on the parties. In a **jury trial**, a panel of people is selected to hear all testimony and make a final decision based on the law, testimony, and instructions from the judge.

An **appeal** is a process that asks a higher court to overturn the judgment of a lower court so as to correct mistakes or an observed injustice. Depending on the particular legal rules applying to each circumstance, a party to a court case who is unhappy with the result *may* be able to challenge the result in an appellate court on specific grounds. These grounds may typically include errors of law, fact, or procedure. Judgments from both court decisions and jury verdicts may be appealed, as well as final judgments or orders on motions that dispose of matters in a case. If a party believes the decision of the court or jury was made because of an error in interpreting the law, because the judge abused his or her discretion or for certain other reasons, that person may appeal the ruling to a court of appeals at the state or federal level. The appeals process is discussed in detail in Chapter 5.

You have just reviewed the civil litigation process and should be confident in applying your own knowledge in this area. In civil litigation and other legal processes, the role of the legal support staff is often to ensure that the process goes smoothly and the documents created are professional and error-free.

Language Focus: Spelling

Are you a good speller? If you answered no, great! Why great? If you do not believe you spell well naturally, then you will be more cautious in your proofreading and will be more inclined to look up words you do not know. People who automatically say yes are less likely to check their work and are thus more prone to error. Some people, of course, *are* naturally good spellers, while others do not recognize misspelled words. Not recognizing misspelled words is a problem if that skill is one of your job duties.

What about a spell checker? *Do* use a spell checker, but do *not rely* on the spell checker or other spelling and grammar-checking software. No one has made a spell checker that is smarter than you! The following are just a few examples of distinctions that a spell checker may miss.

accept and *except*	*wood* and *would*
its and *it's*	*your* and *you're*
manager and *manger*	

Although some spell checker programs can identify spelling errors and common grammatical mistakes, a spell checker will not indicate where an apostrophe should be placed or how to fix a sentence fragment. A spell checker will not show you grammatical mistakes such as *would of* instead of *would have*, nor will it point out proper nouns, such as people's names and the names of companies, like *Sagau Delivery Service* and *Leigh Tae Kwondo Academy*.

If you have chosen to become a legal support person, you *must* question your work and look up words whenever you are unsure of their spellings. The more often you look up words and rules, the more likely these rules are to become second nature to you. You will then become more efficient at your work. Review some of the following basic spelling patterns. Keep in mind that there are always exceptions to patterns and that, when in doubt, you should consult an appropriate style guide or dictionary. Certain style guides will be particularly useful to you in the legal office. A list of suggested style guides appears in the Appendix: Style Guide for your reference.

Common Spelling Patterns

You have probably been introduced to certain spelling "rules" during your years at school. However, many of these rules have exceptions, so it is in your best interest to view them merely as *patterns* instead. The following is a brief list of common spelling patterns that you can apply to your own work. By becoming familiar with these spelling patterns, you will become more confident in your spelling and, eventually, in your editing and proofreading skills.

1. One of the best-remembered spelling patterns is "*i* before *e* except after *c* or when sounding like *a* as in *neighbor* or *weigh*." Note that there are a few exceptions to this pattern (such as *neither*, *either*, and *weird*). Always refer to a dictionary if you are uncertain.

The *i* before *e* except after *c* pattern applies to all *ie* and *ei* words that have "ee" sounds.	Words whose letters create "ay" sounds contain the *ei* pattern.
i before *e*	neighbor
thief	reign
believe	rein
relief	weigh
except after *c*	weight
receive	veil
ceiling	
conceit	

2. All syllables must contain a vowel. That is why the letter *e* appears at the end of *apple*, *bottle*, *table*, etc.

3. In English, the letter *x* is not immediately followed by *s* (*excited*, *boxes*, *exercise*).

4. English words never end in *i*, *u*, or *v*.

5. Words that end with the sound "seed" are spelled with either *-cede*, *-ceed*, or *-sede*. It is important to remember that only the word *supersede* ends in *-sede*, and only three words end in *-ceed* (*exceed*, *proceed*, and *succeed*). If you remember these four words, you will know that every other "seed" word ends in *-cede*, such as *intercede*, *concede*, and *recede*.

Best Practice Tip

OTHER RESOURCES

Other spelling patterns can be found in a variety of writing resources, particularly books on spelling and grammar.

6. A single vowel *y* at the end of a word usually changes to *i* when a suffix is added, except typically not when the suffix is *–ing*.

Base Word	+ Suffix	New Word
dry	+ ing	= drying
cry	+ es	= cries
happy	+ ly	= happily

7. The letters *s* and *h* are combined to form the sound "sh" at the beginning of a word or end of a syllable but not at the beginning of a syllable immediately following the first. When the sound occurs immediately following the first syllable, the letters *ti, si,* and *ci* are used instead.

"sh" at the beginning or end of a syllable	"sh" sound immediately following the first syllable made with *ti, si* and *ci*.
sheriff	motion
relinquish	tension
shoulder	social

8. When you add a suffix that begins with a consonant (-ly, -less, -ment) to a word, the original word typically does not change: state + -ment = statement. There are exceptions to this rule (judgment, truly, etc.).

Base Word	+ Consonant Suffix	New Word
assign	+ ment	= assignment
spite	+ ful	= spiteful
late	+ ly	= lately
judge	+ ment	= judgment (*not* judgement)

9. When you add a suffix that begins with a vowel (-able, -ible, -ous, -ing) to a word that ends in a silent *e*, you must determine whether or not to keep the silent *e*. Suffixes that begin with *e* or *i* typically drop the silent *e* from the main word. Note: While this is a common pattern, do *not* drop the silent *e* if doing so will change the meaning of the word, as in *singeing*.

Original Word	+ Vowel Suffix	New Word
calculate	+ ion	= calculation
expense	+ ive	= expensive
late	+ est	= latest
prestige	+ ious	= pretigious
singe	+ ing	= singeing (not singing)

10. Suffixes that begin with *a* or *o* typically keep the silent *e*.

Original word	+ Vowel Suffix	New Word
change	-able	changeable
notice	-able	noticeable
courage	-ous	courageous

Mnemonic Devices

A mnemonic device is a phrase, image, or trick that helps you to remember information. Most are verbal sayings, such as a rhyme or sentence used to remember the spelling or definition of a word. Many mnemonic devices have been passed along from generation to generation, including those in Table 2.1.

Table 2.1 Mnemonic Devices

Word	Mnemonic Device
Friend	"A friend is a friend until the *end*."
Separate	"The word sep*arat*e has 'a rat' in the middle."
Weird	"We are *weird*."
Dessert	"De*ss*ert is *twice* as good as the desert."
Cemetery	"The lady screamed, 'e-e-e!' as she ran through the cemetery."
Argument	"I lost an *e* in an argument."

Language Focus Exercises

Apply what you have learned previously to the following exercises.

Exercise 2.1 Using the patterns in prvious sections and your current spelling knowledge, circle the correctly spelled words in the following columns. If you are unsure of the correct spelling, look the word up in a hard-copy dictionary or an online dictionary.

Column A

1. receive	6. mysterious	11. preceed	16. height
2. science	7. happyness	12. maintainance	17. paralell
3. consceince	8. ordinarily	13. noticeable	18. fashion
4. conveys	9. greivous	14. truly	19. varyance
5. handfuls	10. reprieve	15. excellant	20. laboratory

Column B

1. recieve	6. mysteryous	11. precede	16. hieght
2. sceince	7. happiness	12. maintenance	17. parallel
3. conscience	8. ordinaryly	13. noticable	18. fasion
4. convays	9. grievous	14. truely	19. variance
5. handfulls	10. repreive	15. excellent	20. labratory

Exercise 2.2 Share with the class any mnemonic devices or tricks you have learned over the years and then brainstorm words that consistently give you and your classmates trouble. As a class, try to come up with a mnemonic device for the words that you have identified. Write your mnemonic devices on the lines below.

_____

_____

_____

_____

_____

_____

Exercise 2.3 Circle the misspelled word and write the correction on the line. Write the letter C on the line if there are no errors.

1. Use parenthesis to enclose metric equivalents. _____

2. Are the Morrises involved in the deposition on Friday? _____

3. Carmen said that the three memorandum of law are to be keyed again. _____

4. The x's are missing from every keyboard in this box. _____

5. All books have been returned to the shelfs. _____

6. The man caught many salmons before he was injured on the job. _____

7. The only important criteria, in our opinion, is the safety of all employees in the plant. _____

8. We are now waiting to hear from our attornies concerning the validity of the documents. _____

9. The company is owned by two brothers— the Reeyes—who have managed to make Reeyes Enterprises a million-dollar business in a very short time. Mr. Humbart Reeyes is in his 80s. _____

10. Because of various government embargos, the defendant does not ship computer equipment to certain nations. _____

11. Here are the instructions for merging both halfs of the manuscript onto one flash drive. _____

12. Sari's hunchs about opposing counsel are usually correct. _____

13. If these figures represent thousands, then please be sure to add three zeroes to each numeral as you retype these columns. _____

14. What one item do you remember as the bases of your decision to reject their offer?

15. The woman is suing the restaurant for allowing the cactuses to grow onto the sidewalk, where she tripped and injured her wrist. _____

16. The lunar eclipse was a spectacular phenomena. _____

17. The case was started in the 1990s and has continued until today. _____

18. Mr. Murphy had two summons served on him on Friday. _____

19. We met with the client to discuss the ups and down's of a long trial. _____

20. Five VIPs have been invited to the training session. _____

Editing: Audience and Language

The revision process begins after a document has been written. Editing is typically the first step of the revision process. Editing a document means rereading the material and deciding if it is organized correctly and written concisely and accurately. Although an editor's attention is usually drawn to grammar, conciseness, and accuracy, the editor must also determine the audience of the document and check that the language used is consistent and appropriate for that audience.

In writing, the audience is the person or persons who are meant to read the document. The audience determines the choice of language. Language choices range from formal to informal English (although in a legal setting, nearly all documents will be formal) and may vary based on the audience's understanding of the subject. All material should be written with a specific audience in mind. While editing, think about who is reading and trying to understand the document. If the material is written for a judge, the writing can be at a judge's level of comprehension. If the material is intended for the client, the material should be written for a person without any legal background. As a legal support person, never be afraid to speak up and say that you do not understand the material, *especially* if it is written for a client. If *you* have trouble understanding a document, it is likely that the client will also have difficulties.

Writing is a common activity for lawyers, and many lawyers are good writers. However, some are not. Legal support staff sometimes have difficulty editing writing given to them because they do not understand the law as well as the lawyer does. This leads them to type what is given to them without editing the document. There are ways to edit legal writing from the legal support staff's perspective without changing the content. For example, wordy noun expressions weaken writing; they can often be converted to verbs such as the following:

Original:	The council **made a decision** to hire a new city manager.
Revised:	The council **decided** to hire a new city manager.

Original:	Our client **made an agreement** to continue talks with the labor union.
Revised:	Our client **agreed** to continue talks with the labor union.

Notice that although the meaning of the sentence does not change, it becomes stronger when a noun is converted into to an action verb.

Editing Exercises

The following exercises will allow you to practice your editing skills using the information discussed in this chapter.

Exercise 2.4 Rewrite the following sentences, correcting the wordy noun phrases while leaving the meaning of the sentences intact.

1. The lead investigator will perform an analysis of the details before sending the information on to the main office.

   _____

2. Our office is involved in preparation for the conference at the end of the week.

   _____

3. The company has the intention of revising the employee handbook over the summer.

   _____

4. We were able to bring the resistance to a halt by allowing questions at the end of the presentation.

   _____

5. The union has come to an agreement with the negotiators on wages as well as benefits.

   _____

Exercise 2.5 Read the following sentences. Imagine that they will have to be read and understood by either a client with no legal background or an attorney. Offer suggestions on how the sentences could be edited to match the intended audience. Apply your edits directly to the sentences, using notes and marks that are easily understood.

1. The client has commenced an action to dissolve the parties' marriage. (client)

2. A cause of action would show that both the person bringing the lawsuit and the person responding to the lawsuit were residents of Davidson County, Tennessee. (attorney)

3. You are asked to show up and defend a civil action filed against you in the Circuit Court. (attorney)

4. As a direct and proximate result of the negligence of the defendant, the plaintiff received extremely severe and permanent injuries to his person. (client)

5. The foregoing motion for a judgment by default has been mailed to Alexis R. Bryant, the defendant, by placing same in a properly addressed, stamped envelope and depositing it for delivery by the mailman. (attorney)

Exercise 2.6 The following paragraph is written informally but will be included within a court document. Without making too many changes, edit the paragraph so that it becomes more formal and can be included in the official court document.

Despite being given tons of opportunity, the defendants didn't examine the building closely and now find that they hate the layout but having an undesirable room layout does not make a building "unfit" and doesn't justify breaching the lease.

Proofreading: Methods of Proofreading

After all editing revisions have been made and the document is considered final, it is time to proofread it for misspelled words, grammatical errors, and faulty punctuation. Does it matter whether you proofread the document? Do not fall into the trap of thinking that it is someone else's responsibility. Others will judge you and your company or firm by how well or poorly your communications are written. As a legal support person, you are the one who must verify that the document makes the best possible impression, and this includes proofreading the document.

If it is your responsibility to both edit and proofread the document, do not begin proofreading until you are completely finished with the editing process. If you attempt to proofread while you edit, you will find that you focus on the more obviously misspelled words, rather than reading for consistency, transition, ideas, and word choices. Retrain your brain to edit first and proofread last. Remind yourself that you will proofread after you have finished editing, and allow your mind to consider the flow of ideas during the editing process. This will allow you to focus more sharply on your proofreading once you feel that the document is polished and ready.

Be sure to let enough time to pass between each task. Some people may choose to set the final document aside for a day or even longer, so as to approach it again

PROOFREADING

It is common for people to avoid proofreading the following parts of letters and documents:

- Dates
- Inside addresses
- Salutations
- Closings
- Signature lines
- Captions
- Date lines
- Signature blocks
- Headers
- Footers

Proofread these sections first. Then concentrate on the body and content of the document.

with "fresh" eyes. This method will not be possible if a deadline will soon be approaching; however, always take a break between editing and proofreading to signal to yourself that you are starting a new project. Even a quick break to stretch your legs or to address another project will give you enough time to focus your attention anew when you begin proofreading the document.

Many people only do a quick "once over" when proofreading, meaning that they briefly scan the document or read it as rapidly as possible. Although timely, this method will miss too many errors. As you learn different methods of proofreading, you will eventually choose the one that works best for you, or you may develop your own proofreading process. Try different methods until you have a system that you feel comfortable with and allows you to find as many errors as possible in the shortest period of time.

Proofreading methods include the following:

- Proofread as you key a final hard-copy document into an electronic file (this method should always include one more review after the document has been keyed).
- Proofread a long document in sections to break it up and allow yourself time to focus.
- Put the proofed document aside for an extended period of time (such as overnight) and proofread it again with a fresh mind.
- Proofread the final document on the computer screen.
- Print the final document and proofread it in hard copy.

Note that this is not an all-inclusive list. You may blend some of these methods or discover others as you gain experience. Talk with your classmates about how they proofread most successfully.

Proofreading Exercises

Apply what you have learned previously to the following proofreading exercises.

Exercise 2.7 Practice proofreading a printed document using your own proofreader's marks. Assume that you are proofreading the following document for your own work and use marks that you understand. Refer to the proofreader's marks in Table 1.3 in chapter 1 if you want to practice common marks. Be sure to proofread the document for errors in spelling, grammar, and punctuation.

1. Open and print the **C02_Proofreading_Ex2.7** file from the Chapter 2 folder in your electronic storage medium.
2. Proofread the document for general spelling, grammar, and punctuation errors.
3. After you have finished proofreading, obtain the answer key from your instructor and compare your marked copy to the answer key.
4. Did you find all the errors? In the space provided, note any discrepancies in your work and how you might avoid such errors in the future.

_____

_____

_____

_____

Exercise 2.8 Practice the method of proofreading a document in two separate stages by completing the following exercise.

1. Open the file titled **C02_Proofreading_Ex2.8** from your electronic storage medium. The file contains an unproofed email. Print the document.

2. Proofread the email for general spelling, grammar, and punctuation errors.

3. Assume that you are proofreading the email for yourself. Use marks that make sense to you if you were going to make the changes.

4. Put this work aside for at least two hours. After at least two hours have passed, proofread the document again. Did you find additional errors?

5. Obtain the answer key from your instructor and compare it with your marked hard copy.

6. Were you able find all of the errors? Did you miss any during your first attempt at proofreading?

7. Summarize your findings on the lines provided and share this information with your instructor and classmates.

_____

_____

_____

_____

Exercise 2.9 Compare the errors found by a spell checker program with the errors that you find on your own.

1. Open **C02_Ex2.9_Proofreading** from your electronic storage medium and immediately resave it as **LastName_C02_Ex2.9_Proofreading**.

2. Run your software's spell checker to quickly check the document for errors.

3. Indicate here how many errors were found by the spell checker: _____ errors.

4. Now, print the document and manually proofread the same material, circling any errors that you find. If you found more errors, indicate the number of additional errors you found. _____

5. Summarize your findings on the lines provided and compare your work with that of your classmates.

_____

_____

_____

_____

Litigation How-To Guide

A legal support person must be able to create and utilize discovery documents, as discussed earlier in this chapter. The following information will explain what the legal support person's role may be in completing these documents. Although offices may differ when it comes to their own procedures, the following is a good representation of what should be done in preparing discovery documents.

Client Information Forms

An injured person or a person accused of injuring another party will usually seek the assistance of an attorney. When the attorney accepts the case, a client information form is used to gather personal information about the client and the case. The attorney will use these details to prepare legal documents for the client. These forms vary according to the focus of the law for the situation. For example, a personal injury case will focus on information such as medical bills or lost wages; a divorce case would require details on the parties' marriage, their jobs, home, financial situation, and children; and a bankruptcy case would require information about the client's finances. Details that will pertain to any situation include the following:

- Client's full legal name
- Name of spouse (if applicable)
- Date of birth
- Social security number
- Employer (if applicable)
- Details of the client's reason for seeking legal representation
- Current contact information, including the client's address, home phone and cell phone numbers, work phone number, fax number, and email address

Other information required on the client information form will depend on the issue the client presents to the attorney. For example, in accident cases, information such as the following would be needed:

- Date, time, place, and circumstances of the incident
- Description of vehicles, people, witnesses, and law enforcement agencies involved
- Insurance information
- Property damage and injuries received
- Time lost from work
- Names and addresses of lifetime medical providers
- Employment and earning history

See Figure 2.3 for an example of a blank client information form. The client information form is usually filled out by the attorney or legal support person at the first appointment with the client. Other times, the form is sent home with the client to be completed and returned. It is common for items on the form to be missing because the client either overlooked the question or did not know the answer at the time the form was submitted.

When the client information form is received by the office, it is the legal support person's responsibility to review the form for missing information. For example, he or she may have to call the police department to obtain details about the accident or witnesses. In most situations, however, calling the client and asking for the missing information may be all that is needed.

Figure 2.3 **Client Information Form**

CLIENT INFORMATION FORM

Today's date: _____

Name: _____

Address: _____

Telephone: _____

Date of birth: _____

Social Security No. _____

Marital status: _____Name of spouse: _____Children: _____

Name, address and telephone of parents: _____

Date and time of accident: _____

Location of accident: _____

Make, model, year, and license no. of your vehicle: _____

Make, model, year, and license no. of other vehicle: _____

Name of other party involved in accident: _____

Address of other party involved in accident: _____

Injuries you received in accident: _____

Name and address of doctors and/or hospitals where you were treated for your injuries:
_____

_____

Treatment received: _____

_____

_____

Time off work (dates): _____

Employer and detail of duties: _____

_____

continues

Figure 2.3 **Client Information Form** (continued)

Wage: _____

Damage to your vehicle: _____

_____

Damage to other vehicle: _____

_____

Cause of accident: _____

_____

_____

_____

Your version of how accident occurred: _____

_____

_____

Witnesses (name, address, phone): _____

_____

Names and addresses of lifetime medical providers: _____

_____

_____

Signature:_____ **Date:** _____

Interviewing attorney: _____

_____

Fee arrangement: _____

_____

Notes from Attorney:

2

Interrogatories

After the attorney receives discovery requests from the opposing party, answers to these requests will be prepared using information from the client information form as well as other sources. One such request is an interrogatory. Recall that interrogatories are written questions from one party to the other and are used to obtain more information about the positions or claims of each party in a lawsuit. The time for returning answers to such questions is governed by the rules of the court where the lawsuit will take place. The time allowed for answering may vary from state to state, between local or federal courts, or by special order of a court. It is important that you refer to your local rules to determine how to compute the time to return answers to the interrogatories. The number of questions allowed in interrogatories, including subparts, is also dictated by the rules of court and may differ among jurisdictions. The answers are put in written form and usually signed under oath by the party to whom the questions were directed. If the answering party is a state, corporation, partnership, or association, an officer or managing agent will sign the answers. The answers will define personal information about the party to whom they are directed, the party's version of the facts, witnesses and exhibits to be offered at trial, and specific information about injuries, wage loss, personal property loss, and other items specific to the case. Usually only the parties to an action are required to answer interrogatories.

Receiving Interrogatories When interrogatories or other discovery requests directed to your client are received, there will usually be a certificate of service with the document telling you when the other attorney "served" or mailed the item to you. Refer to the applicable rules of court and confer with the responsible attorney to determine the date when the answers are due at the opposing attorney's office. Make sufficient entries on your calendar to remind you and your attorney that the answers must be mailed to the opposing attorney on a particular date to comply with the rules.

Obtaining Answers for Interrogatories Answers to some of the questions will be found in the attorney's file, and some questions will have to be supplemented with information from the client. Some questions call for legal conclusions that only the attorney can draw, and there will be questions that only the client can answer.

After receiving the interrogatories, your attorney will dictate a letter or may direct you to draft a letter to the client sending the questions and requesting the client's answers before a certain date.

For time management purposes, it is a good idea to prepare the responsive document in the computer before receiving the answers from the client. The responsive document is what you will eventually complete and serve on the opposing attorney in response to the interrogatories served on your client. You can retype the questions, request them electronically from the other side, or scan the questions if your office has a scanner. Format the document so you can add the responses when they are received from the client. It is not unusual for a client to return his or her answers at the last minute. The responses will be finalized faster and more efficiently if you have the majority of the document prepared in advance. If it is determined that it is not possible to serve the responses within the required time, the attorney may request an extension of time from the opposing party. If an extension is granted, remember to recalculate the reminder dates using the new due date.

After the final answers to interrogatories have been signed by the client and the attorney, your task will be to make the appropriate number of copies of the document, to prepare a letter and certificate of service serving the answers on the

opposing attorney, and to send copies to any other attorneys or unrepresented parties in the lawsuit. In addition, you will send a copy of the signed answers to interrogatories to your client and put a copy in the client's file. You may also prepare a letter to the court filing the document, if required by your local court rules.

The following is a summary of the tasks a legal support person would complete on the job in preparing answers to interrogatories or other discovery requests:

1. Calculate the due date.
2. Calculate the reminder dates.
3. Send the questions to the client.
4. Prepare and format the responsive document before receiving the answers.
5. Add information to the document from the file and client.
6. Send answers to the client to review, sign, and return to your office.
7. Prepare a certificate or affidavit of service and letters to opposing parties.
8. Provide a copy of the document to the opposing attorneys, client, and office file; also file the document with the court, if required.

Critical Thinking: Office Calendars and Reminders

The hints and suggestions in the previous sections relate to an employee's critical thinking skills. Deadlines must be followed in all of the legal office's activities, so it is important to be confident in determining these deadlines. A legal support person should be able to look at the calendar and determine the actual due date of the answers to interrogatories and calculate reminder dates for the parties involved.

The calculation of reminder or review dates for every file or project worked on is a critical task that a legal support person would complete every day on the job. Lack of communication and missed deadlines are two of the most common complaints made by clients. Infrequent review of files and lack of status reports to the client leaves the attorney vulnerable to a malpractice complaint. You can be of value to the attorney or legal team by making sure that you assign a review or reminder date to the file every time you work on it or whenever it crosses your desk.

Updating a Calendar

Knowing your office's calendaring system will allow you to use it to your benefit. Some offices use different terms, such as *calendar, docket,* or *tickler.* Actually, each of these can have a different function.

- Calendar: A tool used to record any appointment or deadline
- Docket: A tool used to record only court dates
- Tickler: A tool used as a reminder of upcoming tasks and events

ASSIGNING REVIEW AND REMINDER DATES

If the attorney does not give you the reminder or review date, you should provide one. Your office may have a policy on this, but if not, four weeks is a good time frame within which to review the file again and remind the attorney to send a status report to the client. This is also a good way to make sure that the file is in good order and to discover oversights or tasks that are yet to be completed.

These tools can be paper or electronic. Many offices use a combination of paper and electronic tools. Some offices keep all attorneys' schedules, appointments, reminders, deadlines, and court dates in one system. Some attorneys keep their own schedules with no connection to the other attorneys in the office. People must be able to trust the office calendar. Keeping your calendaring system simple is the key to making it work!

Some offices may maintain an official office calendar that tracks important dates and deadlines. It is also common for attorneys and legal support staff to keep their own. If the calendar is electronic and "public," everyone would be able to see changes no matter who made them. If the calendar is paper based, a legal support person will have to make a habit of cross-checking the office calendar with the attorneys' calendars to keep track of newly added items. The following tips will keep the office calendaring system accurate and useful.

Task Reminders In addition to calendaring important events such as court dates, hearings, deadlines, and statute of limitations dates, insert reminders before the actual deadline. Reminders include such items as:

- Call _____ to determine meeting date.
- Get investigation details from _____.
- Begin research on _____.
- Review material from _____ before it is too late to use it.

Reminders for Others In addition to calendaring reminders of what *you* are to do, calendar what *other* people are supposed to do too, such as:

- Check that _____ has arrived (send follow-up, if necessary).
- Verify that the call from _____ was received (follow-up, if necessary). Note: Opposing counsel's support staff should also have reminded him or her of the promised information on this date!

Acknowledge Active Files As you replace a file in the cabinet, set a reminder date to remind yourself that the file is still active and check to see what may have to be done. Your attorney will appreciate knowing that you have prevented active files from being overlooked.

Track Changes Use a pen to make entries in a paper calendar. This will prevent you or anyone else from erasing important information. Keep track of changed information so that you can recall what actually occurred. You may also have to prove that you actually did record it! Computerized calendaring systems should have an auditing system so that you can track changes.

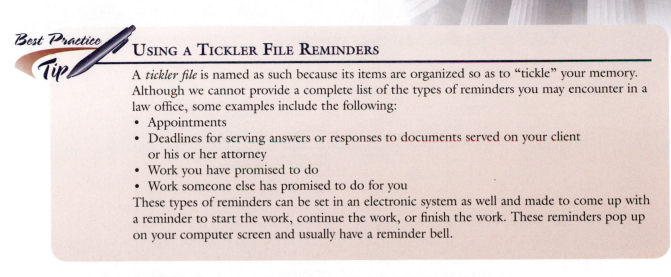

USING A TICKLER FILE REMINDERS

A *tickler file* is named as such because its items are organized so as to "tickle" your memory. Although we cannot provide a complete list of the types of reminders you may encounter in a law office, some examples include the following:

- Appointments
- Deadlines for serving answers or responses to documents served on your client or his or her attorney
- Work you have promised to do
- Work someone else has promised to do for you

These types of reminders can be set in an electronic system as well and made to come up with a reminder to start the work, continue the work, or finish the work. These reminders pop up on your computer screen and usually have a reminder bell.

Incorporate Received Mail It is best if the legal support staff opens and sorts the mail before delivering it to the attorney. This allows the support person to highlight any items that must be recorded in the calendar. Always initial items that are added to the calendar to show that they have been added.

One of the first things you will do each day is make a to-do list based on the reminders in your calendar system whether it is paper or electronic.

Print this list daily and complete the tasks. If you keep these systems updated, they will be invaluable tools for your work in the legal office.

Reminder Date Calculation Process

The following activity will walk you through the reminder date calculation process for answers to interrogatories. Assuming that the questions were mailed to your office on July 1 and the rule requires responses within 30 days after service plus 3 days for mailing, then the answers are due 33 days after July 1. Start counting on July 2 to determine the 33rd day when the answers are actually due to the opposing party, which would be August 3. Calculate your reminder dates *backwards* from the due date. Keep in mind that you must allow time for the mailed document to reach its destination. See Figures 2.4 and 2.5 for a visual of these dates.

- August 3: The date the document is due to the opposing attorney.
- July 31: The date you must mail the final answers to the opposing attorney.
- July 28: The date when the signed document is due at your office.
- July 21: The date you need to mail the completed answers to the client for review and signature. This date should be calculated to allow enough time to prepare the document for service on the opposing attorney.
- July 16: The date you should receive the client's preliminary answers in your office.
- July 3: The date you should mail the questions and letter of instruction to your client with the date by which he or she should return the answers to your office.
- July 1: The date the interrogatories were served upon you by mail.

Keep in mind that we are using the calendar-day method of deadline calculation. This means that you start counting on the day following the date on the certificate of service, *including* weekends and holidays. If the last day ends on a weekend or holiday, the due date is the next working day.

Figure 2.4 July Calendar for Reminder Date Calculation

July 2xxx

Sunday	Monday	Tuesday	Wednesday	Thursday	Friday	Saturday
			1 Date the interrogatories were served upon you by mail. Do not count this day.	2 Start counting 33 days (30 days by rule, plus 3 days for mailing)here. Include weekends and holidays. (Day 1)	3 (Day 2) Mail questions (interrogatories) and letter to client with date by which he/she should return answers.	4 (3)
5 (4)	6 (5)	7 (6)	8 (7)	9 (8)	10 (9)	11 (10)
12 (11)	13 (12)	14 (13)	15 (14)	16 (Day 15) Date you should receive the client's preliminary answers in your office.	17 (16)	18 (17)
19 (18)	20 (19)	21 (Day 20) Date you need to mail the completed answers to the client for review and signature.	22 (21)	23 (22)	24 (23)	25 (24)
26 (25)	27 (26)	28 (Day 27) The date when the signed document is due from client to your office.	29 (28)	30 (29)	31 (Day 30) The date you need to mail the final answers to the opposing attorney.	

Figure 2.5 August Calendar for Reminder Date Calculation

August 2xxx

Sunday	Monday	Tuesday	Wednesday	Thursday	Friday	Saturday
						1 (31)
2 (32)	3 (Day 33) Date the document is due to the opposing attorney.	4	5	6	7	8
9	10	11	12	13	14	15
16	17	18	19	20	21	22
23	24	25	26	27	28	29
30	31					

COURT-IMPOSED DEADLINES

When you are calculating a court-imposed deadline, move the deadline date back one to three days so that the court receives the documents several days earlier than required. The court appreciates receiving the documents in advance of the last due date so that the document can be in the file when needed.

Birth Date Calculation

Some documents require a client's current age, but all you may have is the client's birth date. Other times, you may know that a client is, for example, 54 years old and the birth date is July 9, but you do not know the birth year. Figuring out these dates is a common but important skill. The following are a few quick examples of the process.

Today is July 6, 2014. A legal document requires the client's current age. You know the client's birth date is December 16, 1958. Therefore, the client's current age is 55, and after December 16, 2014, the client will be 56.

2014 − 1958 = 56

56 − 1 year = currently 55 years old
(the current year's birthday has not yet arrived)

Today is May 25, 2014. A legal document requires a client's birth date. You know that the client is 26 years old and that her birthday is May 14. You do not, however, have the client's birth year. Using some simple math skills, you can determine that this client's birth year is 1988.

2014 − 26 = 1988 (the current year's birthday has already arrived)

Remember: If today is May 25 and the person's birthday is July 9, he or she has not yet turned a year older. If today is May 25 and the person's birthday is January 8, that person *has* already turned a year older.

Critical Thinking Exercises

Refer to Figures 2.6 and 2.7 to calculate the due dates in the following exercises. Some are court-imposed deadlines. Some are time management reminders that you would set for yourself to get a project completed on time. In computing time deadlines, *always* review your local rules of court and make a note of the guidelines that apply to your project. Write your answers on the lines provided in the following five exercises.

Exercise 2.10 Your client is served in person on December 2 with a subpoena to produce documents, which are due within 45 days to the opposing attorney.

1. Using the calendars in Figures 2.4 and 2.5, on what date are the documents due?

_____

_____

2. Is the due date a court-imposed deadline or a time management deadline?

_____

3. What date do you suggest the document be ready to be mailed to the opposing attorney? What factors are you considering when you make this suggestion?

_____

_____

_____

Exercise 2.11 A trial date has been set for April 10 of the current year. Jury instructions, trial memoranda, and other documents are due to the court 2 weeks before the trial date.

1. Using the time calculation rules discussed previously and the calendars in Figures 2.6 and 2.7, determine the date on which the documents must be received by the court.

_____

2. Is the due date a court-imposed deadline or a time management deadline?

_____

3. What date do you suggest the documents be mailed to the court so that they arrive by the due date? What factors are you considering when you make this suggestion?

_____

_____

_____

Exercise 2.12 You have made a reservation at a hotel for October 8. The hotel's cancellation policy states that there will be no penalty if you cancel within 30 days of the check-in date. There is a 50 percent penalty for cancelling two weeks before, and for anything less than two weeks there is no refund. Calculate the last date you can cancel with no penalty. Calculate the last day you can cancel and still get a 50 percent refund.

_____

_____

Exercise 2.13 Today is September 15, 2014. A legal document calls for a client's birth date. You know that the client is 77 years old and her birthday is March 21. What is her birth year?

_____

_____

Exercise 2.14 Today is February 2, 2014. A legal document calls for a client's current age. You know that the client's birth date is April 9, 1949. What is the client's current age?

_____

_____

Figure 2.6 **First Year Calendar**

Figure 2.7 **Second Year Calendar**

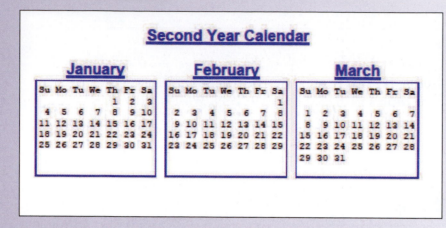

Chapter Summary and Projects

Summary

You have now read an overview of civil litigation and have an understanding of what tasks you might perform working in a legal office that specializes in civil litigation. You have also reviewed procedures that are important to legal support staff in helping the attorney create professional correspondence and legal documents. You have reviewed and practiced applying language, editing, and proofreading skills to legal documents and practiced methods to help your future office meet deadlines in the progression of the client's civil litigation case.

Remember that as a legal support person, it will be your responsibility in a civil litigation case to complete the following tasks:

- Review the client information form for content, determine what information is missing, and obtain the missing information from the client.
- Review the preliminary answers to the interrogatories.
- Compare the preliminary answers with the client information form, looking for any missing information.
- Proofread the answers to interrogatories for errors in grammar, spelling, and punctuation.
- Review the attorney's notes to the file.
- Make a list of tasks to be completed.
- Suggest reminder dates for completing the tasks with applicable back-up dates for starting the work, completing the work, and mailing the items so that they will be received by the deadlines, and then mark those dates on the calendar.

Key Terms

answer, 20
appeal, 23
arbitration, 22
caption, 21
causes of action, 18
civil lawsuit, 18
claimant, 18
client information form, 17
codefendant, 19
complaint, 20
counterclaim or cross-action, 21
court trial, 23
criminal lawsuit, 18
cross-complaint or cross-claim, 21
defendant, 18
defense attorney, 19
deposition, 22
discovery, 22
entity, 18

felony, 18
initial or first pleadings, 20
interrogatories, 22
jurisdiction, 19
jury trial, 23
lawsuit, 17
litigant, 18
litigation, 17
mediation, 23
medical provider, 22
misdemeanor, 18
order, 21
performance, 20
petition, 21
petitioner, 18
plaintiff, 18
plaintiff's attorney, 19
pro se, 19
process server, 20

Local Focus Research

Your local court will have rules and due dates specific to your jurisdiction. Locate the Chapter 2 folder in your electronic storage medium and open the local focus file **C02_LocalFocus_Litigation**. Resave the file as **LastName_C02_LocalFocus_Litigation**. Research the following topics and record your research in the file you just created. Use this information as a reference tool as you start and continue your career as a legal support person. Your instructor may ask you to submit a copy as homework.

Local Focus 2.1   Page 20 discusses common summons and complaint procedures. Refer to your local rules of court to determine the procedure for preparing and serving the summons and complaint in your own state. Write the names that your local court uses for these types of documents, as well as the current filing fee required by your court.

Local Focus 2.2   The process of answering a summons and complaint is described on page 21. Refer to your local rules of court to determine the guidelines for computing due dates for answering a summons and complaint.

Local Focus 2.3   Page 36 discusses interrogatories. Review your local court rules and key the guidelines for computing due dates for answering interrogatories or other discovery requests. Also, note how many questions may be asked in interrogatories.

Scenario

You start out your legal support career in a law office in Detroit, Michigan, called Jordan, Leone & Sanchez, PLLP. You have worked with this law office for 11 months. You know that there is still much to learn, but you are feeling confident that you understand most of the routine situations that occur at the law office. You will work on two different client matters this week.

In the case at hand, Mathias Gruetzmacher, a paralegal working at your office, was instructed by Attorney Sharon Stensrud to meet with the client to get the additional information required to complete the client information form. However, Mathias's wife gave birth to their first baby the day before, and he had to leave the office. Before he left, Mathias asked you to review the client's information form and provide him with a list of information that was not complete. Mathias had planned to contact the client to complete the information when he returned to the office.

When you arrive at work today, however, Attorney Stensrud informs you that Mathias will be out of the office for the next few weeks, and you are now in charge of completing the entire client information form for this particular case. The following projects provide all of the necessary information you need to complete your task.

Several months ago, Attorney Stensrud had an appointment with Jason Johnson. Johnson was involved in a motor vehicle accident a few years ago. He sustained personal injuries and property damage to his truck and horse trailer. The accident also resulted in the deaths of two valuable show horses. Johnson came to the office to meet with Attorney Stensrud to discuss the possibility of a lawsuit against Mark Monroe, the driver of the other vehicle in this accident.

The client explained the following: He (Johnson) was driving down the road pulling his horse trailer with two show horses. As he approached an intersection, Monroe pulled out from a stop sign in front of him. He was not able to take evasive action and collided with Monroe. His vehicle and trailer were a total loss. The horses were severely injured and did not survive. He was off work for seven or eight months due to his injuries.

After his initial meeting with Attorney Stensrud, Johnson hired her to pursue his case. Johnson completed a client information form during this initial meeting, but the information is incomplete. Monroe's attorney has served interrogatories on Johnson, and the lawsuit is in progress. Mediation is scheduled to occur in a few months.

Project 1   Client Information Form

When a person hires your law office to perform certain work, that person becomes your "client." Recall that the client information form is a tool used by the law office to collect personal information about the client and details about his or her legal issue. It is a list of questions the client will answer to the best of his or her ability. This information form will be referred to frequently by various members of the law office while working on the client's case.

Part A The client information form has been completed and provided to Attorney Stensrud. Review the Client Information Form section in the How-To Guide and read all of the following instructions before preparing your answers. Although most legal offices work with electronic documents, you will be asked to print out and correct a hard-copy document to hone your editing and proofreading skills without the use of a spell checker.

1. Open and print **C02_P1_ClientInfoForm** from the Chapter 2 folder in your electronic storage medium.

2. Review the information provided by the client on the first two pages of the client information form, but stop before the line: **Note from Attorney Stensrud - to do by July 1.** Projects 2 to 4 will address the material on the subsequent pages.

3. Determine what information is missing on the form and circle or highlight the parts of the bolded headings where information is missing in the client's response. Write notes in the margins of the document to explain what information is missing.

4. Your instructor will tell you how to submit your work. You may be asked to turn in the printed copy with your handwritten notes or to scan the hard copy and submit it electronically. If you scan your work, save the resulting electronic document as **LastName_C02_P1A_ClientInfoForm** and save it in the Chapter 2 folder on your electronic storage device before you submit the file to your instructor. Note the addition of the letter "A" to the file title—this represents "Part A."

Notes:
- Legal support staff are asked to complete work from multiple supervisors in many different ways. Different supervisors will have differing thought processes and may ask you to complete tasks in the way that they prefer. It is helpful to be confident in creating, editing, and proofreading materials in both electronic and hard-copy documents.
- Dates: Today's date on the client information form is May 15. Assume that references to 2xxx refer to the current year.

Part B The purpose of this project is for you to practice the calculation of dates. Refer to the client information form used in Part A, along with the notes you added about missing content. Answer the following questions and insert the answers in the client information form where appropriate. Save this version as **LastName_C02_P1B_ClientInfoForm**. Your instructor may have you hand in your answers, or you will discuss the answers in class.

1. What is the current date and year?
2. What is the client's date of birth including the year?
3. What is the date of the accident?
4. What year is the client's vehicle?
5. What year is the other vehicle?
6. What are the correct dates for the time the client was unable to work?

7. On what date did the client sign the client information form?

8. What exact years' tax returns should you request?

9. What exact years' medical records should you request?

Project 2 Making a Task List and Calendaring Deadlines and Reminder Dates

You have now reviewed the client information form, found areas that were not complete, and identified some important details. To complete the form, you would call the client on the telephone to clarify issues and obtain the missing details.

This project will ask you to follow instructions and determine diary or reminder dates for the calendar. You have already reviewed and practiced the calculation of deadlines and reminder dates. Go back to the How-To Guide and review that information once more to make sure you understand this process. Then proceed to the following instructions to complete the project.

1. Use the client information form you used for Projects 1A and 1B previously.

2. Starting at the line **Note from Attorney Stensrud—to do by July 1** on the client information form, read and underline or highlight the key words of the tasks to be completed.

3. Open **C02_P2_Jan-DecCalendar** from the student data disc, which is the calendar to use to determine and calculate reminder dates that are necessary to complete the tasks in project 2.

4. Because the attorney will probably, at this point, want this task list to be typed, open **C02_P2_TaskList** from your electronic storage medium and save the document as **LastName_C02_P2_TaskList** in your Chapter 2 folder. This task list may become a checklist later to be certain that you have completed all jobs.

5. Type a list of tasks that need to be completed along with the reminder dates.

6. Save your work and submit it to the instructor.

Project 3 Answers to Interrogatories

Attorney Stensrud was impressed with the work you did on the client information form and deadline dates, so she decided to give you more responsibility. Since you were already familiar with the matter after working on the client information form, Attorney Stensrud asked you to complete a draft of the client's answers to interrogatories. Ms. Stensrud had dictated preliminary answers that were transcribed by your coworker, Nicole Padoch. You are now instructed to review all the questions and see what information is still needed in order to provide complete answers. You recall from your instruction at school that you should read every word of the document and pay attention to names, numbers, addresses, and relationships to make sure that they are correct. These are items that would not be verified by the spell checker in your word processing program.

Note about captions: This project may not have a caption with which you are familiar. Assume that the caption format is correct. Remember to always proofread the information in the caption.

Part A Review the Interrogatories section in the How-To Guide if you need a reminder of the process of interrogatories. Then complete the following project.

1. Open and print **C02_P3_AnswersToInterrog** from the student data disc.

2. Proofread the definitions and the draft of Jason Johnson's answers to interrogatories for errors in grammar, punctuation, and spelling. The format of the caption of this document is correct. Proofread only for completeness and correctness of information.

3. Compare the information in the answers to interrogatories to the client information form, checking for incorrect and missing information. Keep in mind that just because the attorney dictated the material, that does not always mean that it is correct. Attorneys are sometimes so focused on the letter of the law that they make errors in details. You must be aware of the details in the file so that you can find content/context errors as well as typos and errors in grammar and punctuation.

4. Circle the errors and write in missing information on the answers to interrogatories document.

5. Since you are completing this project by hand, your instructor will tell you how to submit this form. You could be handing it in physically, or you could be scanning the completed form and submitting it electronically. If you are asked to submit your work electronically, scan the file and save it as **LastName_C02_P3A_AnswersToInterrog** in the Chapter 2 folder. Note the addition of the letter "A" to the file title—this represents "Part A."

Part B While proofreading Mr. Johnson's answers to interrogatories, you found missing information in addition to grammatical errors. To complete the answers and mail them in time, you called Mr. Johnson and other necessary parties to obtain the missing information.

1. Open **C02_Litigation_P3B_AnswersMissingInfo** from your electronic storage medium. This file contains a list of the missing information.

2. Open **C02_P3_AnswersToInterrog** from the student data disc and resave it as **LastName_C02_P3B_AnswersToInterrog**. Note the addition of the letter "B" to the file title—this represents "Part B."

3. In Project 3, Part A, you circled areas of missing information in the answers to interrogatories. Add the missing information by typing it directly into **LastName_C02_P3B_AnswersToInterrog**.

4. Spell check and manually proofread one more time. Resave **LastName_C02_P3B_AnswersToInterrog** in the Chapter 2 folder.

5. Submit the file to the instructor.

Project 4   Long Letter

Attorney Eduardo Sanchez is also a partner in the law firm at which you work. Nicole Padoch, his assistant, is out of the office on a short vacation. Before she left the office, Nicole quickly transcribed a long letter dictated by Attorney Sanchez. The letter must go out to the client today by mail, so you offer to proofread the letter for Attorney Sanchez.

This is what you currently know about the case: Kelly Neelson is a landlord with rental property. The prospective tenants signed a 1-year lease for a monthly rent of $1,500 and a $1,500 deposit. Neelson agreed to hold the property for 1 month while she installed some new appliances. The tenants were to examine the property to make sure that it was what they wanted. The tenants complained of certain perceived deficiencies in the property, citing state and federal regulations. They then requested the return of their rent and security deposit, and asked to void the lease. Neelson hired Attorney Sanchez to negotiate with the tenants for a resolution of this matter.

Part A   Use the following instructions to complete the project.

1. Open and print **C02_P4_LongLetter** from the Chapter 2 folder in your electronic storage medium.

2. Proofread the letter for proper punctuation, grammar, sentence structure, and office style. Refer to a grammar style manual of your choice.

3. Circle the errors and write in missing information or corrections in the margins of the printed page.

4. Since you are completing this project by hand, your instructor will tell you how to submit this form. You could be handing it in physically or you could be scanning the completed form and submitting electronically. Save the scanned file as **LastName_C02_P4A_LongLetter** into the Chapter 2 folder on your electronic storage medium. Note the addition of the letter "A" to the file title—this represents "Part A."

Part B   Use the following instructions to complete the project.

1. Open the original **C02_P4_LongLetter** from the electronic storage medium.

2. Make any needed corrections in the file.

3. Resave the updated file as **LastName_C02_P4B_LongLetter** into the Chapter 2 folder in the electronic storage medium. Note the addition of the letter "B" to the file title—this represents "Part B."

4. Submit the electronic file to the instructor.

Discuss the Projects

This chapter covered the basics of the litigation process and details about calendaring and reminders. Take a moment to discuss the most efficient methods of calendaring and reminders with your classmates and how you would apply these skills to the projects pesented previously or similar assignments on the job.

1. What might you have to consider when working with a hard-copy document versus an electronic file during an assignment?

2. Project 3 instructed you to "read every word of the document and pay attention to names, numbers, addresses, and relationships to make sure that they are correct." Discuss ways in which you can ensure that you do this step properly.

3. Reread the long letter you saved as **LastName_C02_P4B_LongLetter**. With your classmates, make a list of items that you might note in your calendar after reading this letter. Include an estimate of when you would calendar the reminder and what you would actually write in the calendar.

Family Law/
Domestic Relations

Chapter Objectives

- Understand basic family law procedures and terminology
- Understand dissolution of marriage
- Complete an application for temporary relief
- Proofread a marital termination agreement

Attorneys Brisk, Arnold, and Jackson work for the same law firm. Attorney Brisk is currently representing a man seeking to adopt his recently orphaned nephew and a woman who is suing her ex-husband for spousal maintenance. Attorney Arnold has a client who is seeking visitation rights to see his two young children. Attorney Jackson is representing a client in the client's divorce proceedings. Although these four cases are different, they are all classified as family law.

Family law includes many specific areas of law sometimes called domestic relations. This area of law includes not only marriage and divorce but also diverse issues such as paternity, adoption, emancipated minors, civil unions, domestic partnerships, spousal abuse, annulments, property settlements, spousal maintenance, the establishment or termination of parental rights, child support, child custody, visitation, legitimacy, surrogacy, and child abuse. In some jurisdictions, guardianships, truancy, and matters related to juvenile delinquency are considered part of the law of domestic relations. In this chapter you will review basic family law procedures and terminology, review dissolution of marriage, complete an application for temporary relief, and proofread marital termination documents. This chapter's projects focus on dissolution of marriage (in some states, referred to as divorce).

When a married person or couple decide that they no longer wish to be married, one of the parties initiates a dissolution of marriage (in states that have adopted the no-fault system) or a divorce proceeding (in states that have not adopted the no-fault system). A **divorce** legally ends a marriage with one's spouse by providing grounds (or reasons) in a court of law, while a **no-fault dissolution of marriage** is a legal process for terminating a marriage in any way but annulment, usually on a no-fault basis, where grounds do not have to be proven. **Grounds** for a divorce are the reasons, or proof, needed to obtain a divorce. Grounds include marital misconduct such as adultery, cruel and abusive treatment, desertion, or neglect to provide support. In a dissolution of marriage, neither party is required to prove fault. By statute, the grounds or reasons for a dissolution of marriage are an irretrievable breakdown of the marriage relationship, irreconcilable differences, irremediable breakdown of the marriage, or incompatibility. Nothing needs to be proven in court and neither party is determined to be at fault.

A number of states allow no-fault dissolution of marriage. The laws of other states allow people to choose between either no-fault dissolution of marriage or divorce. In those states, the attorney will advise the client which procedure is best suited for the situation. People who decide upon a divorce are required to prove grounds or reasons for the divorce. A **no-fault divorce system** does not require an allegation or proof of fault of either party to be shown. The matter of grounds basically represents the difference between the two processes, requiring more time to be spent on proving grounds in the fault process.

Whether a state's laws allow divorce or no-fault dissolution, people generally refer to the process as divorce. Sometimes the process is referred to as dissolution of marriage instead of divorce. Either way, the couple legally and personally wish their marital relationship to be dissolved.

A divorce is a civil procedure, so the process is similar to a personal injury lawsuit or other type of civil case. Although there are many differences between these types of cases, you will recognize procedures, terms, and documents that are used for both.

In a state that follows no-fault procedures, the parties involved are the **petitioner** (party who starts the dissolution of marriage) and the **respondent** (party who responds to the documents served in the dissolution of marriage proceedings), as opposed to plaintiff and defendant in states that require proof of fault in a divorce proceeding.

The spouse who decides to start the divorce proceedings will usually contact and meet with an attorney and legal support staff. They will discuss the situation and decide if the attorney will be able to represent the person. Before anything can be done, the attorney must gather information about the parties and their lives. A confidential domestic relations questionnaire is used for this purpose. A **confidential domestic relations questionnaire** is a document that requests answers to questions about a client's life pertinent to dissolving a marriage. The questionnaire is given to the client to complete. It is similar to the client information form discussed in Chapter 2 and is often sent home with the client so that he or she can take the necessary time to gather information for the next appointment. Since the client may not know all the required information, the attorney or legal support staff may assist in gathering that information.

If the client is prepared to move forward with the divorce, the action will be brought in the county where either party resides if there are no children; however, if the children reside with only one parent, the action will be brought in the county where the children reside. The first or **initial pleadings** are the summons and petition (or complaint in fault states). Remember that a summons includes instructions about the length of time the respondent or plaintiff has to respond; in some cases, the back of the summons will contain a form to be completed by the person serving the documents as proof of service. In some states, the summons also includes wording that restrains the parties from selling, encumbering, or spending down assets other than to support themselves. This wording also restrains each party from ending or changing the beneficiary on any insurance coverage or selling any assets without the knowledge of the other.

Recall that a petition is a written request to the court asking for an order of the court. A petition used in family law is a document prepared by the petitioner that gives basic facts about the petitioner and his or her family and specifies what is being sought from the respondent through the divorce, such as child support, custody, spousal maintenance, etc.

In a dissolution proceeding, when initial or first pleadings are served upon the client's spouse, a process server or sheriff's deputy delivers documents to the respondent. Although in most civil procedures personal service of initial pleadings may be required, service by mail is allowed by the rules of court in some areas. The pleadings can be mailed along with an admission of service as proof of service. An **admission of service** serves as proof to the court that the respondent did indeed officially accept (sometimes in person) the summons and petition. Offices may also use the services of a sheriff's deputy to make service. When a sheriff's department is unable to perform the task, a professional process server is retained. Recall that a process server is a professional who is paid to serve legal documents upon people. The respondent can also accept service by appearing in person at the office of the petitioner's attorney.

Most legal pleadings require proof of service. Such proof states the name of the party being served, that party's address, and a brief statement describing how the documents were served. Figure 3.1 provides an example of an affidavit of service by mail. It is important to make certain that this proof of service is signed and dated. In some jurisdictions, this is simply a certificate of service; in other jurisdictions, it is a sworn affidavit of service which must be notarized.

Once the respondent has been served with the initial pleadings, he or she will typically contact an attorney. After obtaining detailed information from the respondent, the respondent's attorney will draft an answer and counterpetition to serve upon the petitioner's attorney. After the initial pleadings are served, responsive pleadings can be served by mail. The **answer and counterpetition** is a document that responds to each item in the petition and sets forth the relief that the respondent is requesting. It is one of the initial pleadings created by the respondent's attorney. As in the petition, the answer and counterpetition will address custody and parenting schedules from the respondent's perspective, along with any other issues.

At this point, both parties will file with the court a certificate of representation and a confidential information form along with a summons and petition and/or answer and counterpetition. The **certificate of representation** is a document required by the court that lists each party, his or her attorney's name, and all contact information. Because most court documents are available to the public, a confidential information form is required by the court. A **confidential information form** is a document filed separately with the court listing confidential information. In family law situations, many private details are needed on the forms required by the court, such as social security numbers, financial information, bank account numbers, children's names, etc. Private information is provided to the court on this form and should not be included on public documents. Figure 3.2 contains an example of a confidential information form.

Figure 3.1 **Affidavit of Service by Mail**

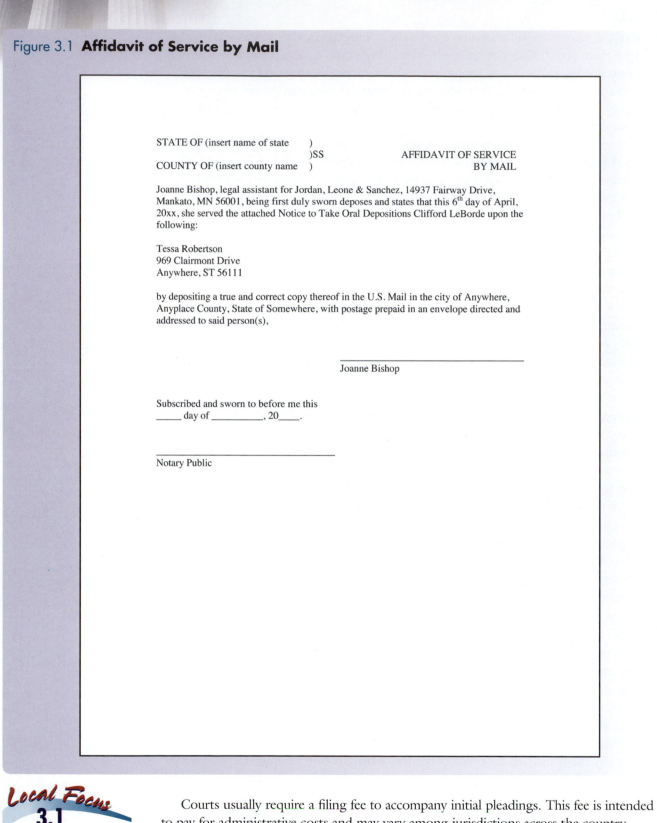

STATE OF (insert name of state   )
)SS   AFFIDAVIT OF SERVICE
COUNTY OF (insert county name   )   BY MAIL

Joanne Bishop, legal assistant for Jordan, Leone & Sanchez, 14937 Fairway Drive, Mankato, MN 56001, being first duly sworn deposes and states that this 6th day of April, 20xx, she served the attached Notice to Take Oral Depositions Clifford LeBorde upon the following:

Tessa Robertson
969 Clairmont Drive
Anywhere, ST 56111

by depositing a true and correct copy thereof in the U.S. Mail in the city of Anywhere, Anyplace County, State of Somewhere, with postage prepaid in an envelope directed and addressed to said person(s),

_____
Joanne Bishop

Subscribed and sworn to before me this
_____ day of _____, 20_____.

_____
Notary Public

Courts usually require a filing fee to accompany initial pleadings. This fee is intended to pay for administrative costs and may vary among jurisdictions across the country.

After initial pleadings have been filed with the court, a court file number and judge are assigned to the case. In some states an **informational statement** is due within a certain time after the court file is opened. An informational statement is a

Figure 3.2 **Confidential Information Form**

STATE OF MINNESOTA

COUNTY OF RICE

5-Dissolution without Children
IN DISTRICT COURT

THIRD JUDICIAL DISTRICT
Court File No.: 10-XT-12-41
Judge Robert Beecher

In Re the Marriage of:

Juliet Amphros,

       Petitioner,

v.

Harmon Amphros,

       Respondent.

CONFIDENTIAL INFORMATION FORM

The information on this form is confidential and shall not be placed in a publicly accessible portion of a file.

	Name	Social Security Number, Employer Identification Number, or Financial Account Numbers
Petitioner:	Juliet Amphros	SSN: 000-486-2081
	Juliet Amphros	American Bank Acct. No.: 376333-8359
Respondent:	Harmon Amphros	SSN: 000-104-1269
	Harmon Amphros	Prairie Bank Acct. No.: 48962-92867
Minor Children:	Ryan Amphros	SSN: 000-782-0927

Information supplied by Petitioner and counsel, Jessica D. Jordan

Dated:_____ _____

       Jessica D. Jordan
       JORDAN, LEONE & SANCHEZ
       14937 Fairway Drive
       Mankato, MN 56001
       Telephone: 507-389-6746
       Facsimile: 507-388-6740
       Attorney license number: 715MY3
       ATTORNEY FOR PETITION

document that provides the court with a summary of the issues involved in the case and an estimate of when both parties will be ready for trial.

Since a pending divorce affects almost everything involved with being a couple and/or a family, many issues will have to be addressed early in the process. Therefore, both parties have the right to file a **motion for temporary relief**, which allows

the court to consider immediate issues such as custody, child support, spousal maintenance, possession of the home, and other matters as the client's case may dictate. This motion, as its name implies, is temporary. In filing a motion for temporary relief, the following documents must be submitted to the court:

Motion A written request to the court.

Affidavit A formal sworn statement of fact signed by the **affiant** (person making the affidavit) and witnessed by a notary public.

Application for temporary relief A request to the court asking for an award of temporary custody, child support, spousal maintenance, possession of the home, and other matters as the client's case may dictate.

If the parties do not settle the case between themselves, the court does have jurisdiction to enter a final judgment and decree based upon the evidence presented at trial and information presented in the temporary motions. At this point, the parties can either agree to settlement by stipulation, or they may choose nonbinding mediation to settle their differences through a neutral third party. A **stipulation** is a court document in any legal process that includes details that the parties agree upon. It can also mean an agreement made between lawyers on opposite sides of a lawsuit.

Settlement by stipulation occurs if the parties can agree on all issues. In this case, the respondent does not have to file an answer to the first pleadings. Instead, agreed upon details are documented in a marital termination agreement for submission to the judge. The **marital termination agreement** is an agreement made by the divorcing spouses regarding the division of property, custody and parenting time, child support, and alimony/maintenance. The agreement must be put in writing, signed by the parties, and accepted by the court. It becomes part of the divorce decree and does away with the necessity of having a trial on the issues covered by the agreement. A marital termination agreement may also be called a *divorce agreement*, a *marital settlement agreement*, or a *settlement agreement*.

The other settlement option, other than a trial, is nonbinding mediation. **Mediation** is an informal voluntary process in which a mediator, trained in facilitation and negotiation techniques, helps the parties reach a mutually acceptable solution. The mediator does not impose a solution. Instead, he or she helps the parties to create their own understanding of what the settlement should entail. This process, whereby the parties are helped to craft their own agreements, often leads to unique solutions to specific situations that may not have been possible through litigation. Mediation is nonbinding unless both parties agree to a settlement. If the parties do agree, they may sign a marital termination agreement at this time.

If no trial is planned owing to an executed marital termination agreement, then one of the following actions will occur:

• If both parties are represented (regardless of whether there are children involved), the parties will sign the marital termination agreement and findings of fact and there is no hearing.

• If there are *no* children and one person is not represented and the parties have reached an agreement, there is no need for a hearing. Documents are simply submitted to the judge for signature. However, if there are no children and one person is not represented and that person fails to respond and no agreement is reached between the parties, there is a default hearing that must be attended by the petitioner. The respondent must be notified of the default hearing and may or may not attend.

- If there *are* children and one party is not represented, there is a default hearing that must be attended by the petitioner. The respondent must be notified of the default hearing; however, the respondent's attendance is optional.

If, however, there is disagreement and the answer and counterpetition are filed, the parties proceed toward trial. This process starts with discovery, including interrogatories, depositions, requests for documents, and requests for admissions, in order to clarify financial, custodial, and parenting time issues.

After the trial, each party creates a legal document called findings of fact, conclusions of law, order for judgment, and judgment and decree based upon testimony at trial. The judge has an allotted number of days (determined by state rules) to make a decision based upon the findings of fact submitted by one or both parties or a combination thereof. Once the judge has made his or her decision, the judge will sign a document called findings of fact, conclusions of law, order for judgment, and judgment and decree, which the court clerk will mail to both attorneys. The **findings of fact, conclusions of law, order for judgment, and judgment and decree** (all one document) sets forth the facts the judge found to be true and the conclusions of law he or she reached regarding those facts. This allows the parties to know how and why the judge reached a decision and whether an appeal is warranted. In a divorce situation, the parties want legal closure, so the judge also includes an order for judgment as well and the final judgment and decree, which is recorded with the county. The final judgment and decree is the document that finalizes the divorce or dissolution of marriage. A **final judgment and decree** is the final document that resolves all contested issues and terminates the legal proceedings.

ASSISTING THE COURT IN DEVELOPING FINDINGS OF FACT

Because each party has the ability to submit findings of fact to the judge and the judge then drafts his or her version (sometimes a combination of the two documents), the legal support person should send an electronic file of the findings of fact by email to the judge or the judge's clerk. Sending the file allows the judge to cut and paste from both parties' documents and create the binding final document.

Language Focus: Possessives

Legal documents are technical in many ways and require special attention and thought, so legal office staff must apply their knowledge of grammar and punctuation before the document is final. Possessives may seem routine, but because singular possessives can sound just like plural words, it is easy to make mistakes.

Possessives show that one noun has ownership of another noun. This is typically accomplished by adding an apostrophe and an *s* (*'s*) to the noun that possesses the other. Possessives show ownership, authorship, origin, or measurement. In the course of your work, you will encounter situations where you must determine whether a word is possessive and whether the possessive form is applied accurately. A simple way to understand possessive forms is to rewrite them. You should be able to easily identify the object that is being possessed and the noun that possesses it. Although this requires a little reworking, it is a simple and effective method. Consider the examples presented in Table 3.1.

Table 3.1 Rewritten Possessive Forms

Possessive Form	Type	Rewritten Phrase
Judge Sentory's decision	ownership	the decision of Judge Sentory
opposing counsel's brief	authorship	the brief of the opposing counsel
Wyoming's mountains	origin	the mountains of Wyoming
two weeks' vacation	measurement	a vacation of two weeks

Either version may be used in a written document; however, the possessive construction is shorter and more concise.

You have probably noticed that it is the *s* sound that makes a word sound possessive. Most people understand that to make a singular noun possessive, an apostrophe and an *s* would be added to the noun. But what about words that already contain an *s* sound? Possessive errors usually occur when a singular noun already end in *s* (Francis, Christmas); when a noun is plural (bosses, judges); and when a noun is plural but it does not end in *s* (children, women).

Possessives typically follow the standard construction as shown in Table 3.2:

Table 3.2 Standard Possessive Construction

Original	To Create the Possessive Form
Singular nouns that do *not* end with an *s* sound (client, lawyer)	Add an apostrophe *s* (*'s*) (a *client's* address, the *lawyer's* work)
Plural nouns that do *not* contain an *s* sound (children, men):	Add an apostrophe *s* (*'s*) (the *children's* mother, the *men's* dispute)
Singular nouns that *do* end in an *s* sound (Francis, Christmas)	Add an apostrophe *s* (*'s*) (*Francis's* case, *Christmas's* origin)
Plural nouns that *do* end with an *s* sound (judges, bosses)	Add an apostrophe (*'*) (the *judges'* conference, the *bosses'* bonuses)

Best Practice Tip

AVOID DOUBLE S SOUND IN POSSESSIVES

Most editors try to avoid the double *s* sound that is created when a possessive noun already contains an *s* sound. If possible, one might rewrite the sentence to avoid the sound. For example, you might choose to change the phrase "the business's lawsuit" to "the company's lawsuit."

Best Practice Tip

DOUBLE S SOUND AND OFFICE STYLE

You may work for a company that avoids the double *s* sound by *only* adding an apostrophe to singular nouns that end in an *s* sound and not including the additional *s*. In this situation, "Francis' case" would be considered correct. Be sure that you follow your office's style when you are editing documents. The key here is to be consistent in every case and to become familiar with your office's style.

When you encounter what may be a possessive word, the first thing to determine is whether it should be singular or plural. Use your prior knowledge and context clues from surrounding material to determine if a word should be plural or singular. Verify that the word is spelled correctly. Now decide whether the word is possessive or not. If a word *is* possessive, it will always have a noun following it. Only nouns (persons, places, things, concepts) can belong to someone or something. The following is an example.

> Pursuant to Minnesota Rules of Civil Procedure, Mr. Miller's request is not supported.

Rules is plural but not possessive because it is followed by a preposition. *Mr. Miller* is singular and possessive because it is followed by the noun *request*—the request of Mr. Miller. *Request* is the object of possession.

> The Millers are on vacation this week.

Millers is just plural and not possessive here. *Are* is a verb.

> The Millers' home was burglarized while they were on vacation.

Millers' is plural *and* possessive here because it is the home of the Millers and *home* is the object of possession.

Other Tricky Possessives

Do not use an apostrophe with nonpossessive descriptive words that end in *s*. *Legal* in *legal department* does not end in *s*, so do not be tempted to make *legal* possessive. *Legal* is an adjective describing *department*. Nouns, not adjectives, are the only words that are made possessive. On the other hand, because *electronics* in *electronics department* does end in *s*, you may be tempted to use an apostrophe and make it possessive. However, *electronics* is, once again, an adjective in *electronics department* and does not require an apostrophe.

> The attorney's lecture encouraged me to transfer from our human resources division to our legal division.

Always put the apostrophe on the END of a possessive compound word. Remember that the plural *s* is on the most important word, as in *brothers-in-law*.

> I met my brothers-in-law to discuss their company. (plural, not possessive)
>
> My brothers-in-law's company made a profit this quarter. (plural and possessive)
>
> My father-in-law's legal rights to the company have been questioned. (singular, possessive)

People's names are made possessive the same way as other nouns except that the spelling should not be changed.

> The Kellys' adopted son has arrived. (not the Kellies' adopted son)

The word *the* before a family name indicates that the name is plural.

> The Joneses are going through a divorce.
>
> Have you heard that the Joneses' divorce has been finalized?

If the object of possession at the end of the sentence is unstated, the owner noun should still be treated as possessive.

> Do you prefer Attorney Johnson's suggestion or Attorney Smith's? (Smith's *suggestion* is implied, so *Smith* must be possessive, too.)

When two nouns come before an object of possession and express *separate* ownership, make both nouns possessive. In other words, each owner has his or her own object of possession.

> Ronaldo's and William's law offices are both attracting the same types of clients.

When two nouns come before an object of possession and express *combined* ownership, make the second noun only possessive. In other words, the owners own the object together.

> Mark and Diane's son is filing to become an emancipated minor.
>
> The Thomases and Hoods' cabin has been owned jointly since 2007.

Remember that a gerund looks like a verb (because it ends in *ing*) but acts like a noun. Because a gerund acts like a noun, it can be an object of possession and the noun before it needs an apostrophe.

> We were not happy about Chad's telling the opposing attorney too much about the situation.

Remember that while nouns use apostrophes to show possession, pronouns change their spelling and do not use apostrophes.

> *He, she, they, it* ➡ *his, her, their, and its*
>
> Ryan's education came in handy as he looked for a job.
> His education came in handy as he looked for a job.
>
> The girls' athletic program was on par with the boys'.
> Their athletic program was on par with the boys'.
>
> Every section of the rules has its own regulations.
> Do you think it's a good idea to balance the accounts before we finalize the monthly entries? (It's is a contraction for *it is*.)

Best Practice Tip

POSSESSIVE OR CONTRACTION?

Remember that *it's* is a contraction for *it is* and should never be used as a possessive form. This is a common error in writing. For example, *It's* a successful company, but *its* stock has dropped significantly during this past year. Keep in mind that in professional writing, legal writers avoid contractions such as *it's*, *can't*, *doesn't*, *let's*, and others. Contractions are acceptable in informal interoffice communications.

Language Focus Exercises

Apply what you have learned previously to the following exercises.

Exercise 3.1 Use the following sentences to practice the lesson. Determine if the underlined word should be singular or plural and whether it should be possessive. In the space provided, rewrite the underlined word to correct each sentence.

1. I was expecting to receive briefs from multiple attorneys early in the week; unfortunately, several of the <u>attorneys</u> briefs were delivered to the office on Friday.

   _____

2. The two minor <u>child</u> school is in the same neighborhood as both parents.

   _____

3. The two minor <u>child</u> will be attending that school in the fall.

   _____

4. The <u>witness</u> attention was flagging by the end of the day. She was the only one who showed boredom.

   _____

5. The <u>witnesses</u> asked if he had to answer the question.

   _____

6. Mr. Swinghammer, Mr. Schleicher, and Ms. Jacobs all witnessed the accident. The <u>witness</u> testimony were recorded before they all left town.

   _____

7. All the <u>witness</u> had to stay the entire day.

   _____

Exercise 3.2 Read the following sentences and correct any errors directly to the sentences. Write "C" in the left margin if the sentence is correct.

1. Jessica Harms is our legal assistant. It was our legal assistants idea to add the jurat clause to the affidavit.

2. Our two next-door neighbors objected to him running the mower late at night.

3. We have been invited to the Molstad's home on Friday night. Phoebe Molstad will be home on Thursday.

4. Did you know that the antique store downtown has lost it's lease?

5. Valentin's and Timothy's pool takes up most of their backyard.

6. The attorneys' luncheon will be held at 11 a.m. for all of the attorneys in the office.

7. Anderson Fox will be granted a 6-month leave in January.

8. How many Macintosh's have been ordered?

9. My sisters'-in-laws houses are just blocks from each other.

10. The mayor's opponents are all informed of the details.

11. Even though I like Jack's work, I am inspired by Lilys.

12. The Sales' Department will need to work overtime this weekend.

13. It's hard to manage two bosses' work at the same time.

14. Their catalog is a lot smaller than our's.

15. Elliot has 16 year's experience at mediating contracts.

Editing: Methods of Staying Focused

Documents in many areas of the law are quite long. Editing is an important task, whether the documents are long or short. Of course it is easier to edit shorter documents because the editor is not required to focus for a long period of time. It is important, however, to keep your mind sharp and focused on content as well as details no matter the document's length. The following contains ideas to keep the editor's mind sharp and focused in order to edit efficiently.

Take Breaks Edit for a preset period of time; then set the work aside and do something else. Return to the work after doing something other than editing or proofreading.

Edit Twice Edit your document completely. Then, if possible, set it aside until the next day. Edit again to find errors missed the day before. The only problem with setting work aside until the following day is that employees in a busy law office rarely have time to spare, and the work may have to be sent out on the same day. Instead of setting it aside overnight, set it aside for an hour. Focus on something entirely different before finishing the project.

Consider the Time of Day Do this more detailed work early in the day so that your mind and eyes are fresh.

Experiment with Music If you have done editing and proofreading before, you know that it can often become tedious and boring. Can you concentrate on your work with music on? Does the type of music make a difference in your concentration? Determine whether music with vocals distracts you. Would instrumental music be a better choice? Or, no music at all?

LIGHTING

If you work in an office with fluorescent lighting, consider having a desk lamp to use when you are editing and proofreading documents.

Use Proper Lighting Do not proofread under fluorescent lighting. Because fluorescent lights have a lower "flicker" rate than other lights, our eyes do not pick up inconsistencies as easily. *Light flicker* refers to quick, repeated changes in light intensity, which can make light sources appear to flutter and be unsteady. Flicker is caused when the voltage supplied to a light source changes or when the voltage of the power line itself fluctuates. A lower flicker rate can cause the page to be dim for a fraction of a second; our eyes may then miss small inconsistencies, such as minute changes in font size or very small indents.

Rest Your Eyes Rest your eyes every 15 to 20 minutes. Look up from your copy and focus on a far object for 10 seconds. Then focus on your close copy for 5 seconds. Do that three or four times. Close your eyes for 30 seconds at the end of the exercise.

Add Variety Read something else between edits to clear your mind of what you expect to see on the page.

REVIEW GRAMMAR MANUALS

Spend 30 minutes per month reviewing grammar rules. This not only gives you a break from the editing and proofreading tasks at hand but also improves your confidence. Consider reading these manuals when you need to add variety to your editing schedule.

Editing Exercise

The following exercise will allow you to practice your editing skills using the information discussed in this chapter.

Exercise 3.3 Practice the focusing methods discussed earlier in this chapter while completing the following exercise.

1. Open and print the PDF file **C03_Ex3.3** from the Chapter 03 folder in your electronic storage medium.
2. Edit the document for content and formatting, marking all errors and changes in black pen.
3. Put the document away for 24 hours.
4. Take the marked document out again the next day and edit it one more time. Mark any additional changes with a red pen.
5. Discuss with your classmates if you found more errors the second time around.
6. Submit the edited document according to your instructor's directives.

Proofreading: Moving Between Hard Copy and Electronic Documents

Although it is important to determine whether you prefer to edit and proofread materials on the computer screen or on a printed copy, your employer will expect you to be comfortable with both methods. It is necessary to be confident working with both types, as you may need to transfer hard-copy documentation to an electronic file or proof an electronic document against a hard copy document.

The number of interruptions that a legal support person has to contend with each day makes it easy to return to the wrong place in a printed or electronic document. Use the following tips to assist in proofreading between hard copy documents and electronic documents.

Use a Straight Edge It is important to always know your place in a document. Use a straight edge (such as a ruler or the edge of another sheet of paper or folder) to draw your eye down the page of hard copy that you are proofing. Doing so will keep your eyes focused on the correct line and allow you to move your eyes easily from the hard copy to the screen.

Mark Your Place When you are interrupted, take a second to mark your current location in the documents you are proofreading. In the document, draw or type a slash (/), underline, or highlight the last word you typed or proofed before you were interrupted.

Ask for Assistance When you return to your work after an interuption, ask a colleague to read the original document to you and proofread what you have typed.

Watch for Repetitive Numbers When you proofread documents for a divorce, be aware that you may encounter repetitive information regarding real estate. Married couples frequently own real estate together. When these couples divorce, they must decide to sell the property or arrange to have one of the parties buy out the other. Divorce documents must show this decision; therefore, the property's legal description will appear within the documents that the legal support person will edit and proofread. The legal description in Figure 3.3 is a good example of repeated words and figures; these can draw your eye away from the spot to which you should return when you are typing the description.

A legal description of property is not the mailing address. It is the official physical description of the property determined by surveyors and used to locate the property. It can be complicated to type since there are many repetitive numbers and words. In typing these descriptions, concentrate and return your eyes to the correct location if you are interrupted.

As often as possible, type the legal description from an official document, such as an abstract or a Torrens certificate of title. If you have to use handwritten legal descriptions or other unreliable sources like letters, follow up with the official legal description to confirm accuracy.

Best Practice Tip

ELECTRONIC EDITING AND PROOFREADING

In a busy legal office, there is often very little time to transfer your handwritten editing work to an electronic file. Working electronically can save both time and paper, so it in your best interest to become skilled at editing and proofreading directly in an electronic document.

Figure 3.3 **Legal Description Example**

A certain tract or parcel of land containing 1.766 acres, more or less, being a portion of Lots 1 & 2, Block E, Unit 13, River Oaks Subdivision, in Section 35, Township 18 North, Range 3 East, Land District North of Red River, Ouachita Parish, Louisiana, as per plat recorded in Plat Book 17, page 47, records of Ouachita Parish, Louisiana, and being more particularly described as follows:

Beginning at the Northwest corner of Lot 1, Block E, Unit 13, River Oaks Subdivision, said point being the intersection of the South right-of-way line of Deborah Drive with the East right-of-way line of Barbados Boulevard; thence South 80°53'42" East along the North line of said Lot 1 and the South right-of-way line of Deborah Drive a distance of 260.00 feet; thence South 09°06'18" West for a distance of 258.00 feet; thence South 46°39'37" West for a distance of 119.91 feet to a point on the Northeasterly right-of-way line of "M" Street and the South line of said Lot 2; thence North 44°07'18"West along said Northeasterly line of "M" Street for a distance of 101.21 feet to the Southwest corner of said Lot 2 and the point of curvature of a curve to the left; thence North along said curve to the left, said curve having a radius of 175.0 feet (chord bearing North 62°30'30" West—length 110.40 feet) for a distance of 112.32 feet; thence North 80°62'42" West 1.08 feet to the Southwest corner of said Lot 1 and the intersection of the East right-of-way line of Barbados Boulevard with the North right-of-way line of "M" Street; thence North 09°06'18" East along the West line of said Lot 1 and the East right-of-way line of Barbados Boulevard a distance of 257.65 feet to the Point of Beginning and subject to a 12-foot-wide servitude along Barbados Boulevard, Deborah Drive, and "M" Street and all other rights-of-way, easements, and servitudes of record or of use.

These legal descriptions are difficult to type as well as proofread, since they do not read like a typical paragraph. Once the description is typed, team proofread with an office colleague. Since you have already read and typed the description, have your colleague proofread and make corrections on the computer screen as you read from the original. As you read, include how a word is abbreviated, whether a number is spelled out or in numerals, and say every mark of punctuation. The description may have been typed from an old deed or survey that is difficult to read because the font is small, print has faded, or a typewriter was used. A 6 can look like an 8, and other words and numbers may be hard to read. In this situation, two people should review the original, and if there are two opinions about a number or letter, it should be investigated further.

Check for Common Errors

Pay attention to your editing and proofreading and notice the types of errors you tend to miss. Be watchful of the parties' titles throughout the document. Keep in mind who your client is as well as the client's relationship to other parties referred to in the document.

Make a list of these items and scan the list periodically to remind yourself to look specifically for these errors or omissions. The following is a sample list showing what may be on a legal support person's list of frequently missed editing and proofreading details.

CHECK:
- Spelling of people's names
- All addresses (house number, street name, city, state, zip)
- That there are page numbers
- Double and single spacing throughout document

Pay special attention to numbers and dollar amounts. In addition to recalculating the figures used in family law documents, focus on whether the figures make sense. In a family law situation, the marital termination agreement (MTA) is based upon the figures in the application for temporary relief (ATR). Figure 3.4 shows page 5 in the ATR. Compare this figure to pages 3 and 4 of the marital termination agreement in Figure 3.5.

In proofreading these documents, one should consider the differing net amounts of take-home pay between the ATR and the MTA shown in Figures 3.4 and 3.5. Upon inspection, the proofreader can verify that the net take-home pay for the petitioner in the ATR is $82 less because the petitioner is paying the respondent for the children's health insurance. The net take-home pay for the respondent in the ATR is $82 more because the respondent is receiving $82 from the petitioner as reimbursement for the children's health insurance. It is important that these numbers be proofread before the final draft is completed.

Best Practice Tip

FREQUENTLY USED INFORMATION

Pay close attention to addresses, cities, counties, and states. There may be several parties to a transaction from different locations. It is easy to mix up these locations. Make a cover sheet for each file with important and frequently used information on the top sheet. Keep this sheet up to date as you receive information. Always keep the sheet current in the computer file since the attorney may retrieve the file from his or her wireless device as well.

Figure 3.4 **Page 5 of an application for temporary relief (ATR)**

Employment Data	Husband	Wife
Federal Income Tax	301	82
State Withholding	128	46
Social Security (FICA)	219	185
Pension Deduction		192
Union Dues		
Medical Insurance		240
Dental Coverage		44
Subtotal of Statutory Deductions:	B. 648	B. 789
Net Income: (Line A – Line B)	C. 3,219	C. 3,461
Other Paycheck Deductions:		
Life Insurance		189
Long-Term Disability		
Subtotal of Other Paycheck Deductions:	D.	D. 189
NET TAKE-HOME PAY (Line C – Line D)	3,219	3,272
Tax withholdings above are based on married/single with # of exemptions:	S-1	S-2
Employer-reimbursed expenses—specify below:		
Other Income:		
Public Assistance		
Social Security Benefits for party or child(ren)		
Unemployment/Workers' Compensation		
Interest Income		
Dividend Income per quarter		11
Other Income		

Figure 3.5 **Pages 3 and 4 from a marital termination agreement (MTA)**

Petitioner's Employment. The Petitioner is employed as a mechanic at Gavin's Machinery, Inc. The Petitioner's earned income in the past year was approximately $44,500. After allowable statutory deductions and reimbursements to Respondent of $82 per month for the children's health insurance, Petitioner has net monthly income of **$3,137**.

Respondent's Employment. The Respondent is employed as an accountant at W. B. Accounting, Inc. The Respondent has been so employed for 8 years. The Respondent's earned income in the past year was approximately $51,000. After allowable statutory deductions and reimbursement from Petitioner of $82 per month for the children's health insurance, Respondent has net monthly income of **$3,354**.

Proofreading Exercise

Complete the following proofreading exercises using the tips described previously.

Exercise 3.4

1. Open and print **C03_Ex3.4_LegalDescription**.
2. Quickly move your eyes through the legal description to see if your eyes are drawn to repeated words or numbers.
3. Highlight these repeated items.
4. Compare with your classmates the items you feel may cause you to mistype this legal description.

Exercise 3.5

1. Key the legal description from the hard copy you printed for Exercise 3.4.
2. Use techniques that help you to keep your eyes on the correct line as you are typing.
3. Save the legal description periodically as you key it as **LastName_C03_Ex3.5**.
4. Find someone willing to proofread this description with you. Have him or her proofread what you have keyed (on the computer screen or a printout) while you read the original description from which you typed. Remind the helper that all marks and punctuation must be proofread, such as *abbreviations, commas, periods, semicolons, parentheses, end parentheses, degrees, minutes,* and *seconds.*

5. Make corrections and resave.

6. On the lines below, write what techniques you used to keep your eyes on the correct line of the description as you typed. Also, write how many errors you found proofreading with a partner and what difficulties you may have encountered during the team proofreading process.

_____

_____

_____

7. Share your findings with your classmates and instructor.

Family Law/Domestic Relations How-To Guide

In working in a family law office, one becomes familiar with caption requirements for court documents. A **caption** is the first section of any written legal pleading to be filed with the court. It contains the names of the parties involved in the legal situation, the court name, the case number, and the title of the document (complaint, answer, motion, etc.). Each jurisdiction has its own rules as to the exact format of the caption. The following discussion uses a specific state style; however, the details described can be applied to any state's caption requirements. Always check your local requirements before creating the caption for a court document. Your office will have previous files to view as samples as well.

Captions

The office that initiates the lawsuit is the one required to determine the details needed for the caption. Any responsive pleadings would use the same caption as the initial pleadings except that the name of the document would change. A **responsive pleading** is any court document that is created in response to another court document.

Figure 3.6 shows the rules that apply to court captions in court documents according to the *Minnesota Rules of Civil Procedure*. The entire rule is available in the Chapter 03 folder of the student data disc for your reference: **C03_MinnCivilRules_Rules10-11_effective102210**. Figure 3.7 shows a diagram and format explanations of a caption.

Best Practice Tip

CAPTIONS

Whether your client is initiating the lawsuit or the court proceeding, remember that all documents pertaining to one lawsuit/proceeding have the same caption. The only things that change are the name of the document and the body. Having the same caption allows office staff to create and save the caption once, making certain that it is perfectly correct. You can start every court document then by inserting the caption from the saved file. This eliminates repeated errors. Keep in mind that the caption must be entirely correct, so that you do not perpetuate a saved error from document to document. Having the same caption also allows court staff to make a clear connection among the documents for one case.

Taken from *Minnesota Rules of Civil Procedures, Updated: 10-22-10*

Rule 10. Form of Pleadings

10.01 Names of Parties

Every pleading shall have a caption setting forth the name of the court and the county in which the action is brought, the title of the action, the court file number if one has been assigned, and a designation as in Rule 7, and, in the upper right hand corner, the appropriate case type indicator as set forth in the subject matter index included in the appendix as Form 23. If a case is assigned to a particular judge for all subsequent proceedings, the name of that judge shall be included in the caption and adjacent to the file number. In the complaint, the title of the action shall include the names of all the parties, but in other pleadings it is sufficient to state the first party on each side with an appropriate indication of other parties.

(Amended effective March 1, 2001.)

Advisory Committee Comments - 2000 Amendments

Rule 10.01 is amended to facilitate case management and document management in cases where a judge has been assigned to the case. By placing the judge's name on the caption, it is often possible to expedite the delivery of filed documents to that judge. This provision is commonly required in federal court cases where all matters are assigned to a judge, including in the United States District Court for the District of Minnesota. See LR 5.1 (D. Minn.). The rule is also amended to require the inclusion of a court file number if one has been assigned.

10.02 Paragraph; Separate Statements

All averments of claim or defense shall be made in numbered paragraphs, the contents of each of which shall be limited as far as practicable to a statement of a single set of circumstances; and a paragraph may be referred to by number in all succeeding pleadings. Each claim founded upon a separate transaction or occurrence and each defense other than denials shall be stated in a separate count or defense whenever a separation facilitates the clear presentation of the matters set forth.

10.03 Adoption by Reference; Exhibits

Statements in a pleading may be adopted by reference in a different part of the same pleading or in another pleading or in any motion. A copy of any written instrument which is an exhibit to a pleading is a part of the statement of claim or defense set forth in the pleading.

10.04 Failure to Comply

If a pleading, motion or other paper fails to indicate the case type as required by Rule 10.01, it may be stricken by the court unless the appropriate case type indicator is communicated to the court administrator promptly after the omission is called to the attention of the pleader or movant.

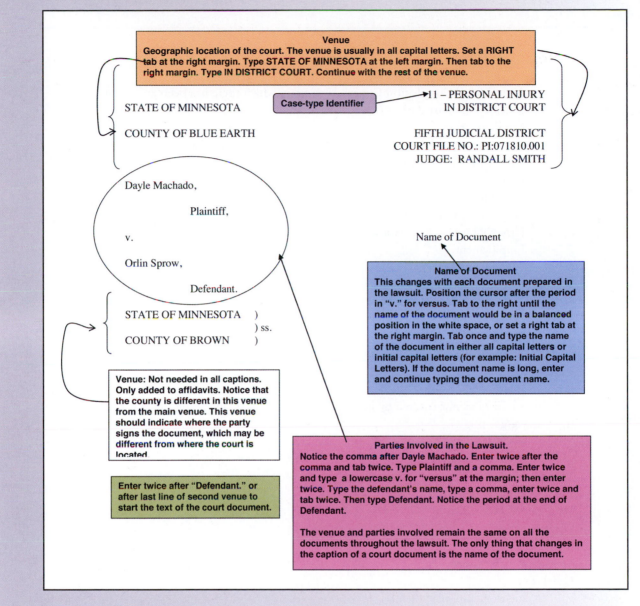

The first time you create a court document for a client, you will most likely be working with the attorney or another legal support person. Creating the correct caption will be a joint effort. Some of the items you may be responsible for obtaining and verifying are the case type identifier, county name, judicial district number, court file number, party names and designations, document name, and optional venue.

Case-type Identifier Some states require that the caption include a case-type identifier to allow for faster filing and organizing by the court and gathering of statistical data. Figure 3.8 shows the Appendix of Forms, Form 23, the subject matter index for civil cases found in the *Minnesota Rules of Civil Procedure*. Insert the

FORM 23—SUBJECT MATTER INDEX FOR CIVIL CASES

1. Appeal from Conciliation Court (All cases in which there has been an appeal from a conciliation court decision)
2. Condemnation
3A. Consumer Credit Contract (Plaintiff is a corporation or organization, not an individual; defendant is an individual; and contract amount does not exceed $20,000)
3B. Other Contracts (All other contracts not included in 3A, above)
4. Dissolution With Children
5. Dissolution Without Children
6. Driver's License Revocation (Implied consent)
7. Employment
8. Harassment (Except for employment-related cases)
9. Medical Malpractice
10. Property Damage
11. Personal Injury
12. Unlawful Detainer
13. Wrongful Death
14. Other Civil

(All other civil cases not covered by items 1 through 13 above, including but not limited to the following:

        Appeals from Administrative Agencies
        Attorney Malpractice
Change of Name
Corporate Dissolution
Declaratory Judgment
Discrimination
Minor Settlement
Mortgage Foreclosure
Quiet Title
Real Estate Tax Petitions
Receivership
Torrens
Writs of Attachment, Certiorari,
Habeas Corpus, Mandamus
and Prohibition)

(Amended effective January 1, 2009.)

REFERENCE LISTS

You may find lists like this one in Figure 3.8 that you refer to frequently. Post these lists in a convenient spot at your desk for easy reference.

number and the name of the subject matter of the case into the upper-right corner, first line, followed by the caption. Figure 3.7 shows where this case-type identifier should be placed. For example, if the case is a dissolution of marriage with children, then the case-type identifier would be as follows:

4—Dissolution with Children

County Name In a dissolution of marriage, if there are no children, the court with jurisdiction will generally be in the county where either party resides. However, if the two parties have children and the children live with only one parent, the judicial hearings would be held in the county where the children reside. You may have to search online for the appropriate county name based on where the children and/or parties reside.

Judicial District Number Once the appropriate county has been determined, go to your state court system's website to determine the judicial district. You can find which judicial district a city and county are in by going to the state's website. For example, Minnesota courts can be found at http://lep.emcp.net/mncourts.

Court File Number One of the parties will file initial documents with the court (summons and complaint or petition) and notify the court of the names and addresses of the other involved parties and/or their attorneys. Court administration will open a file, assign a court file number to the matter, and mail out a notice of case filing to all parties or attorneys on record. The notice will identify the court file number and the address to which future filings should be sent to the court. It may include the name of the judge assigned to the case. This notice may also include deadlines by which the parties must give the court additional information about the case. Therefore, it only makes sense that the first pleadings *will not* have a court file number to insert into the caption. Figure 3.9 shows an example of a notice of case filing and assignment.

Party Names and Designations Party names must be checked and spelled correctly. Double check the file. In addition to spelling the parties' names correctly, determine the correct title or party designation for the particular type of case. For example, a personal injury case or a criminal case will most likely have a plaintiff and defendant. However, in a state that has no-fault divorce, the party initiating the dissolution of marriage is the petitioner and the other party is the respondent.

Local Focus 3.4

Document Name One of the simplest mistakes made in creating court documents is leaving out the document name. If you look at Figure 3.7 again, you will see that it is easy to complete the "parties involved" section of the caption and simply enter it several times and continue with the body of the document. In the example given in Figure 3.7, the name of the document is to the right of the *versus* line. Some offices prefer to center the name of the document a double space after the last party title. Always follow the style used in your own office.

Figure 3.9 **Completed Notice of Case Filing and Assignment**

5-Dissolution without Children

STATE OF MINNESOTA   IN DISTRICT COURT

COUNTY OF WASECA   THIRD JUDICIAL DISTRICT
                                                      Court File No.: 70-BE-90-93

NOTICE OF CASE FILING & ASSIGNMENT

PHILLIP WALSH
491 TIMBER BORDER, SUITE 21
JANESVILLE, MN 56231

Nick R. Stewart vs. Scott P. Tomsen

Date Case Filed: 12-03-11

Court file number 70-BE-90-93 has been assigned to this matter.

Pursuant to M.S. 542.13, 542.16 and Rules of Civil Procedures 63.03, you are hereby notified that this case has been assigned to District Court Judge Bradley M. Montebrand.

All future correspondence must include this file number, the attorney identification number, and must otherwise conform to format requirements or they WILL BE RETURNED. Correspondence and communication on this matter should be directed to the following court address:

      Waseca County Court Administration
      Justice Center, 104 Morris Drive, P.O. Box 743
      Waseca, MN 56710

If ADR applies, a list of neutrals is available at any court facility. Please direct all inquiries on this matter to the judicial staff at 507-555-0564.

Dated: December 3, 2011   Judith Jamison
                                                      Court Administrator
                                                      Waseca County

cc: Paige J. Donahoe

XX_____ Certificate of Representation is due pursuant to Rule 104 Rules of General Practice.
XX_____ Information Statement is due within 60 days pursuant to Rules 111.02 and 304.02 of Rules of General Practice.

Additional, Optional Venue An additional, optional venue is added as a double space below the second party's title on affidavits and applications, such as this:

STATE OF MINNESOTA)
) ss.

COUNTY OF _____)

The blank indicates the county in which the document will be signed. Remember that *venue* means the geographic location. All court documents include the geographic location of the court that is to hear the case indicated in the main part of the caption. In addition, if the document is to be signed by the client, it is usually notarized. Documents such as affidavits and applications are notarized and require the additional venue to indicate the location of the party at the time the document is signed.

As an example, assume that the court venue for a case you are handling is the state of Minnesota, county of Sibley. This information would be at the top of the page in the court caption. You are submitting a sworn affidavit in support of a motion, and this affidavit will be signed by your client's relative who lives in Scott County.

Figure 3.10 shows an example of the affidavit. Notice the venue (geographic location of the lawsuit) in the court caption. Also, notice that there is an additional venue below the court caption that identifies where this affidavit is being signed.

A legal support person should know when to add a second venue. But if the attorney is dictating an entire document, he or she will typically indicate in the dictation when this second venue is to be added. If you have been asked to fill in variable information in a premade form, the second venue will likely have been previously inserted into the form.

Jurat Clause (added to the signature area of affidavits and applications)

On an affidavit or application, remember to add a jurat clause to the end of the document next to or a double space after the signature line. A **jurat clause** is certification declaring when, where, and before whom a document was sworn. Jurat clauses are added to all affidavits and applications.

Some states prefer that the jurat clause be typed across the entire page. Other states use a jurat clause that is formatted just to the left of the center of the page. See examples of both formats in Figures 3.11 and 3.12 on the next page:

The notary public will sign jurat clauses of both styles. In the full-page jurat clause, the notary will handwrite when his or her commission expires. A rubber stamp may or may not be added over the jurat clause, showing the state seal. In the left-to-the-center formatting, the expiration date of the commission is in the rubber stamp used over the jurat clause.

Best Practice Tip

DOCUMENT SIGNING

If the document will not be signed in your presence, always find out where the document signing will occur and fill in the correct location. You can also leave it blank so that it can be written in during the signing. Apply a colorful tab pointing to the blank as a reminder for the client to fill in the location.

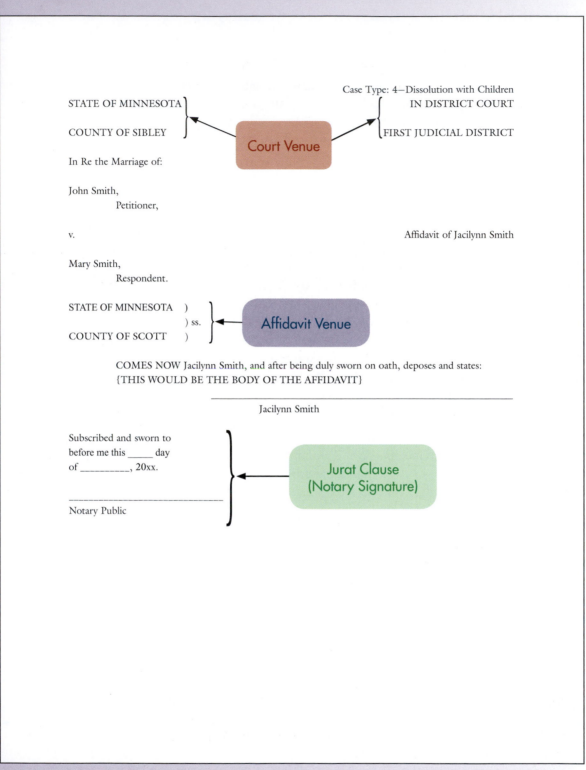

Figure 3.11 Example of jurat clause formatted across full page

Subscribed and sworn to before me this _____ day of _____, 20xx.

_____
Notary Public

My Commission Expires _____

Figure 3.12 Example of a jurat clause formatted on the left to the center of the page

Subscribed and sworn to
before me this _____ day
of _____, 20xx.

_____
Notary Public

How-To Guide Exercises

Complete the following exercises using the information found in the How-To Guide section.

Exercise 3.6 Read the following situations. Apply what you have learned in this section to determine the answers to the following questions. Write your answers on the lines provided.

In the first case you assist with, your client, Anthony Bandalona, lives in Roseau, Minnesota, and is the defendant in a personal injury case. The plaintiff is Marc Oline, from Owatonna, Minnesota. Mr. Oline is suing Mr. Bandalona for injuries suffered in a car accident. Your client has already been served with initial pleadings. You are now creating answers to interrogatories for your client.

In your second case, Brittany Woodruff, your client, lives in Watonwan County, Minnesota, and is the petitioner in a dissolution of marriage case in which Allen Jones is the respondent. The parties have no children. Your client has already served the initial pleadings. You are now creating answers to interrogatories for your client.

1. Which of the two cases described does not require your office to provide the necessary details to use in the caption? Explain why on the lines provided.

_____

_____

_____

_____

2. Which of the two cases described requires your office to find and provide the details necessary to use in the caption? Explain why on the lines provided and then answer questions 3 through 9 based on your response.

_____

_____

_____

_____

3. What will be the case-type identifier (use the information provided in Figure 3.8)?

_____

4. In what county will the case be brought?

_____

5. In what judicial district is the county?

_____

6. Will a court file number be assigned to the case at this point? Why or why not?

_____

_____

7. Who are the parties involved and what are their titles?

_____

8. What is the name of the document you are creating?

_____

9. Will this document require an optional venue?

_____

Critical Thinking: Goal Setting and Working with Clients

The legal workplace is competitive, and it is necessary to separate yourself from your competition. To succeed, you must be willing to go above and beyond the expectations of your position. To obtain and maintain your position in a legal office, you have to make yourself indispensable to your employer. This means always having your work completed on time, being efficient in interpreting instructions, thinking ahead, making sure that the office runs smoothly, and always working in a professional manner.

A typical employer is looking for an employee who can think about the consequences of current actions and plan for possible future outcomes. This is the primary objective of critical thinking skills. For every action there is a reaction, and for every task there are needs and obstacles that must be anticipated. Critical thinking is work. Just as an athlete must train his or her body, the brain must be exercised to make it stronger. This process takes time and energy, but it will save you and your employer time and energy in the long run.

Setting Goals to Encourage Critical Thinking

Ambition is a key characteristic of successful workers. Consider the goals that you have for your own career. You might want to work for a particularly well-known law firm, receive an early promotion, or even manage the work of other employees. By establishing goals for yourself, you will feel encouraged to do your best in the office and become an effective critical thinker.

Brainstorm three goals you have for your own career. Record these goals on the lines provided and make a list of the ways in which you might achieve these goals. Identify which actions will help you be most successful.

_____

_____

_____

_____

_____

_____

_____

_____

One way to ensure that you will achieve your goals in the workplace is by representing yourself in a professional manner. Behaving professionally both in person and on the telephone is important in any office. You represent your employer every time you do business with a client, an office supply company, a printing company, and even the grocery store if you are in charge of buying supplies for the break room. When you start a new job, it is essential for you to understand and maintain the image that your office wants to convey to the public. This may include how you communicate with clients and other law firms, your professional appearance, and how you behave toward your coworkers.

By helping the company maintain its image, you serve your own career goals. This is because employers value employees who maintain the company's image in all aspects of their work. In addition to understanding the company's image, knowing its professional goals will help you to become an important member of its staff.

Your employer is in business not only to make a profit but also, very likely, to help people in need of legal advice as well as to make the law firm become well-known and respected. This goal cannot be met by lackluster performance on the part of the employer or the employees. Be proud of your work. You are part of the team that is ensuring the firm's success. Your services, consequently, are related to the services that the office provides to the client. The employee who has the "what's in it for me" attitude in the workplace will most likely find it difficult to keep his or her job. It is essential that you use your skills to perform to the best of your ability. That includes helping coworkers and employers to make sure that the company reaches it professional goals.

Working with Clients

An important skill to have is that of working successfully with clients. It will be difficult for you to reach your career goals in a legal office if clients do not want to work with you or if you cannot manage the office–client relationship successfully. If you work for a family law attorney, you will likely have extensive contact with clients. The client's first contact may be with you while calling the office to make an appointment with a family law attorney. Your future contact with the client will involve collecting and organizing financial information and other items required to process petitions, applications, affidavits, and other necessary legal documents.

Remember that there are a lot of emotions involved in this area of law. It is important that these emotions belong to the client and not to the attorney or legal support staff. The client's life is changing, and that can be upsetting to the client no matter which side of the legal proceeding her or she is on. You must stay calm and be attentive but also remain somewhat detached in talking with clients.

If you receive a call from an angry, emotionally upset, or demanding client, it is your job to listen patiently and politely, get as much information as you can about the problem at hand, then summarize and repeat the client's concerns to verify that you understand the problem. Let the client know that you will give the attorney a memo regarding the client's call and that the attorney will call the client as soon as he or she is able. This will give the attorney time to review your memo and the file and prepare for the return call.

OFFICE ATTIRE

Some offices require employees to wear suits to work; others may allow for more casual business attire. Determine the office dress code *before* your first day of work. This guarantees that you will make the right first impression. If your goal is to be promoted to a higher position within the firm, dress like those who currently hold those positions. This ensures that your work attire will not be a factor in your supervisor's recommendation and allows other people to "see" you in the new role.

It is the legal support staff's responsibility to be attentive to the client by listening and recording the client's concerns and to convey these concerns clearly to the attorney. It is the attorney's responsibility to give advice and suggestions to the client and manage client behavior.

Critical Thinking Exercise

Apply what you have learned in this section to the following exercises.

Exercise 3.7 If you were assigned an e-mentor in an earlier chapter, contact that person and ask the following questions about professional goals. If you were not assigned an e-mentor, contact someone you know who is employed in any office and ask them the following questions:

- Does your office set professional goals during the year? If so, can you give me examples?
- Does the office ask you to set personal career goals? If so, can you give me examples of your goals?
- Do you and your office make action plans to accomplish the goals?
- Do you and your office examine accomplishments at the end of the year and reset your goals?
- Do you ever have to reevaluate and restate goals?

Summarize your e-mentor's answers on the lines provided.

_____

_____

_____

_____

_____

_____

_____

Share what you have discovered with your classmates. Your instructor will let you know how to go about sharing this information. Analyze and formulate your own thoughts on how you might integrate professional goal setting into your own life.

Best Practice Tip

EMERGENCIES

Some clients may believe that every problem is an emergency situation and demand to talk to the attorney immediately. If you believe the problem needs immediate attention, put the client's call on hold, give the attorney a quick summary of the situation, and then transfer the call to the attorney. If the attorney is not available, explain this to the client and then follow your typical office procedures. Your office may have you direct the client to a different attorney or simply leave a message.

Chapter Summary and Projects

Summary

You have now read an overview of family law and have an understanding of what tasks you might perform while working in a legal office that specializes in family law. You have reviewed the basic procedures of dissolution of marriage (divorce) and have reviewed terms that apply to this area of law. You have also reviewed and practiced identifying errors in possessives; read about and practiced staying focused while editing; learned the skills needed to work in both hard copy documents and electronic documents; and considered professional goals for your career. The skills you have developed here in editing, proofreading, and critical thinking will help you to progress successfully through your career in the future.

Remember that as a legal support person, it will be your responsibility in a family law case to complete the following tasks:

- Know and understand basic family law procedures and terminology
- Effectively work with angry or emotionally distraught clients
- Understand and prepare correct court document captions
- Correctly type and proofread a complicated legal description
- Edit and proofread applications for temporary relief and marital termination agreements

Key Terms

admission of service, 55
affiant, 58
affidavit, 58
answer and counterpetition, 55
application for temporary relief, 58
caption, 71
certificate of representation, 55
confidential domestic relations
    questionnaire, 54
confidential information form, 55
divorce, 54
final judgment and decree, 59
findings of fact, conclusions of law, order
    for judgment, judgment and decree, 59

grounds, 54
informational statement, 56
initial pleadings, 54
jurat clause, 77
marital termination agreement, 58
mediation, 58
motion, 58
motion for temporary relief, 57
no-fault dissolution of marriage, 54
no-fault divorce system, 54
petitioner, 54
respondent, 54
responsive pleading, 71
stipulation, 58

Local Focus Research

The Local Focus icons that appear in the chapter indicate that your local court may have different rules, due dates, terminology, and/or procedures than what has been discussed. The following Local Focus assignments will help you acknowledge these differences. Locate the Chapter 03 folder in your electronic storage medium and open the local focus file **C03_LocalFocus_FamilyLaw**. Resave the file as **LastName_C03_LocalFocus_FamilyLaw**. Research the following topics and record your research in the file that you just created. Use this information as a reference tool as you start and continue your career as a legal support person. Your instructor may ask you to submit a copy as homework. Insert a printed copy into your portfolio.

Local Focus 3.1   Page 56 discusses the confidential information form. Refer to your local rules of court or rules of evidence to determine if your state requires such confidential information to be filed as a separate document.

Local Focus 3.2   Page 57 discusses filing fees. Your local court will have rules specific to your jurisdiction regarding these fees. Determine the filing fee for family law documents required by the courts in your area.

Local Focus 3.3   Captions are discussed on page 73 of the text. Your local court will have rules specific to your jurisdiction regarding the official requirements of a caption on a court document. Determine the proper format and details for a court caption in your area.

Local Focus 3.4   Court file numbers are discussed on page 75 of the text. Call your local court administrator's office and ask when the court file numbers are assigned to cases and how attorneys are made aware of those numbers.

Scenario

You work as a legal support person in the office of Jordan, Leone & Sanchez, PLLP, as the assistant to Amie Roberts, who specializes in family law. Ava Joy Miller has been a client of Jordan, Leone & Sanchez for several months as the respondent in dissolution of marriage.

Throughout the next weeks, Ms. Roberts will be completing an application for temporary relief for Ms. Miller to temporarily settle some of the financial and child custody issues. Once that is completed, you and Ms. Roberts will be working together to complete the marital termination agreement. The findings of fact, conclusions of law, order for judgment, and judgment and decree document will also have to be completed, but this will be done later.

Ava Joy Miller's husband, Seth Michael Miller, is requesting a divorce from his wife of 15 years. The parties have two minor children, both boys, from their marriage. Ms. Miller works as an accountant at W. B. Accounting, Inc., and makes $51,000 annually. Mr. Miller works as a mechanic at Gavin's Machinery, Inc., and makes approximately $44,500 annually. Ms. Miller moved the boys and herself back to Dundee, Minnesota, where her family resides in Nobles County, before commencement of the proceedings. Mr. Miller stayed at the family residence in Dundas, Minnesota, located in Rice County. The parties have assets, including a parcel of property in Rice County, the site of the family residence.

The couple's children currently reside with Ava Miller. She believes that she should be awarded sole legal and physical custody and that the residence of the parties' minor children be with her. The husband wants joint legal and physical custody. The client believes that her husband is not able to provide for the minor children as he has tendencies toward alcoholism and may endanger the children's lives when he is drinking. The client is requesting spousal maintenance and child support. Mr. Miller wants to pay nothing.

Ultimately, Mr. and Ms. Miller compromise and agree to joint legal custody with sole physical custody and the residence of the parties' minor children awarded to the client. Mr. Miller does not have to pay spousal maintenance but agrees to pay child support in the amount of $726 per month.

Project 1   Complete a Template for an Application for Temporary Relief (ATR)

1. Before starting the ATR, open the file titled **C03_P1_ DomesticRelationsQuestionnaire** from the Chapter 03 folder in your electronic storage medium. Familiarize yourself with the information supplied to you by your client Ava Joy Miller on this confidential domestic relations questionnaire. The client completed this form as best she could at the time.

Print the document and use it as a reference. In a legal office, you would have this document printed and stored in your client's folder.

2. Open **C03_P1_ATR** created as a Microsoft Word template file in the Chapter 03 folder in your electronic storage medium.

3. Save this file as **LastName_C03_P1_ATR**. This is a protected fill-in document. You will not be able to change the document other than the fill-in fields.

4. Find the information needed to complete the ATR in the confidential domestic relations questionnaire that you printed in step 1. Use the tab key to move through the fields, entering the appropriate information as you go. Be sure to tab first. If you click into the first box, you will have to delete the wording before you can insert information. Some fields will require you to select from a drop-down list. If a certain field requires no information, tab to that field and touch the space bar to make sure that nothing prints in that area.

5. As you work your way through the ATR, keep a list of the fields for which you cannot find information or that are confusing to you. Record these empty fields in your notebook to refer to later. Resave the file before closing.

6. Submit the updated file to your instructor.

Project 2 Monthly Expense Information to Supplement the Application for Temporary Relief (ATR)

You have started the ATR for Ava Joy Miller but have found that the monthly expense figures are missing. Thankfully, the client stopped by the office earlier today to drop off the monthly expense form she had been asked to complete. Later in the afternoon, you return to your desk to find that the attorney has left you a message on your voice mail.

1. Open and listen to **C03_P2_AudioInstructions**. As you listen to the audio instructions, make notes in your notebook as to what you need to add to the ATR.

2. Open and print **C03_P2_MonthlyExpenseReport** from your electronic storage medium. This is the expense form that the client delivered.

3. Open **LastName_C03_P1_ATR** from your electronic storage medium.

4. Resave the file as **LastName_C03_P2_Expenses**.

5. Using the monthly expense report and the notes you created from the audio instructions, add the missing information into the **LastName_C03_P2_Expenses** file.

6. Save the updated document in your electronic storage medium and submit to your instructor.

Project 3   Proofread the Marital Termination Agreement

You come in to work today to find that Ms. Roberts has dictated the marital termination agreement and Sean Kahler, an assistant working in the office, has typed it. Your job is to prepare it for signature by editing and proofreading it. It is due by the end of the day.

1. Take out the confidential domestic relations questionnaire that you printed in Project 1 (file **C03_P1_DomesticRelationsQuestionnaire**). Have it in a convenient location for reference.

2. Open **C03_P3_MTA** from the Chapter 03 folder on the student data disc.

3. Save the document as **LastName_C03_P3_MTA** in the Chapter 03 folder of your electronic storage medium.

4. Begin editing and proofreading for typos, incorrect numbers, misspelled words, incorrect word choices, and any other mistakes you find. Review the editing and proofreading sections for reminders on how to proofread an electronic document, if necessary.

5. Since Sean Kahler is not familiar with the case, pay close attention to details that may have been missed.

6. Make all necessary changes in the file and resave the document.

7. Submit the final document to your instructor.

Discuss the Projects

Family law office files usually contain large amounts of background documents to be used by the lawyer in organizing and verifying details for the client.

1. In groups of two or three, brainstorm the various types of papers you might have gathered from the client.

2. The client's folder (usually a brown pocket file) will typically contain the normal filing categories, such as correspondence, pleadings, and billing. Discuss with your group what other categories might be added to the file—for example, insurance papers, etc.

3. If you have obtained an e-mentor currently working as a legal office staff person, email him or her and ask what filing categories the office usually prepares for a dissolution of marriage or divorce client.

4. After you have gathered this information, share it with your classmates and listen to their own suggestions.

Criminal Law

Chapter Objectives

- Complete a client contact sheet based on information provided by the client
- Prepare a certificate of representation
- Review a police report, witness statements, investigation, and client information
- Use critical thinking to compare information in documents and create a memo addressing any discrepancies
- Prepare a motion to compel discovery, a pretrial motion, and notice of witnesses and exhibits
- Prepare a plea petition
- Prepare transmittal letters
- Create letters to the opposing attorney serving documents
- Write a letter to the client sending copies of documents

Before beginning the exercises for this chapter, copy to your storage medium the Chapter 04 folder from the Student Resources disc that accompanies this textbook. Do this for each chapter before starting the chapter's exercises.

Attorney Davis is contacted by a young man seeking legal advice. The young man, Marshall Miller, explains that he had been wrongly accused of vandalizing a local establishment. He says that although he was near the location of the crime, he was there only to pick up his sister and was not aware that a crime had been committed until he was pulled over by a police officer. He feels that he was identified as the perpetrator only because his clothing contained paint stains—evidence of his enrollment in a painting course and not of his connection to the crime—and that he matched the vague description of "a tall teenager with a black hooded sweatshirt." Attorney Davis plans now to discuss Miller's options with him.

Davis and Casey, Attorneys at Law, specialize in criminal law and have nearly 200 active clients. This week they are working on 30 cases. These cases are in a variety of phases in the legal process. Several involve new clients currently being held by law enforcement and who are eager to talk with an attorney. Others are at home or working because they have posted bail. The attorneys may be investigating the charges in some of these cases. In others, they may be working out plea agreements with the prosecutors. The legal office staff and attorneys may be preparing for trial on some cases or preparing for sentencing in others. As you continue through this chapter, you will not only review the criminal law process but also gather information, analyze investigation reports, and prepare forms. This information will then be relayed to the attorneys as they continue with their clients through the criminal law process.

Attorneys who decide to practice criminal law depend on their office staff to learn and understand the forms and timelines in a criminal lawsuit. Recall that a **criminal lawsuit** deals with a crime against members of the public on both the state and federal levels. It includes all procedures through arrest, charging, trial, sentencing, and appeal. An **arrest** is the taking of a person into custody for the purpose of charging him or her with a criminal offense. In order to issue arrest warrants, search property, or hold a person in jail, law enforcement officials as well as judges must have **probable cause** or a reasonable belief that a crime was committed and that the accused person committed the crime.

Constitutional law protects the rights of the accused. A person accused of committing a state crime will be prosecuted under that state's laws of criminal procedure. A **state crime** is an action or lack of action that violates the criminal laws of a state. A **federal crime** is a crime that violates the federal laws of the United States. A person accused of committing a federal crime will be prosecuted under federal laws of criminal procedure as contained in the amendments to the U.S. Constitution.

As discussed in Chapter 2, there are different types of crimes and different levels of offense. A **misdemeanor** is a less serious crime punishable by a fine, county jail time of less than one year, probation, or community service. Examples of misdemeanors are petty theft, disturbing the peace, some traffic violations, and public drunkenness. A **felony**, in contrast, is a crime serious enough to be punishable by death or incarceration in a state or federal prison for more than one year. Examples of felonies are assault, murder, rape, robbery, arson, and possession or sale of certain drugs. A person convicted of a felony will lose several constitutional rights, including but not limited to the right to vote and the right to bear arms.

Cities, states, and the federal government each have their own criminal codes defining crimes. State and local rules of criminal procedure usually closely follow the federal rules. It is important for legal support persons who work in any form of criminal law to understand the rules of procedure that govern their local city, county, and state.

The criminal law process starts when a person is arrested after an alleged crime has been committed, reported, and investigated. A criminal procedure will typically involve the following measures:

- **Booking**—an administrative procedure at a police station or other law enforcement facility to record the accused person's name, address, telephone number, photograph, fingerprints, and the crime being charged
- **Arraignment**—a procedure where the accused appears in court to enter a plea of guilty or not guilty (in which case a trial date will be set)
- **Bail hearing**—a hearing to determine if the accused will be released on bail or detained in jail until trial
- **Preliminary hearing**—a hearing at which the prosecutor must present enough evidence to convince the judge that the accused committed a crime

- Discovery procedures by both defense and prosecuting attorneys
- Trial, either by jury or judge
- Sentencing—a procedure at which a penalty is ordered by the court, consisting of punishment by payment of a fine, serving probation, or serving time in jail, to name a few
- A possible appeal if the accused can prove that an error occurred during trial or that there was insufficient evidence to convict him or her of the crime

As in a civil case, the parties in a criminal matter are also the plaintiff and the defendant. What is different between civil and criminal law, however, is that the plaintiff is not the victim but a prosecuting attorney who brings a claim on behalf of the victim. In the United States, citizens have surrendered their personal right to seek justice against another party. Instead, they have given tacit approval for the formation of a civil government. This protects all individuals' rights and allows the government to pursue justice on behalf of the individual or society itself. Therefore, if Mary steals from Jose, Jose must contact authorities to protect his right to his property. Jose cannot mete out justice against Mary.

Because the government has the role of protecting individuals' rights, the government is the representative of the victim in the crime. The plaintiff in a criminal case is the government, state, city, or complainant. The **prosecuting attorney** (or district attorney or United States attorney) represents the government as plaintiff. The prosecuting attorney has the burden of proof and must prove the case against the defendant. The **burden of proof** is a duty placed on the prosecution to prove or disprove a disputed fact.

The **defense attorney** represents the defendant. Sometimes a defendant, with permission of the court, will choose to represent himself or herself without the advice of an attorney; in that case he or she is referred to as defendant pro se. A defendant may also hire a private attorney. The attorney will meet with the client to talk about the background and the facts, complete an investigation, and prepare for settlement or trial. In that instance, the defendant must pay the attorney using personal funds. If a defendant cannot afford an attorney, he or she will be provided with a public defender. A **public defender** is a court-appointed attorney who represents individuals who cannot afford to hire an attorney.

In addition to guaranteeing the right to an attorney, the Sixth Amendment to the U.S. Constitution guarantees a criminal defendant a speedy trial by an impartial jury. A **speedy trial** is a constitutional right granted to the defendant to be tried for alleged crimes within a reasonable time after being arrested. Most states have laws that set forth the time by which a trial must take place after charges have been filed. An **impartial jury** is a panel of people selected to serve on a jury who have no prior knowledge of the situation and no preconceived opinions as to the defendant's guilt or innocence. They are selected by the attorneys on the case from a random group of citizens. In most crimes, the defendant has a constitutional right to be tried by a jury, which must find the defendant guilty beyond a reasonable doubt. The phrase "**beyond a reasonable doubt**" means that the jury must not have any reasonable doubts about its decision.

The defendant in a criminal case can demand an omnibus (evidentiary) hearing; at that hearing, he or she demands a speedy trial. An **omnibus** (evidentiary) **hearing** determines the admissibility of testimony and evidence seized at the time of arrest.

The defense attorney makes certain that the civil rights of the defendant were not violated during the investigation and arrest and will not be violated during trial.

The defense attorney must also force the prosecutor to prove the case. The defense attorney must analyze the case and discuss with the client the advantages and disadvantages of going to trial or working out a plea agreement. Additionally, because it can be expensive to defend a client through trial, the attorney will explain to the client the options and the approximate cost and consequences associated with each option. If, after considering all the facts and possible defenses, the client decides to resolve the matter without a trial, the defense attorney will attempt to work out a plea agreement. A **plea agreement** is the negotiated disposition of a case where a defendant may, if other charges are dropped, plead guilty to lesser charges or to only some of the charges.

Sentencing is the imposition of a penalty ordered by the court after a plea agreement or a trial by jury or before a judge. To assist in sentencing, a **presentence investigation** might be conducted by a probation department. It may contain details about the defendant's prior convictions and arrests, work history, and family circumstances.

A defendant may appear to be guilty from a reading of the complaint. However, under the U.S. Constitution, a person is presumed innocent until the prosecuting attorney has proven guilt beyond a reasonable doubt. If the prosecuting attorney has proven to the jury beyond a reasonable doubt that the defendant is guilty, then the jury's verdict must be unanimous to convict. The accused is not required to testify at trial, and the choice to exercise this right to remain silent cannot be used against him or her by the prosecuting attorney.

The result of a trial could be a hung jury, a verdict of guilty, or a verdict of not guilty. A **hung jury** is a jury that has not been able to come to a decision after deliberating for a given period of time. A defendant is said to be **acquitted** of the crime if a judge or jury has found him or her to be not guilty of the criminal charge. If an accused person is acquitted of criminal charges, he or she is protected from being charged and prosecuted for the same set of facts or circumstances at any time in the future by the law of **double jeopardy**.

Like many areas of law, criminal law is driven by forms. Criminal law attorneys typically manage many cases all at the same time; therefore, templates are created to save time and energy. Some law offices pay for subscriptions to premade fillable forms from legal form supply companies. Other offices make their own fillable forms using their word processing software. Forms are also made available by courts and the American Bar Association. Legal support staff are expected not only to be able to use these forms but also to create, edit, and proofread them.

Best Practice Tip

CASE AND CLIENT PRIVACY

As a legal support person, your job is to keep the client's information confidential at all times. In dealing with a case that is attracting media attention, remember that the attorney is the only one authorized to communicate with the media. Even allowing any member of the public to believe that you are working with a particular client constitutes providing too much information.

Language Focus: Pronouns

Police officers and other law enforcement officials often write their reports using words and phrases such as *witness 1*, *witness 2*, *suspect*, or *person*. Later in the report, these individuals may be referred to as *he, she, him,* or *her*. It is the legal support staff's responsibility to make certain that pronouns used within a document are clear and accurate. In transferring information from police reports to your own notes, it is essential that you keep these names and references organized.

Attorneys who practice criminal law may use premade fill-in forms. The legal office support staff will have to select pronouns from drop-down menus. Since pronouns take the place of nouns, they are used in the same manner as nouns in sentences. Nouns and pronouns are categorized as either subjective (the subject of the sentence), objective (the object of the sentence), or possessive. Of course, the reason that people have more trouble with pronouns than nouns is that there are more pronouns to choose from for any one particular noun. For example, the noun *client* could be subjective or objective, depending on whether it is used as a subject or an object in a sentence. The choices for the pronoun that could take the noun's place include *he, she, him, her, his,* and *hers*.

> The client (subject) is due to arrive in 10 minutes.
>
> He or she is due to arrive in 10 minutes.
>
> I have asked our attorney to contact the client (object).
>
> I have asked our attorney to contact him or her.

In choosing the correct pronouns in a sentence, it is important to remember exactly which pronouns are subjective and which are objective. Table 4.1 provides a list of pronouns. If you have difficulty selecting the correct pronouns for a sentence, either memorize the cases or keep a list near your work until you have them memorized.

Table 4.1 Pronouns

	Subjective Case (Subject Case)		Objective Case (Object Case)		Possessive Case	
	Singular	*Plural*	*Singular*	*Plural*	*Singular*	*Plural*
First person (person speaking)	I	we	me	us	my mine	our ours
Second person (person spoken to)	you	you	you	you	your yours	your yours
Third person (person or things spoken of)	he she it	they	him her it	them	his her hers its	their theirs
	who		whom		whose	

People do not typically make mistakes with subjects of verbs and incorrect pronouns when they are speaking. Our own ears usually will not allow an incorrect pronoun case because it just does not sound right. For example, "Him has been treated at the hospital." Most people would not like the sound of the objective case "him" in this sentence. In addition to relying on how the sentence sounds, the following rules and patterns will be helpful in determining the correct pronoun case in a sentence.

The Subjective Case

A **subjective case pronoun** is used when the pronoun is the subject of a sentence or the subject of a verb in an independent or dependent clause. Subjective case pronouns usually precede a verb unless the sentence is a question or in inverted order.

Subject of a verb Verifying the correct subject of a verb should be fairly easy. Simply select the action (verb) in the sentence and ask, "who or what is doing the action?" The answer to this question will be the correct subject and a subjective pronoun.

Independent clause: He has been treated at the hospital.

> *He* is the subject of the verb *has been treated.*

Dependent clause: Although she wanted Mr. Johnson to review the interrogatories on Wednesday, he did not have time until Friday.

> *She* is the subject of the verb *wanted.*

The first part of the second sentence, *Although* through *Wednesday*, is a dependent clause since it cannot stand alone. **Dependent clauses** have subjects and verbs but cannot stand alone as complete sentences.

Inverted vs. Normal Order The previous examples are in **normal order**, meaning that the subject appears before the verb. Sentences can also be in **inverted order**, meaning that all or part of the verb appears before the subject. Questions are generally in inverted order:

Why is she going to the deposition?

> The subject is *she*. The verb is *is going.*

Notice that part of the verb is before the subject. In some inverted sentence structures, all of the verb appears before the subject.

The Objective Case

An **objective case pronoun** is used when it is the direct or indirect object of a verb, the object of a preposition, or the object of an infinitive. An objective case pronoun usually *follows* a verb, preposition, or infinitive.

Object of a verb In picking out the object of a verb, select the verb (for example, *gave*) and ask, "gave who or what?" The answer to the question is the direct object (such as *draft* in the following example). To find the indirect object, continue by asking "To whom?" The answer to this question is the indirect object. In the following example, the indirect object is the pronoun *them*, which has to be in the objective case.

The attorney gave them the draft for review.

> *Gave* is the verb and *them* is the object.

Object of a preposition Recall that a preposition shows the relationship between its object—a noun or a pronoun—and another word in a sentence. Common prepositions include *after, around, at, behind, beside, off, through, until, upon,* and *with.*

Ms. Stensrud made an appointment with him 2 weeks before mediation.

> *With* is a preposition. The word that follows a preposition is typically the object of the sentence.

Note that objects generally follow the words of which they are the object. Prepositions are always used in prepositional phrases. Prepositional phrases always *start* with a preposition and *end* with a noun or a pronoun. Since the pronoun follows the preposition, the pronoun is the object of the preposition and must be in the objective case (see Table 4.1). To make correct pronoun choices, one has to recognize prepositions. Until you can recognize them and are making correct grammar choices, create a list of common prepositions and keep it by your work area.

Object of an infinitive Remember that an infinitive is *to* combined with a verb. Examples of phrases that include infinitives are:

"…*to help* **him**"

"…*to wish* **them** good luck"

"…*to call* **us**"

Dianne Finlayson wanted *to give* **her** advice about international travel.

> The pronoun *her* is the object of the infinitive *to give.*

Possessive Cases

A **possessive case pronoun** is used when the pronoun shows ownership. Unlike possessive nouns, possessive pronouns never require apostrophes. Although this rule is easy enough to remember, confusion occurs when pronouns are used as contractions, which do require apostrophes. Remember that the apostrophe in a contraction takes the place of the left-out letter.

Table 4.2 Possessive Pronouns and Contractions

Possessive Pronouns vs. Contractions	
its	it's (it is)
their	they're (they are)
theirs	there's (there is)

Possessive Case Examples:

Theirs is the first contract to be processed.

The company must complete its review by next Monday.

Contraction Examples:

There's only one contract left.

It's going to take all day to complete.

Compound Subjects and Objects

It can be difficult to choose the correct pronoun in a compound structure. For some reason when the pronoun is alone, it is easier to tell which pronoun case is correct based on how the sentence sounds. However, as soon as that same pronoun is used in a compound structure, both options may sound correct. With the following pronoun tips and suggestions, you will be less likely to be led astray by your ear!

Pronoun Tip 1 In choosing a single pronoun in a compound structure, ignore the other part of the compound to determine if the pronoun should be in the subjective or objective case.

The Robertsons and he were referred to early in the contract negotiations.

This example might not sound accurate right away. Notice that the compound subject (Robertsons and he) is on the left side of the verb in this normal-order sentence. Therefore, the pronoun must be in the subjective or subject case (he vs. him). Practice the tip by ignoring *The Robertsons and* and rephrase the sentence only using *he* as the subject. This new sentence "He was referred to early in the contract negotiations" sounds more correct than the objective use of *him* in "Him was referred to...." The rules and your ear verify that the use of the subjective *he* is correct in this sentence.

Pronoun Tip 2 In choosing pronouns in a compound structure where both words are pronouns, test that the correct pronoun case was used by ignoring one pronoun while analyzing and choosing the other. Then ignore the pronoun you just chose to analyze and choose the second.

On Monday the county recorder's office called him and her to verify the legal description.

Him and *her* are the compound objects of the verb *called* in this sentence. Notice that the words *him* and *her* are on the right side of the verb, which supports the fact that they are in the objective case (and not *he* and *she*). To choose the correct pronouns in this compound structure, follow the steps described in Pronoun Tip 2. First, ignore the second pronoun (*her*), along with the word *and*, and check that the first pronoun works in the sentence:

On Monday the county recorder's office called him ~~and her~~ to verify the legal description.

Then, ignore the first pronoun (*him*), along with the word *and*, to check that the second pronoun works in the sentence.

> On Monday the county recorder's office called ~~him and~~ her to verify the legal description.

By verifying that both pronouns work in the sentence by themselves, you can confirm that the original sentence is correct and the compound pronouns are used properly. Now consider this example.

> The Robertsons agreed with Ms. Neelson and her that the arrest warrant would be approved in two days.

Robertsons is the subject of the verb *agreed*.

With is the preposition in this phrase. *Ms. Neelson and her* is the compound object.

Since the subject *The Robertsons* is on the left side of the verb in this normal-order sentence, one can assume that it is in the subjective case. Notice also that the compound object *Ms. Neelson and her* is on the right side of the preposition. Apply the preceding tips to check the accuracy of the pronouns. First, ignore *Ms. Neelson.* Then say, "The Robertson agreed with her." *Her* is the object of the preposition *with* and is used correctly. Refer to the pronoun chart to verify that *her* is the objective case.

Advanced Use of the Subjective Case

Any pronoun that follows a *being* verb (*am, is, are, was, were, be, been, being*) must be in the subjective case. Subjective case pronouns function as subjects in sentences. Sometimes the pronoun is the subject complement, which means that the subject *follows* a "being" verb in the sentence. Compare the following sentences:

> They *sent* the package.

> It might have been they who sent the package.

They is in the subject case in both sentences. Your ear probably tells you that *them* would not be the correct pronoun choice in the first sentence. However, when the pronoun is the subject complement (when it follows a "being" verb, as in "it might have been"), your ear may not lead you to the correct pronoun. You might be comfortable with the statement "It might have been them who sent the package," which is incorrect. By knowing the subject complement rule, you will always make the right pronoun choice.

Best Practice Tip

PRONOUN CHOICES

You might think it is important to know whom *her* refers to in this example. "Her" identity is not relevant to making pronoun choices. Remember that this is just an example sentence extracted from a paragraph. In reality there would be more information in the actual communication.

Who and Whom

Determine the correct use of *who* and *whom* by reworking the sentence and seeing whether the words *he* or *him* work best in the reworded sentence. As noted in Table 4.1, both *who* and *he* are subjective pronouns, while *whom* and *him* are objective pronouns. Remembering this will help you select the right use of *who* and *whom* within a sentence.

In reworking a sentence, always start with *who/whom* wherever it happens to be in the sentence.

    a. If the sentence is in normal order, substitute *he* for *who* or *him* for *whom* to verify the correct pronoun choice.

    b. If the sentence is in inverted order (i.e., if you start with *who/whom* and it does not make sense), then start with the next word and insert *he/him* where it does make sense.

Who/Whom is interested in interviewing for the position?

The entire question is the "who/whom" clause. Substitute *he* for *who* or *him* for *whom*. "Him is interested" is not a grammatically correct statement. "He is interested..." is correct. Since *He* is the subject of the verb *is interested*, then the subjective case *Who* is the correct choice. The subjective case is required in this instance.

Ryley is the person *who/whom* I want to hire.

As noted previously, always start at the *who/whom*. Again, substitute *he* for *who* or *him* for *whom*. Does either of them make sense? The options are either "he I want to hire" or "him I want to hire." Neither option sounds perfectly correct. Since it does not make sense to substitute and read in normal order, you then have to start reading right after the *who/whom* choice and insert *he/him* where it makes sense. For example, "I want to hire him" makes sense. *Him* is the object of the infinitive *to hire*. Therefore, the sentence should read, "Ryley is the person whom I want to hire."

It is important to know which pronouns are subjective and which are objective. Eventually, these guidelines and suggestions will not be necessary because you will be more familiar with pronouns and their proper use. You might study the guidelines now and feel that you understand them. However, what will you do when you know that you need an objective case pronoun but you do not know which pronoun is objective? Print the C04_PronounTable from the student data disc and post it near your computer for reference until you automatically know which pronouns are subjective and which are objective.

As you start the process of editing and proofreading for pronoun choice, remember the following:

- Identify the pronoun(s) in the sentence
- Determine if the pronoun is acting as a subject or object in the sentence

Best Practice Tip

WHO AND WHOM

How will you remember which word to substitute? Remember that both *who* and *he* do not have an *m* in their spelling, while both *whom* and *him* do contain an *m*.

- If the pronoun is on the left side of the subject, it will typically be the subjective case (*he, she, they*, etc.). It will be on the left side of the subject only, of course, if the sentence is in normal order
- If the pronoun is on the right side of the verb, preposition, or infinitive, the pronoun will typically be in the objective or object case (*him, her, me, them*, etc.)
- If the pronoun follows a "being" verb, the pronoun will be in subjective case
- *Who/Whom* choices: Substitute *he* for *who* and *him* for *whom*

APPLYING WHAT YOU KNOW

Notice that the examples in this section are very basic. The legal documents in a law office will be more lengthy and complicated. To be a good editor and proofreader, you must analyze the sentences and notice that these more complicated sentences are made up of basic parts similar to the ones used in the examples.

Language Focus Exercises

Apply what you have learned previously to the following exercises.

Exercise 4.1 Review the following sentences and circle the correct pronoun choice for each. Support your choice by writing a brief explanation on the line provided.

Example: (I)/me would like to give good advice.   *Rule 1: Subject of a verb*

1. I thought Jackson and he/him did a superb job in finishing the report.

2. The Patrices and we/us have a meeting to negotiate a solution.

3. They have invited Attorney Windom and I/me to the grand opening of the business they started.

4. We faxed they/them the documents for the hearing.

5. Kara feels she/her should be allowed to set her/hers own hours.

6. When asked on the phone whether she was available, Rita answered by saying, "This is she/her."

7. Who/whom should I expect at the meeting with the governor?

8. The defendants will be present when they're/their attorney is sworn in for testimony.

9. The plaintiffs both testified that the doctor talked with both he/him and she/her at the time of the diagnosis.

10. It might have been he/him who informed the police.

Exercise 4.2 After reading the following sentences, circle any errors you find and write the corrected word on the line provided. Write the letter "C" on the line if the word is already correct. Finally, write the rule that applies to your decision on the second line provided.

	Correction	Rule
1. Then theirs the question of what car was used as the getaway car.	_____	_____
2. The first task is to decide whom used the car the night of the incident.	_____	_____
3. Whom did you say you called yesterday at the court administrator's office?	_____	_____
4. Its not a job that we look forward to doing!	_____	_____
5. Then we must decide who's responsibility it is to retrieve the car from impound.	_____	_____
6. The matter involves no one except the defendant and I.	_____	_____
7. Just between you and I, there will be layoffs at the county by fall.	_____	_____
8. Whom do you think will be nominated for vice president at the forthcoming American Bar Association convention?	_____	_____
9. Neither Craig nor I think it's you're responsibility.	_____	_____
10. The defendant, whom the judge spoke to on Friday, will be here in 20 minutes.	_____	_____

Editing: Creating Clear and Organized Documents

When attorneys draft documents or letters to their clients, one can assume that they are thinking more about the client's case than they are about formatting and text organization. As they dictate or draft these documents themselves, information may emerge in a disorganized fashion. It is not uncommon for busy attorneys to dictate or draft documents exactly as they think! While this method ensures that they cover all of the necessary topics, it may make for disorganized work.

As a legal support person, you may be asked to edit letters and other documents for organization. One important factor in doing so is to include transitional words and phrases that help the reader understand the document. You may need to reorganize the paragraphs so that similar topics are grouped together and the letter or document develops in a logical, comprehensible manner.

Transitions

The use of transitional words and phrases helps to make a document read more smoothly. These "links" provide logical organization and understandability by making connections between ideas and topics. Transitional words and phrases show relationships between words, sentences, and even entire documents.

Consider the following two paragraphs:

> Many legal documents you encounter will need to follow court-imposed formatting guidelines and requirements. It will be clear what information should be included and in what order the information should appear. Other documents will not have an assigned format.

> Many legal documents you encounter will need to follow court-imposed formatting guidelines and requirements. If so, it will be clear what information should be included and in what order the information should appear. However, other documents, such as letters or correspondence, will not have an assigned format.

The first paragraph, although accurate, may be difficult to understand. The second paragraph utilizes transitional words to explain concepts.

Table 4.3 lists possible relationships between concepts and the transitional words and phrases that could be used to connect them.

You should not only add transitional words to organize and correctly connect ideas, but also edit for clarity and organization by paying close attention that the thoughts expressed in the document are in a logical order. You may need to move certain sentences or paragraphs to help the document make sense. Items should be in order by time, completion sequence, or similar guidelines.

Table 4.3 Transitions

addition	also, again, as well as, besides, coupled with, furthermore, in addition, likewise, moreover, similarly
consequence	accordingly, as a result, consequently, for this reason, for this purpose, hence, otherwise, so then, subsequently, therefore, thus, thereupon, wherefore
contrast and comparison	by the same token, conversely, instead, likewise, on one hand, on the other hand, on the contrary, rather, similarly, yet, but, however, still, nevertheless, in contrast
direction	here, there, over there, beyond, nearly, opposite, under, above, to the left, to the right, in the distance
diversion	by the way, incidentally
emphasis	above all, chiefly, with attention to, especially, particularly, singularly
exception	aside from, barring, besides, except, excepting, excluding, exclusive of, other than, outside of, save
exemplifying	chiefly, especially, for instance, in particular, markedly, namely, particularly, including, specifically, such as
generalizing	as a rule, as usual, for the most part, generally, generally speaking, ordinarily, usually
illustration	for example, for instance, for one thing, as an illustration, illustrated with, as an example, in this case
restatement	in essence, in other words, namely, that is, that is to say, in short, in brief, to put it differently
similarity	comparatively, coupled with, correspondingly, identically, likewise, similar, moreover, together with
sequence	at first, first of all, to begin with, in the first place, at the same time, for now, for the time being, the next step, in time, in turn, later, later on, meanwhile, next, then, soon, the meantime, while, earlier, simultaneously, afterward, in conclusion, with this in mind
summarizing	after all, all in all, all things considered, briefly, by and large, in any case, in any event, in brief, in conclusion, on the whole, in short, in summary, in the final analysis, in the long run, on balance, to sum up, to summarize, finally

Editing Exercises

The following exercises will allow you to practice your editing skills using the information discussed in this chapter.

Exercise 4.3 Practice using transitions in the following exercise.

1. Open the file **C04_Ex4.3** from the Chapter 04 folder in your electronic storage medium and read a letter to a client created by an attorney.

2. With a classmate, discuss the organization of this letter. Are there topics that should be in different paragraphs?

3. Rewrite and key the letter to read more clearly and concisely.

4. Save the document as **LastName_C04_Ex4.3**.

Exercise 4.4 Apply what you have learned to the following exercise.

1. Open file **C04_Ex4.4** and read how this attorney drafted the body of a letter to be sent to a client.

2. With a classmate, discuss the organization of this letter. Are there topics that should be in different paragraphs?

3. Rewrite and key the letter to read more clearly and concisely.

4. Save the document as **LastName_C04_Ex4.4**.

Proofreading: Tips for Proofreading Forms

As mentioned earlier, criminal law procedures include many forms, and most offices either purchase forms from a legal forms supply company or make their own forms using their word processing software. One expects that the purchased forms will be made perfectly. However, if the forms are made by you or someone else in the office, you will need to verify that everything is correct and that the forms work properly. While it is rare to find an error in a preprinted form purchased from a supply company, it is a good practice to read the entire form, as there may be provisions in it that do not apply to your use or some other error nobody caught before the form was printed. When a form is made, it is locked to prevent the user from changing the consistent wording. The form will have fill-in blanks, choice fields, check boxes, or other fields. When you are instructed to proofread these forms, you will have to unlock the form, proofread the document, and then lock the form again before saving your changes.

In proofreading a form, a legal support person should do the following:

- Verify that the wording of the entire form is exactly what is required by the court.
- Make certain that the form fields are in the correct places so that the form makes sense.
- Check the spacing and punctuation of the form so that the form fields are inserted correctly.

Use Program Tools Proofread templates by first turning on the show/hide button to more easily see the spaces and paragraph markers. The show/hide button in Microsoft Word is the one represented by ¶ on the toolbar. In Corel WordPerfect, "reveal codes" will show the same type of information. Viewing the template in this setting will allow you to easily identify formatting errors or inconsistencies.

In Microsoft Word, the default is set so that it does not spell check words that appear in all capital letters. Change the settings to include spell checking all capital letters.

Test the Template After the template has been created, test it by filling in sample language to verify that the spacing and formatting are correct and that the fields work properly.

Add Help Text Insert help text designed to help the user determine what to insert in the field. Help text consists of nonprinting explanatory words inserted in a form when it is being made to ensure that it is filled out correctly.

In order for forms and templates to remain consistent, an office may choose to assign the task of creating and proofreading forms to a specific person or group of people. You may be asked to be on the team that creates and revises templates and forms. You may also be employed at an office where employees are expected to make their own forms. Therefore, knowing how to make corrections in forms is a necessary skill for legal support staff. Because not all offices use the same word processing programs, you must know and understand the form-protecting procedures in your office's word processing program.

Proofreading Exercises

Complete the following exercises by applying the information given previously in the proofreading section.

Exercise 4.5 Checklist for proofreading premade forms.
1. Open the "Help" menu in your own word processing program.
2. Search for the procedures to follow to unprotect and make changes to a protected form or template.
3. Type a checklist to use when you are proofreading and correcting errors on a protected form.
4. Save the check list as **LastName_C04_Ex4.5_ProtectedFormChecklist**.
5. Submit it to your instructor.

Exercise 4.6 Apply your understanding of proofreading to the following exercise.
1. Open **C04_Ex4.6_ DefenseWitnessesExhibits** as a template from Chapter 04 of your electronic storage medium.
2. Unprotect the template and proofread it, using the techniques that work for your particular word processing program.
3. Make the necessary changes.
4. Reprotect and save this as a template as **LastName_C04_Ex4.6_ DefenseWitnessesExhibits**.
5. Submit it to your instructor.

Criminal Law How-To Guide

In working on a criminal law case in a legal office, a legal support person may be asked to join the attorney and client after they have discussed whether the attorney will accept the case. If you are unable to join them, you could be asked to listen to or transcribe a recorded initial interview between the client and the attorney. The attorney asks questions and the client provides answers. You will use this information to complete a client contact sheet. A client contact sheet can be known by other names. In civil litigation, this form is called a client information form. In family law, a similar form, called a domestic relations questionnaire, focuses on family law details.

Figure 4.1 **Example of a Proofread Form**

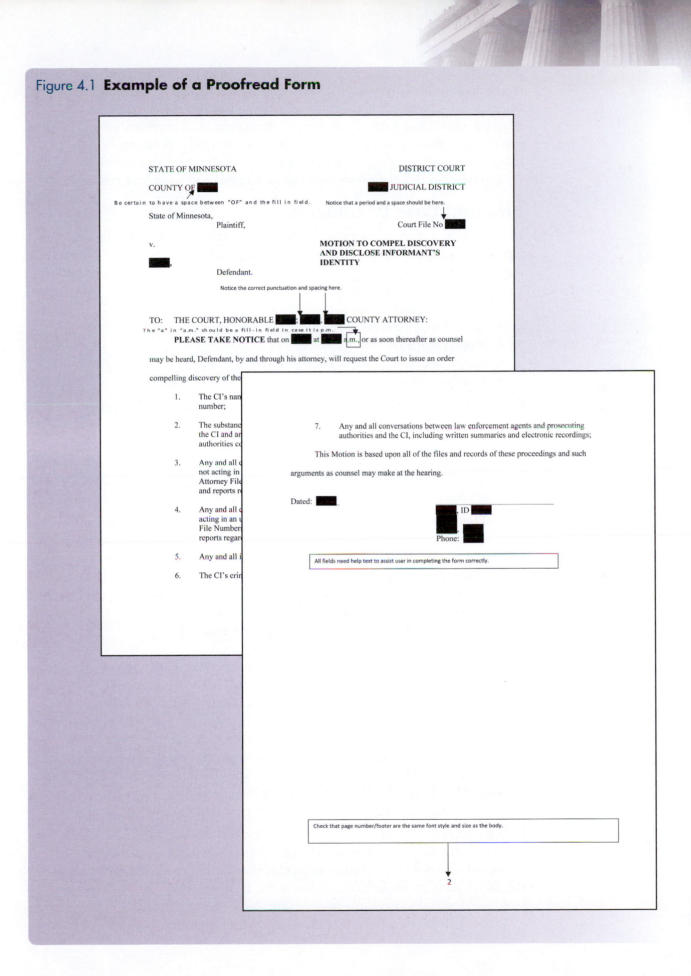

STATE OF MINNESOTA   DISTRICT COURT

COUNTY OF ███   ███ JUDICIAL DISTRICT

Be certain to have a space between "OF" and the fill in field.   Notice that a period and a space should be here.

State of Minnesota,
      Plaintiff,   Court File No ███

v.   **MOTION TO COMPEL DISCOVERY
███,   AND DISCLOSE INFORMANT'S
      Defendant.   IDENTITY**

Notice the correct punctuation and spacing here.

TO: THE COURT, HONORABLE ███; ███ COUNTY ATTORNEY:

The "a" in "a.m." should be a fill-in field in case it is p.m.

PLEASE TAKE NOTICE that on ███ at ███ a.m., or as soon thereafter as counsel

may be heard, Defendant, by and through his attorney, will request the Court to issue an order

compelling discovery of the

   1.   The CI's nam
       number;

   2.   The substanc
       the CI and an
       authorities co

   3.   Any and all
       not acting in
       Attorney File
       and reports r

   4.   Any and all
       acting in an u
       File Number
       reports regar

   5.   Any and all i

   6.   The CI's cri

   7.   Any and all conversations between law enforcement agents and prosecuting
       authorities and the CI, including written summaries and electronic recordings;

     This Motion is based upon all of the files and records of these proceedings and such

arguments as counsel may make at the hearing.

Dated: ███   ███, ID ███
                      ███
                      Phone: ███

All fields need help text to assist user in completing the form correctly.

Check that page number/footer are the same font style and size as the body.

2

All areas of law require that information be gathered from the client for effective representation. These forms will be used to gather differing types of information depending on the details needed. Like a client information form and domestic relations questionnaire, the client contact sheet contains all necessary information pertaining to the case and the client. To be used efficiently, all information must be summarized and organized within this document and clipped into the client file as the top page, so that the information can be accessed easily and kept current.

Criminal Case Documents

In addition to a client contact sheet, you will want to be familiar with the following types of documents. This will be beneficial to you and to the law firm as you assist on criminal cases.

- Certificate of representation
- Case discrepancy memo
- Motion to compel discovery
- Motion in limine
- Notice of defense witnesses and exhibits
- Petition to enter a plea

Certificate of Representation Once the client and attorney have agreed to work together, they must come to an agreement on fees. The client and attorney will both sign a representation agreement. In a criminal law case, it is important that the court and prosecuting attorney know who is representing the defendant. The defense attorney will file a **certificate of representation** or notice of appearance, which will tell the court and the prosecutor involved in the case who is representing the defendant.

Case Discrepancy Memo After filing and serving the certificate of representation, the attorney may ask the legal support person to help with the case by reviewing the case information and identifying any discrepancies that may exist among the different parties' accounts. This memo provides the attorney with a second person's perspective of the details. To perform this task, you would review:

- Information about the case provided by the client
- The complaint by the police and the charges filed
- Investigation information

In your analysis, review the police report, witness statements, and investigation reports, and compare them with the client's version of the facts. Look for discrepancies, missing information, or information that does not make sense. You would then create a memo to the attorney that discusses any differences you discovered between the various versions of facts. Even though the attorney will carefully review everything in the file, your review would help the attorney as he or she reviews the file. There may be occasions when your perspective will help the attorney make decisions and see things in a different way.

Motion to Compel Discovery Just as in civil litigation, criminal litigation includes discovery. Recall that discovery is the process of requesting from others information that the attorney does not have. Sometimes the other parties must be compelled or ordered by the court to provide the information. Remember that a *motion* is a formal communication between the attorney and the court and that the term *compel* means to force or apply pressure. Both sides of this case have the right to discovery. If the other party is not providing the information, the attorney has the ability to request the court (by motion) to order that party to produce the requested details. As a legal support person, you will likely be instructed to prepare a motion to compel discovery, serve it on the opposing attorney, file it with the court, and send a copy to your client.

Motion in Limine In addition to asking the court to compel discovery, the attorney may ask the court to suppress certain evidence. You may also be instructed to prepare a motion in limine, which can either be a pretrial evidence motion or motion to suppress evidence. *In limine* is Latin for "at the threshold." A **motion in limine** is a motion made before the start of a trial asking that the judge rule, with regard to certain evidence, whether it may or may not be introduced to the jury at trial. This, of course, may be done in the judge's chambers or in open court, but it must always occur out of hearing of the jury. If a question is to be decided in limine, it will be for the judge to decide. Usually it is used to shield the jury from possible inadmissible and unfairly prejudicial evidence. Remember that the attorney always makes the decisions about what goes into motions, and the legal support staff person prepares, files, and serves the documents. Sometimes these motions are made in writing and provided in advance of a pretrial hearing. At other times, they may be made verbally during a hearing.

Notice of Defense Witnesses and Exhibits Each side of the case must notify the other as well as the court of the identity of witnesses and of the exhibits to be used at trial. Some states may require that a notice of defense witnesses and exhibits be completed and provided to the court and the opposing attorney disclosing this information. The attorney will be making the decisions about witnesses and exhibits to be used at trial. The legal support person might review the file with the attorney and discuss what to include in these documents. In addition, he or she would prepare the document, file it with the court, and serve it on opposing counsel.

Petition to Enter a Plea Bargain The prosecutor and defense attorney may negotiate a plea bargain to eliminate the need for a trial. In that event, the attorney may ask you to prepare a petition to enter a plea of guilty, setting forth the charges agreed upon during the negotiations. Your office forms may include petitions to plead guilty to misdemeanors as well as petitions to plead guilty to felonies. Think clearly about which form you will need. You may have several clients at the same point in their cases, but they may be pleading to different charges.

The Use of Forms in Criminal Law

As mentioned earlier, criminal procedure consists mostly of completing premade templates or forms. Some offices will purchase a subscription to premade forms for the state in which the law firm is located. Because of the subscription, these types of forms are kept up to date by the company. There are also offices that create the forms themselves and will even share them with other offices if asked.

Best Practice Tip

DEADLINES

Be sure that you check on court deadlines and file documents with the court on time. Put reminders into your calendar so that the attorney does not miss deadlines. Because of the right to a speedy trial, most criminal cases do not usually last very long, so your efficient and timely work will be appreciated.

The various people creating the forms in different offices will each have personal preferences about the style, including the pleading captions and the remainder of the document as well. Some people format the caption using a table, while others may insert tab stops or create fillable forms. It does not matter what method is used to format the caption as long as it contains the elements set out in the court rules. When you are employed at a law office, it is recommended that you follow the format already in place within the office. You could also be asked to create the forms. In that event, find a style you prefer, document it, and use it consistently.

In completing a form for a particular case, the legal support person would have to locate information to be inserted into the form. To find the correct information, you would:

- look in the file,
- call the client,
- talk with the attorney, or
- contact other people who have the missing information.

Prior to filing with the court or serving the document on the opposing attorney, every blank fill-in field would have had information inserted.

Handwritten Agreements

You may become accustomed to a routine where the attorney leaves instructions for you to complete a form in the office, print it, and have it signed. These types of forms are neat and tidy. However, criminal practice is also fast paced. Some criminal law attorneys carry printed template forms along with them in their briefcases. If they resolve a matter while at the courthouse, they will take out the appropriate form and complete it in pen on the spot and immediately file the document with the court. Choices will be circled and agreements will be handwritten into paragraphs.

Figure 4.2 features a page—an example from a handwritten agreement showing typical word choices—from a petition to enter plea of guilty in a felony or gross misdemeanor case.

FORM LIBRARY

Save time by making a library of those premade fill-in form documents that are frequently used in criminal files. Save copies of the forms in the client's computer file and fill in the blanks when the forms are needed.

KEEPING THE CLIENT FILE UP TO DATE

Because forms can be created on the run at the courthouse, the legal office support staff would need to follow up with each file to be certain it contains copies of the documents the attorney created outside the office. In addition, attorneys communicate with their support staff in many ways including email and office voice mail. Always print the emails and type out voice mail to be included in the client's file. Because you will be working with so many details, do not test your memory. The attorney sends these messages to get details out of mind and into the file. He or she will need the information the next time the file is reviewed. Print out all instructions and details for the file.

2. I (do) (do not) make the claim that I was so drunk or so under the influence of drugs or medicine that I did not know what I was doing at the time of the crime.

3. I (do) (do not) make the claim that I was acting in self-defense or merely protecting myself or others at the time of the crime.

4. I (do) (do not) make the claim that the fact that I have been held in jail since my arrest and could not post bail caused me to decide to plead guilty in order to get the thing over with rather than waiting for my turn at trial.

5. I (was) (was not) represented by an attorney when I had a probable cause hearing. (If I have not had a probable cause hearing):
   a. I know that I could now move that the complaint against me be dismissed for lack of probable cause and I know that if I do not make such a motion and go ahead with entering my plea of guilty, I waive all right to successfully object to the absence of a probable cause hearing.
   b. I also know that I waive all right to successfully object to any errors in the probable cause hearing when I enter my plea of guilty.
   c. For Gross Misdemeanor driving while intoxicated under ILCS169.121 or ILCS 169.129 if a complaint has not been filed, I know that I could request that a complaint be filed and that I waive my right to do so. I know that I could move that any complaint filed against me be dismissed for lack of probable cause. I also know that if I plead guilty, I waive all right to object to the absence of a probable cause hearing.

6. My attorney has told me and I understand:
   a. That the prosecutor for the case against me, has:
      ✓ i. physical evidence obtained as a result of searching for and seizing the evidence;
      _____ ii. evidence in the form of statements, oral or written, that I made to police or others regarding this crime;
      _____ iii. evidence discovered as a result of my statements or as a result of the evidence seized in a search;
      ✓ iv. identification evidence from a line-up or photographic identification;
      _____ v. evidence the prosecution believes indicates that I committed one or more other crimes.
   b. That I have a right to a pretrial hearing before a judge to determine whether or not the evidence the prosecution has could be used against me if I went to trial in this case.
   c. That if I requested such a pretrial hearing I could testify at the hearing if I wanted to, but my testimony could not be used against me as substantive evidence if I went to trial and could only be used against me if I was charged with the crime of perjury. (Perjury means testifying falsely.)
   d. That I (do) (do not) now request such a pretrial hearing and I specifically (do) (do not) now waive my right to have such a pretrial hearing.

2

Critical Thinking: Contact Sheets and the Formatting of Letters and Documents

To stay organized and always have current information at your fingertips, create a contact sheet for each file. The contact sheet will contain frequently used information such as the court file number as well as the name, address, telephone number, fax number, and email address of the client, prosecuting attorney, court administrator, judge's clerk, probation officer, and any other important information that may be needed often for the case at hand. In addition to saving the contact sheet as a computer file, print the contact sheet and keep it in a visible location in the paper file so that the information will be quickly available to anyone working on the case.

As time goes on, make changes to the contact information as it becomes known to you. It is important to keep calendars and contact sheets current in both the computer and paper files. Many attorneys use portable information devices (cell phone, Blackberry, etc.) that make it possible for them to access office files and calendars from an external location.

As discussed and demonstrated in Chapter 2, remember the importance of maintaining a system for calendaring of deadlines, court dates, meetings with the client, reminder dates for work that needs to be done on the file by either you or the attorney, and information you are expecting from others. When you receive a notice that a meeting or hearing has been set for a certain date, enter that date on the calendar and put a small check mark by the date on the notice to confirm that you put the information on the calendar. Prepare a letter to the client and include a copy of the notice of hearing for the client's information. Record a reminder to yourself to contact the client and remind him or her of the hearing date.

When you contact clients, attorneys, and courts, it is important to include all of the information that is necessary to communicate clearly and effectively.

Drafting Transmittal Letters

In drafting transmittal letters to accompany legal documents, determine the correct person and organization to which the letter is to be addressed and think about exactly what you want to convey to the recipient.

You will find that the wording of the letters you draft to file or serve documents with is quite different from the wording of business letters you may have learned to write in a business communications class. Although business letters typically have an introduction, body, and conclusion, legal letters are sometimes referred to as "here you are" letters—meaning that they are very short and to the point. Such a letter may consist of only one sentence clearly telling the receiver what is being sent.

Questions to consider in drafting a transmittal letter:

- Is a particular case being discussed? Include the case name and court file number in the subject line. Sometimes the recipient's and sender's own office file numbers are included for ease of filing within the office.
- Are you filing (at the court), serving (on an opposing party), or simply providing a copy of a document? Include such wording in the letter. For example, "Enclosed for filing...," "Enclosed and served upon you...," or "Enclosed for your information...."
- What are you providing, filing, or serving? Include the document name in the letter.
- What is the recipient supposed to do with this information and/or the enclosure(s)?
- Is there a deadline for any activities? If so, state the deadline clearly.
- Are additional notations necessary at the end of the letter to indicate enclosures? Enclosures should be clearly listed within the body of the letter or itemized near the enclosure notation following the signature area of the letter.
- Does the recipient of the letter need to know if anyone else is receiving the letter? Include that information in the letter or as a copy notation.
- Although a particular person will be receiving a copy of this letter, you may not want the recipient of the original to know that person's identity. In that case,

include a blind copy notation. A **blind copy notation** is shown as bcc (blind courtesy copy) and means that the original recipient does not and should not know that a third person is receiving a copy of your communication. This bcc notation is *not* shown on the original letter. It is placed on the copy to the third person receiving the letter and on the file copy.

Figure 4.3 Blind copy and enclosure notation shown on third-person copy and file copy

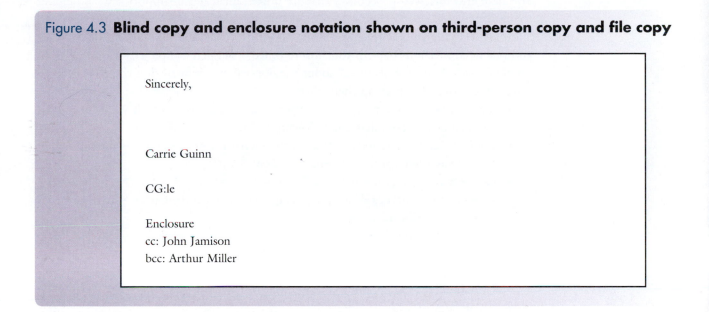

Sincerely,

Carrie Guinn

CG:le

Enclosure
cc: John Jamison
bcc: Arthur Miller

Critical Thinking Exercises

Use the information provided in the critical thinking section to complete the following exercises.

Exercise 4.7 Discuss with a small group of classmates what you would write in a letter to each of the following people:
- A court administrator, asking him or her to file the enclosed certificate of representation
- The opposing attorney, to serve the certificate of representation
- The client, to provide him or her with a copy of the certificate of representation

Exercise 4.8 Draft the following letters. You will be enclosing the motion to compel discovery, the motion in limine, and the notice of witnesses and exhibits in each letter.
1. Draft letter 1 to the court administrator asking him or her to file the enclosed documents.
2. Draft letter 2 to the opposing attorney, to serve him or her with the previously-mentioned documents.
3. Draft letter 3 to the client to provide him or her with copies of the previously-mentioned documents.

Save each letter with this file name: **LastName_Ex4.8_ltr#**. Adjust each file name to reflect the proper letter number and submit the files to your instructor as directed.

The letters referred to in Exercises 4.7 and 4.8 are very common. Generally, you will send these documents for filing and service as you prepare them, enclosing just one document. In other situations, you may enclose several documents, as in Exercise 4.8.

Chapter Summary and Projects

Summary

You have now read an overview of criminal law procedures and have an understanding of what tasks you might perform working in a legal office in the area of criminal law. You have also reviewed procedures that are important to legal support staff in helping the attorney create professional correspondence and legal documents. You reviewed and practiced applying language, editing, and proofreading skills to legal documents and practiced methods to help your future office effectively handle fast-paced criminal cases. You have also read about the importance of analyzing the content of transmittal letters and making them clear.

Remember that as a legal support person in a criminal law case, it will likely be your responsibility to complete the following tasks:

- Prepare a client contact sheet, determine what information is missing, and obtain missing information from the client
- Create a certificate of representation
- Review the client's case and provide an analysis of discrepancies for the attorney
- Prepare a motion to compel
- Prepare a motion in limine
- Complete a notice of defense witnesses and exhibits
- Prepare a petition to enter a plea bargain
- Update files with incoming information from attorneys
- Create and proofread criminal forms and templates
- Keep contact sheets updated and available to anyone needing the information
- Inform the attorney of upcoming deadlines

Key Terms

acquitted, 92

arraignment, 90

arrest, 90

bail hearing, 90

beyond a reasonable doubt, 91

blind option notation, 111

booking, 90

burden of proof, 91

certificate of representation, 106

criminal lawsuit, 90

defense attorney, 91

dependent clause, 94

double jeopardy, 92

federal crime, 90

felony, 90

hung jury, 92

impartial jury, 91

inverted order, 94

misdemeanor, 90

motion in limine, 107

normal order, 94

objective case pronoun, 94

omnibus hearing, 91

plea agreement, 92

possessive case pronoun, 95

presentence investigation, 92

preliminary hearing, 90

probable cause, 90

prosecuting attorney, 91

public defender or court appointed
   attorney, 91

sentencing, 92

speedy trial, 91

state crime, 90

stay of execution, 120

subjective case pronoun, 94

Local Focus Research

Your local court will have rules and due dates specific to your jurisdiction. Locate the Chapter 04 folder in your electronic storage medium and open the local focus file **C04_LocalFocus_CriminalLaw**. Resave the file as **LastName_ C04_LocalFocus_CriminalLaw**. Research the following topics and record your research in the file you just created. Use this information as a reference tool as you start and continue your career as a legal support staff member. Your instructor may ask you to submit a copy as homework.

Local Focus 4.1   The levels of criminal offenses are described on page 90. Look up what the different levels of crimes are called in your state. Do you have crimes called petty misdemeanor, gross misdemeanor, misdemeanor, and felony? Or, do those crimes have different names in your state? Make a list of these levels and their definitions and save your work in the Local Focus file.

Local Focus 4.2   Page 90 discusses rules of procedure. Find the criminal rules of procedure for your state and make a list of the rule numbers dealing with appeals of pretrial orders, motions to compel discovery, pretrial notices of witnesses and exhibits, and plea petitions. Save the rule numbers in your Local Focus file for future reference.

Local Focus 4.3   Page 92 discusses templates and forms provided by other companies through subscription, the court, the American Bar Association, or a law office. Go to your local court website and find forms that may be provided. Review the forms to determine the name for your state form similar to the notice of representation used in this text. Write the name of this document in your Local Focus file and include the URL of where the other forms are located.

Scenario 1: Matthew James, Client

Attorney Jessica Jordan from the Riverside, Illinois, office of Jordan, Leone & Sanchez, is defending Matthew James on a charge of possession with intent to sell cocaine, a felony. You are the legal support person working with the attorney on this case, and you know that the prosecuting attorney, Mick Stuart, has charged Matthew James with unlawfully selling one or more mixtures containing cocaine. The prosecuting attorney's address is 15 Acoma Court, Riverside, IL 33211. He can be reached by telephone at 312-555-9322. His attorney identification number is 592491X.

The prosecuting attorney has provided the complaint, the police report, and part of the police investigation, including portions of witness statements and videotape. Attorney Jordan has done her own investigation by sending an investigator to take additional photographs and get statements from the witnesses named by the client.

You sat in on the initial client interview and took notes on the case because you knew you would have to prepare a client contact sheet using details provided by the client. When you arrived at work today, you found a memo from attorney Jordan requesting your help on a number of documents.

Project 1   Prepare a Checklist of Tasks to Complete

1. Review the memo from Attorney Jordan found in Figure 4.4 or open the memo from Attorney Jordan. It is saved as **C04_P1_AttyMemoClientJames** and can be found in the Chapter 04 folder on your electronic storage medium. Note that she has created a separate folder for you containing forms and files for the case. The folder is named **C04_MaterialsFromAttyJordan**.

2. Read the memo carefully.

3. Highlight and make a checklist of:
   a. The documents you are asked to read/review
   b. Tasks you are asked to do
   c. Notes and reminders

4. Save your checklist as **LastName_C04_P1_Checklist**.

5. Find a partner and compare your lists. Add or delete items.

6. Your instructor will make a list as each group shares items on its list. Make certain that you have done everything you are being asked to do by the attorney.

Figure 4.4 **Memo from Attorney Jordan**

CONFIDENTIAL INTEROFFICE MEMO

DATE: JULY 25

TO: LEGAL ASSISTANT

FROM: JESSICA JORDAN

RE: STATE OF ILLINOIS V. MATTHEW JAMES

Matthew James, the client you met this morning, is a new client who has been charged with a Third Degree Controlled Substance Crime and is facing serious consequences if convicted. Mr. James has retained our office to represent him. We will begin preparing for a trial immediately.

Mr. James is currently on probation for a similar offense. He pled guilty seven months ago and received a 21-month stayed sentence, which will be vacated if he is convicted again. According to the Sentencing Guidelines, this is a Level VI felony. We need to be aware that there is a mandatory minimum of six months in prison with any subsequent drug offense. (ILCS §152.01, Subd. 1). I have already checked the client's criminal history in all available databases and all are consistent with the information provided by the client.

I am attaching the file, including the Complaint (labeled as Summons and Statement of Probable Cause), the police reports, the interview transcript between Agent Patterson and the confidential informant, the memo from the investigator, photos 1-10, and an aerial view map. The prosecuting attorney provided the copy of the Complaint, along with a CD containing video footage of the incident and an audio recording of the alleged sale. I have listened to the audio recording and reviewed the videotape several times. The audio is nothing but loud rap music. The prosecuting attorney has already advised me he will not be using it at trial. I have made notes identifying all relevant portions of the video. Most notably, much of the video is obstructed by overgrown bushes, and no transfer of money or drugs can be seen on the video. I would like you to review all information we have and complete the following documents:

    a. Client Contact Sheet; and

    b. Certificate of Representation.

The certificate of representation must be served on the prosecuting attorney and filed with court administration, so please prepare the appropriate letters. Because this is a situation involving a confidential informant, I would like you to complete a motion to compel discovery. Even though the client believes the confidential informant is James Snyder, we still have to make certain and obtain the entire file kept by the Drug Task Force regarding Mr. Snyder. I have scheduled a motion hearing for November 13 at 9:00 a.m. Therefore, please prepare a

    c. Motion to Compel Discovery.

We must notify the prosecution of our witnesses and the exhibits we are aware of, so please prepare a

    d. Notice of Defense Witnesses and Exhibits

I also want to make a request to the Court for an order suppressing any evidence of our client's prior record should he choose to testify. So with regard to that issue, please prepare a

continues

Figure 4.4 **Memo from Attorney Jordan** (continued)

e. Motion in Limine.

I have prepared the same motion before in other files, so a form does exist that refers to a request for sequestration (keeping the witnesses from hearing testimony of others before they testify), and a request regarding the client's criminal history, citing the *Jones* case, among others, in support. Use that form.

Please prepare items b, c, d, e, and appropriate letters.

Alison Yumi, Private Investigator, has been retained and has provided us with pictures from different viewpoints in and around the scene of the alleged crime, and an aerial view map of the area, all of which will be used as exhibits at trial. She also interviewed one witness, Lisa Rum, and has obtained a transcript of the testimony of Agent Paul Patterson taken at the Omnibus Hearing of Ms. Rum. Ms. Yumi has advised me that she has checked all available criminal history databases on both witnesses, Rum and Acoma, and neither have any prior convictions of any kind. If you need any further information from Ms. Yumi, you can contact her by phone at (312) 555-1212. Her mailing address is P. O. Box 222, Riverside, IL 56001.

Finally, I would like you to review the entire contents of our file and watch for inconsistencies among the police evidence, the investigation, and the facts given to us by the client. Prepare a memo to me listing the inconsistencies you find, your thoughts about the evidence, and a summary of facts that are both favorable and unfavorable to the client.

The documents I have requested should be prepared and served within a couple days. I would like to review your memo within two weeks. Thank you.

Jessica Jordan

Project 2   Transcribe Initial Client Interview Recording

To complete the client contact sheet, you must transcribe the recording of the client interview with Attorney Jordan.

1. Referring to your checklist, start the work for Mr. James.
2. Using transcription equipment, transcribe the recording of the initial interview with the client. The recording is saved in the Chapter 04 folder on your electronic storage medium as **C04_P2_InitialInterviewAudioFile**.
3. Save the transcript as **LastName_C04_P2_InitialClientInterviewTranscript** in the Chapter 04 folder on your storage medium.
4. Proofread the transcript carefully, make changes, and resave.
5. Print the transcript to be used in the next project.
6. Submit the transcript to the instructor.

Project 3   Prepare the Client Contact Sheet

1. Using the memo from the attorney and the transcript of the recording of the initial client interview, complete the client contact sheet. The template is provided for you saved as **C04_P3_ClientContactSheet** in the Chapter 04 folder on your storage medium.
2. Save the client contact sheet as **LastName_C04_P3ClientContactSheet** in the Chapter 04 folder on your storage medium. Add appropriate information to complete the client contact sheet.
3. Resave, print the completed contact sheet, and circle any missing information on the hard copy.
4. Submit the marked copy to the instructor.

Project 4   Create a Certificate of Representation

After Attorney Jordan and Mr. James agree on the terms of representation, the next step is to prepare a certificate of representation to file with the court, as noted by Attorney Jordan in her memo.

1. Use the information provided in the **C04_MaterialsFromAttyJordan** folder to create a certificate of representation. A template named **C04_P4_CertRep** is provided for you in the Chapter 04 folder.
2. Save the final document as **LastName_C04_P4_CertRep** in the Chapter 04 folder on your storage medium. Add the appropriate information and resave.
3. Print the completed certificate of representation and circle any missing information on the hard copy.
4. Submit the marked copy to the instructor.

Project 5   Create a Memo

Attorney Jordan asked you to review the materials in the file and compare them to the investigation done by your office investigator. Prepare a memo to her listing any differences you find between the two investigations.

1. Examine the documents located in the **C04_MaterialsFromAttyJordan** folder in the Chapter 04 folder on your storage medium. These should include the following:

   - Information provided previously by the attorney in the memo
   - Police complaint (**C04_JamesCriminalComplaint**)
   - Police report (**C04_JamesCriminalPoliceReport**)
   - Interview transcript between Agent Patterson and the confidential informant (**C04_JamesInterviewAgentPattersonAndConfidentialInformant**)
   - Testimony of Agent Patterson at the Omnibus Hearing (**C04_JamesTestimonyAgentPattersonOmnibusHearing**)
   - Transcript of video (**C04_JamesVideoPlayByPlay**)
   - Memo regarding investigation from Alison Yumi (**C04_JamesMemoFromPrivateInvestAlisonYumi**)

   You can also view the aerial maps and photographs provided in the folder. Note anything you think the attorney should pay attention to in reviewing the information.

2. Create and save the memo as **LastName_C04_P5_MemoToAtty** in the Chapter 04 folder on your storage medium.

Project 6   Create a Motion to Compel Discovery and Disclose Informant's Identity

According to the memo to you from the attorney, Ms. Jordan wants to confirm the identity of the confidential informant (also abbreviated as CI in investigative reports). To do so, she asks you to prepare a motion to compel discovery and disclose the informant's identity.

1. Use the information provided in the **C04_MaterialsFromAttyJordan** folder to create a motion to compel discovery. A template named **C04_P6_MotionCompelDiscovery** is provided for you in the Chapter 04 folder.

2. Complete the form with the appropriate information and save the final document as **LastName_C04_P6_MotionCompelDiscovery** in the Chapter 04 folder on your storage medium.

3. Print the completed motion to compel discovery and disclose informant's identity and circle any missing information on the hard copy.

4. Submit the marked copy to the instructor.

Project 7   Notice of Defense Witnesses and Exhibits

The prosecuting attorney as well as the defense attorney have the right to know the opposing party's potential witnesses and exhibits. Since you have created a notice of defense witnesses and exhibits before, Attorney Jordan asks you to create one again for her client, Mr. James.

1. Use the information provided in the **C04_MaterialsFromAttyJordan** folder to create a notice of defense witnesses and exhibits. A template named **C04_P7_NoticeDefenseWitnessesExhibits** is provided for you in the Chapter 04 folder.

2. Save the final document as **LastName_C04_P7_NoticeDefenseWitnessesExhibits** in the Chapter 04 folder on your storage medium.

3. Print the completed notice of defense witnesses and exhibits and circle any missing information on the hard copy.

4. Submit the marked copy to the instructor.

Project 8   Create a Motion in Limine

In this case Ms. Jordan wants to suppress evidence of her client's previous drug record. The office form available for your use is a standard form with standard language. Attorney Jordan always uses this form. If there are other items she wants suppressed, she will give you further instructions.

1. Use the information provided in the **C04_MaterialsFromAttyJordan** folder to create a motion in limine. A template named **C04_P8_MotionLimine** is provided for you in the Chapter 04 folder. Complete the form using the standard language.

2. Save the final document as **LastName_C04_P8_MotionLimine** in the Chapter 04 folder on your storage medium.

3. Print the completed motion in limine and circle any missing information on the hard copy.

4. Submit the marked copy to the instructor.

Scenario 2: Wanda Elizabeth Betters, Client

Attorney Jordan also represents Wanda Elizabeth Betters. Ms. Betters is 36 years old, her date of birth is August 1, 19xx, and her address is 112 Main Street, Riverside, IL 33211. She has a ninth-grade education but did obtain her GED in her early twenties. Ms. Betters suffers from an anxiety disorder. She has never been admitted to a mental hospital but has been treated for a mental health condition. She is otherwise in good health and had not been using alcohol or drugs for a period of 18 months prior to this incident. She is currently using drugs, however. The medication she was prescribed for her anxiety has helped.

Ms. Betters has been charged by Complaint in File No. CR-05-10943 with:

Count I: one felony count of aiding and abetting the manufacture of methamphetamine, a controlled substance

Count II: one felony count of aiding and abetting the sale of methamphetamine, a controlled substance, in violation of 720 ILCS 570.401 (d-5). The maximum penalty for each count is 3 to 7 years and/or a $200,000.00 fine. There is no mandatory minimum. The crime was allegedly committed on June 10, 20xx.

The prosecuting attorney is John Smith of Cook County. His address is P.O. Box 1001, Riverside, IL 33211.

Ms. Betters has been held in jail since her arrest, as she could not post bail or bond. She demanded a speedy omnibus (evidentiary) hearing and at that hearing she demanded a speedy trial.

Her trial is quickly approaching. She will have completed 60 days in jail by the date of her trial. The prosecutor has offered a plea agreement requiring Ms. Betters to plead guilty to one count of the complaint. The other count would be dismissed, she would receive a **stay of execution** (this temporarily delays the carrying out of an order [execution] based on certain conditions) of any further jail time, and credit for the time she has already served. She would be sentenced after a presentence investigation is completed.

Although Ms. Betters admits to having been under the influence of drugs at the time she was arrested, she does not claim that she was so impaired that she did not know what she was doing. It is contemplated by both parties that a condition of probation would be completion of an inpatient chemical dependency treatment program. In fact, they have agreed that she will not be released from jail until a bed in a treatment facility is available for her.

Ms. Betters did have a probable cause hearing, at which time it was determined that the state's evidence included (1) actual methamphetamine confiscated from the defendant's residence as the result of a search warrant; (2) statements of witnesses who saw the manufacturing operation on the defendant's premises; (3) the defendant's statement, which includes incriminating admissions; and (4) discussion with her attorney about the lack of any viable defenses. Ms. Betters agreed to plead guilty and take advantage of the plea agreement being offered. Therefore, a further pretrial hearing to determine the admissibility of evidence is not necessary and will be waived by the client. Both parties agree that if the court does not accept the plea agreement, Ms. Betters can withdraw her plea and again exercise her right to trial.

Attorney Jordan has negotiated a plea agreement with the prosecuting attorney and has discussed it with Ms. Betters. Ms. Betters has accepted the prosecutor's offer. Attorney Jordan has sent you a dictation file with the details for completing the petition to enter plea of guilty in felony or gross misdemeanor case.

Project 9   Prepare a Petition to Enter Plea of Guilty in Felony or Gross Misdemeanor Case

You receive a message from Attorney Jordan, who is away from the office but asks you to prepare a petition to enter a plea of guilty for her client. Listen to the message and add the appropriate information to the form as requested.

1. Open the appropriate petition from the Chapter 04 folder in your student data disc.
2. Save the document as **LastName_C04_P9_PetitionPleadGuilty**.
3. Open and listen to the instructions left by the attorney. The audio file is named **C04_P9_PetitionPleadGuilty_AudioFile**.
4. Apply the instructions in the audio file to the correct petition.
5. Resave the document and submit it to the instructor.

Discuss the Projects

While you were completing the chapter and projects, you learned:
- Criminal terminology
- How to find and access court rules pertaining to a project
- How to become familiar with the various aspects of the client's file, analyze the information, and apply your knowledge of the facts to your assignments
- How to think critically and independently to prove yourself a valued legal support person in the criminal process

Your education about the criminal process should not end with your work here. A successful legal support person will take the initiative to do additional reading and self-instruction during the course of his or her career.

As a class, discuss tips and other things you found helpful in completing the projects. Make a list of your own suggestions and the suggestions of those in your class.

Appeals

Chapter Objectives

- Understand the rules and terminology of appellate courts
- Know how to format a formal appellate brief, locate answers to questions, and determine deadlines for filing appellate briefs
- Know where to find appellate court rules in various states
- Successfully proofread text and focus on details of formatting a brief as prescribed by the court rules
- Be familiar with evaluating a reenactment of an actual argument to a court of appeals
- Understand how critical and independent thinking skills are applied to the appellate process by an employee of a legal office

Before beginning the exercises for this chapter, copy to your storage medium the Chapter 05 folder from the Student Resources disc that accompanies this textbook. Do this for each chapter before starting the chapter's exercises.

In 2010, the law offices of Blake, Wyler, and Whitney lost a case. The district court ordered their client to pay over $85,000 in damages to the plaintiff. Owing to their client's and Attorney Wyler's belief that the court had erred in refusing to allow certain evidence, the law office of Blake, Wyler, and Whitney decided to file an appeal with a higher court. They hoped that after the appellate process, the higher court would decide in their client's favor and overturn the original judgment.

In this chapter you will review the rules and terminology of appellate courts, format a formal appeal brief, find answers to questions regarding appellate court rules and formatting of briefs, and determine deadlines for filing. Later you will edit and proofread appellate documents to abide by court rules and evaluate an argument. You will also be asked to think critically and apply your knowledge to a set of projects at the end of the chapter.

To make an **appeal** means to ask a higher court to reverse a verdict, decision, order, final judgment, or other legal ruling made by a lower court. An appeal can be made if the attorney believes that the judge in the original case erred in interpreting the law, that the judge abused his or her discretion during the trial, that there was jury misconduct, or simply that the attorney disagreed with the judgment made against his or her client. A **notice of appeal** is written notice to the lower court and all parties and attorneys involved in a case that the losing party wishes to have a higher court review the decision made in the lower court.

In all state court systems, there are different levels of courts. Decisions are made in courts of original jurisdiction or the lowest courts. These decisions can be appealed to the next level of the court system. These *higher courts* in the state court structure have **appellate jurisdiction**, which means that higher courts have the authority to review and reverse, change, or agree with the decisions of lower courts. Names for these courts vary. Notice the differing court structures and names for Nebraska, Oregon, and Minnesota in Figures 5.1, 5.2, and 5.3.

Figure 5.1 **Nebraska Court Structure**

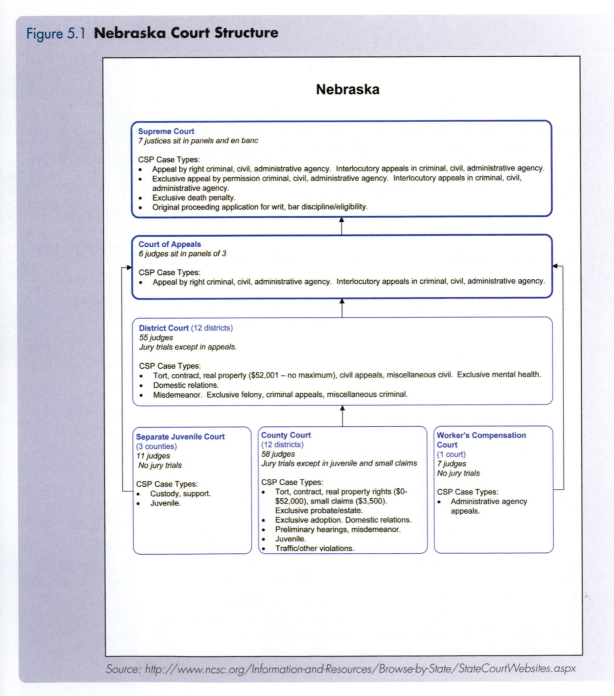

Source: http://www.ncsc.org/Information-and-Resources/Browse-by-State/StateCourtWebsites.aspx

Recall from Chapter 2 that an order is a document stating the ruling or opinion of a court or judge, and a judgment is a final determination of a matter by a court or judge. An appeal may be made to a court of appeals or higher court on either the state or the federal level. An **appellate brief** is a written argument by either party to the appeal and provides the appellate judges with reasons to rule in favor of the party presenting the brief. Although numerous steps are involved in an appeal from beginning to end, this chapter addresses the process and format of a formal appellate brief. An informal brief is done when not many issues are in the case. The rules do allow for informal briefs with the permission of the court. The attorney can request permission to file an informal brief, which has the same elements as a formal brief but is usually unbound.

Figure 5.2 Oregon Court Structure

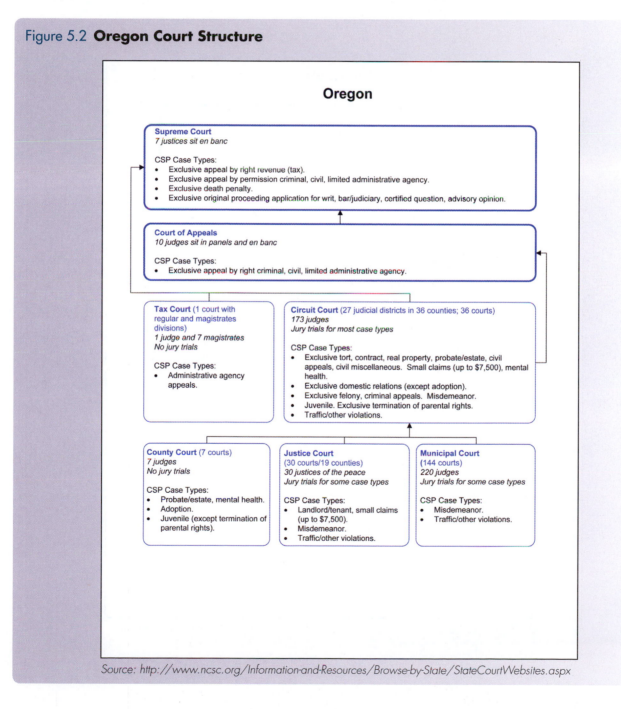

Source: http://www.ncsc.org/Information-and-Resources/Browse-by-State/StateCourtWebsites.aspx

In an appeal, the **appellant** is the party making the appeal to a higher court to change a judgment made in a lower court. The appellant files his or her initial (or principal) brief, after which the respondent or appellee files his or her reply brief. The respondent, or **appellee**, is the party who responds to an appeal arguing that the ruling of the lower court should stand. Some appellate terminology may differ from state to state. During the appeals process, the appellant will have the opportunity to file an additional brief in response to the position taken by the respondent in his or her brief.

Figure 5.3 **Minnesota Court Structure**

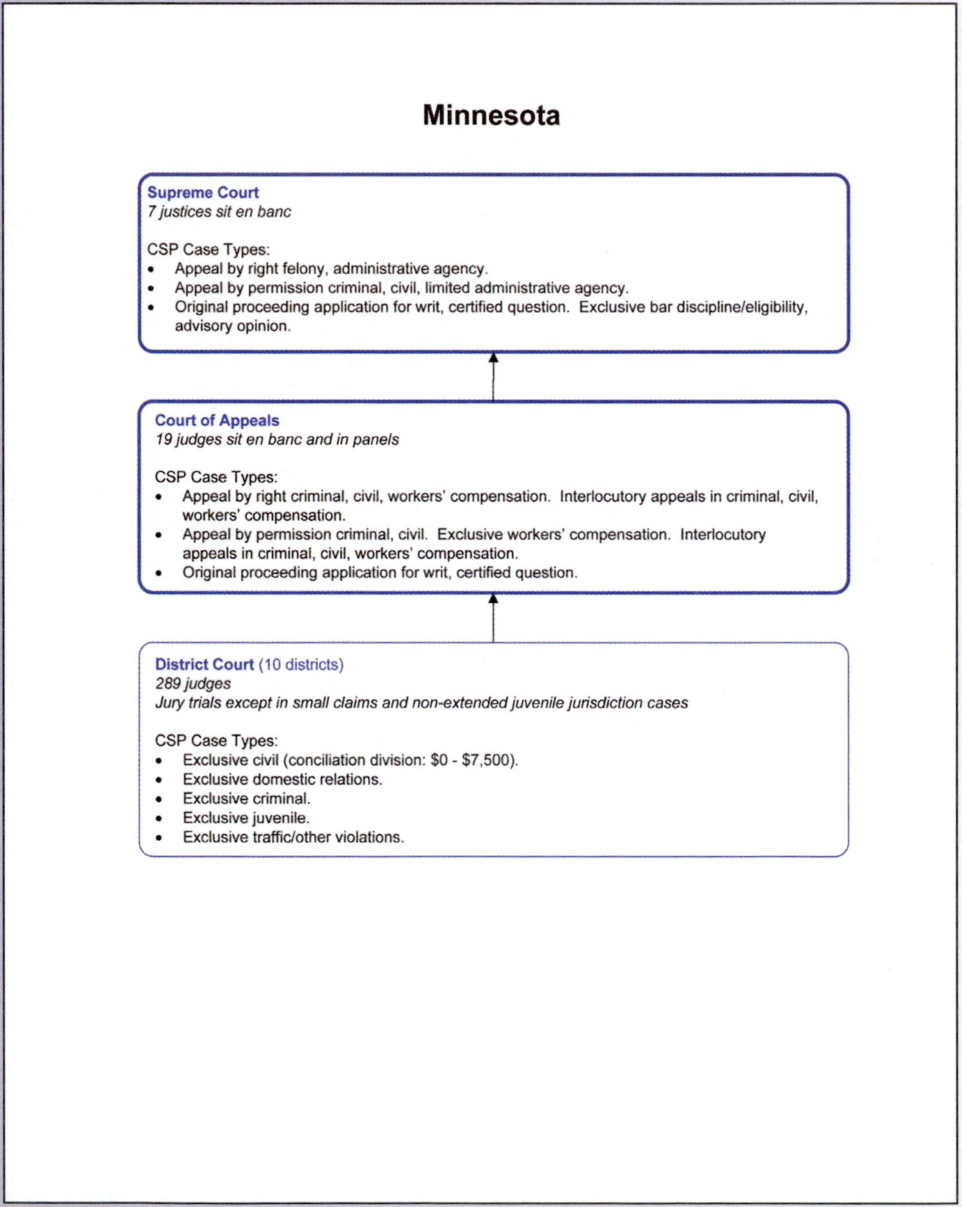

Minnesota

Supreme Court
7 justices sit en banc

CSP Case Types:
- Appeal by right felony, administrative agency.
- Appeal by permission criminal, civil, limited administrative agency.
- Original proceeding application for writ, certified question. Exclusive bar discipline/eligibility, advisory opinion.

Court of Appeals
19 judges sit en banc and in panels

CSP Case Types:
- Appeal by right criminal, civil, workers' compensation. Interlocutory appeals in criminal, civil, workers' compensation.
- Appeal by permission criminal, civil. Exclusive workers' compensation. Interlocutory appeals in criminal, civil, workers' compensation.
- Original proceeding application for writ, certified question.

District Court (10 districts)
289 judges
Jury trials except in small claims and non-extended juvenile jurisdiction cases

CSP Case Types:
- Exclusive civil (conciliation division: $0 - $7,500).
- Exclusive domestic relations.
- Exclusive criminal.
- Exclusive juvenile.
- Exclusive traffic/other violations.

Source: http://www.ncsc.org/Information-and-Resources/Browse-by-State/StateCourtWebsites.aspx

TERMINOLOGY

Be aware that terminology varies from state to state. For example, in Nebraska, the person bringing the appeal is the appellant. The person responding is the appellee. However, in Minnesota, these people are referred to as the appellant and the respondent, respectively.

Contents of a Formal Appellate Brief

A thorough review of appellate court rules will provide a solid understanding of the appellate process from beginning to end. These rules are found on the particular appellate court's website. The appellate rules are written in the order in which an actual appeal occurs. Formal appellate briefs typically contain a brief cover page, table of contents, table of authorities, issues, argument, certificate of brief length, addendum, and appendix.

The formal brief is prepared in a format prescribed by the court and is always bound. The brief cover page of an appellate brief is also prepared in a format prescribed by the court and indicates the level of the appellate court to which the case is being presented. The **brief cover page** is color coded and includes the court's case number, the case title containing the names of the appellant and respondent, the title of the document, and the contact information for all attorneys involved in the case. The case caption is part of the brief cover page; it contains information about the court, parties, and attorneys.

Figure 5.4 shows Appendix 5.95 of the Oregon rules of appellate procedure, which contains an example given by the court of a brief cover page with two document title options. This type of brief cover page is required if a brief contains confidential information that must be redacted. To **redact** means to carefully edit a document for the purpose of removing confidential references or other stated material. According to Oregon court rules, one may use this form but should choose the title depending upon whether the information is redacted pursuant to statute or court order.

The **table of contents** outlines each element of the brief and lists the page number on which that element may be found within the brief. A table of contents can be created manually or by using a function within the word processing program used to create the brief.

The **table of authorities** is a categorized outline of all legal cases, statutes, and precedents that supports the parties' arguments to the court and lists the page numbers on which each case, statute, or precedent appears in the brief. A table of authorities can be created by using a specially designed software program or a function within the word processing program used to create the brief.

All the required elements of a brief are defined by the rules of the court considering the appeal. One of the first elements that appears in the brief is the issue or **issues on appeal**. The appeal is restricted to the issues addressed or ruled upon in the lower court. These issues are called the issue(s) on appeal. No new issues can be brought up in an appeal if they were not addressed in the lower court.

The **argument section** of the brief is where the attorney cites case law and discusses how the case law supports each party's position on the issues on appeal.

If required by the rules, a certificate of brief length follows the last page (signature page) of the brief. The **certificate of brief length** indicates the word or line count of a brief as defined in the court rules. It indicates the font style and size in which the brief is typed as well as the version of the word processing program used to create the brief.

Figure 5.4 Appendix 5.95 of the Oregon Rules of Appellate Procedure

1. Sample Brief Caption for Brief Containing Confidential Material

IN THE COURT OF APPEALS OF THE
STATE OF OREGON

STATE OF OREGON,	)	_____ County
Plaintiff-Respondent,	)	Circuit Court No. _____
v.	)	CA A _____
JOHN DOE,	)	
Defendant-Appellant.	)	
	)	

CONFIDENTIAL BRIEF UNDER ORS 137.077
[or]
CONFIDENTIAL BRIEF UNDER TRIAL COURT ORDER
DATED JANUARY 1, 20xx
APPELLANT'S OPENING BRIEF AND
EXCERPT OF RECORD

---

2. Sample Brief Caption for Brief with Confidential Material Redacted

IN THE COURT OF APPEALS OF THE
STATE OF OREGON

STATE OF OREGON,	)	_____
Plaintiff-Respondent,	)	Circuit Court No. _____
v.	)	CA A _____
JOHN DOE,	)	
Defendant-Appellant.	)	
	)	

REDACTED BRIEF UNDER ORS 137.077
[or]
REDACTED BRIEF UNDER TRIAL COURT ORDER
DATED JANUARY 1, 20xx
APPELLANT'S OPENING BRIEF AND
EXCERPT OF RECORD

The brief's **addendum** contains an index and copies of the order, judgment, and so on, relating to the issues on appeal and short excerpts from the record that would be of assistance to a person reading the brief without referencing the appendix. Following the addendum is the brief's appendix. The **appendix** contains an index and copies of certain documents from the lower court, the notice of appeal, and constitutional challenges.

Local Focus 5.1

Once you are comfortable with finding and reviewing rules of appellate procedure, it will not matter what state you work in or in what level of the court system your appeal brief is being prepared. Knowing that you need to find certain details, finding those details, and applying them to your work are advanced skills that can be applied to different jobs, in different areas of law, and in different careers.

LOCAL RULES

As with most legal processes, the rules, procedures, documents, and terminology will vary among states and among different levels of the courts. Each level in the appellate court system will have its own set of rules. You should always locate and review the rules that pertain to the particular court in which you are filing your brief. It is not necessary to memorize rule numbers. Make a list of the appellate court rule numbers for your state that apply to the formatting of an appeal brief. Include in that list the rules pertaining to the time line deadlines for filing briefs. Keep these lists for future reference. Bookmark the website for the court rules for your state.

Appellate Procedure

If a party believes the decision of the court or jury was made because of an error interpreting the law or that the judge abused his or her discretion, then that party may appeal the ruling to a court of appeals at the state or federal level. An attorney might believe that a judge abused discretion by denying a motion to exclude evidence, incorrectly instructing the jury, or incorrectly ruling on objections made by attorneys regarding testimony. Appeals to a higher court are made to a state or federal court of appeals, circuit court, or the U.S. Supreme Court. An appeal may not bring up issues that were not discussed in or decided by the lower court. As mentioned earlier, the appellant is the party who first makes an appeal and asks a higher court to review or overturn a decision made in a lower court. Note that terminology may differ from state to state.

In addition to the preceding parties to an appeal, an outside party called an intervenor may be involved. An **intervenor** is one who has some right or interest in a case that already exists between other parties. He or she must ask the court's permission to enter the case and will be allowed to do so only if his or her interest will not unduly prejudice the movement of the original case. Similarly, a party or organization can become involved in a case based solely on its interest in the issue and not because of any direct involvement. These parties are known as **amicus curiae**, a Latin term meaning "friends of the court." A friend of the court is a party who participates in a case for the greater good of business or society.

Knowing the terminology that applies to the appeal will help you to understand the appellate procedures. The **rules of appellate procedure** set the rules and procedures to be followed during the appeal as well as the deadlines for performing certain actions. These rules are listed in the order in which an appeal will proceed

FIND THE FORMS APPENDIX WITHIN THE APPELLATE COURT RULES OF PROCEDURES

Most court rules have an appendix that provides examples of the wording and format for standard selected appellate documents. For example, the Minnesota Rules of Civil Appellate Procedure provide over 20 different examples of appellate documents. Form 128 in the appendix to the rules shows an example of the brief cover page and the various sections of an appellate brief from the brief cover page to the end of the brief. Each section is separated by a short row of asterisks (******). Take advantage of this support tool.

from the start of the appeals process through the appellate court's decision and, if necessary, possible appeal of that decision to a higher court. Strict time deadlines and procedures must be followed in appeals. The time limitation to bring an appeal begins to run only after a final decision has been made. Failure to file an appeal by the deadline will bar the right to appeal unless special permission from the appellate court is obtained. The attorney will determine the time limitation for the appeal. The legal support staff does not decide the deadline.

The rules of appellate procedure vary among states. Always know where to find the rules for your state or the federal rules, if applicable, and become familiar with them. Work with your supervising attorney to establish the correct deadlines and record them in a prominent place in the client's file. You and the attorney must always work together in determining these deadlines, since it is ultimately the attorney's responsibility to meet them. Timing rules for appeals are strictly enforced. If the appeal is not filed and served in a timely manner, the court will dismiss the appeal. Your appeal papers must also conform to the rules of the appellate court or they will not be accepted for filing and will be returned to you. The date of your attempted filing will not be preserved, meaning that the court will have no record of your attempt to file a notice of appeal. The court may decline to open a file on an appeal if there is a deficiency (or error) in the filing paperwork. There may or may not be time to make the necessary corrections and refile by the deadline. There is no grace period.

After the briefs have been submitted, the court will set a time for oral argument. **Oral argument** is an attorney's opportunity to present a brief oral summary supporting his or her case in a limited amount of time to a panel of appellate judges. In some cases the attorneys agree that no oral argument is necessary; then the judges decide the case based on the briefs submitted.

Language Focus: Verbs

As an employee in a law office, you must be able to combine the procedures of the law with the process of creating clear, concise, and correctly written documents. Using the correct and consistent verb tenses is important and should be a point of focus in editing documents. Being able to correctly identify the types of verbs within a document and how to conjugate them accurately will clarify your editing choices.

Action and linking verbs are the words that tell what is going on or what is happening in a sentence. Table 5.1 provides examples of action verbs, and Table 5.2 provides examples of linking verbs.

Table 5.1 Action Verbs

agree	disagree	require
appeal	intervene	serve
argue	move	speculate
bring	prepare	stipulate
contemplate		

Table 5.2 Linking Verbs

True Linking Verbs	Other Linking Verbs
be (and all of its variations such as am, is, are, was, were, has been, are being, might have been, etc.) become seem	appear feel grow look prove remain smell sound taste turn

An **action verb** is a verb that expresses physical or mental action, while a **linking verb** connects the subject with a word or words in the predicate. Recall that every sentence consists of a subject and a predicate. The predicate provides information about the subject and includes a verb or verb phrase. The verb in a predicate will be either an action or a linking verb with or without a helping verb. A list of common helping verbs is given in Table 5.3.

Table 5.3 Helping Verbs

am	has
are	have
be	is
been	may
being	might
can	must
could	shall
did	should
do	was
does	will
had	would

Use the helping verbs *am, is, are, was, were,* and *be* with main verbs ending with *ing.* These helping verbs focus on progress of action (progressive tense).

I am thinking.

He is thinking.

They are thinking.

She was thinking.

They were thinking.

He will be thinking.

The helping verbs *have*, *had*, and *has* allow action to continue over time (perfect tense).

I have thought.

I had thought.

I will have thought.

Verbs have principal parts that tell the time at which something happened. These are called the simple tenses: present tense, past tense, and past participle. You can make the singular form of verbs by adding *s* and *ing* (present participle). You can make the principal part of a verb past tense in a "regular" way (by adding *ed* to the present tense) called a **regular verb** or in an irregular way (by changing the spelling of the present tense) called an **irregular verb**.

Regular Verbs

Table 5.4 shows a list of regular verb tenses. It shows that the past tense and the past participles of regular verbs both end in *ed*. The table also shows that the past tense and past participles are differentiated by the fact that the past tense "never has a helping verb" and the past participle "always has a helping verb."

The writer chooses the past tense to indicate something that has happened in the past and is finished.

The court **determined** that the evidence was admissible.

The writer chooses the past participle, the past tense verb plus a helping verb, to indicate a past action and that that action applies to something happening currently.

The court **has determined** that the evidence is admissible."

Table 5.4 Regular Verb Tenses

Present Tense			Past Tense	
Singular Form	Plural Form	Present Participle	Singular or Plural Form	Past Participle
Test: The child walks...The child helps...	Test: The children walk... The children help...	Present tense + ing	Never has a helping verb	Always has a helping verb
argues	argue	arguing	argued	argued
calculates	calculate	calculating	calculated	calculated
evaluates	evaluate	evaluating	evaluated	evaluated
helps	help	helping	helped	helped
investigates	investigate	investigating	investigated	investigated
listens	listen	listening	listened	listened
processes	process	processing	processed	processed
researches	research	researching	researched	researched
responds	respond	responding	responded	responded
transcribes	transcribe	transcribing	transcribed	transcribed

Irregular Verbs

Table 5.5 provides a partial listing of irregular verbs. Memorize key irregular verbs and use the dictionary to confirm the correct form of an irregular verb.

Table 5.5 Irregular Verbs

Present Tense			Past Tense	
Singular Form	**Plural Form**	**Present Participle**	**Singular or Plural Form**	**Past Participle**
Test: The child walks...The child helps...	Test: The children walk... The children help...	Present tense + ing	Never has a helping verb	Always has a helping verb
begins	begin	beginning	began	begun
strives	strive	striving	strove	striven
chooses	choose	choosing	chose	chosen
drinks	drink	drinking	drank	drunk
forbids	forbid	forbidding	forbade	forbidden
lies	lie	lying	lay	laid
rises	rise	rising	rose	risen

Unlike the regular verbs shown in Table 5.4, the past tense and the past participle forms of the irregular verbs in Table 5.5 do not share the same endings. Therefore, it is possible to make a mistake in choosing between the past tense form, to indicate an action that is done, and the past participle form, to indicate an action that occurred in the past but is also currently happening. For example, if a writer or editor is unfamiliar with the irregular verb, *to strive*, it might be difficult to decide which form to use with a helping verb.

We strive to treat all clients fairly. (present tense)

We strove to treat all clients fairly. (past tense)

We have striven to treat all clients fairly. (past participle)

Best Practice Tip

USING AN UNABRIDGED DICTIONARY

An unabridged dictionary is one that has not been shortened by leaving out certain terms or definitions in the interest of making the dictionary smaller and easier to carry. An unabridged dictionary will list how to spell the plural of regular and irregular verbs, for example; it will show the present tense of a verb as well as all of its principle parts. It will show, among other items, all the definitions of words and its history and how it is used in a sentence. Unabridged dictionaries are obviously going to be the "really big" ones at the library and bookstore! Most free online dictionaries work very well for most purposes and are readily available on the Internet. Companies such as Merriam-Webster and Cambridge offer online unabridged versions for a fee. These fee-driven online dictionaries include twice as many words as the free versions. Reputable online dictionaries have appeared on the Internet and have no unabridged versions. Choose a paper-based or an online dictionary that fits your needs.

It is important to remember that the singular or plural form of a verb in the past tense will *never* have a helping verb paired with it, but the past participle form will *always* have a helping verb paired with it. The choice between a past-tense verb form and a past-participle verb form with a helping verb will depend on the time when the action happened or if it continues to happen.

We **began** our work on Monday morning. (correct)

We **have began** our work on Monday morning. (incorrect)

The work, which continues throughout this week, **was begun** on Monday morning. (correct)

The work, which continues throughout this week, **began** on Monday morning. (incorrect)

Language Focus Exercises

In the following exercises, use a bound dictionary or an online dictionary to verify your answers.

Exercise 5.1 Fill in the tenses of the regular verbs in the rows of the following chart. Share your answers with your classmates and see how many other regular verbs can be found.

	Present Tense			Past Tense	
	Singular Form	Plural Form	Present Participle	Singular or Plural Form	Past Participle
1.	accepts				
2.		clean			
3.			frightening		
4.				noticed	
5.					searched

Exercise 5.2 Think of five irregular verbs not listed in Table 5.4 and fill in the tenses in the rows of the following chart. Share your answers with your classmates and see how many other regular verbs can be found.

	Present Tense			Past Tense	
	Singular Form	Plural Form	Present Participle	Singular or Plural Form	Past Participle
1.	bleeds				
2.		hit			
3.			leading		
4.				threw	
5.					written

Exercise 5.3 Read the following sentences and underline the verb or verb phrase. Write on the line provided whether the main verb is a regular or irregular verb.

1. Appellant failed to appear for his deposition. _____
2. The trial court dismissed appellant's complaint. _____
3. Respondent brought a motion for sanctions. _____
4. The judge set the hearing for Monday, November 8, at 8:45 a.m. _____
5. The deposition revealed how the accident occurred. _____

Exercise 5.4 Read the following sentences. Underline the verb or verb phrase. Determine whether the main verb is correct or not. Write the correction on the line provided. Write "C" on the line if the sentence is correct as is.

1. The contract has been laying in the outbox for two days. _____
2. The visitors can sit their luggage in the reception area. _____
3. I seen the link for the new rules of appellate procedure. _____
4. He had wound the rope so tightly that it was impossible to untangle. _____
5. The site of injury had swelled so much that the plaintiff could not remove her hockey skate. _____

Editing: Verb Tense Consistency

In many instances, the first impression formed by a client, another attorney, local businessperson, court administrator, or judge is made in response to written documents created by a law firm. Mistakes of any kind, including mistakes related to verb tense, may create an impression that other legal work from your office is flawed as well.

Shifts in verb tense throughout a sentence or paragraph can cause confusion, especially if those shifts are unintentional or distort the actual time line of events being described. In editing documents, it is important to watch for verb tense consistency at both the sentence and paragraph levels. Change tense in a sentence or paragraph only when necessary—for example, to indicate a change in time from one action or state to another.

The following examples show a shift in verb tense at the sentence level, with incorrect and correct verb tense choices.

Incorrect: During the deposition, the court reporter stood up and drops her water glass.

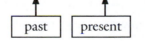

| past | present |

Correct: During the deposition, the court reporter stood up and dropped her water glass.

| past | present |

Incorrect: When the attorney in cowboy boots and gold chains <u>walks</u> into the courtroom, everyone <u>will stare</u>.

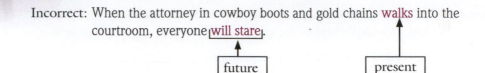

| future | | present |

Correct: When the attorney in cowboy boots and gold chains walks into the courtroom, everyone stares.

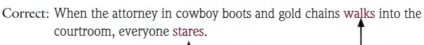

| present | | present |

Sometimes it is necessary to change the verb tense within a sentence, but such instances should be reviewed carefully, to confirm that the time line being described accords with the author's intentions.

Correct: Ms. Sullivan reached for the completed brief after she had already completed the research.

| past, indicates second action happened in the past | past, indicated second action happened in the past | past participle, indicates first action happened before the past action |

Ideally, paragraphs will establish a primary tense and will keep that tense consistent from sentence to sentence. Watch for changes in tense that are not required by the author's intention. Although both of the following examples show a shift in tense within the paragraph, both are correctly written and do not require editing changes to the tenses of the verbs.

Correct: The child sits on the ground, close to the bench. She cries out for her mother. Several people pass by and look at her, but no one does anything. If her grandmother sees the child, she will pick her up. However, the grandmother seems to be nowhere in sight.

present tense

future tense

Correct: The child sat on the ground, close to the bench. She cried out for her mother. Several people passed by and looked at her, but no one did anything. If her grandmother saw the child, she would pick her up. However, the grandmother seemed to be nowhere in sight.

past tense

conditional future tense

Editing Exercises

The following exercises will allow you to practice your editing skills using the information discussed in this chapter.

Exercise 5.5 Read the following sentences and underline the verbs or verb phrases. Write "C" on the line provided if the verbs are consistent. If they are not, circle the verb that should be changed and write the change on the line.

1. People recall very little about the first landing on the moon other than news clips they watch in the 1960s.

    _____

2. At 3 p.m. the sun popped out of the clouds, the wind died down, and the birds announce their presence.

    _____

3. Last week I had walked downtown but rode home with a friend.

    _____

4. Maria is in charge of finance; she always keeps her office locked.

    _____

5. A few countries produce almost all of the world's illegal drugs, but addiction affected many countries.

    _____

6. When the tickets are ready, the travel agent notifies the client. Each ticket is then listed on a daily register form, and a copy of the itinerary is filed.

    _____

7. The self-help mania of the 1980s gave way to the greed of the 1990s, which in turn gives way to the occupational insecurity of the 2000s.

    _____

8. Janet worked on the interrogatories as we complete the cover letters and envelopes.

    _____

9. Spring comes early in Pennsylvania. First, the lilacs burst into blossom; then the dogwood trees began to bloom.

    _____

10. The moderator asks for questions as soon as the speaker has finished.

    _____

Exercise 5.6 Edit the following paragraph, paying close attention to verb tenses. Rewrite the paragraph on the lines provided. Discuss your changes with your classmates and instructor.

When I was in high school, I used to think I want to major in psychology. After taking a psychology class my first semester, however, I realize that perhaps psychology was not for me. While other students are choosing their majors, I did not know what I want. I decided not to worry about it and to just take classes that fulfill my core requirements. I took an introduction to law class and love it. I decided to major in prelaw, and I felt confident that this is the right decision.

_____

_____

_____

_____

_____

_____

_____

_____

_____

Proofreading: Legal Documents

Earlier in the chapter, you read about the requirements for appellate court documents and how to research them. In addition to the more difficult and time-consuming tasks of confirming that appellate court documents follow the necessary requirements, proofreading of these and other legal documents must include confirming the correct spelling and accuracy of names, street addresses, and unusual city names. Next to formatting the brief properly by following the court rules, proofreading the text of the final copy is the most important task you will perform in assisting an attorney who is writing an appeal brief.

You will be expected to proofread the entire brief from the front cover to the last page of the appendix. You must track many details, so you should refer to the formatting requirements in the court rules as you perform your review. In addition to making sure that the cover page includes all the necessary information and the content of the attorney's signature block is correct on the final page of the brief, you should also ensure that the brief reads well. If a sentence or paragraph does not read well in your opinion or seems incomplete based on your knowledge of the file, it is likely that the panel of judges reading the brief will also find it difficult to understand.

One important way in which you will assist the attorney is to proofread the text of the brief, watching for errors in spelling, grammar, spacing, font style, and font size. Be aware of who the parties are in the case and watch for transposition of parties as you read. No matter where it appears, whether in an appellate brief, criminal complaint, civil interrogatories, or family document, always double check that the address details and the dates are correct. It is common to reuse a letter as a template and forget to change the date or other parts of the letter. Sometimes more than one attorney will create and sign documents on a file. Make sure that you have the correct signature block(s). Proofread these each and every time. Remember that a spell checker will not catch many of these types of errors.

Proofreading is essential in all document creation and should be taken seriously no matter if the document or letter is going to a supreme court judge or to the local court administrator. This section focuses on proofreading the repetitive parts of documents, including letters. In a legal office, a letter is not considered to be a legal document. Generally, court rules do not govern the formatting of correspondence.

Tips for Proofreading Legal Documents

The following will identify parts of legal documents and the key issues that should be checked as part of the proofreading process. Make these proofreading checks a habit.

Top and Bottom Margins According to some court rules, the minimum top and bottom margins on the first and subsequent pages should be 1 inch. Always check court rules to determine what is required in your local area. Check each document as you proofread to see that your top and bottom margins are set at what is required in your office style guide.

Left and Right Margins Court rules may also specify left and right margins. Some rules may state the maximum typing area, such as 6.5 by 9.5 inches. In that case, the left and right margins would be set at 1 inch each. The top and bottom margins would be 0.75 inches each.

Until you verify what your local court rules specify, use default margins on the first draft of a document.

Caption Formatting and Information Requirement Proofread repetitive locations in the caption of the court document such as the court file number, judge's name, and document title. It is easy to leave out the document title or forget to replace the title if you are using a different file as an example or a starting point. To eliminate repeated proofreading of this area of a court document, create one that is absolutely correct and save it. Insert the caption on all documents that require it. The only thing that will be different on each will be the document name. Continue to proofread that section.

Header, Footer, Footnote, and Page Number Style Check that the font style and size of the document's header, footer, and page numbers match the font style and size of the body of the document. In general legal document creation, page numbers are suppressed on the first page. However, appellate briefs are different. The court rules specify that all pages be numbered including first pages. The only page not numbered is the brief cover page. In addition, footnote font style and size are addressed in court rules for appellate documents and must be followed.

Paragraph Numbering Style and Format Sometimes you will number paragraphs by using the automatic numbering or outlining feature in your word processing program. However, in many legal documents—such as affidavits, complaints, legal briefs, and petitions—you will turn off the numbering or outline feature and number the paragraphs yourself because it is easier to format the numbered paragraphs manually especially if there are headings between paragraphs. Depending upon the attorney's personal writing style, some appellate briefs will have sections labeled with roman numerals, but the internal numbered lists may use arabic numerals.

Documents should employ a consistent numbering style. For example, the paragraphs in the document may be numbered with roman numerals that are centered above the paragraphs (as shown in Figure 5.5), or the paragraphs may be numbered with arabic numerals located at the left margin (as shown in Figure 5.6). Either format may be acceptable, but the same, consistent format must be used throughout the document.

The format of second and subsequent lines of numbered paragraphs should be consistent within a given document, but more than one correct way to format these lines is used. Figure 5.6 shows the first line of each numbered paragraph indented, with the turnover lines set flush to the margin. Figure 5.7 shows the same text formatted so that the turnover lines are indented and aligned under the text above. The format shown in Figure 5.7 is sometimes called a *hanging indent*. Either format may be acceptable, but a consistent format should be used throughout a document. If the document is very long, the format in Figure 5.5 may be preferred because it will result in a more economical layout (fewer printed pages).

Figure 5.5 Roman numbers

> I.
>
> Whether Appellant was provided with effective assistance of counsel guaranteed under the Sixth and Fourteenth Amendments to the United States Constitution and Article I, Section 6 of the Montana Constitution?
>
> II.
>
> Whether the trial court was within its broad discretion in excluding defense testimony as a sanction for defense counsel's discovery violation and did not violate any of Appellant's constitutional rights?

Figure 5.6 Arabic numbers in paragraph formatting

> 1. Whether Appellant was provided with effective assistance of counsel guaranteed under the Sixth and Fourteenth Amendments to the United States Constitution and Article I, Section 6 of the Montana Constitution?
>
> 2. Whether the trial court was within its broad discretion in excluding defense testimony as a sanction for defense counsel's discovery violation and did not violate any of Appellant's constitutional rights?

Figure 5.7 Arabic numbers with hanging indent formatting

> 1. Whether Appellant was provided with effective assistance of counsel guaranteed under the Sixth and Fourteenth Amendments to the United States Constitution and Article I, Section 6 of the Montana Constitution?
>
> 2. Whether the trial court was within its broad discretion in excluding defense testimony as a sanction for defense counsel's discovery violation and did not violate any of Appellant's constitutional rights?

Document Line Spacing The rules of your local court will specify the required line spacing for legal documents. Generally, legal documents are double spaced. More recent rules are showing single spacing in some documents, such as summonses. Some states do not require the filing of discovery documents with the court, which has led some offices to adopt single spacing simply to save paper. Letter style dictates single spacing.

Date Format Be consistent with date formats. Some attorneys prefer the date with the signature block to read "Dated this _____ day of _____, 20XX," whereas others prefer a simple "Dated: [month day, year]." Depending upon where you are working, you could run into a military-style or foreign date format such as "2 January 20XX."

In addition to checking the format of the date, always make certain that a date *is* on the document. Although the date line is not typically part of the signature block, one approach is to create a template that includes the date line as part of the signature block to reduce the chance of leaving it out. Attorneys do not always dictate a date, but all legal documents must be dated.

In typing a legal document, leave the actual date out of the date line. The attorney can handwrite the date in at the time the document is signed. The date indicates the date on which the document was signed—not the date on which it was created.

Signature Line/Block Format and Information The signature block, along with other parts of documents such as captions, can be tedious to type. Make a template to insert a signature line with the following information below it:

- Attorney name and identification number
- Firm name
- Attorney for [plaintiff or defendant, etc.]
- Address
- Telephone number

Check your local court rules because the court may specify signature block format and other required information such as fax number and email address.

Always try to get the signature block on the same page as the last paragraph of the legal document. A document is more professional and harder to commit fraud with if the signature block is not on a page by itself. It is possible that your word processing program has a feature that will, if used, automatically keep the signature block on the same page as the last paragraph.

Proofreading Exercises

Complete the following proofreading exercises to apply the tips described previously.

Exercise 5.7 Complete the following exercise to develop a proofreading checklist.

1. Brainstorm with a group of students to create a checklist you can use when you are proofreading documents.
2. Key the checklist and save the file with the file name **LastName_C05_Ex5.7_ ProofreadingChecklist**.
3. Share the checklist check points your group has identified with the other class groups. If other groups come up with check points not included in your group's list and your group finds them helpful, add them to your file and resave the file.

Exercise 5.8 Complete the following exercise to practice identifying stylistic inconsistencies within a legal document.

1. Open **LEP_StyleGuide** and review the preferences for the law office of Jordan, Leone & Sanchez.
2. Open and print **C05_Ex5.8_ProofStyleInconsistencies.**
3. Proofread the printed document, circling stylistic inconsistencies and marking how they should be corrected.
4. Make the necessary changes in the original file, saving the file as **LastName_ C05_Ex5.8_ProofStyleInconsistencies**.
5. Submit the marked document and corrected file as directed by your instructor.

Exercise 5.9 Complete the following exercise to practice identifying stylistic inconsistencies within a noncourt document.

1. Open and print **C05_ Ex5.9_NonCourtDoc**.
2. Using the style guide opened in Exercise 5.8, proofread the printed document, circling stylistic inconsistencies and marking how they should be corrected.
3. Make the necessary changes in the original file, saving the file as **LastName_ C05_Ex5.9_NonCourtDoc**.
4. Submit the marked document and corrected file as directed by your instructor.

Exercise 5.10 Complete the following proofreading exercise relating to parties in a case.

1. Open and print **C05_Ex5.10_Proofreading**.
2. Proofread the printed document, marking any errors you find.
3. Make the necessary changes into the original file, saving the file as **LastName_ C05_Ex5.10_Proofreading**.
4. Submit the marked document and corrected file as directed by your instructor.

Exercise 5.11 Complete the following proofreading exercise of part of an appeal brief.

1. Open and print **C05_Ex5.11_Appeal**.
2. Proofread the printed document, marking any errors you find. Watch for spelling, grammar, punctuation, and subtle differences in the appearance of text.
3. Make the necessary changes in the original file, saving the file as **LastName_ C05_Ex5.11_Appeal**.
4. Submit the marked document and corrected file as directed by your instructor.

Appeals How-To Guide

Many attorneys are too busy to produce a brief that complies with the many formatting details set out in the court rules. Most attorneys will draft a brief and then rely on their support staff to edit and proofread the document and verify that the brief conforms to the requirements of the court. First impressions are important. A carelessly formatted or edited brief may lead a judge to think that the brief writer was also careless with its contents and supporting material.

The main role of the legal support staff in the appeals process involves compiling the body of the appeal brief and its related parts. The person in this role will review the appropriate court rules of appellate procedure to determine specific guidelines on how to complete the appeal brief. For example, a legal support person is responsible for determining the following information:

- Requirements for formatting, including font size, caption style, margins, spacing, and binding
- Working with the attorney to determine time computation and deadlines for filing certain documents with the court
- Service rules, such as how many copies are to be filed with the court and provided to all parties

Appeal briefs are usually bound. The acceptable methods for binding are set out in the court rules. Some law offices may have their own equipment for the brief-binding process and will copy and bind briefs in house. Other law offices use a brief printing service to put the brief into final form. A **brief printing service** is a vendor hired to bind, copy, and file the formal appeal brief based on an office's specifications. Such a service will make the appropriate number of copies, serve copies on opposing counsel, and file the brief with the court by the deadline you give them. A reputable brief printer is an invaluable resource to the law office.

Figure 5.8 is an example of a legal brief order form that a brief printing service may provide for you to fill out. Forms such as these would be completed and provided to the printer with your brief cover page and your completed brief. You will send your final brief containing an original signature as well as its addendum and/or appendix to the printer by mail, express service, email in pdf format, or according to the printer's preference. To learn the preference of the printing service, you would refer to the service's website or call to learn details.

When your office works with an outside vendor, great care should be taken to ensure that deadlines are met and information is delivered in a timely fashion. It is important to identify the things you will need to know from the brief printer so this vendor can get your brief prepared, filed, and served by the date it is due. The printer will need a specific amount of time to complete the project, and this time will be dependent on the details of the work the printing service needs to do, the length of the brief and appendices, the number of copies that must be made and bound, and the delivery method for the completed brief. By allowing the printer enough time, you will be confident that your brief will be prepared and served before the court's deadline.

Local Focus 5.2

When you contact the printing service staff, you will need to tell them the date your brief is due to the court and ask them by what date they must receive your final brief so that they will have enough time to perform their service. The printer will appreciate your foresight in asking this question so that an appropriate work schedule can be set up. You are not the only customer for whom the printer is performing a service. You should discuss the printer's deadline with the attorney writing the brief so that you can determine your internal office deadline for the final proofreading of the brief and the date by which it must sent to the printer.

Best Practice Tip

BRIEF PRINTING CHECKLIST

Whether your office uses a legal brief printing service or performs this service in house, you will need to gather certain information to accomplish the task of filing your brief with the court and serving it on all parties to the appeal. It is a good idea to have your own checklist so that you can easily make sure that all details are covered.

Figure 5.8 **Legal brief order form**

LEGAL BRIEF ORDER FORM

ACE LEGAL PRINTING

123 Market Square
Minneapolis, MN 50061

Fax: 123-555-0160
Email: acelegalprinting@emcp.com
Phone: 507-555-0160

Today's Date: _____

Firm Name: _____

Firm Street Address: _____

Firm City/State/Zip: _____

Attorney Filing Brief: _____

Contact Person: _____

Phone Number: _____

Fax Number: _____

Email: _____

Your Office File Number: _____

Court Case Number: _____

Court: (Select One)
❏ State Court of Appeals
❏ State Supreme Court
❏ Circuit Court
❏ U.S. Supreme Court

CHECKLIST
❏ Did you sign your brief?
❏ Is your case number correct?
❏ Are attorney registration numbers and phone numbers on the cover?
❏ Is your table of contents, table of authorities, appendix index, and addendum index included?
❏ Did you number your appendix and addendum?

Manner of filing and service:

Court: (Select One)
❏ Personal delivery
❏ Overnight express service
❏ First-Class Mail

Service on opposing attorneys: (Select One)
❏ Personal delivery
❏ Overnight express service
❏ First-Class Mail

Delivery to your firm: (Select One)
❏ Personal delivery
❏ Overnight express service
❏ First-Class Mail

Deadline date to file with court: _____

Fax your cover page and we will prepare your cover in advance.

Number of copies required:

Unbound to court:

Bound to court:

Bound to opposing attorney:

Bound to your firm:

Type of Brief (Select One):
❏ Appellant
❏ Respondent
❏ Appellee
❏ Reply
❏ Amicus
❏ Other

Critical Thinking: Rule References

In your work as a legal support person in any area of law, an important task you will be expected to do is to find the court rules that pertain to the project on which you are working. You will then have to read and comprehend the details within the rules that refer you to additional information.

These rules are available online or in a printed rule book. As a legal support person, you will not be required to memorize these rules. However, you will be expected to find and interpret their meaning. A suggestion is to make a list of frequently used rules so that you will be able to find them quickly. Some people print the applicable pages. Check for updated rules periodically. Online rules are updated as changes occur, so they are always up to date. For printed references, supplements will be provided with the updated rules.

In reviewing court rules, you will sometimes see comments at the end of the rule. These comments give historical information about amendments to the rules over the years. You should rely only on the printed rule. If you are confused about how to interpret a particular rule, you should always talk to the attorney who is responsible for preparing the brief for clarification.

A particular rule may refer to an additional civil, criminal, or appellate rule. In that case, you will need to look up the rule referred to and decide if it applies to your project. Minnesota Rule of Civil Procedure 59.04 contains an example of a reference within a rule, which addresses the time allowed for serving affidavits. This set of rules is cited as Minn. R. Civ. App. P. (specific rules in this section hereafter referred to as MN Rule ##.##). MN Rule 59.04 states: "When a motion for a new trial is based upon affidavits, they *shall be served with the notice of motion. The opposing party shall have 10 days* after such service in which to serve opposing affidavits, *which period may be extended by the court pursuant to Rule 59.03 . . .*" (emphasis added). This rule tells you that if the affidavit you need to file is in support of a motion, you must do further research to learn the timing for serving a motion.

Because MN Rule 59.04 references MN Rule 59.03, you should read MN Rule 59.03, which addresses time for serving motions. MN Rule 59.03 states: "A notice of *motion for a new trial shall be served within 30 days* after a general verdict or service of notice by a party . . . *and shall be heard within 60 days after . . . unless the time for hearing be extended by the court within the 60-day period . . .*" (emphasis added). After reading MN Rule 59.03, you can work with the attorney to create the time line for preparing and serving the motion and affidavits.

FINDING STATE RULES

You can find court rules for all 50 states, including details about each state, by doing your own Internet search or using the website www.50states.com. Choose a state and then find the link for courts/judicial system. Move around in the menu items on the court's site to see what information the court has posted. Most courts have a self-help center as well as court forms, rules of procedure, and a lot of other helpful and interesting information.

When you have the time in the future, look at websites for court rules in other states and compare the formatting of briefs, differences in terminology for the naming of the parties, titles of briefs for the various parties, etc.

Later in this chapter, you will be doing a project based on a review of the Minnesota Rules of Civil Appellate Procedure (found at www.mncourts.gov). The following are examples of references one might encounter within these rules.

When the attorney is drafting the statement of the case that must be filed with the notice of appeal, the attorney must indicate if he or she will request oral argument to the court. MN Rule 133.03 talks about the statement of the case and states: "If a party desires oral argument *at a location other than that provided by Rule 134.09, subdivision 2(a) to (e)*, the location requested shall be included in the statement of the case" (emphasis added).

The reference to MN Rule 134.09 indicates that the legal support person should further refer to MN Rule 134.09, which addresses the place for oral argument. This rule states the physical locations where oral arguments will be heard. "Argument to the Supreme Court shall take place at the State Capitol or Minnesota Judicial Center in St. Paul or at any other place designated by the Supreme Court." If the attorney wants to request a different location for argument, that request should be made in the statement of the case. Frequently, the panels of appellate judges hearing cases will travel within the state and will hear several cases during a week at various locations. This saves long travel times for attorneys located in remote areas and gives the general public an opportunity to attend arguments and see how the system works.

Critical Thinking Exercises

The first exercise will provide practice on finding and interpreting references within a rule. This exercise will help you to better understand how to locate, review, and interpret the various references in rules you will find as you perform your job. The following exercises will provide other opportunities to develop skills related to rules.

Exercise 5.12 The attorney writing an appellate brief asks you to find the rules explaining computation or limitation of time to determine when the appellate brief is due to the court. Note that you will look at two different sets of rules.

1. Review MN Appellate Rule 126.01 and Civil Rules 6.01 and 6.05, available at the Minnesota court website.
2. Open the student data file **C05_Ex5.12_MNApp_TimeComp**.
3. Using the information about the specific rules, answer the questions in the student data file.
4. Save the revised file with the answers inserted as **LastName_C05_Ex5.12_MNApp_TimeComp**.
5. Submit the file as directed by your instructor.

Exercise 5.13 In this exercise, you will read the excerpts from the state of Nebraska's court rules of appellate practice and will be instructed to highlight key points of each rule and answer specific questions. The excerpts from the rules are included in **C05_Ex5.13_NERules**. A complete set of the rules is posted at the Nebraska court website.

1. Complete the following work in the textbook. Because you should include this exercise in your portfolio, open **C05_Ex5.13_NERules** and transfer your highlights and answers onto the electronic copy. Save the file as **LastName_C05_Ex5.13_NERules**. Submit the file to your instructor.

2. Read § 2-102 (D). This rule tells you where and when a brief should be filed and how many copies are to be filed. Highlight the information in the file and indicate the information in the space below.

a. Where should the brief be filed?

_____

b. When should the brief be filed?

_____

c. How many copies must be filed?

_____

d. What additional item must be filed with the brief?

_____

3. Because § 2-102 references § 2-109, read the portions of § 2-109 to learn the timing requirements and deadlines for filing certain briefs. Highlight this information in the rule found in **LastName_C05_Ex5.13_NERules**, answer the questions in the document, and save the file.

a. If the appellant has served and filed the brief on August 15, when must the appellee's brief be served and filed?

_____

b. By how many days is the deadline extended to allow for mailing of the appellee's brief?

_____

c. If the appellee's brief is served and filed on the date of your answer to question "3.a", how many days does the appellant have to serve the appellant's reply brief?

_____

d. By how many days is the deadline extended to allow for mailing of the appellant's reply brief?

_____

4. Read and highlight the portions of § 2-109 given in **LastName_C05_Ex5.13_NERules** that identify the formatting requirements for typewritten and computer-generated briefs. Answer the following questions. Resave the file. Pay attention to the differences between the types of briefs. Section B(1) refers to briefs that are typeset or professionally printed. Section B(2) refers to the types of briefs that would be created in the law office.

a. What is the required paper size for a typewritten brief?

_____

b. At what location should the brief be fastened or stapled?

_____

c. What side, top, and bottom margins are required?

_____

d. What font size and style are required for computer-generated briefs?

_____

e. What line spacing is required for computer-generated briefs?

_____

5. Read and highlight the portions of § 2-109 given in **LastName_C05_Ex5.13_ NERules** that identify the formatting requirements for a brief cover page. Answer the questions below and resave as **LastName_C05_Ex5.13_NERules**.

a. What are the six things that must be on the brief cover page?

_____

b. What should be the color of the appellant's brief cover page?

_____

c. What should be the color of the appellee's brief cover page?

_____

d. What should be the color of the brief cover pages of an amicus brief?

_____

6. Read and highlight the portions of § 2-109 given in **LastName_C05_Ex5.13_ NERules** to identify the length requirements for a brief and answer the questions in the document. Resave the file as **LastName_C05_Ex5.13_NERules**.

a. How many pages are the appellant and appellee allowed for their briefs?

_____

b. How many pages are allowed for motions and amicus briefs?

_____

c. Which pages of the brief are not included in the number of pages allowed?

_____

7. Read and highlight the portions of § 2-109 given in **LastName_C05_ Ex5.13_NERules** to identify the rules for serving and filing a brief. Answer the questions. Resave the file as **LastName_C05_Ex5.13_NERules**.

a. How many copies of the brief must be served on any party participating in an appeal?

_____

b. By what methods may service be made?

_____

c. How do you prove service was made?

_____

d. How many copies of the brief must be filed in a case in the supreme court?

_____

e. How many copies of the brief must be filed in a case in the court of appeals?

_____

8. Read the portions of § 2-109 that explain the elements or sections that must be included in all briefs. These sections will be written by the attorney. A table of contents and title or cover page will likely be created by a member of the legal support staff after the brief is completed. Highlight the portions of § 2-109 briefly identifying the sections required to be included in the brief. Answer the questions on the lines provided and resave as **LastName_C05_Ex5.13_NERules**.

a. What are the nine elements or sections that must be included in the appellant's brief?

_____

b. What are the seven elements or sections that must be included in the appellee's brief?

_____

c. How does the appellee indicate that his or her brief contains a cross-appeal?

_____

d. How is the reply brief to be prepared?

_____

e. How does the appellant respond to a cross-appeal?

_____

Exercise 5.14 In this exercise, you will read the excerpts from the state of Oregon's court rules of appellate procedure and will be instructed to highlight key points of each rule and answer specific questions. The excerpts for the rules are included in **C05_Ex5.14_ORRules**. A complete set of the rules is at the Oregon court website.

1. Complete the following work in the textbook. Because you should also include this exercise in your portfolio, open **C05_Ex5.14_ORRules**, and save the file as **LastName_C05_Ex5.14_ORRules**. Highlight the key points in the electronic copy. Answer the following questions and tranfer them onto the electronic copy. Submit the completed file to your instructor.

2. Read OR Rule 5.95 in the **LastName_C05_Ex5.14_ORRules** document. Highlight the key points related to actions to be performed to assist the attorney and then summarize those actions. List four actions you would perform to assist the attorney.

_____

_____

_____

_____

3. Read the footnote included in **LastName_Ch05_Ex5.14.** This footnote was referenced in OR Rule 5.95 and also references an Appendix 5.95, which is shown in Figure 5.4 on page 128. This footnote gives examples of information considered confidential. Using the footnote text and Appendix 5.95, highlight the types of information considered confidential. Answer the following questions and resave.

a. How could you determine if the attorney needs to comply with this rule?

_____

b. How could you assist the attorney in complying with this rule?

_____

Exercise 5.15 Confidential Brief Cover Pages Recall from earlier in this chapter that in preparing an appeal brief in Oregon (OR) that does not contain confidential information, the brief cover page will be prepared according to OR Rules. However, when the appeal brief (also in Oregon) contains confidential information, the OR Rules require you to submit two briefs each having a different brief cover page—one brief with the confidential information included and one with the confidential information redacted. You would find what is defined as confidential information in either a trial court order or a state statute. After determining if your brief has confidential information, the OR Rules provide examples of the types of brief cover pages that be must submitted with each brief.

Figure 5.4 shows examples of each. The only difference between each type of brief cover page is a statement as to whether the information is confidential according to an order or a statute.

1. Using Figure 5.4, create the correct brief cover pages using the following information:
   - Client: Mary Jones
   - Jurisdiction: Marion County, Circuit #3
   - Court file number: CA-A-1233X
2. Prepare these two brief cover pages assuming that the brief contains information deemed confidential under a trial court order.
3. Save the files as **Lastname_C05_Ex5.15_Example1** and **Lastname_C05_Ex5.15_Example2**.

Chapter Summary and Projects

Summary

You have now read an overview of appeals and have an understanding of what tasks you might perform for an appeal. You have also reviewed procedures that are important to legal support staff in helping the attorney format documents. You reviewed verb tenses and consistency; practiced applying language, editing, and proofreading skills to legal documents; and reviewed court rules pertaining to the creation and formatting of appellate briefs.

Remember that as a legal support person, it will be your responsibility in an appellate case to complete the following tasks:

- Locate rules
- Review rules regarding format of appellate briefs
- Determine deadlines according to the rules
- Proofread text in an appellate brief
- Review court websites
- Create a brief order form

Key Terms

action verbs, 131
addendum, 128
amicus curiae, 129
appeal, 123
appellant, 126
appellate brief, 125
appellate jurisdiction, 124
appellee, 126
appendix, 128
argument section, 127
brief cover page, 127
brief printing service, 144

certificate of brief length, 127
intervenor, 129
irregular verbs, 132
issues on appeal, 127
linking verbs, 131
notice of appeal, 123
oral argument, 130
redact, 127
regular verbs, 132
rules of appellate procedure, 129
table of authorities, 127
table of contents, 127

Local Focus Research

The Local Focus icons that appear in the chapter indicate that your local court may have different rules, due dates, terminology, and/or procedures than what has been discussed. The following Local Focus assignments will help you acknowledge these differences. Locate the Chapter 05 folder in your electronic storage medium and open the local focus file **C05_LocalFocus_Appeals**. Resave the file as **LastName_C05_LocalFocus_Appeals**. Research the following topics below and record your research in the file you just created. Use this information as a reference tool as you start and continue your career as a legal support person. Your instructor may ask you to submit a copy as homework.

Local Focus 5.1   Page 128 discusses the contents of an appellate brief and notes that rules may differ between states.

1. Use www.50states.com to locate a website that contains the appellate court's rules for any of the following: your own state, a state of your choosing, or a state that is assigned to you by your instructor. Record the website's URL on the following line.

_____

2. Find the appendix of forms in your local rules of appellate procedure. List here three different forms you find in that appendix.

_____

_____

_____

3. Find out what the appellant and respondent are called in that state. Write those terms here for future reference.

_____

4. Using the same method of research, find out what the appellant and respondent are called in two other states. Record that information here and share your findings with your classmates.

_____

_____

Local Focus 5.2   Legal printing services are described on page 144. Look in the Yellow Pages of your local phone book for legal brief printing services or do an Internet search to find the contact information for one or more legal brief printing services in your area.

1. Record your findings and share what you find out with your classmates.

_____

_____

2. Make a list of brief printing services on the lines below for future reference. Using the Internet, find a website for each printing service and find out if it has a legal brief order form on its website. Print a copy of the form for future reference.

_____

_____

Scenario

Attorney Jessica D. Jordan is a partner at the law firm of Jordan, Leone & Sanchez, PLLP. You work as a legal support person for the firm. Ms. Jordan's client is Sally Peckman, defendant/respondent. Attorney Jordan represented Sally Peckman as the defendant in a criminal matter in which Peckman won her case and the charges against her were dismissed by the trial court. The plaintiff, State of Minnesota, lost that case and appealed the trial court's decision to the Minnesota Court of Appeals. The court file number is A12-004. Ms. Jordan received the plaintiff's notice of appeal and initial brief on April 7. Now she must file a timely responsive brief on behalf of her client. Remember that a notice of appeal is a formal written notice to the lower court and all parties and attorneys involved in a case that the losing party wishes to have a higher court review the decision in the lower court.

You arrived at work this morning and found a memo from Attorney Jordan asking for your assistance.

Figure 5.9 **Memo from Attorney Jordan**

CONFIDENTIAL INTEROFFICE MEMO

DATE: August 7
TO: Legal Support
FROM: Jessica Jordan
RE: Our Client: Sally Peckman

Good morning! I need your help with the following items. Please:

*   Research the court rules governing the formatting of appellate briefs and list the rule numbers supporting the requirements.
*   List the time deadline for filing the client's brief.
*   Prepare a brief cover page.
*   Prepare, serve, and file the final copy of the brief using a brief printing service. Service should be made by regular mail on the attorney with the number of copies as required by the rules. Filing with the court should be by personal delivery.

Here is some additional information to help you complete these tasks:

The office file number is 442.1234.
The opposing party is State of Minnesota, Plaintiff/Appellant
The opposing attorney and contact information are as follows:
   Bob Benjamin
   Assistant Attorney General
   P.O. Box 4000
   St. Paul, MN 55104
   Telephone: 612-222-2222
   Attorney identification number: W99911

Thank you.
Jessica Jordan

Project 1   Rules for Formatting a Formal Appeal Brief

To help Attorney Jordan, you must review the Minnesota Rules of Civil Appellate Procedure to help with the responsive brief. Demonstrate your understanding of the rules by answering questions regarding the formatting requirements for an appellate brief and cite the court rule that provides that information.

1. Open **C05_P1_QuestionsForm** from your active Chapter05 folder.
2. Locate and study the Minnesota Rules of Civil Appellate Procedure.
3. Use the Rules of Civil Appellate Procedure to answer the questions listed on the question form.
4. Type in the answers and the rule numbers that support the answers.
5. Save the document as **LastName_C05_P1_QuestionsForm** in the Chapter05 folder on your personal storage device.
6. Submit either a printout of the completed form or the file to your instructor as directed.

Portfolio

Project 2   Special Requirements in a Rule

The Minnesota Rules of Civil Appellate Procedure govern how exhibits, diagrams, and other aids that are not included in the appendix to a brief are to be handled during oral argument to the court. Exhibits, diagrams, other aids may consist of trial court exhibits, plats, diagrams, or other aids used to help the court and attorneys understand the facts or issues involved in the case.

1. Open the data file named **C05_P2_MNRule134.07** and save the file as **LastName_C05_P2_MNRule134.07**.
2. Highlight the key points that are important in complying with this rule.
3. Type a list in the file of the specific actions you will take to help Attorney Jordan comply with this rule.
4. Be prepared to share your answers with your classmates during class discussion.
5. Save the file and submit it to the instructor.

Project 3   Appeal Brief Cover Page

After reviewing the Minnesota Rules of Civil Appellate Procedure, you will prepare a brief cover page for Attorney Jordan's appellate brief following the formatting requirements set out in the court rules.

1. Refer to the list of answers to questions about Minnesota Rules that you prepared in Project 1.
2. Based on what you know about the client's case, prepare and print a brief cover page for a respondent's appeal brief following the requirements set out in the court rules. Go to the Minnesota Rules of Civil Appellate Procedure

and find Form 128, which includes an example of a brief cover page. Use this example to complete this project.

3. Save your cover page as **LastName_C05_P3_MNAppealCoverPage**.

4. Either print your cover page on the appropriate color paper or identify the color on the top right corner of the cover page you create.

5. Submit the cover page to the instructor.

Project 4   Proofread a Section of an Appellate Brief

In addition to your work on Attorney Jordan's case, you have been asked to proofread a section of the appellate brief for another attorney. The attorney has given you the electronic file and would like you to finish the work as soon as possible.

1. Open file **C05_P4_AppealProofread** and save the file as **LastName_C05_P4_AppealProofread**.

2. Review your work from Project 1 in the file **LastName_C05_P1_QuestionsForm** to refresh your memory of the court's formatting rules.

3. Proofread the contents of the file and make the necessary corrections. Watch for errors in margin size, spacing, font style, font size, spelling, grammar, and punctuation. The required font for this brief is Times New Roman 13.

4. Save the file when you have completed your corrections.

5. Submit the file as directed by the instructor.

Project 5 . Legal Brief Order Form

You have been asked to complete a legal brief order form for the Peckman appeal that will provide the brief printing vendor the details needed to print, bind, serve, and file a final brief by the court's deadline. Apply the information given to you in this section's scenario and the memo from the attorney shown in Figure 5.9 to complete the following tasks:

1. Open **C05_P5_LegalBriefOrderForm** from the student data disc and save the file as **LastName_C05_P5_LegalBriefOrderForm**.

2. Complete the order form with the information from the scenario and the memo.

3. Save the file.

4. Submit the completed form as directed by the instructor.

Discuss the Projects

If you were to help your attorney by reviewing the Rules of Civil Appellate Procedure before he or she prepares a responsive brief, what would you do with the results? Discuss with your classmates ways to keep the research results so that you don't have to do so much the next time. Will you ever need to research this same topic again? Yes/No Why or why not?

Real Estate

Chapter Objectives

- Review the process of purchasing/selling real estate
- Manage real estate information
- Research title information
- Think critically about the final title opinion
- Edit and proofread a closing statement

Ryan Baboila and Taylor Bollinger are legal support staff at Jagdish and Faaborg, Attorneys at Law. Baboila and the attorneys work daily with clients who are buying and selling real estate. Others in the firm are involved in lawsuits with people who have broken their contracts for the sale of real estate. The employees from local lending institutions and real estate sales offices regularly refer customers to Jagdish and Faaborg for title searches, title opinions, title transfer, and other legal services.

A legal support person may work for an attorney or law firm that specializes in real estate law or perhaps for a firm that works on real estate cases in addition to other types of cases. It is not uncommon for law firms in nonmetropolitan areas to practice many types of law. Since many people will have some interaction with a real estate transaction during their lives, no shortage of clients are in this area of law.

Real estate sales offices, bank lending departments, title companies, county recorders, registrars, and land records departments are a few of the other offices a legal support person will encounter while working in real estate law. A person with legal support training and an understanding of real estate procedures may find employment in any of these offices because these offices play a role in the process of real estate title transfer.

The Real Estate Title Transfer Process

The purchase of real estate can be one of the largest investments (as well as greatest satisfactions) with which a person will ever be involved. Property can be described in two ways—real property (also referred to as real estate) and personal property. **Real property** is defined as land and anything attached to it, such as a building. **Personal property** is any property that is movable, such as cars, trucks, farm equipment, jewelry, lawn mowers, etc. Most personal property does not have a title, but some personal property, such as a vehicle and certain types of farm equipment, may have a title. Personal property can be sold very easily with just the exchange of money for the property. Other personal property of more value can be sold with a bill of sale, the title document, and the property exchanged for money.

All real property has a title and can be sold. **Title** is a legal term designating the ownership rights that a person has in a piece of property. This term may also refer to a formal document that serves as evidence of ownership. **Conveyance** (giving) of the title document is usually required to transfer ownership in the property to another person. The concept of title is separate from **possession**, a right that often accompanies ownership but is not necessarily sufficient to prove it. In many cases, both possession and title may be transferred independently of each other.

This chapter focuses on the process of selling real property. People can start the process of buying and selling real property by either doing the work themselves or by hiring a real estate agent.

A professional **real estate agent**, or **realtor**, is an individual who is licensed to negotiate and arrange real estate sales and works under the authority and supervision of a real estate broker. Negotiating and arranging a sale can include showing property, listing property, and completing listing agreements and purchase contracts. States vary in their licensing requirements. In some states real estate salespeople are also brokers. In other states real estate professionals generally are licensed to operate under a **real estate broker**, who has a higher-level license than a real estate agent and is authorized to hire and supervise real estate agents as well as to manage a brokerage business. The broker hires sales agents and manages the fees between the buyer's agent and the seller's agent.

When sellers decide to work with a real estate agent, the seller and real estate agent sign a **listing agreement**, which is a contract describing the services to be rendered and the property for sale; it also states the terms of payment for the realtor's services. The payment usually includes a commission that is generally payable to the realtor/broker upon closing.

Interested buyers also contact real estate offices. Generally, the realtor works for the seller and will focus on selling the property for the best possible price. Many realtors are members of a **multiple listing service (MLS)**, which is a marketing database set up by a group of cooperating real estate brokers. This service provides accurate and structured data about properties for sale. It is also a mechanism for listing brokers offering compensation to buyer brokers who bring in buyers for their listed properties. Having access to the MLS allows realtors to provide more property choices for their buyers and more interested buyers for their sellers.

Since the multiple listing service is national and online, buyers find it convenient to search the properties available and then contact the realtor.

Purchase Agreement

When the realtor locates an interested buyer, the realtor will show the property and negotiate the terms between the seller and the potential buyer. The two parties (buyer and seller) will eventually sign a purchase agreement. A **purchase agreement** is a legal, binding agreement between the buyer and seller setting out price and terms of sale. In different states, this document may be referred to as a *real estate contract, bid, binder*, or *offer to purchase*. For this discussion, the document will be called a purchase agreement. A purchase agreement can be created by the individual buyer and seller, by a real estate professional, or at a law office. Because there are so many regulations and requirements for disclosure regarding property, most people rely on the expertise of a real estate professional in buying or selling property.

The purchase agreement includes the following:

1. Purchase price and how it is to be paid.
2. Legal description of the property. A **real estate legal description** is the official description written by the county recorder to indicate the official location of the property. It is not the mailing address; it is more technical and is created by a civil engineer.
3. Good and marketable title furnished by the seller, as indicated by an abstract of title or a registered property abstract.
4. Warranty of title, which comprises promises made by a seller guaranteeing possession of clear title sufficient to transfer ownership to a buyer including title restrictions and any other rights and limitations to which the title may be subject.
5. Date of transfer of possession.
6. Prorations of utility bills, property taxes, and similar expenses.
7. Party responsible for risk of fire or other hazard pending closing or transfer of possession.
8. Itemization of furnishings, appliances and utility equipment, shrubbery, fixtures, and other personal property included in the sale.
9. Basic terms of any escrow agreement.
10. Wording about the return of earnest money if the sale is not completed.
11. Signatures of the parties.

When the purchase agreement is signed, the buyer usually makes a down payment to the seller or the seller's real estate broker. A **down payment** (sometimes called **earnest money**) is money paid to show that the prospective buyer has serious intentions to purchase the property. The funds that make up the down payment are not refundable. The buyer may lose the money if he or she does not follow the terms of the purchase agreement. Of course, a seller is liable for damages for not following the terms as well. Buyers and sellers should have lawyers review the purchase agreement, but many do not. If a purchase agreement is well thought out, it will carry all parties successfully from signing to the closing.

Financing

When a person wants to obtain a loan for a vehicle purchase, to attend college, or to start a business, he or she will contact a bank or other lender. The same is true for those who need financing to purchase a home. If financing has to be secured, a clause in the purchase agreement may say that the purchase is contingent upon the buyer's obtaining financing.

Because most real estate purchases are financed, potential buyers contact lending institutions early enough to find the best loan terms for their situation. Preapproval prior to bidding on a property is important because some purchase forms require buyers to apply for financing within a certain time period. By being preapproved, buyers do not have to rush through the financing process. A lender will review a buyer's financial situation and write a preapproval letter assuring a seller and the realtor of the buyer's ability to pay. The real estate law office will not be involved in the preapproval process for potential buyers, but the legal support staff assisting clients with real estate transactions do need to be familiar with the financing process to best assist the clients.

When a bank decides to lend money, it usually needs some type of **collateral (security)** given by the borrower to guarantee that if the borrower cannot pay, the bank has the right to seize and sell the collateral to cover the amount of the loan. In this situation, a promissory note is signed by the borrower agreeing to the terms of repayment. A **promissory note** is a contract stating that a person or entity owes money to another person or entity. The signer of a promissory note promises to repay to the lender a certain amount of money at a certain time and according to certain terms and conditions. A promissory note may be unsecured or secured. If a lender takes an **unsecured promissory note**, the lender is lending the money based solely on the signer's cash flow. If a lender takes out a **secured promissory note**, the lender is lending the money based on cash flow as well as other assets that could be sold to cover the amount of the debt, if necessary.

A **mortgage** is a document that pledges property to the lender to secure the payment of a debt. The debt is paid in installments over a period of time. The mortgage guarantees that the money will be repaid or the lender will foreclose or seize the property, which can be sold to repay the lender. Note that the **mortgagor** (sometimes spelled mortgager) is the party that borrows money in a mortgage agreement. The lender of the money in a mortgage agreement is known as the **mortgagee**.

The borrower may also be eligible for certain government-insured loan situations such as **first-time home buyer loans**, **FHA-insured loans**, and **VA-guaranteed loans**. These loans are financing insured by the government and provided through local banking institutions.

A **real estate installment sales contract** (also called a land sales contract or a contract for deed) is an agreement between the seller and buyer indicating the purchase price and method of payment made directly to the seller, as well as other rights and duties. The buyer in this type of sales contract usually does not receive a

Best Practice Tip

MORTGAGOR VS. MORTGAGEE

For help remembering which word to use for which party, go to the Critical Thinking section in this chapter. It contains more information on selecting the correct *-or* or *-ee* words.

deed (or legal title) to the property until all required payments are made. In the event that the buyer discontinues payments, previous payments may be forfeited and the buyer's interest in the property may be lost.

When a buyer makes an offer on property, the realtor will present that offer to the seller or the seller's representative. Of course, the seller has several options. He or she can accept the offer, reject the offer, or make a counteroffer. A **counteroffer**, which is common, allows for negotiation between the buyer and the seller before settling on a mutually agreeable price.

When an offer is officially accepted and financing is secured, it is time for the parties to determine if the seller has a marketable and insurable title to the property.

Ownership and Title

Unlike personal property, real property, such as real estate, is titled to convey ownership. This title must be transferred when assets are sold and must be cleared (free of liens or encumbrances) in order for transfer to take place. Real estate ownership can take several forms, each of which has implications on how ownership can be transferred and can affect how they can be financed, improved, or used as collateral. These forms of ownership are listed and explained below:

- Joint tenancy
- Tenancy in common
- Tenants by entirety
- Sole ownership
- Community property

Joint Tenancy **Joint tenancy** occurs when two or more people hold title to real estate jointly with equal rights to enjoy the property during their lives; in the event of the death of one of the partners, their rights of ownership pass to the surviving tenant(s). A joint tenant is said to have "rights of survivorship."

Tenancy In Common With **tenancy in common**, two or more persons hold title to real estate jointly with equal rights to enjoy the property during their lives. Unlike joint tenancy, however, tenants in common hold title individually for their respective part of the property and can dispose of or encumber it as they wish. Ownership can be willed to other parties, and in the event of death, ownership will transfer to that owner's heirs undivided.

Tenants By Entirety **Tenants by entirety** is ownership in real estate under the fictional assumption that husband and wife are one person for legal purposes. This method conveys ownership to them as one person, with title transferred to the other in entirety if one of them dies. This method can only be used when owners are legally husband and wife.

Sole Ownership **Sole ownership** can be characterized as ownership by an individual or entity legally capable of holding title. The most common sole ownerships are held by single men and women, married men or women who hold property apart from their spouse, and businesses with corporate structure allowing it to invest in or hold interest in real estate.

Community Property **Community property** is a form of ownership by husband and wife during their marriage that they intend to own together. Under community property, either spouse has the right to dispose of one half of the property or will it to another party. Outside of real estate, property acquired during one's marriage is usually deemed community property.

A **title** is a document that shows formal ownership of property, meaning the legal right to own, possess, use, control, enjoy, and dispose of property. After making an offer and starting the process of securing financing, the buyer will inform the lending institution that the offer has been accepted. The lender now must determine whether the title is good, marketable, and insurable. A **marketable title** describes a real estate title in which a reasonable purchaser could note no discoverable defects (such as tax liens, mechanic's liens, mortgages, or unpaid assessments). An **insurable title** is a title that can be insured by a title company—in other words, title to a piece of real estate that is reasonably free from risk of litigation because of possible defects. Even though an insurable title is not perfect in its title, it is free from or reasonable objections and is one that a court of law would order the buyer to accept. A **title company** is a firm that verifies ownership of real property, often in connection with a conveyance of real property from buyer to seller. The valid owner is determined through a thorough examination of property records in a title search. The company issues a title certificate based on its examination. The lending institution could have a title company search the property's title, or they might hire an attorney at this point. If the lender chooses to work with an attorney, the bank or lending institution will have to fill out a title work order form similar to the one shown in Figure 6.1, requesting a *title search* and *preliminary or final title opinion*. Sometimes this is the only service a law office will provide to the lender.

Title Search and Title Opinion

A **title search** is a search of the public records to determine the status of a title, including any encumbrances, liens, mortgages, and future interests affecting the property. Normally, a title search is conducted by a real estate attorney or by a title company at the request of a prospective buyer or lender. A **title opinion** is an attorney's professional judgment of the owner's rights to the property following a title search by the attorney's office. This opinion is usually in the form of a letter addressed to the lender or whoever requested the title search. The lender will send the following information to an attorney for use in searching the title:

- Buyer's name
- Seller's name
- Selling price
- Mortgage amount
- Property address
- Legal description

Most attorneys will have experienced staff carry out the title search. Many counties make current title information available from a database via the Internet; however, older title information may not be available electronically and will have to be researched in person at a land records office. The older, nonelectronic records are usually handwritten and recorded in large books that are typically 3 feet tall and 2 feet wide. Land records offices usually do not accept requests, and the searching of the records has to be done in person at the specific records location.

An experienced legal support person will have a form or checklist on which to record the information needed by the attorney to create the title opinion. After the information is gathered from the county, the legal support person will either draft the title opinion or pass the information on by giving the attorney a copy of the

Figure 6.1 **Title Work Order Form**

TITLE WORK ORDER

TO: Jordan, Leone & Sanchez

Attention: _____ Date: _____

From: _____

Buyers: _____ Selling Price: _____

Sellers: _____ Mortgage for: $_____

Property Address: _____

Legal Description: _____

Items Delivered: _____ Abstract of Title

Prepare: _____

_____ Title Commitment/Title Policy

_____ Preliminary Opinion/Final Opinion

_____ Owners and Encumbrances (O & E)

_____ Expense Statement

_____ Other _____

Other Instructions:

_____ Record all documents
_____ Continue abstracts with/without certificates
_____ Closing at Jordan, Leone & Sanchez

_____ Other: _____

Need papers by: _____ Received by: _____

Closing date: _____ Today's Date: _____

researched information or emailing the information to the attorney for use in drafting the document. Figure 6.2 is an example of a completed form showing information gathered for the attorney in anticipation of a title opinion. The form is used to gather information, and the filled-out form would be put in the case file for reference.

The title opinion gives the attorney's opinion of the ownership of real property (land and buildings attached to it) and may indicate defects in the chain of title or incorrect or unclear instruments in the public record. The title opinion may also suggest ways to correct the title as recorded to match the actual use and possession of the land, such as in the following extract from an opinion:

> To cure the title defect, this examiner requires the owner of the subject parcel to exchange quitclaim deeds with the owner of the parcel immediately east of the subject parcel.

The attorney usually prepares a **preliminary title opinion**. This document is typically referred to as "preliminary" because the opinion states the current condition of the title prior to any adjustments. If something needs to be changed or fixed, these changes can be made to the lender's and/or buyer's satisfaction. Then the title is searched again and a **final title opinion** is created to indicate that all required changes have been made.

Researching a title is not what an entry-level legal support person will be assigned to do early in his or her career. Accuracy and thoroughness is of utmost importance in preparing a title opinion. An inexperienced legal support person will generally observe and assist until the attorney and the experienced support person are both confident in the research of the less experienced legal support person. Some attorneys, however, prefer that the legal support person research the title and pass the information on so that the attorney drafts and dictates the title opinion. The legal support person would then transcribe, edit, and proofread the attorney's title opinion. In transcribing, it is important to key the information and details exactly as they are dictated. However, it is also important for the legal support person to verify the transcribed information by proofreading it, editing it, and checking the accuracy of the information against the notes taken during the research process. It is important to watch for these specific editing and proofreading errors:

- Letter format
- Spelling of names
- Correct numbers
- Correct legal descriptions
- Correct dates

Evidence of Title

Ownership of real property (another name for real estate) is shown by possession of the title. When a parcel of real estate changes ownership, the owner has to provide evidence of title in the form of an abstract or a Torrens certificate. The following sections review these documents.

Abstract All property starts out as abstract property. An **abstract of title** is a document that summarizes the history of ownership and lists all owners and all transactions since the property began having a recorded history. For example, a property's first entry could be granting ownership from the U. S. Government, James Buchanan, President, to John D. Zimmerman, in 1856. Many properties were given to Civil War veterans as a bonus for serving during the war.

When a person plans to buy property, he or she must know or find out whether there are any claims by others on the property, such as taxes or liens against the title. A **lien** is the legal claim of one person upon the property of another to secure the payment of a debt or the satisfaction of an obligation. This claim would have to be

Figure 6.2 **Completed Title Search Notes**

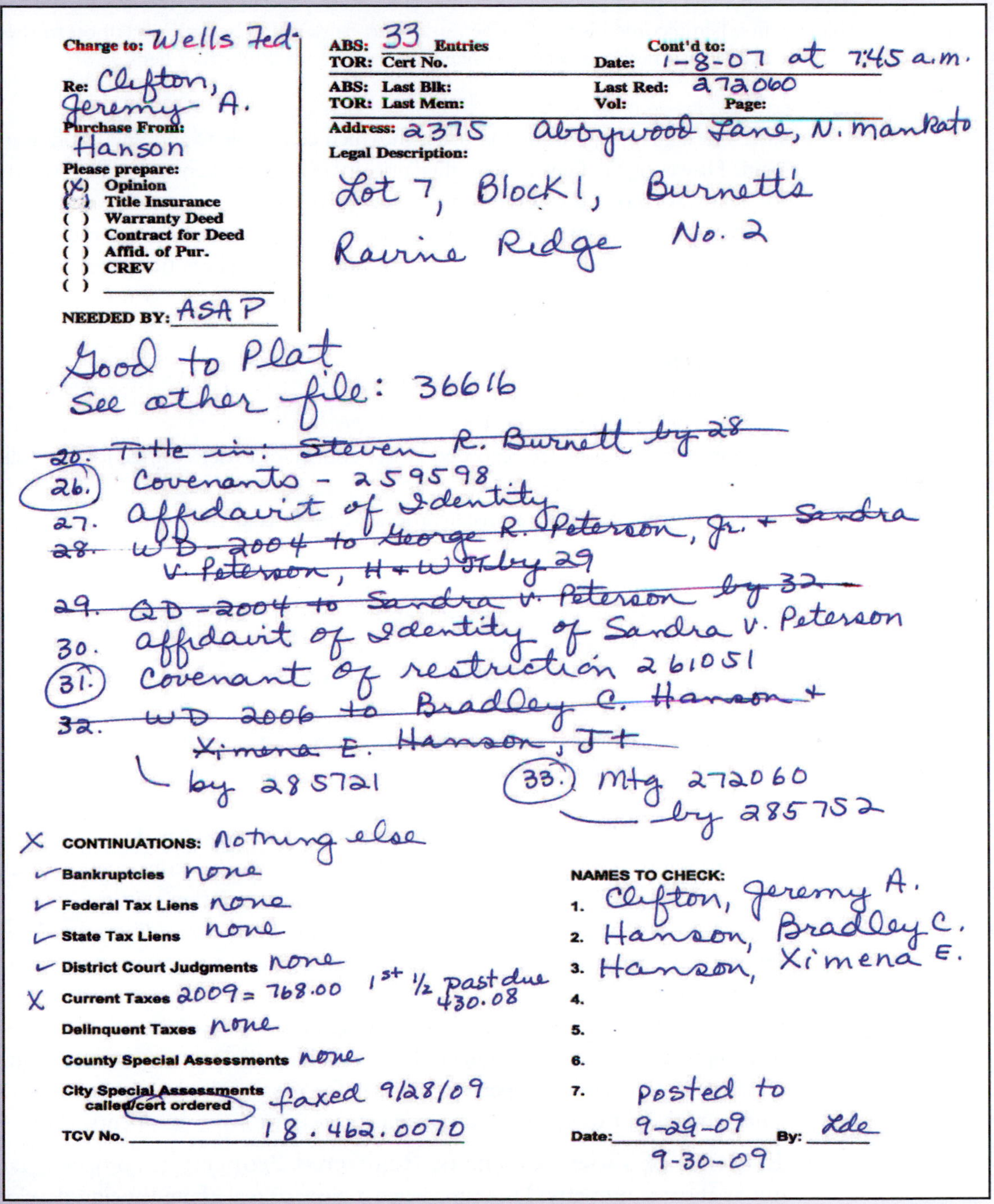

Charge to: Wells Fed.

Re: Clifton, Jeremy A.

Purchase From: Hanson

Please prepare:
- (X) Opinion
- ( ) Title Insurance
- ( ) Warranty Deed
- ( ) Contract for Deed
- ( ) Affid. of Pur.
- ( ) CREV
- ( ) _____

NEEDED BY: ASAP

ABS: 33 Entries
TOR: Cert No.
ABS: Last Blk:
TOR: Last Mem:
Address: 2375 Abbywood Lane, N. Mankato
Legal Description:

Cont'd to:
Date: 1-8-07 at 7:45 a.m.
Last Red: 272060
Vol: Page:

Lot 7, Block 1, Burnett's Ravine Ridge No. 2

Good to Plat
See other file: 36616

20. Title in: Steven R. Burnett by 28
26. Covenants – 259598
27. affidavit of Identity
28. WD-2004 to George R. Peterson, Jr. + Sandra V. Peterson, H+W Jtly by 29
29. QD-2004 to Sandra V. Peterson by 32
30. affidavit of Identity of Sandra V. Peterson
31. Covenant of restriction 261051
32. WD 2006 to Bradley C. Hanson + Ximena E. Hanson, J+
    by 285721
33. Mtg 272060
    by 285752

X CONTINUATIONS: Nothing else
Bankruptcies none
Federal Tax Liens none
State Tax Liens none
District Court Judgments none
X Current Taxes 2009 = 768.00 1st ½ past due 430.08
Delinquent Taxes none
County Special Assessments none
City Special Assessments called/cert ordered faxed 9/28/09
TCV No. 18.462.0070

NAMES TO CHECK:
1. Clifton, Jeremy A.
2. Hanson, Bradley C.
3. Hanson, Ximena E.
4.
5.
6.
7. posted to
Date: 9-29-09 By: Lde
9-30-09

paid before a clear title could be passed to the next owner. For example, if a carpenter worked for the current owner and the owner did not pay for the carpentry work, the carpenter could have placed a lien on the title at the recorder's office.

The order in which these claims are recorded is important because liens are given priority by the date of their recording, with earlier liens having higher priority than

Best Practice Tip

REMEMBERING THE RULE

To remember the rule of priority, remember the phrase "first in time, first in line"; meaning that the first lien recorded is the first lien in line to be repaid. The only exception to this rule is when a tax lien is involved, since tax liens take priority over all other liens.

later ones. **Priority** means the order in which certain liens and encumbrances must be paid. However, tax liens have higher priority over other liens regardless of when the tax lien was recorded or even if it was recorded.

When transactions related to the property occur, the transactions must be recorded in the county recorder's office (office of land records). These transactions include:

- Sale of property resulting in new ownership
- Mortgages
- Tax liens
- Easements
- Mechanic's and other liens

These transactions are recorded at the county recorder's office for the following reasons:

- The real estate title transfer process requires that the ownership change be recorded soon after the sale is made.
- Banks are motivated to record mortgages against the title at the county recorder's office so that mortgagors are forced to pay the mortgage before selling again.
- The government wants its tax liens recorded against the title as well to obtain payment. (Tax liens take first priority over all other liens, even when other liens have been recorded earlier.)
- An **easement** is an official right to use property not belonging to the user. Easements are recorded so that owners and users all have proof of the use of the property.
- A **mechanic** in a legal title situation is a person who has done work on the property—such as a carpenter, a plumber, or another construction worker—and wants to be paid before the property is sold to another owner.

The process of updating the abstract with any of the preceding transactions is called a **continuation**. The continuation work is done at the county recorder's office. The actual abstract has added to it the transactions that have occurred since the last time the abstract was updated. This updating process or continuation costs money to complete, so it is usually done only when selling the property or when the owner is using the title to the property as security for a loan. The new owners and/or the bank would want to know about any mortgages, tax liens, easements, etc.

Evidence of Title: Torrens or Registered Property All property starts out as abstract property. However, when a piece of real estate is being developed or split into smaller parcels of land, it is common to change the evidence of title from abstract to Torrens or registered property. **Torrens or registered property** is a system for land titles under which a court directs the issuance of a certificate of title upon application by the landowner. The actual document that evidences title in the Torrens system is called a certificate of title. The **certificate of title** shows the legal description of the real estate along with the current owner and any liens or encumbrances made by this current owner. The certificate of title does not show any previous owners or their liens and encumbrances.

Remember that all property starts out as abstract property because that was the only way to identify property when title was being applied to American land. Every time there is a transaction regarding the property, it is recorded at the county recorder's office and continued on the abstract. Every time abstract property is sold, the same entries on the abstract all the way back to the original owners are searched to assure that the property has a clear title. This is repetitious, costly, and time-consuming—*and* this process happens *every* time property is sold!

If property is subdivided during development, each new lot will need its own evidence of title. Because creating an abstract for each of the lots is costly (it would have to include all the entries from the original, larger tract of land), the developer usually has a certificate of title created for each new lot instead. Creating an initial certificate of title for each newly divided parcel from the original parcel is costly, but the process of changing from abstract property to Torrens property occurs just once. The following basic discussion explains how the abstract property is changed over to Torrens property.

When property title is changed from abstract property to Torrens or registered property:

- The attorney for the person requesting that the title be changed from abstract to Torrens searches the public record one last time for every entry on the abstract starting with the original owner to the most current owner.
- The abstract entries are certified as being correct and showing clear title through a court proceeding.
- The abstract is destroyed and each lot becomes registered property and has a certificate of title as its evidence of the title.
- The previous transactions that were searched over and over again in the abstract are permanently deleted from the evidence of title for this particular parcel of land. The only transactions listed on a certificate of title are the most recent owner and any mortgages, liens, etc., that the most recent owner has incurred.

When a buyer purchases registered property, all that has to be researched is the current owner's transactions. (Remember that with abstract property, all owners and all transactions are researched every time a piece of property is sold.)

When registered or Torrens property title is transferred, the previous owner's ownership and transactions are deleted and the new owner's ownership is added. These new documents are created at the county recorder's office for the new owner.

In summary, the one drawback to a Torrens system is the initial cost of registering the property. The system is most effective when undeveloped land is subdivided for the first time because it reduces the number of deed entries an examiner must review. When these developed lots are sold in the future, much less time and money is spent verifying clear title.

The modern trend is for property to have a certificate of title under the Torrens system. Remember, however, that all property first transferred from the U.S. government to a citizen had evidence of title in the form of an abstract. The abstract system went on for many years. It is true that transferring title with an abstract has always been repetitious and cumbersome. Today, however, if property is being developed from original abstract property, the developer will take the time and go to the expense of providing the new owners with the more streamlined certificate of title.

Title Policy

A **title policy** is an insurance policy that protects the owner of property against loss that occurs from a defect in the title for real estate, among other things (see Table 6.1). For instance, if you buy a piece of property and at a later date another person proves ownership of it, the insurance will pay your losses (with a few exceptions). A variety of options are available to consumers as well as lenders, such as a basic owner's policy and a basic lender's policy. When a property is mortgaged, the lending institution has a separate title policy to protect its interests (**basic lender's policy**). In addition to a **basic owner's policy**, which protects the owner against loss that occurs from a defect in title, an owner can also get an extended owner's policy. Table 6.1 shows more specifically what is covered under a basic owner's policy, a basic lender's policy, and an extended owner's policy.

Table 6.1 Coverage of Three Types of Policies

Basic Owner's Title Policy Coverage
• Clear title to the property
• Incorrect signatures on documents
• Forgery, fraud
• Defective recordation
• Restrictive covenants
• Encumbrances or judgments
Basic Lender's Title Policy Coverage
• Mechanic's liens and unrecorded liens
• Unrecorded easements and access rights
• Defects and other unrecorded documents
Extended Owner's Coverage
• Building permit violations from previous owners
• Subdivision maps
• Covenant violations from previous owners
• Living trusts
• Structure damage from mineral extractions
• Variety of encroachments and forgeries after title insurance is issued

Deeds

A **deed** is an official title document transferring title from one person to another. The following types of deeds are used for differing reasons.

- Warranty deed
- Quitclaim deed
- Contract for deed
- Trustee deed
- Probate deed

The attorney will advise the buyer which of these title transfer documents is most appropriate for the situation. Official title to real estate does not actually transfer to the new owner until this title is recorded in the recorder's office in the county in which the real estate is located.

Warranty Deed A **warranty deed** is the most secure type of deed for the buyer because the **grantor** (or maker of the deed) warrants the following:

- He or she is the lawful owner of the property and has the right to convey title.
- No liens or encumbrances are on the title unless specified in the deed.
- The buyer is guaranteed that the title is good against a third party.
- He or she will provide all documents required to make the title good.

Quitclaim Deed A **quitclaim deed** transfers or "quits" any interest in real property. The grantor may not have a claim on the title at all, so the **grantee** (the receiver of the deed) cannot assume that the grantor has any real interest to convey. The following is an example:

> Mr. Roberts was asked to sign a quitclaim deed on property that his father had owned and sold many years ago. The father had been deceased for several years when the current property owner attempted to sell the property. The father's name appeared during the title search, probably as a result of a recording mistake made years ago. An attorney contacted Mr. Roberts, as personal representative to his father's estate, asking him to sign a quitclaim deed "quitting his paper claim" on the property. This quitclaim deed was recorded and, upon another search of the title, the title appeared clear and marketable to pass on to another owner.

Contract for Deed A **contract for deed** (sometimes known as a land contract or an installment sale agreement) is a contract between a seller and buyer of real property in which the seller provides financing to the buyer of the property for an agreed-upon purchase price and interest, and the buyer repays the loan in installments. The buyer does not receive the deed until the final payment is made.

Trustee Deed A **trustee deed** is a deed executed by a person serving as a trustee; for example, a trustee deed is often used by a trustee in bankruptcy to sell the property of the debtor.

Probate Deed A **probate deed** is a deed executed by the executor (personal representative) of an estate when the executor conveys the real estate owned by the decedent.

Recording

When the buyer and seller have agreed on a price and a deed is executed, it must be recorded at the county recorder's or land records' office. **Recording** is the process of writing into the official documents data pertaining to real estate in the public record, which, in most cases, is in the courthouse of the county in which the real estate is located. By recording these documents, information is made available to government authorities and prospective buyers of real estate in the county about

SPELLING

Quitclaim deed is commonly misspelled as *quickclaim*, *quick claim*, or *quit claim*. The words quick, claim, and quit are not individually misspelled, so a spell checker will not catch this error. Quickclaim will, of course, be highlighted as misspelled. It is up to the editor and proofreader of the document to catch these errors.

the current owners, encumbrances, liens, and other interests in the real estate. Most states require that any document that affects either the title or the interests in the land be recorded.

Before a document can be recorded, it must satisfy the requirements of the recording laws of the state in which the property is located. For instance, state law may require that the documents be a certain size, color, or quality. Some states require witnesses or that names be printed below the signatures. Some states also require a certificate of real estate value and the payment of current property taxes before recording. The law office staff may be involved in this process by preparing the deed and facilitating the closing at which documents are signed and money is exchanged. A title does not actually transfer until the deed is recorded at the county recorder's or land records office. Therefore, it is important that the law office staff deliver the deed immediately and in the correct format for recording.

Local Focus
6.3

Certificate of Real Estate Value

Some states must account for the property transfers on the local and state levels. The form used is called a **certificate of real estate value** and offers the taxation controllers documentation of the selling price of the property and any special terms associated with the transaction. The form accompanies the deed when it is submitted for recording. If the forms are not complete and correct, the property transfer cannot be finalized.

Certain states use property taxes to help pay for schools and other community purposes. Buyers of real property in these states must file a certificate of real estate value with the county auditor in the county where the property is located if the sale price or other consideration is more than $1,000 and the deed is a warranty deed, contract for deed, quitclaim deed, trustee deed, executor deed, or probate deed. If the price is $1,000 or less, a certificate of real estate value does not have to be filed. The following must be written on the back of a deed sold for less than $1,000: "The sale price or other consideration given for this property was $1,000 or less."

Closing

A **real estate closing**, sometimes called a real estate *settlement*, is the meeting that is the final step in executing or finishing a real estate transaction. The closing meeting could actually be closing two different processes—the buying and selling of real estate and the signing and finalizing of a mortgage. The closing will occur when both parties have finalized details and documents and are ready to close or finish the deal.

Several things happen during closing:
- The buyer or the bank delivers a check or cashier's check for the balance owed on the purchase price. Remember that the buyer most likely paid earnest money to secure the offer in the early stages of negotiations.
- The seller signs the deed over to the buyer and delivers the keys.
- The seller receives a check for the proceeds of the sale listed on the closing (or settlement) statement minus closing costs and mortgage payouts.

After the closing, the deed is recorded with the county recorder or land registry office. For the buyer and seller, it is important to know that the title officially transfers at that time—not when the deed is signed and not even if the title is physically handed over to the buyer or his or her representative. This concept is important in the event that the property is damaged or becomes damaged.

In a closing in escrow, a title company or other trusted party, instead of a lawyer, holds the money and the signed deed and arranges for the transfer. This is primarily so that the seller can give up ownership of the property and the buyer can hand over the payment without both parties having to be present at the same time. A **real estate closing in escrow** is a process in which a third party takes over the important duties of holding the money, holding the signed deed, and making title transfer arrangements. Having a closing in escrow ensures an orderly transaction, or, if something goes wrong, an orderly termination of the agreement.

A **closing statement** (or **settlement statement**) is a document commonly used in real estate transactions that details the fees, commissions, insurance, etc., that must be taken care of for a successful transfer of ownership to occur. The closing statement is usually prepared by a closing agent or the staff at a law office. The person conducting the closing goes through the closing statement line by line so that all parties are clear as to who is paying what amount and that the totals are equal.

Real Estate in Litigation

Law offices do not work only with real estate title transfer. They also deal with many other issues that can arise dealing with real estate, such as:

- Boundary disputes
- Easement issues
- Breach of contract
- Unlawful use
- Mobile home/association issues
- Landlord/tenant issues
- Development and commercial situations
- Loan litigation
- Property defects
- Property damage claims

Some of these situations can be dealt with by the attorney, who sends a well-researched, well-written letter explaining the issues and the alternatives. The recipient of the letter can then comply, retain his or her own attorney, or simply ignore the letter, in which case the attorney may send another letter.

Other work that a legal office would do includes being on retainer to be available for an organization when legal advice is needed. Other issues may include litigation situations where the office would follow the process of a civil litigation (discussed in Chapter 2).

Language Focus: Subject-Verb Agreement

Recall that you learned about verbs and how to edit for verb tense consistency in Chapter 5. Another essential step in editing is to verify that subjects and verbs "agree." This means that when the subject in a sentence is singular, the corresponding verb should also be singular, and when the subject is plural, the corresponding verb should also be plural. Remember that in writing, a subject (a noun) is the person, place, or thing that performs the action, and a verb is a word that expresses an action or a state of being. Consider the sentence: "Attorneys review evidence of title before signing title opinions." Both the subject *attorneys* and the verb *review* are plural. If the subject is singular, the verb would have to be singular as well: "An attorney reviews evidence of title before signing title opinions."

Basic Rules for Subject-Verb Agreement

If a subject (noun) is singular, the verb must also be singular. Singular nouns generally *do not* end in *s*. However, singular verbs *do* end in *s*. If a subject (noun) is plural, the verb must also be plural. Plural nouns generally *do* end in *s*. Plural verbs *do not* end in *s*.

Sometimes people can pick out the correct subject and determine if it is singular or plural, but they have trouble determining whether the verb is singular or plural. If that happens to you, just use a simple sentence with a simple subject to help you determine whether a verb is singular or plural. Consider the sentences:

Singular noun and verb: The boy plays with the toy.

Plural noun and verb: The girls play with the toys.

Table 6.2 provides a sampling of common verbs in both their singular and plural form. Consider creating your own table of verbs that regularly confuse you during the editing and proofreading process. For example, *am* is an exception that can confuse people because it is a singular verb that is used with the singular pronoun *I*.

Table 6.2 Singular and Plural Forms of Common Verbs

Singular Verbs (DO end in *s*) (Test it by starting with "The boy...")	Plural Verbs (DO NOT end in *s*) (Test it by starting with "The girls...")
is	are
was	were
has	have
does	do
seems	seem
appears	appear
likes	like
walks	walk
types	type
listens	listen

Best Practice Tip

SUBJECT-VERB AGREEMENT

The following sentence may help you remember the subject/verb agreement rule: *Singular verbs end in S.*

Best Practice Tip

IRREGULAR PLURAL SUBJECTS

Not all plural subjects end in *s*. Examples include *children, women, men, oxen,* and *salmon*. These words will still need a corresponding plural verb.

Identifying the Correct Subject and Verb

While the grammatical rule for subject and verb agreement is fairly straightforward, mistakes are inevitable and often overlooked. Making a mistake with subject-verb agreement generally occurs for three reasons:

- Choosing the wrong subject or pronoun in the sentence
- Choosing the wrong verb even if the correct subject is chosen
- Not recognizing whether that subject is singular or plural

It helps to remember the following steps when choosing the correct subject: First, pick out the verb (the action), and ask "who or what completes the action?" The answer to that question will be the subject. Apply this method to the following sentence.

Attorneys review evidence of title before signing title opinions.

The verb is *review*. Ask yourself "who reviews?" The correct answer is *attorneys*. Since both verb and subject are plural—you are able to confirm that the subject and verb agree.

Second, while all verbs in a sentence have subjects, the subjects are not always immediately obvious. They can be difficult to find for the following reasons:

- An intervening element between the subject and the verb such as a prepositional phrase
- Inverted sentences
- Sentences that start with *here* or *there*
- Contractions

Intervening Elements Intervening elements are phrases or clauses that come between the subject and verb. Words in these intervening elements can lead the editor to choose the wrong subject. Prepositional phrases are examples of intervening elements. A prepositional phrase always starts with a preposition and ends with a noun. Because the subject of the sentence will never be in a prepositional phrase, be careful not to choose that noun as the subject.

The following are examples of prepositional phrases as well as other types of intervening elements to watch for.

Only one of our lake properties is insured.

The prepositional phrase in this sentence is "of our lake properties." *Properties* is *not* the subject of the sentence. The word *one* is the singular subject, which agrees with the singular verb *is*.

Other clients such as Marcus have completed the refinancing process.

In the previous example, the phrase "such as Marcus" is an intervening phrase since it divides the true subject *clients* from the verb *have*. The name *Marcus* is singular and can cause the writer to incorrectly assume that the subject should be singular.

Inverted Sentences Some sentences, including questions, are in inverted order, which means that all or part of the verb comes before the subject. Examples include:

Have the form requirements been reviewed by the client?

In this example the plural *requirements* is the subject. In an inverted sentence or question, look for all or part of the verb placed before the subject.

There are nine clients returning the certificate of real estate value forms.

In the previous example sentence, since the subject *clients* is plural, the verb must be plural. *Are* is plural. Notice that part of the verb appears before the subject, making this sentence inverted. The words *here* and *there* are clues that the sentence is inverted. *Here* or *there* at the beginning of a sentence is never the subject. Always look for some other word to function as the subject.

Contractions Contractions are a shortened form of a word, group of words, or an ordinal (*she is = she's, do not=don't, they are=they're, first=1st*). Contractions should agree in number with their subjects. If the contraction includes a negative (such as *not*), treat the negative words as an intervening expression. A helpful hint when testing contractions is to write out the full form of the words in the contraction and verify that the subject and verb agree.

The attorney doesn't proofread the brief = The attorney does not proofread the brief.

Special Rules for Subject-Verb Agreement

The following are rules that are less straightforward than the general subject-verb rule.

Subjects Joined by *And* The verb must be plural when the subject is joined by *and*. In the example below, *were* is the plural verb describing the two subjects (*the apple and the orange*).

The apple and the orange were in the bag.

Subjects Joined by *Or* or *Nor* The verb must agree with the subject(s) that *follow(s) or* or *nor*.

Neither the customers nor the designer was happy with the results.

The words *designer* and *customers* are the subjects. Since the singular *designer* follows *nor*, it is the subject that dictates that the verb (*was*) should be singular.

Indefinite Pronouns as Subjects Table 6.3 lists indefinite pronouns. Some are singular and some are plural. Until you memorize which are which, keep this table close at hand.

Table 6.3 Indefinite Pronouns

Always Singular	Always Plural	Singular or Plural
anybody	both	all
anyone	few	any
anything	many	more
each	several	most
either		none
every		some
everybody		
everyone		
everything		
many a/an		
neither		
nobody		
nothing		
somebody		
someone		
something		

Someone always leaves the door open.

The word *someone* is a singular subject. The verb *leaves* is singular (note that it ends in *s*) and agrees with the singular subject.

Neither of the two witnesses is available on that date.

Since *Neither* is the subject and, from the previous table, you know that it is always singular, the verb *is* is singular, too (note that *is* ends in *s*). The section "of the two witnesses" is a prepositional phrase, so *witnesses* is not the subject.

Parts and Portions Parts and portions may be either singular or plural depending on the noun to which they refer. If the subject in a sentence is *half*, then ask "half of what?" The answer to that will determine whether the subject is singular or plural. Words that refer to parts and portions include:

all	minority
some	most
part	all fractions (such as half, one-third, a fourth, etc.)
majority	

Over half of the pie was eaten by the time I got there.

The word *half* is the subject. To determine if it is singular or plural, ask yourself, "half of what?" The answer is "half of the pie." *Pie* indicates that *half* is a singular subject, so the verb must be singular, too. *Was* is singular (it ends in *s*) and is correct in this sentence. If the subject of the sentence, *half*, referred to a plural noun, such as *pies*, then the verb would also have to be plural.

Over half of the pies were eaten by the time I got there.

Table 6.4 lists a summary of the subject-verb agreement rules you will need to know.

Table 6.4 Subject-Verb Agreement Rules

1. Singular subjects require singular verbs.
2. Plural subjects require plural verbs.
3. Prepositional phrases and intervening phrases will not contain the subject.
4. The verb must be plural when the subject is joined by *and*.
5. Test contractions to be certain that the verb is correct.
6. When subjects are joined by *or* or *nor*, the verb must agree with the subject that follows *or* or *nor*.
7. Some indefinite pronouns are singular and some are plural. (See Table 6.3.)
8. Parts and portions may be either singular or plural depending upon the noun to which they refer.
9. *There* and *here* will never be the subject. These sentences, along with questions, are probably inverted.

GRAMMAR

As the office member in charge of making certain the documents leaving the office are correct and professional, your role on the office team is an important one. Sloppy grammar and punctuation mistakes can lead clients to believe that the office creates flawed documents in other legal procedures as well. One dissatisfied client or customer can pass on dissatisfaction to several people who may then advise potential clients to avoid your office. It seems that bad news travels faster than good news! Clients who are satisfied do share their satisfaction with friends, but not as fast as they share dissatisfaction.

Language Focus Exercises

Apply what you have learned in the previous section on subject-verb agreement to the following language focus exercises.

Exercise 6.1 Read through the following sentences and determine the subject and noun in each. Circle the correct subject and underline the corresponding verb.

1. Our neighbors hire the lawyer.

2. The court accepts our appeal.

3. Brian works over the weekend.

4. The attorneys disagree with our proposal.

5. The appeal surprises the judge.

Exercise 6.2 Circle the correct verb choice in the following sentences. Use the rule numbers from Table 6.4 to note which rule applied to your choice of verb. Write the corresponding rule number on the line provided. The first one has been done as a sample.

Rule Number from Table 6.4

1. They has/have been creating a new

   policy for the company. _____

2. Luis and Gregory is/are to attend the

   hearing on Friday. _____

3. Either Miranda or her mother has/have

   signed the contract. _____

4. Jessica Pankle doesn't/don't handle

   irate callers very well. _____

5. The orders on the computer is/are going

   to be distributed first. _____

6. The maintenance workers, along with the office

   assistant, works/work overtime every Wednesday. _____

7. Every error and correction slows/slow

   down the process. _____

8. One of the lawn mowers was/were

   in for repair. _____

9. Three-fourths of the community supports/support

   the bonding issue. _____

10. The Petitioner and the parties' minor child

    receive/receives medical and dental insurance

    through Respondent's employment. _____

Exercise 6.3 Read the following sentences, circle any errors, and write the correct word on the line to the right. If the sentence is correct, write "C" on the correction line. On the second line, write the rule from Table 6.4, if one applies.

	Correction	Rule
1. There has been a thorough search of the title.	_____	_____
2. As opposed to abstract title, there have been a change to Torrens title.	_____	_____
3. Neither the (buyer) nor the seller are the recipient of advice from an attorney.	*Rule 2 plural subject/verb*	_____
4. Neither the attorney nor the client is subject to an order to clear title.	_____	_____
5. Either of the parties are responsible for the costs.	_____	_____
6. The parties, in the name of Mr. Jacob, is the owners of three acres of land in Pine County.	_____	_____

Editing: Office Style and Formatting Letters

Efficient offices generally have common style rules that all employees use. These style rules are often referred to as "office styles," "house styles," or "style guides." They may have been created specifically for the office, or they may be published guides that the office uses for reference. These guides may contain the expected formatting used in the office or simply a collection of suggested guidelines. Typically, these style guides will describe all formatting, including font types, font sizes, line spaces, and margins. Such a guide may also explain the desired treatment for captions, titles, and document names. These rules should be followed by all employees. This adherence eliminates inconsistencies and eliminates the need for employees to remember for whom they are working and what format that person or department uses. In addition, a common format shows unity within a company.

When you are on the job, check to see if your office uses a specific house style or style guide. If so, always abide by this style. If your office does not use a style guide,

Best Practice Tip

LETTERHEAD

Many law offices have their own letterhead, which should be used on all official correspondence. If you are required to create your own letter formatting template, you will have to make sure that your formatting works with the office letterhead. Be sure to verify that the letter does not conflict with any letterhead graphics.

you may be expected to adhere to the style preferences of the individual attorneys and supervisors with whom you work. Be aware that each might have his or her own style. Consider ways that will help you adjust to variances in style within your office, such as keeping department- or attorney-specific style guides on hand or creating a file to reference as you work.

Letter Style

Legal documents are frequently served, filed, and shared to ensure clarity. A cover letter should always accompany documents that are sent on to others. Sometimes these letters are very short and simply list what is being sent and what the recipient is to do with the items. These letters are often called "here you go" letters. Even though several business letter formats have been used over the years, the most efficient is block style (see Figure 6.3). In a **block-style letter**, all parts of the letter start at the left margin. Time is not wasted tabbing to the center for the date and closing. Simply press enter the appropriate number times after each letter part. The block-style letter is the preferred style simply because it saves time.

Formatting a Letter

Letter formatting is not difficult. Letters typically contain the following parts:
- Date
- Address of recipient
- Salutation
- Body
- Closing

Many offices will have a template for you to follow or will provide a specific style that dictates spacing, margins, and basic formatting. You may even find proper templates on your word processing program. Always follow your house style guide if one exists; otherwise, create a consistent style that you can apply to the documents you create.

Date and Address Of course, every letter starts with the date, name, and address of the intended recipient. Including the date in legal correspondence is extremely important. Do not forget to include the date in your letters, which appears on its own line.

Salutation Just as you would not jump into a conversation with a person without first greeting him or her, you should not send a letter without addressing it to the proper party and greeting the party at the start of the letter.

DATE CODES IN LETTER TEMPLATES

Frequently, letter templates in word processing software will include a "date code" that automatically updates every time you open or print the file. It is best to delete this code and simply type in the date. Using the date code can cause problems in instances where you open and print an additional copy of the letter at a later date. The date will update to the current one and lose the original date. It is extremely important to the legal situation that it be the original date. In addition, if you resave the letter, it will have the current date instead of the original date. (In some software, you can check a box so that the date is not automatically changed.)

Figure 6.3 **Block Letter Style**

Use default left-right and top-bottom margins. Enter several times at the top if the letter is short. The margins should be even white space to resemble a white picture frame.

Current Date

{3 blank lines (4 enters)} ⟶

{1 blank line (2 enters)} ⟶ CERTIFIED MAIL [Mailing Notation, such as: PERSONAL MAIL, REGISTERED MAIL]

Recipient's full name including title [Mr., Mrs., Ms., Miss, Dr., etc.]
Company Name
Address
{1 blank line (2 enters)} ⟶ City, State Zip

{1 blank line (2 enters)} ⟶ Dear Mr. Safler [Salutation. Notice no colon after salutation and no comma after closing]

{1 blank line (2 enters)} ⟶ Subject [or Re:]: brief summary of letter

Body of the letter. Do not indent paragraphs. Enter twice to leave a double space between each paragraph.
{1 blank line (2 enters)} ⟶ Body of the letter. Do not indent paragraphs. Enter twice to leave a double space between each paragraph.

Body of the letter. Do not indent paragraphs. Enter twice to leave a double space between each paragraph.
Body of the letter. Do not indent paragraphs. Enter twice to leave a double space between each paragraph.
Body of the letter. Do not indent paragraphs. Enter twice to leave a double space between each paragraph.
{1 blank line (2 enters)} ⟶ Body of the letter. Do not indent paragraphs. Enter twice to leave a double space between each paragraph.

{1 blank line (2 enters)} ⟶ Sincerely [Closing]

{3 blank lines (4 enters)} ⟶

{1 blank line (2 enters)} ⟶ Roberta T. Thomas [Writer's Typed Name]

Identification Initials [RTT:wfe RTT is the dictator or writer's initials. wfe is the typist's initials]
Enclosure: [insert number of enclosures and short description]
{1 blank line (2 enters)} ⟶ c: [copy notation—include name to which copy is going]

Preprinted Return Address

REGISTERED MAIL   CONFIDENTIAL

MR AUGUST SAFLER
227 MERAY BOULEVARD
OTISCO MN 56077

Give several seconds of special attention during the editing process to the inside address and salutation. According to good business writing practices, the salutation should always match the first line of the inside address in name and number. For example, if the first line of the inside address is Mr. Jonathon Smalzer, then the salutation is Dear Mr. Smalzer. (It is up to the writer to decide if he or she knows the receiver well enough to use Dear Jon or Dear Jonathon).

Follow these tips about courtesy titles such as Mr., Ms., Mrs., Miss, Dr., etc., in the inside address and salutation of a business letter, such as those created in a legal environment:

- Always use a courtesy title in the inside address even if you address the reader by his first name, such as Dear Steven.
- Use a courtesy title in the salutation unless you greet the person with his or her first name.
- Use a courtesy title in the salutation along with the recipient's last name.
- Do not include the person's first name in the salutation if you use a courtesy title.

Consider the following examples:

	Inside Address	Salutation
Correct:	Mr. Roberto Ashrafi	Dear Mr. Ashrafi
Correct:	Mr. William Ernesto	Dear Bill
Incorrect:	Ms. Phyllis Scherer	Dear Ms. Phyllis Scherer

In considering what salutation to use, you must also consider who else is getting a copy of this letter. If you are sending a letter to opposing counsel, Ms. Emily Jones, you would not want to address it as Dear Emily. If a copy is being sent to the client, the client may get the impression that his or her attorney is too friendly with opposing counsel.

If the first line of the inside address is Smalzer Corporation, the salutation should be Ladies and Gentlemen. Ladies and Gentlemen is correct because you can assume there is more than one person in the corporation, and you do not know if they are men or women. If the first line is Human Resources Director, then the salutation should be Dear Sir or Madam. The title Human Resources Director indicates one person but not whether that person is a man or woman. It is best, however, in the last example, to find out who the human resources director is and use his or her name, such as Ms. Marlene Trippman. The salutation, in this case, would be Dear Ms. Trippman.

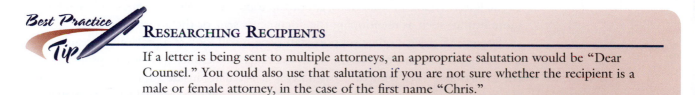

RESEARCHING RECIPIENTS

If a letter is being sent to multiple attorneys, an appropriate salutation would be "Dear Counsel." You could also use that salutation if you are not sure whether the recipient is a male or female attorney, in the case of the first name "Chris."

Table 6.5 Salutation Choices and When to Use Them

Salutation	Context
Dear John	Addressing a colleague with whom you are friends and at a similar level in the company or firm. The first line of the inside address would be *Mr. John Smith*.
Dear Mr. Smith	Addressing a person at a similar level of management and one you are not necessarily acquainted with.
Dear Sir/Madam	Used when the name of the receiver of the letter is unknown and you do not know that it is a man or woman.
To Whom It May Concern	This salutation is not encouraged when you address someone in a senior position and when you wish to gain something in cash or in kind from the recipient. Use a little effort and determine the name of the person you are addressing.
Respected Sir/Madam	Used to address someone in a senior position whose name you do not know.
Dear Counsel	Used to address an attorney when you do not know the gender of the attorney. Also, used to address a group of attorneys receiving the letter. The trend is to use more gender neutral language such as Counsel, Chair, Judge, Justice, etc., instead of pointing out the person's gender.
To the (title of recipient's position)	Best used when referring to someone whose name you do not know but whose position you do know. The first line of the inside address would be *Records Manager*, for example.

Letter writers sometimes use an attention line, but the modern preference in letter formatting is not to use an attention line. If you know to whom the letter is being sent, then use the name in the first line of the inside address and eliminate the attention line. It would probably be to your advantage to put some effort into researching and finding the name of the person to whom you are addressing the letter. People like letters to be more personal.

Body Text The body of the letter should be clear and understandable. If an introduction or some background information needs to be given, it should be done at the start of the body text. The paragraphs within the body text should be in a logical order. It is common to close letters with a repetitive sentence such as, "If you have any questions about the documents I am sending you, please call me." This sentence may seem repetitive to you, but it is not necessarily repetitive to the receiver of the letter. Weave in something about the topic of the letter to make this sentence more fitting, such as mentioning the documents sent or the attorney's advice.

Sometimes a legal office support staff person will look at a previously created letter from a different case to use as an example. Remember to edit and proofread the format and basic content of such items as the date, inside address, salutation, and closing. It is common to forget to change details from the original letter to match the current situation.

Closing and Signature The end of the letter should contain a complimentary closing and should be signed by the attorney or whoever is sending the letter. Common complimentary closings are a personal choice of the writer but should be something professional such as Sincerely or Sincerely yours. The sender's name is 3 to 4 blank lines below the closing. Be sure to leave enough room between the closing and the sender's typed name for the sender to write his or her signature.

Envelope Do not forget to review the envelope as well. You can probably assume that the envelope has a preprinted return address. Think about whether the letter and envelope require mailing and delivery notations. See the format of an envelope in Figure 6.3. In using the mailing feature in your word processing software, the inside address is usually taken from the letter automatically. To add the mailing and delivery notations, you will need to click on the envelope on the screen once it is created to key them in yourself—an easy thing to forget to do!

Editing Exercises

The following exercises will allow you to practice your editing skills using the information discussed in this chapter.

Exercise 6.4 Read the items in the first column. These items are the first line of an inside address in a letter. Decide what the appropriate salutation would be and write it on the line provided. You may have to use a reference manual.

First Line of Inside Address	Appropriate Salutation
1. Files Specialist	
2. Mr. Noah Nustad	
3. SP15/Sign Professionals	
4. Gamble's Do It Best Hardware	
5. Dr. Marybeth Flack and Mr. Kyle Flack	
6. Seen First Realty	
7. Parts Manager	
8. The Honorable Judge James R. Painter	
9. Ms. Tiffany's Jewelers	
10. Maintenance Department	

Exercise 6.5 Refer to Appendix: Style Guide and answer the following questions about letter formatting using the style guide for Jordan, Leone & Sanchez. Write your answers on the lines provided.

1. What letter style does the firm use?

2. Does the firm require punctuation after the salutation and closing?

3. Which comes first, an enclosure notation or reference initials?

_____

4. Does the date start at the center of the page or at the left margin?

_____

5. Is a letter single- or double-spaced?

_____

Exercise 6.6 Proofread the letter in **C06_Ex6.6_Letter** correcting format according to the Appendix: Style Guide.

1. Open **C06_Ex6.6_Letter**.
2. Using the style guide that you used in Exercise 6.5, edit the letter to match the guide.
3. Save the letter as **LastName_C06_Ex6.6_Letter**.
4. Submit the completed letter as directed by your instructor.

Proofreading: Proof for Inconsistencies— Check Your Office Style Guide

Verifying details is important in all areas of law and especially in proofreading for inconsistencies. As noted in the previous section, most offices have a house or office style. If your future office does not have its own style guide, consider talking with the other office staff about starting one. Add to it as you all agree on a standard style. Note that you should know your office staffing arrangement. Sometimes individual attorneys share the cost of office space and staff. In that case, you will need to continually be aware of whom you are working for and what style that attorney prefers.

Once you know the office style, proofread all correspondence for inconsistencies, such as the following:

Letters:
- Preferred letter style
- Font style and size
- Second page header, if needed
- Commonly used closing (Sincerely, Sincerely yours, etc.)
- Enclosure notation format (enclosures listed or not)
- Date of the letter
- Recipient's name
- Entire street address including number and street name
- City, state, and zip code
- Writer's name
- Writer's title
- Identification initials
- Enclosure notation (is the notation included, if necessary?)
- Copy notation (is the notation included, if necessary?)

It is common to create and print envelopes and labels on the computer, but some offices still type them on typewriters. Proofread the delivery address on the envelope. If you use word processing software to create the envelope, proofread the inside address in the letter because it will be automatically taken from the letter and inserted onto the envelope.

Specifically, in proofreading a letter, scan the set up or format of the letter to see that the parts are in the appropriate places. Each office will have a preferred style. Make certain that the letter is set up the same as all other letters sent out by your firm.

Notice that in Figure 6.3 of the editing section, the subject line (Re:) appears below the salutation. You will find this format in most style guides. However, many offices prefer the subject line between the last line of the inside address and the salutation. See, for example Figure 6.4 below:

In addition, the example in Figure 6.3 shows no punctuation after the salutation as well as the closing. Several methods of punctuating a salutation/closing are actually used. If you use a colon after the salutation, use a comma after the closing (mixed punctuation—commonly used in the United States). If you do not use a colon, do not use a comma (open punctuation). Follow your office's preferred style. (Note: A comma after the salutation (and closing) is less formal and used in personal or personal business letters.)

Figure 6.4 Example of Subject and Salutation Line

July 15, 20xx

Mr. Bjorn Johanson
183933 154th Street
Chamberlain, SD 66699

Re: Hunting Lease

Dear Mr. Johanson:

Proofreading Exercises

Complete the following proofreading exercises using the tips described previously.

Exercise 6.7 Proofread the following letters and check for inconsistencies using a style guide.

1. Open and print each of the following files:

   C06_Ex6.7a_CanoLetter

   C06_Ex6.7b_CanoLetter

   C06_Ex6.7c_CareCenterLetter

2. Use the Appendix: Style Guide, if necessary, and Figure 6.3 to verify details.

3. If necessary, use your word processing program to determine errors in font style and size or font spacing errors.

4. On each letter circle or underline grammar, punctuation, or typographical errors and write in the correction. Use lines and arrows to indicate format changes.

5. Submit handwritten corrections to your instructor.

6. If your instructor asks you to make the changes in the files, save the corrected files as:

   LastName_C06_Ex6.7a_CanoLetter

   LastName_C06_Ex6.7b_CanoLetter

   LastName_C06_Ex6.7c_CareCenterLetter

7. Submit corrected files to your instructor.

Real Estate How-To Guide

In real estate law, the most common assignments given to a legal support person will relate to a real estate transaction. The following how-to guide will help you understand the role of support staff within a legal office that specializes in real estate, a law office that has no specialty, or in other offices that work with the transfer of real estate titles. Real estate title transfer procedures and documents may vary slightly from state to state, and offices may vary in their expectations of how a legal support person performs these duties.

Buying and selling real estate includes an entire spectrum of professional offices in a community. Real estate sales offices, law offices, county offices, and lenders all work closely together to complete a real estate transaction.

Real Estate Legal Descriptions

Support staff in real estate sales offices, law offices, land records (county recorders) offices, and title companies all need to type legal descriptions accurately. Recall from Chapter 3 that legal support staff in other areas of law (such as family law) need to be familiar with real estate descriptions. A real estate legal description is the official description written by the county recorder to indicate the official location of the property. It is not the mailing address; it is more technical and is created by a civil engineer. The accuracy of a real estate legal description is extremely important in this area of law. Think about the confusion that would result from even the slightest error. Mistakes in legal descriptions cause not only immediate problems but can also cause problems in the future for both buyers and sellers.

Real estate can be described in a number of ways, depending upon its history and location, such as the following:

- Government survey descriptions
- Metes and bounds descriptions
- Block, Lot, and subdivision descriptions

These descriptions must be absolutely accurate. To ensure this accuracy:

1. Always key from the official abstract or other official title documents. Cross check the description with an official document if you have to key from a letter or handwritten note.

2. Always team proofread. Team proofreading is when one person reads from the original while the other verifies it against what appears in the file that was just typed.

Legal descriptions, no matter what type, are keyed single-spaced and indented ½ inch on the left and ½ inch on the right.

In addition, it is entirely possible to have a legal description given to you handwritten on a sheet of yellow legal paper or even a restaurant napkin! Obviously, you should key it from what you have until you can check it with the official description on the abstract or other evidence of title before sending it to the next step.

Team proofreading is essential in working with legal descriptions. Even in very small law offices, attorneys are usually willing to take the time needed to proofread long, complicated descriptions as a team in the name of accuracy. Be sure to have the person reading the description read all individual parts of the description, such as numbers, direction letters, capital letters, and all punctuation marks including commas, semicolons, and parentheses.

Completing Deeds

In a law office that works in real estate, many different kinds of deeds will be prepared over time. Earlier in this chapter, warranty deeds and other deeds were described. This section discusses how to complete these documents. Real estate deeds are almost always fill-in forms. Either the law firm purchases a subscription from a company that provides fill-in forms or the law firm has legal support staff create the forms for office use.

Figure 6.5 shows a warranty deed—joint tenants to joint tenants with numbered callouts. The following is a discussion of each of the numbers on the deed. (For your convenience, an electronic copy of Figure 6.5 [C06_WarrantyDeed_CalloutNumbers] can be found on the Student Data Disc.

Warranty Deed Blank Explanations The following numbered items refer to the numbered callouts in Figure 6.5. Notice that the top two inches of a warranty deed is left blank. This is done to leave room for the county recorder's office and other county offices to stamp and write information on the deed when it is recorded.

1. This line says "DEED TAX DUE," which is tax that is assessed by some states, such as the state of Minnesota. To calculate this tax, multiply the purchase price by 0.0033. Type in the tax amount.

Figure 6.5 **Warranty deed—joint tenants to joint tenants with numbered callouts**

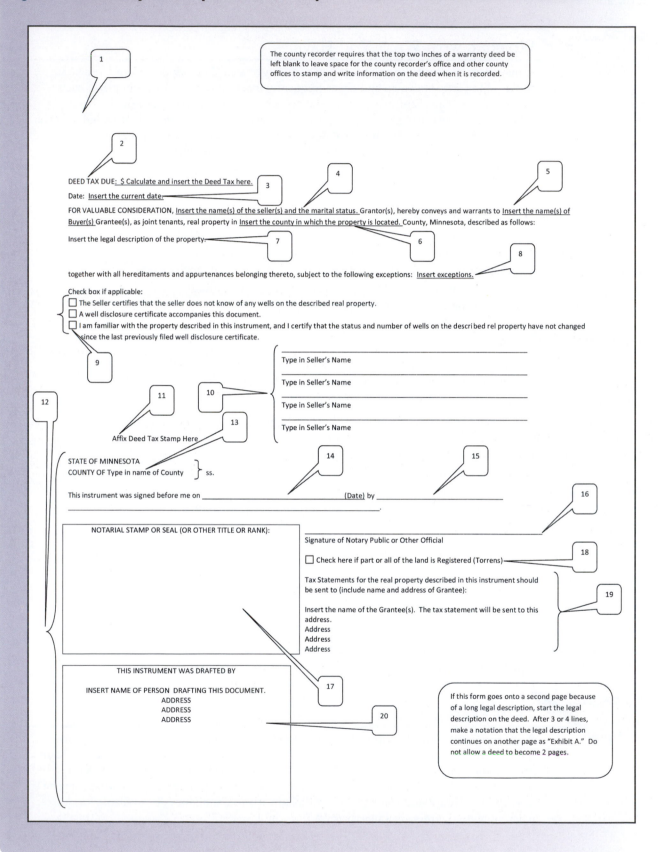

1

The county recorder requires that the top two inches of a warranty deed be left blank to leave space for the county recorder's office and other county offices to stamp and write information on the deed when it is recorded.

2

DEED TAX DUE: $ Calculate and insert the Deed Tax here.

3

Date: Insert the current date.

FOR VALUABLE CONSIDERATION, Insert the name(s) of the seller(s) and the marital status. Grantor(s), hereby conveys and warrants to Insert the name(s) of Buyer(s) Grantee(s), as joint tenants, real property in Insert the county in which the property is located. County, Minnesota, described as follows:

4

5

Insert the legal description of the property:

7

6

8

together with all hereditaments and appurtenances belonging thereto, subject to the following exceptions: Insert exceptions.

Check box if applicable:

☐ The Seller certifies that the seller does not know of any wells on the described real property.
☐ A well disclosure certificate accompanies this document.
☐ I am familiar with the property described in this instrument, and I certify that the status and number of wells on the described rel property have not changed since the last previously filed well disclosure certificate.

9

_____
Type in Seller's Name

_____
Type in Seller's Name

11

10

_____
Type in Seller's Name

13

_____
Type in Seller's Name

Affix Deed Tax Stamp Here

STATE OF MINNESOTA
COUNTY OF Type in name of County } ss.

14

15

This instrument was signed before me on _____ (Date) by _____

16

_____

NOTARIAL STAMP OR SEAL (OR OTHER TITLE OR RANK):

_____
Signature of Notary Public or Other Official

18

☐ Check here if part or all of the land is Registered (Torrens)

Tax Statements for the real property described in this instrument should be sent to (include name and address of Grantee):

19

Insert the name of the Grantee(s). The tax statement will be sent to this address.
Address
Address
Address

12

THIS INSTRUMENT WAS DRAFTED BY

INSERT NAME OF PERSON DRAFTING THIS DOCUMENT.
ADDRESS
ADDRESS
ADDRESS

17

20

If this form goes onto a second page because of a long legal description, start the legal description on the deed. After 3 or 4 lines, make a notation that the legal description continues on another page as "Exhibit A." Do not allow a deed to become 2 pages.

2. Insert the current date.

3. Insert the name of the seller(s). The seller is called the grantor in a deed. Because this deed asks for the marital status of the grantors, you know that this warranty deed is joint tenants to joint tenants. Type in all names of multiple grantors. Indicate marital status, if applicable.

4. Insert the name of the buyers. The buyer is called the grantee in a deed. No marital status is necessary for the grantee.

5. Insert the county in which the property is located.

6. The legal description is typed in this area. Leave a blank line between the preceding paragraph and the legal description. Remember to single-space the legal description and indent ½ inch more than paragraph. The following is an example of the formatting:

   This is an example of a legal description. It is indented ½ inch from the left margin and ½ inch from the right margin. This is an example of a legal description. This is an example of a legal description. This is an example of a legal description.

7. Exceptions to the legal description are listed in this location, such as an easement, for example. The attorney will instruct the legal support person as to any exceptions there must be included in this area.

8. The preparer of this deed must check the appropriate box for whether a well is on the property. The attorney will instruct which boxes to check.

9. Type the name of the grantor under this line. *Only* the seller (grantor) signs a deed. Type the name of another grantor under the next line. Add other names of grantors, as necessary.

10. During the actual recording process, the auditor will stamp here that the deed tax has been paid.

11. This section is the acknowledgment, which is signed by a notary, who verifies that the person or persons signing the deed are who they say they are.

12. Type in the name of the county in which the deed is to be signed.

13. The notary inserts date here.

14. The notary inserts the name of the seller(s) or (grantor(s). Sellers are the only ones who sign a deed and must have their signatures notarized.

15. The notary signs here.

16. The notary stamps or imprints his or her seal.

17. The typist check marks if the land is registered (Torrens) property.

18. The name and address of the buyer (grantee) is typed here. When the transaction is complete, the tax statements must be sent to the new owner.

19. The name, address, and phone number of the person or office preparing the deed is inserted here to make it easy to contact the preparer.

How-To Guide Exercises

Complete the following exercises using the information found in the How-To Guide section. Remember that as a legal support person, you will be creating new documents such as deeds and title opinions that contain legal descriptions. The only way for that legal description to get into the deed, is for the legal support person to type it in. It may come from messy handwriting or it may come directly from the abstract or Torrens certificate. In any event, every legal description must be proofread carefully. You may have been interrupted several times while keying the description; therefore, what was typed must be proofread even if it came from a clean and accurate file.

Exercise 6.8 Practice typing an accurate real estate legal description from handwritten copy. The following steps will walk you through the exercise.

1. Open the **C06_Ex6.8_LegalDesc_Handwritten** file.
2. Type the legal description that you see handwritten there.
3. Save the typed file as **LastName_C06_Ex6.8_LegalDesc**.
4. When you are finished, your instructor will provide you with a paper copy of the official legal description of the property taken directly from the caption of the abstract.
5. Find someone to proofread with you. Your proofreading partner does not have to be a classmate.
6. While your partner reads, out loud, the official description from the printed copy from the instructor, you will follow along on the computer screen and proofread what you typed from the handwritten version, making corrections as you find them. Your teammate should be careful to read every word, every mark of punctuation, and every capital letter in the file given to you by the instructor.
7. Discuss with your classmates how accurately you interpreted the handwriting.
8. Save the file again and submit to your instructor.

Exercise 6.9 Again, as in Exercise 6.8, practice typing a real estate legal description from handwritten copy.

1. Open the **C06_Ex6.9_LegalDesc_Handwritten** file.
2. Type the legal description that you see handwritten there.
3. Save the typed file as **LastName_C06_Ex6.9_LegalDesc**.
4. When you are finished, your instructor will provide you with a paper copy of the official legal description of the property taken directly from the caption of the abstract.
5. Find someone to proofread with you. Your proofreading partner does not have to be a classmate.
6. While your partner reads, out loud, the official description from the printed copy from the instructor, you will follow along on the computer screen and proofread what you typed from the handwritten version, making corrections as you find them. Your teammate should be careful to read every word, every mark of punctuation, and every capital letter in the file.
7. Discuss with your classmates how accurately you interpreted the handwriting.
8. Save the file again and submit to your instructor.

Exercise 6.10 In the event that a legal support person must type a legal description from a clear and accurate source file (such as the caption in the abstract), the resulting electronic file will still have to be proofread to verify that the information was typed accurately. The following exercise will help you practice these skills.

1. Open and print the file **C06_Ex6.10_LegalDesc_AbstractCopy**.

2. Key the legal description found within **C06_Ex6.10_LegalDesc_AbstractCopy** and assume that it is correct.

3. Save the typed file as **LastName_C06_Ex6.10_LegalDesc**.

4. Find someone to proofread with you. Your proofreading partner does not have to be a classmate.

5. While your partner reads, out loud, the official description from the **C06_Ex6.10_LegalDesc_AbstractCopy** copy you typed from, you will follow along on the computer screen, making corrections that you think need to be made. Your teammate should be careful to read every word, every mark of punctuation, and every capital letter.

6. Save as **LastName_C06_Ex6.10_LegalDesc**.

7. Submit the saved file to your instructor.

Exercise 6.11 Practice accurate typing and proofreading by completing the following exercise.

1. Open and print the file **C06_Ex6.11_LegalDesc_AbstractCopy**.

2. Key the legal description from **C06_Ex6.11_LegalDesc_AbstractCopy** and assume that the source material is correct.

3. Save the typed file as **LastName_C06_Ex6.11_LegalDesc**.

4. Find someone to proofread with you. Your proofreading partner does not have to be a classmate.

5. While your partner reads, out loud, the official description from the **C06_Ex6.11_LegalDesc_AbstractCopy** copy you typed from, you will follow along on the computer screen, making corrections that you think need to be made. Your teammate should be careful to read every word, every mark of punctuation, and every capital letter.

6. Save as **LastName_C06_Ex6.11_LegalDesc**.

7. Submit the saved document to your instructor.

Critical Thinking: Accurate Terms and Good Judgment

For most people, purchasing real estate is the largest and most serious financial commitment they will ever make. In a legal office, it is important to clearly understand the definitions and terms referring to the parties involved in the transaction. A mistake in labeling can cause confusion and frustration and require additional time and money to solve the problem. The need to use one's best judgment always exists in a legal office, as many occasions will occur when the legal support person must question the accuracy of a document.

The Suffixes –ee and –or

Being an employee of a law office, real estate office, bank, or other such office, one must clearly understand who is being referred to in words such as *mortgagor*, *mortgagee*, *debtor*, *creditor*, *lessor* (or *leasor*), *lessee*, *grantor*, and *grantee*.

Understanding the suffixes *–or* and *–ee* will help you use these words correctly. A **suffix** is one or more letters added to the end of a word or word stem to create a different word (*–ing*, *–est*, and *–ed* are common suffixes).

The suffix *-er*, *–or* means the "maker, giver, or actor" of the word to which it is attached.

mortgagor	"maker" of the mortgage
debtor	"maker" of the debt
creditor	"giver" of the credit
lessor or leaser	"giver" of the lease
employer	"giver" of employment
donor	"maker or giver" of a donation

The suffix *-ee* means "receiver" of the word to which it is attached. (Tip: The long *e* sound in *receiver* is similar to the long *e* sound of *–ee* in words such as *mortgagee*.)

mortgagee	"receiver" of the mortgage
lessee	"receiver" of the lease

Office employees are not the only ones who become confused by the terms *mortgagor* and *mortgagee*; buyers, sellers, and even realtors misuse these words. The confusion comes from the fact that most people do not understand who is actually doing the mortgaging. You will commonly hear people say that they are going to the bank to "get a mortgage." That is incorrect. The bank does not give the mortgage. The real estate buyer (the borrower) is the one "giving" the mortgage. A mortgage is technically a document that the borrower signs saying that the bank can take the borrower's property if he or she does not repay money lent. Figure 6.6 shows a diagram of who actually gives a mortgage. In other words, you as a borrower are the mortgagor, and the lender is the mortgagee until the debt is repaid.

In review, since a mortgage is the document that pledges property to the lender to secure the payment of a debt, the mortgagor (giver or maker of the mortgage) is the person borrowing money and pledging property as security. The receiver of the mortgage (mortgagee) is the bank, which takes the mortgage document (and title to property) as security for lending money to the mortgagor. Here are examples:

Figure 6.6 **Diagram illustrating who actually gives a mortgage**

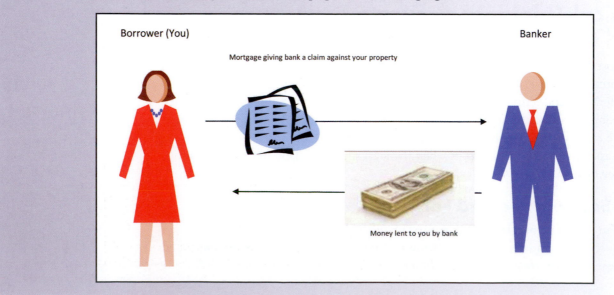

Borrower (You) Banker

Mortgage giving bank a claim against your property

Money lent to you by bank

- The bank became the mortgagee when it accepted our mortgage.
- We became mortgagors when the bank accepted our mortgage and lent us the money to buy our new home.

Consider the confusion that would arise if the terms were entered incorrectly in a legal document!

The Verbs *Borrow* and *Lend*

Borrow is a verb meaning to obtain or receive money with the promise or understanding of returning it. The principal parts of *borrow* are *borrow, borrowed, has/have borrowed,* and *borrowing*.

Lend is also a verb meaning to provide money temporarily on condition that the amount be returned, usually with interest. The principal parts of *lend* are *lend, lent, has/have lent,* and *lending*.

Loan can be either a noun or a verb. *Loan* is verb when there is a physical action. It is a noun when referring to a physical object such as the document identifying the fact that someone has received money from someone else. Examples include:

- The local bank gave me a loan. (noun)
- She loaned me her car. (verb)

All of these terms can apply to borrowing or lending items other than money.

People sometimes make mistakes such as *Will you borrow the money to me?*

The word *borrow* is incorrect here because the writer is actually asking someone to "provide money" to him or her, which is *lending*. The sentence should read *Will you lend the money to me?* Or, *Will you loan the money to me?* Or, *May I borrow the money from you?*

Another incorrect example is *Ms. Seorongo borrowed the money to Hans and Rita Grimm.*

Borrow is incorrect here because Ms. Seorongo is actually lending the money to Hans and Rita Grimm. This sentence should read *Ms. Seorongo lent the money to Hans and Rita Grimm* or *She loaned them the money.* The statement *Hans and Rita Grimm borrowed the money from Ms. Seorongo* is also correct.

Generally, the verb *borrow* is followed by the preposition *from* and the verb *lend* is followed by *to.*

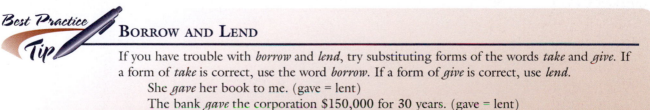

BRING AND TAKE

Frequently, the legal support person must interpret clients' phone calls into understandable messages for the attorney. *Bring* and *take* are commonly misused.

Bring is a verb, and its principal parts are *bring, brought, has/have brought,* and *bringing.*

Take is a verb, and its principal parts are *take, took, has/have taken,* and *taking.*

You would ask someone to *bring* something to your current location, and you would *take* something to another location. Examples include:

- Please bring the file to me so that I can take it to the client's home.
- I took the file to the client's home after it was brought to me at my office.

Good Judgment

Along with spotting misused terms, a legal support person must always be watchful for things that do not seem to make sense. Always keep your mind sharp and think about what you are looking at. Think about the client or situation at hand. Does everything make sense?

If you know that the client is selling a property, you should know where his or her name should appear in a legal document or form. If you discover that the name was used in place of a buyer's name, you should fix or flag the mistake to make sure that it does not move forward without being addressed.

In addition, before you go to the attorney and/or a supervisor with a question, always search for an answer yourself in places such as the case file or other office reference tools (including the Internet).

Do not spend too much time looking for the answer. If you cannot find it within 30 minutes, it is appropriate to ask. Spending more time is actually just wasting time. It is the responsibility of the attorney to have all of the correct details. He or she will not mind helping you if you have already attempted to find the answer yourself.

It is easy to become comfortable with your routine, but forms, processes, deadlines, procedures, technology, workmates, and bosses all change over time. You must be able to continue to be efficient in your work as these changes occur.

Using good judgment and making connections between what you know and whatever you are working on will help you to be a more effective and valuable worker.

Critical Thinking Exercises

Apply what you have learned to the following exercises.

Exercise 6.12 Circle any incorrectly used words in the followiung sentences. Write the correct word on the line provided. Write "C" if the sentence is correct.

1. The donee gave $5,000 to the foundation.

   _____

2. The creditor was anxious over the number of bills he had to pay.

   _____

3. The creditor was eager to get paid for the work he had done on the customer's car.

   _____

4. The employee hired eight people last month and had to create a new employer manual.

   _____

5. The lessor signed the lease agreeing to stay in the apartment for six months.

   _____

6. The grantee gave two acres of land to his son.

   _____

7. The creditor expected the debtor to pay the bill by Tuesday.

   _____

8. The mortgagor started a foreclosure action because the home owner was six months delinquent on payments.

   _____

9. The lessee agreed to rent the apartment to the couple.

   _____

10. The donor was recognized at the reception for her generosity.

   _____

Chapter Summary and Projects

Summary

You have now read an overview of real estate law and understand what tasks you might perform working in a legal office that specializes in real estate. You have also reviewed procedures that are important to legal support staff in helping the attorneys. You have reviewed and practiced recognizing problems with subject-verb agreement, editing documents using office style guides, formatting letters, and proofreading for inconsistencies. You also reviewed important differences in the terms used in real estate to ensure that your work is clear and accurate.

Remember that as a legal support person, it will be your responsibility in a real estate case to complete the following tasks:

- Assist attorneys in creating and proofreading title opinions, including preliminary and final opinions.
- Type and proofread real estate legal descriptions from a variety of original copy.
- Recognize errors in word choices such as mortgagor/mortgagee and lend/loan.
- Recognize content errors by applying good judgment and focusing on the current client and details.

Key Terms

abstract of title, 164
basic lender's policy, 168
basic owner's policy, 168
block-style letter, 179
certificate of real estate value, 170
certificate of title, 166
closing statement, 171
collateral (security), 160
community property, 161
continuation, 166
contract for deed, land contract,
   installment sales agreement, 169
conveyance, 158
counteroffer, 161
deed, 168
down payment, 159
earnest money, 159
easement, 166
FHA-insured loan, 160
final title opinion, 164
first-time home buyer loans, 160
grantee, 169
grantor, 169
insurable title, 162
joint tenancy, 161
land sales contract, 160

lien, 164
listing agreement, 158
marketable title, 162
mechanic (as in mechanic's lien), 166
mortgage, 160
mortgagee, 160
mortgagor, 160
multiple listing service (MLS), 158
personal property, 158
possession, 158
preliminary title opinion, 164
priority, 166
probate deed, 169
promissory note, 160
purchase agreement, 159
quitclaim deed, 169
real estate agent, 158
real estate broker, 158
real estate closing, 170
real estate closing in escrow, 171
real estate installment sales contract, 160
real estate legal description, 159
real property, 158
realtor, 158
recording, 169
secured promissory note, 160

Local Focus Research

The Local Focus icons that appear in the chapter indicate that your local court may have different rules, due dates, terminology, and/or procedures than what has been discussed. The following Local Focus assignments will help you acknowledge these differences. Locate the Chapter 06 folder in your electronic storage medium and open the local focus file **C06_LocalFocus_RealEstate**. Resave the file as **LastName_C06_LocalFocus_RealEstate**. Research the following topics described and record your research in the file you just created. Use this information as a reference tool as you start and continue your career as a legal support person. Your instructor may ask you to submit a copy as homework.

Local Focus 6.1 Page 162 discusses how real estate transfer documents are included in the public record. In your local area, what public office holds the responsibility of recording real estate transfer documents into the public record? Record your findings in your local focus file.

Local Focus 6.2 The process of recording written documents pertaining to real estate in the public record is discussed on page 169. Research the real estate document recording requirements and document standards for your local area. List the local recording requirements along with the statute number in your local focus file. To find this information, you should find the website for your local county recorder or land records office. They may have a link to the document recording requirements and the formatting standards for real estate title transfer documents that must be recorded into the public record. Save your findings in your local focus file.

Local Focus 6.3 Page 170 discusses filing a certificate of real estate value with a county auditor. Research your local county to determine if the auditor's or recorder's office requires documents in a real estate transaction to inform the auditor's office of the value of the real estate. Record the information you find in your local focus file.

Scenario

You are currently employed with the law firm of Jordan, Leone, & Sanchez, PLLP. One of the real estate attorneys, Attorney Shamariyah Thompson, has requested your help on a number of projects. Attorney Thompson has sent you a list of information about her client and has asked that you familiarize yourself with the information and apply it to the work whenever necessary.

When you arrived at work today, you saw that Attorney Thompson left you a note requesting that you prepare a warranty deed from her handwritten notes for her clients, Gary and Louise Albright. She had typed all the required information and saved it as Warranty Deed Information, which she attached to an email.

Project 1   Create and Proofread a Warranty Deed

1. Open the warranty deed fill-in form titled **C06_P1_WarrantyDeedFill-inForm**.
2. Complete the warranty deed form using the information provided by the attorney in the file **C06_P1_WarrantyDeedInformation**.
3. Proofread the warranty deed carefully, make necessary corrections, and save the file as **LastName_C06_P1_CompletedWarrantyDeed**.
4. Submit the file to the instructor.

Project 2   Revise Warranty Deed

1. Open **LastName_C06_P1_CompletedWarrantyDeed** that you completed in Project 1.
2. Make the following revisions.
   a. Change the property description to say that the property is in Robinson County instead of Kellogg County.
   b. Change the zip code of the buyer to 88842.
   c. The purchase price has changed to $139,999.
3. Resave as **LastName_C06_P2_RevisedWarrantyDeed**.

Project 3   Proofread a Preliminary Title Opinion

Attorney Thompson emails to ask you to proofread a preliminary title opinion that was drafted by Sean Kahler, one of your peers in the office. Read her email in Figure 6.7 and complete the requested task.

Figure 6.7 **Email from attorney**

To:	legalsupportperson@jlslaw.emcp.com
From:	Shamariyah@jlslaw.emcp.com
Date:	April 15
Subject:	Before you leave!

Hi ... I know you are about to leave for the day but will you do this for me before you go? Sean drafted a preliminary title opinion on the Juntunen Loan, Parcel No. 39-10-10-200-010. Could you proofread it and make any necessary changes? You will find it by opening **C06_P3_PreTitleOpin**. Print, proof, and return it to me when you are finished. I may make changes, or I may just sign and send it. Thanks!

-Shami

1. Open **C06_P3_PreTitleOpin** from the student data disc.
2. Proofread this preliminary title opinion watching for items such as those discussed in the title opinion section in this chapter.
3. Open **C06_P3_PreTitleOpinInfo** and use this document as a reference assuming this is information you would find in the file or would have gotten as instructions from the attorney during dictation.
4. Proofread on the computer screen, highlighting the errors.
5. Save the highlighted document as **LastName_C06_P3_PreTitleOpin_proofed**.
6. Submit the highlighted document to your instructor.
7. With the same document open, correct the errors on the screen.
8. Save the corrected document as **LastName_C06_P3_PreTitleOpin_corrected**.
9. Submit the corrected file to the instructor.

Project 4   Proofread a Final Title Opinion

In order for the parties to continue with the loan and sale of property, ABC Bank has asked Attorney Thompson to do a final search of the county records to verify that the title of the property is clear. She has asked you to research the title of the Juntunen Loan, Parcel No. 39-10-10-200-010, so she can write a final title opinion. After performing the necessary research, you give the title search form with the results of the search information to the attorney. Attorney Thompson has dictated the final title opinion, and you have transcribed it. In the next project, you will proofread the final title opinion that you transcribed.

1. Open **C06_P4_FinalTitleOpin** from the student data disc.
2. Proofread this final title opinion, watching for items such as those discussed in the Title Opinion section in this chapter.
3. Open **C06_P4_FinalTitleOpinInfo** which contains information received from the attorney. Use this document as a reference to complete your assignment.
4. Proofread on the computer screen by correcting any errors you see using track changes in your word processing software.
5. Save your document as **LastName_C06_P4_FinalTitleOpin_edited**.
6. Submit the document to the instructor.

Project 5   HUD-1 Settlement Statement

Attorney Thompson gave you a rough copy of a handwritten HUD-1 Settlement Statement yesterday, and you completed typing the final copy this morning. Your last task today is to proofread the settlement statement.

1. Open and print the file **C06_P5_HUD-1_FinalTypedForm**. This file is the same file you typed from Attorney Thompson's handwritten notes.
2. Open the file **C06_P5_HUD-1Form_HandwrittenOrig**, which contains Attorney Thompson's rough copy of a handwritten HUD-1 settlement statement.
3. Compare the final typed HUD-1 settlement statement form with the handwritten original form and proofread the final typed form. Highlight all remaining errors with a highlighter pen. Write in the corrections with a pencil.
4. Submit the highlighted HUD-1 form with added corrections to the instructor.

Discuss the Projects

a. Now that you have worked with preliminary and final title opinions, think about what you might do to make yourself more efficient if you were to work in an office that practices real estate law.
b. Think about how you completed Project 5, HUD-1 Settlement Statement. How might you make completing this project more accurate and efficient.

Share your thoughts with your classmates.

Business, Corporate, and Employment

Chapter Objectives

- Review the different types of business entities and the purpose of each
- Review terminology in business, corporate, and employment law
- Search the Internet to determine where to file business documents and the applicable filing fees
- Prepare documents for a limited liability company
- Make changes to a company's existing employment policy handbook
- Prepare an employment agreement
- Prepare a noncompetition agreement

Ms. Swanson has been operating her business as a sole proprietor. Her business is growing and she needs to hire employees. On the advice of her accountant, Ms. Swanson now wants to change her business entity to a limited liability company (LLC), which will protect her business and personal assets. She makes an appointment to see a business/employment law attorney in a legal office to discuss the advantages of this possible change and find out what else she should be doing to protect her business and personal assets and operate her company in an efficient, legal, and profitable manner. Ms. Swanson's new attorney will acquaint her with the terminology, procedures, and documents used in business, corporate, and employment law. Ms. Swanson is advised that the attorney will have to prepare the necessary organizational documents and also create policies and procedures consistent with state laws to ensure smooth business operation and management of employees.

The areas of business law, corporate law, and employment law often overlap. The laws in these areas guide business owners and their advisers through the range of legal matters that can arise between companies, between employers and their employees, between owners of companies, and between companies and their clients. **Business law** (or commercial law) refers to laws that apply to small business entities; it covers the various types of organizations a person can use in starting and setting up a new business or changing the structure of an existing business. A business works closely with its attorney and its accountant to choose the type of business entity that will be most advantageous to the business owner. **Business entity** is a general term for a corporation, limited liability company, institution, or organization. This attorney is generally an outside-the-business attorney (one who is not a member of the business's staff) who is hired individually or on retainer.

Corporate law is a broad area covering the governing, financing, mergers, and acquisitions of the big business world as well as the relationships among corporations, companies, shareholders, boards of directors, and consumers.

Depending on the corporation's size, it will have either an in-house legal department with its own corporate attorneys or it will hire an outside law office to represent it in dealing with its legal needs. An in-house legal department advises the corporation in areas such as contract law and employment law. When a minor legal situation arises, the in-house corporate lawyers will handle it themselves. When more complicated legal issues arise, a company will look to an experienced outside team of business litigation attorneys to help sort out the legal issues and reach a satisfactory resolution or defend a lawsuit.

An attorney can work in business/corporate law either as an in-house attorney as an employee of the corporation, with offices and staff within the corporation. In that case the legal support staff would also be employees of the corporation.

An attorney can also practice business/corporate law by working alone or within a law office with other attorneys. The attorney would be hired by individual clients who may have a variety of business needs, such as starting a business, reorganizing the business structure of a current business, needing advice on employment policies, etc. Such individual clients are generally companies that do not have their own corporate legal departments. The legal support staff in this situation would be employed by the law firm.

In addition to the day-to-day needs of businesses, sometimes the company may be involved in litigation that involves claims against the company by a customer, employee, or another company. These claims can be costly and may involve a deluge of business records and documents as well as many hours spent by attorneys attempting to resolve the matter on both sides of a case. Many business, corporate, and employment law attorneys do not get involved in litigation matters on behalf of their clients. They will consult with a civil litigation attorney to assist the client in the resolution of a claim the business has made or a claim against the business. An employment law attorney can represent employees, employers, or both. Always keep in mind that a conflict of interest cannot exist among any of an attorney's clients.

Attorneys A and B work together in the same office. Attorney A represents only companies. Attorney B represents only employees. Attorney B is contacted by an employee who wants to make a claim against a company represented by attorney A. That would be a conflict of interest, and attorney B must refuse the case.

Common Types of Entities

The five common types of business organizations are: sole proprietorships, partnerships, limited liability companies (LLCs), limited liability partnerships (LLPs), and corporations.

In a **sole proprietorship**, the business and its owner (or sole proprietor) is considered one and the same; there is usually just one owner. If the business is

sued or defaults on a debt, the owner is fully responsible for any losses, debts, or judgments against the business.

A **partnership** is comprised of multiple owners (or partners) who have chosen not to be set up as a formal corporation or limited liability company. The owners are personally liable for any losses, debts, or judgments against the partnership.

In a **limited liability company (LLC)**, owners (or members) are not generally personally liable for any debts or losses incurred by the business. Many state laws do not allow lawyers or doctors to form LLCs. In such states, these professionals will often form a limited liability partnership instead. Even though multiple types of business organizations exist, the LLC is most commonly chosen because it is inexpensive to set up and offers the owners personal protection from the company's debts and liabilities.

A **limited liability partnership (LLP)** is a type of business entity usually used by professional groups (such as doctors and lawyers) when the law or rules of ethics do not allow them to use a different business type. Owners (or partners) of an LLP are not personally liable for the negligence of other partners but remain liable for their own negligence and for the debts and liabilities of the business.

Corporation

A **corporation** is a separate legal entity from its owners (or shareholders). Owners are not personally liable for losses, debts, or obligations of the business. Corporations are useful for raising money and capital, as they can sell shares of stock, allowing investors to become partial owners. The law is more controlling of corporations, requiring that various formalities be strictly followed. Many states do not allow certain lawyers or doctors to operate as a corporation. The daily management of a corporation is handled by officers such as the president/ chief executive officer (CEO), a corporate secretary, and a treasurer/chief financial officer (CFO). There may also be a chief operating officer (COO) and one or more vice presidents (VP). In addition, a corporation will have a board of directors that oversees the work of the officers. Table 7.1 lists the officers in a corporation.

Other types of corporate structures include domestic, foreign, alien, for profit, not for profit, public, and professional associations. These other structures allow business owners to tailor their business's legal organization, usually for tax purposes.

Table 7.1 Officers in a Corporation

President/chief executive officer (CEO)	The executive who is responsible for company/corporation operations.
Chief operating officer (COO)	The executive in a company who is responsible for (1) the day-to-day operation of critical departments such as production, marketing and sales, and distribution; (2) establishing procedures and processes to ensure that the company functions smoothly; and (3) providing timely operational information and assistance to the CEO. The COO is also called the general manager.
Vice president	A deputy to the president of a corporation who is in charge of a specific department or location; for example, vice president of sales and marketing.
Corporate secretary	The person who is in charge of keeping corporate minute books up to date, documenting actions taken by the company, and sending out notices of meetings to shareholders. The person in this position may complete these tasks independently or the corporation may ask its in-house or out-of-house attorneys to complete these tasks. The person holding the corporate secretary position is in charge of making sure that this work is done no matter who performs it. Do not confuse corporate secretary with the former title for an administrative assistant. The corporation may also have administrative assistants doing the company business, but the corporate secretary is an official officer of the corporation.
Treasurer/chief financial officer (CFO)	The executive responsible for a company's financial control and planning. He or she is in charge of all accounting functions including (1) credit control, (2) preparing budgets and financial statements, (3) coordinating financing and fund raising, (4) monitoring expenditures and liquidity, (5) managing investment and taxation issues, (6) reporting financial performance to the board, and (7) providing timely financial data to the CEO. The CFO is also called the chief finance officer, comptroller, controller, or finance controller.
Board of directors	The individuals elected by a corporation's shareholders to oversee the management of the corporation. The members of a board of directors are paid in cash and/or stock, meet several times each year, and assume legal responsibility for corporate activities. This group of people could also be called the directorate.

Employment Law

An area of practice related to business/corporate law is the challenging area of employment law. **Employment law** covers the relationships between businesses and their employees. Relationships between people in the workplace are complex and emotional on all sides. An employment law attorney may choose to represent only businesses or may choose to represent only employees. When an attorney focuses on representing businesses, he or she will advise the company on creating employment policy handbooks; defining policies on antiharassment and antidiscrimination; creating disciplinary processes; setting policies on drug and alcohol testing; drafting employment contracts, severance agreements, and noncompetition agreements; defining disability accommodations; and defending unemployment claims and other claims against the business, among many other things. Business attorneys, like other attorneys, rely on their support staff to assist them in creating the necessary documents and meeting deadlines.

An employment law attorney may also choose to represent employees on civil claims they bring against their employers, such as sexual harassment, age or racial discrimination, hostile work environment, and wrongful termination. These cases can be handled in state or federal court. Although an employee may believe that he or she has been wronged by the employer or was not treated fairly, the law may not always support the employee's claim. The attorney will have the difficult task of informing an emotional client that he or she does not have a valid claim. Dealing with distraught clients is the attorney's responsibility. The legal office staff person's responsibility in this type of situation is to always remain even-tempered and pleasant, making the client feel comfortable in the office setting. Many complicated federal laws govern employment situations, and the employment law attorney must stay up to date on the latest developments in the law, examples of which may include the Americans with Disabilities Act, Family Medical Leave Act, and others. It is challenging and time-consuming for an attorney to keep abreast of all the minute details of the many state and federal labor and employment laws. Because the laws governing these situations are available online, attorneys receive electronic updates and are themselves responsible for keeping up to date on the laws. Sometimes legal support staff will be assigned to watch for law updates and may be asked to summarize changes to laws so that the attorneys will immediately be made aware of the changes and prompted to review the complete law later.

Language Focus: Adjectives and Adverbs

Adjectives and adverbs can cause trouble for many people. This section examines the difference between these two parts of speech and identifies adjective and adverb pairs that are known to be more difficult than others.

Adjectives

Adjectives are words that modify or describe nouns and pronouns—words that allow us to describe characteristics of nouns. Adjectives explain how many, which one, and/ or what kind. Consider how a person would describe where his or her car is located. Without adjectives, the most one could say would be "The car is in the lot." Without adjectives, one could not say the color, type, or age of the car. Nor would one be able to describe the type of lot (parking) in which the car is located. Adjectives are important.

IDENTIFY YOUR COMMON ERRORS

As you become more proficient at basic language skills, you will find fewer and fewer mistakes in your writing and proofreading. We all have certain areas of our language, however, that give us trouble, and these areas will be different from individual to individual. As you gain more experience, you will notice a trend in the types of errors you make. When you notice something you struggle with, jot it down along with a brief explanation of how to make the correct choice. You may even want to put a colored tab on that page of your notes, so you can flip back to it until you are consistent in handling the grammar, proofreading, writing, or spelling issues.

Adjectives can come before a noun or appear in the predicate following linking verbs such as *are, was, were, appear(s), seem(s)*, and so on. Consider the following examples:

We all rose as the distinguished judge entered the room.

The judge appears distinguished.

The lengthy presentations made us all sleepy.

The presentations were lengthy.

Adjectives can be used to compare qualities as well. In describing one noun, the adjective is said to be in the **positive form**. In comparing two nouns, the adjective is said to be in the **comparative form**. In comparing three or more nouns, the adjective is said to be in the **superlative form**. Use Table 7.2 as a tool in helping you make correct comparisons.

Table 7.2 Adjective Comparison Table

	Positive one person or thing	**Comparative** two persons or things	**Superlative** three or more persons or things
One-syllable words	thin	**-er** thinner	**-est** thinnest
Two-syllable words	happy	**some are –er** happier	**some are –est** happiest
	careful	**some are more/less** more/less careful	**some are most/least** most/least careful
Three-syllable words	important	**more/less** more/less important	**most/least** most/least important
Words that change form	good much bad little	better more worse less	best most worst least

Adverbs

Adverbs modify or describe action verbs, adjectives, and other adverbs whereas adjectives describe characteristics of nouns and follow linking verbs, adverbs tell us more about action verbs and answer questions such as *how, when, where,* and *why.* In addition, many, but not all adverbs end in *–ly.* Here are some examples.

The witness easily described the accident.

How did the witness *describe* the accident? Answer: *easily* (adverb). *Describe* is the verb and *easily* tells us how the witness described the accident.

We will use the new testing software tomorrow.

When will we *use* the new testing software? Answer: *tomorrow* (adverb)

The defendant admitted that he hid the gun nearby.

Where did the defendant *hide* the gun? Answer: *nearby* (adverb)

Keep in mind that adjectives describe nouns and pronouns. Adjectives can appear before nouns or after linking verbs. Adverbs describe and give more information

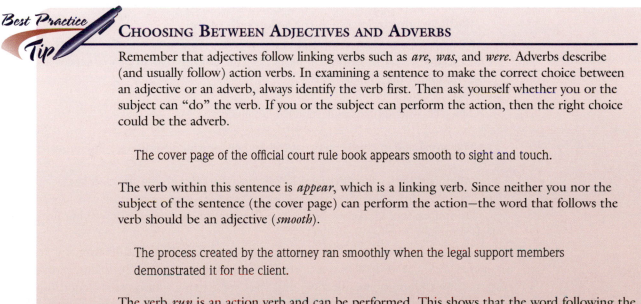

about action verbs (not linking verbs). Carefully examine the parts of speech in sentences to determine if you should be choosing an adjective or an adverb.

Many adjectives also have adverbial forms such as *careful* and *carefully*, *quick* and *quickly*, and *efficient* and *efficiently*. Writers and speakers of English generally do not make mistakes in using adverbs when adjectives are correctly used.

> Our employees are a quietly group of people.

The correction, of course, is "Our employees are a quiet group of people" where *quiet* is an adjective describing *group*. *Quietly*, on the other hand, is an adverb and should be used to tell us more about an action word such as *worked* in *He worked quietly*, or *entered*, in *He entered the room quietly*.

Troublesome Adjective/Adverb Pairs

Have you ever heard someone speak and thought that what had just been said did not sound correct? The words may have been correct, but you have been accustomed to hearing them used incorrectly your entire life. What you have heard for a long time will sound better even though it is incorrect.

Good/Well Often, when people are asked how they are doing, they will respond by saying "good" instead of "well." It is common to hear both responses, and so both may sound accurate; however, responding with the word *good* is grammatically incorrect. Remember that *good* is an adjective (all the time), and *well* is an adverb (some of the time).

> We have a good day when all clients are happy.

Good is an adjective describing the noun *day*.

> The paid time off clause works well in this section of the handbook.

Well is an adverb describing the action verb *works*.

Note that there is an exception to the pattern. *Well* can also be an adjective when it is describing health. In describing health, the adjective form of *well* acts as an adjective following a linking verb.

> She feels well although she sprained her ankle.

The word *well* in this sentence refers to her health and follows a linking verb.

> After leaving the doctor's office, Kelsey looked good with the smile on her face.

Do not be fooled. Kelsey was leaving the doctor, but *good* is describing how Kelsey looked, not her health.

To use adjectives and adverbs correctly, you must sometimes determine if verbs such as *feel(s)*, *appear(s)*, *seem(s)*, *smell(s)*, *taste(s)*, etc., are really linking verbs (requiring the use of an adjective) or if they are actually action verbs (requiring the use of an adverb). For example, *I taste the cinnamon clearly in this recipe* shows that *taste* is an action verb. The adverb *clearly* is the correct choice.

However, when an adjective is needed, the word *taste* will be a linking verb. Because "being verbs," such as *am, is, are, was, were, be, been,* and *being,* are *always* linking verbs, substitute a "being verb" to determine if *taste* is actually a linking verb. For example, in this sentence, *The recipe tastes wonderful,* substitute *is* for *tastes* to prove that *tastes* is a linking verb. Therefore, the adjective choice *wonderful* is correct, instead of the adverb *wonderfully.*

> The employees at Johnson Drilling appear happy with the revisions in the employee handbook.

Substitute a being verb for *appear* and notice that it makes sense.

> The employees at Johnson Drilling are happy with the revisions in the employee handbook.

This means that *appear* is a linking verb and an adjective (*happy*) follows a linking verb. Here is another example:

> All employees at Johnson Drilling appear quickly at 3:15 p.m. for a break.

Appear in this sentence is an action verb. You cannot substitute a being verb for *appear,* so it must be an action verb. *Quickly* describes how the employees appear.

Bad/Badly *Bad* is an adjective and *badly* is an adverb. It is not uncommon for writers and speakers to misuse these two words, but they can also be tested by determining if they are used with linking verbs or with action verbs. Take the sentence *Travis Hammerstein feels bad about the results of the survey.* If you substitute a being verb for *feels* to determine if *feels* is a linking verb, it reads this way: *Travis Hammerstein is bad about the results of the survey.* We know that this is incorrect since Travis is not "bad" like a *bad* hair day or a *bad* apple—both adjectives—he simply feels *sad.* In the case of *bad* versus *badly,* a simple method of testing is to substitute the word *sad* for *bad* to make your decision. You can also simply determine what type of verb it follows.

> Travis Hammerstein feels bad about the results of the survey.

> Travis Hammerstein is sad about the results of the survey.

The second example is actually what is meant. Since this example shows that *feels* is a linking verb, you must choose the adjective *bad* instead of the adverb *badly.*

> Our client's leg was injured badly in the accident.

The word *injured* is an action word, so it should be followed by an adverb (badly). *Badly* modifies the action verb and explains how severely the client was injured.

Real/Really *Real* is an adjective and *really* is an adverb. Sometimes it is easier to substitute another adverb for *really* to make a quick choice. Speed and efficiency in editing and proofreading are important. Since *really* is an adverb meaning *very* or *certainly* (both adverbs) and if you can substitute *very* or *certainly* for really, then you know that *really* is the right choice. Here are some examples:

The profits are real, since the company sold the stocks.

The word *real* describes the noun *profits* and follows a linking verb.

The value is in the real diamond.

The word *real* is the adjective describing the noun *diamond*.

The employees at the union meeting were really happy about the result of the vote.

The attorney was really concerned when the CEO refused to speak to the employees about the changes in the contract.

Since *very* or *certainly* can be substituted for *really* in these last two sentences, the adverb *really* is correct.

Language Focus Exercises

Use the information from the previous section to complete the following exercises.

Exercise 7.1 Circle the adjectives in the following sentences. Underline what they modify.

1. Our new client was furious about the glaring errors in the documents.
2. The human resources director is careful not to use the old contract's wording again.

Exercise 7.2 Using Table 7.2 and what you know about adjective comparisons, fill in the correct word or words in the following sentences. On the line provided, write whether the adjective is in the positive form, comparative form, or superlative form. Note: You may need to add the word *the* in some situations.

1. Although both sides presented strong arguments, the union representative's case was _____(strong).

   _____

2. The instructions were _____(difficult) to understand.

   _____

3. Since two budgets were recommended, the committee had to decide which budget was the _____(good).

   _____

4. The management negotiators were _____(strong) at the most recent talks than they have ever been.

   _____

5. We spent several months negotiating many contracts, but we feel that the Duck Callers, LLC, contract had _____ (fast) turnaround time.

Exercise 7.3 Circle the word that best completes the following sentences.

1. The law requires an employer to check the valves (careful, carefully) on a monthly basis.
2. The inspector visits (frequent, frequently).
3. Because of the noisy equipment, you must speak (loud, loudly), or the team will not hear you.
4. The plaintiff took the defendant's words (personal, personally), causing the situation to escalate into a lawsuit.
5. The images on the monitor in the break room are (bright, brightly).

Exercise 7.4 Circle the word that best completes the following sentences.

1. Mr. Chan completed the client questionnaire as (good, well) as he could.
2. To my palate, the food in the company's cafeteria tasted (strong, strongly).
3. The children in the company's daycare center played so (noisy, noisily) that they disturbed the meeting.
4. Sofyia cannot be expected to look (good, well) after her employment review.
5. Brady purchased a (real, really) fast laptop computer after he received his bonus.
6. Walking in the door, the client could smell the flowers (distinct, distinctly).
7. I am (real, really) pleased with the results of our work with Road Resurfacers, Inc.
8. Allyson felt (bad, badly) when she got lost on the way to the courthouse.
9. The overhead music in the office was playing too (loud, loudly).
10. Ms. Brown's staff work (good, well) together.

Editing: Word Choices; Avoiding Idioms and Redundancies

Remember that the editing process focuses on improving content, sentence structure, and formatting. Unless a communication is short, the first draft is rarely satisfactory. Many times you or the attorney will draft a letter or document and immediately make revisions. The other member of the team will then read and make revisions. Finally, on the third review, the writer may be satisfied that the writing is clear and concise and communicates exactly what it was created to communicate.

Most documents are easier to understand when they are written concisely. Conciseness in writing means that unnecessary and unclear words and phrases (such as redundancies, buzzwords, and idioms) are removed.

Redundancies Redundancies are repetitive words or phrases that do not add useful meaning to a sentence. Table 7.3 contains examples of redundancies and the words one might choose instead.

Table 7.3 Redundancies

Redundant Phrases	Concise Words
repeat **again**	repeat
consensus **of opinion**	consensus
free gift	gift
advance planning	planning
invited guests	guests
foreign imports	imports
close proximity	proximity or closeness
end result	result
usual custom	custom
written down	written or recorded
new beginning	beginning
merge together	merge
exact same thing	exact or same

Buzzwords Buzzwords are words or phrases from specialized fields or groups that usually sound important or technical. These words are used primarily to impress others. In fact, the word *buzzword* is a buzzword! These words are usually popular, overused, and sometimes not widely understood. Table 7.4 contains examples of buzzwords along with their definitions.

Table 7.4 Buzzwords

Buzzword	Meaning
paradigm shift	changing your way of looking at a subject or idea
outside the box	solving an issue by looking at it in a completely different way
cloud computing	hosted services delivered over the Internet
proactive	thinking about and deciding on an issue before it becomes an emergency
step up to the plate	come forward and participate
bleeding edge	having and learning the very latest in technology
generation X	anyone born between 1965 and 1981
ballpark figure	an estimated number or dollar amount

Idioms In professional writing, it is important not only to remove redundant language and buzzwords, but also to remove figures of speech such as idioms, colloquialisms, and metaphors. Idioms are words, phrases, or expressions whose meaning cannot be taken literally. Idioms are usually understood by native speakers of a language, but people from other countries or cultures, for example, may not understand the idiom's meaning. Table 7.5 contains idioms along with their meaning in the English language.

Table 7.5 Idioms

Idiom	Meaning in the English Language
fuddy-duddy	an old-fashioned and foolish type of person
spitting image	the exact likeness or kind
play our cards right	to make the right decisions at the right time
kick the bucket	die
six feet under	dead
kiss of death	that which causes the death or end of anything
graveyard shift	working overnight hours
as easy as pie	being easy to complete
at the eleventh hour	to complete at the last minute
elbow grease	putting hard work into a task
fender-bender	a minor automobile crash
hit the hay	to go to bed
if I had my druthers	if i could have my way
let sleeping dogs lie	do not ask questions; just let the situation be
make a mountain out of a molehill	to exaggerate

Legal writing is formal writing. The primary goal is to communicate ideas clearly and efficiently. An occasional flourish can be useful to emphasize a point, particularly in persuasive writing; however, one should not run the risk of confusing the point. The following are examples of idioms that can be easily corrected.

Informal: On arriving at the scene of the crime, the police officer tore up the stairs in search of the big enchilada.

Improved: On arriving at the scene of the crime, the police officer ran up the stairs in search of the leader of the crime syndicate.

Informal: On December 9, 1987, Ms. DeWinter kicked the bucket.

On December 9, 1987, Ms. DeWinter passed on to her heavenly reward.

Improved: Ms. DeWinter died on December 9, 1987.

Colloquialisms Colloquialisms are informal and sometimes slang expressions that are often specific to a region or specific area. Like idioms, these expressions should not be used in legal correspondence and documents. These include words and expressions such as *gonna* (going to), *wanna* (want to), and *ya'll* (you all). Although you may use these expressions in an informal email or phone call, you would never use them in a formal communication such as a letter written in a law office or in speaking directly with clients.

If you are drafting, editing, or proofreading original writing, leave out the figures of speech discussed in this section. Your writing will be clearer and to the point. However, if you are quoting someone who has used these figures of speech, you must leave them in. You cannot change wording in a direct quote.

Editing Exercises

Apply what you have learned in the editing section to the following exercises.

Exercise 7.5 Edit the following redundant phrases by crossing out the redundant words within the phrase.

1. collaborate together
2. definite decision
3. postpone until later
4. join together
5. close scrutiny
6. consensus of opinion
7. spell out in detail
8. absolutely essential
9. first began
10. filled up to capacity

Exercise 7.6 In small groups or individually, brainstorm buzzwords and determine how the buzzwords could be replaced in professional writing. Write your examples on the following lines. After you are finished, go online and find additional examples. Add them to your list and provide possible alternatives.

_____

_____

_____

_____

_____

_____

_____

_____

Exercise 7.7 In a small group or on your own, brainstorm idioms and how you might replace them in professional writing. Write your examples on the following lines. After you are finished, go online and find additional examples. Add them to your list.

_____

_____

_____

_____

_____

_____

_____

_____

Exercise 7.8 List 5 to 10 modern idioms or colloquialisms on the provided lines and give the meanings of each. Consider idioms and expressions you encounter on the Internet or in social media. After you have finished, go online and find additional examples. Add them to your list.

_____

_____

_____

_____

_____

_____

_____

_____

Exercise 7.9 Practice editing for proper word choices in a legal document by completing the following steps.

1. Open **C07_Ex7.9_WordChoices**.
2. Save as **LastName_C07_Ex7.9_WordChoices**.
3. Edit the memo, paying specific attention to word choices within the document.
4. Delete the figures of speech discussed in this section. Some should be replaced and others can be deleted.
5. Resave and submit the file to the instructor.

Proofreading: Difficult Formatting

Although most people focus on misspelled words and punctuation during their proofreading pass, one must not forget to double check that the document was formatted properly. Formatting errors might have been missed in the editing process, so it is important to watch for these specific issues:

- Columns
- Hard enters and automatic wraps
- Spaces after periods
- Lines between items in numbered or bulleted lists

When you receive a file to proofread for formatting, the first thing you should do is select the tool that shows formatting marks and hidden symbols. This tool is typically titled "show/hide ¶," and the associated icon is the paragraph symbol (¶). This tool will display all of the keystrokes and formatting methods that were used when the document was created. It is likely that the forms and documents you proofread will be produced from a standard template; however, you may encounter changes to the template or original documents created from scratch. Always check with your office style guide to determine if preset formatting rules are required for specific documents and forms.

Columns

When you encounter information that is best understood when presented in column format, do not use the space bar to align the information. You may be familiar using the program's columns feature to set up columns within a document, but it is more efficient to use tabs and tables than it is to use the column feature. Nothing is wrong with the column feature; however, one must insert section breaks to change back to full-line text. When a file is created that requires columns, the columns should be created using one of two methods:

- Set tabs across the page in the locations the material should be aligned.
- Use a table and hide the gridlines.

As you may be required to create the formatting for documents, the following instruction describes how you would go about formatting the document. Use this same information to fix formatting errors in documents you encounter while proofreading.

Using Tabs to Create Columns Set tabs across the page in the locations you want the material to be aligned. Remember that you can set left tabs, center tabs, and right tabs, along with several other varieties. Sometimes you can set them manually on a visible ruler bar. To get more specific, such as setting leader tabs, you can open a tabs dialog box to make the tab settings more specific. For more information about how to set tabs in your own word processing program, search the help topics.

Avoid placing material in columns or other specific locations by using the space bar. These spaces stay within the line where you inserted them, making large spaces appear in a paragraph if you decide to add material later. Use of the tab key avoids this possibility.

Using Tables and Gridlines to Create Columns Using a table and hiding the gridlines to place information into columns works just as well. See Figures 7.1, 7.2, and 7.3 for examples of how columns can be created using two different methods. Note that Figures 7.2 and 7.3 show the same formatting method, but Figure 7.2 displays the nonprinting gridlines of the table.

Figure 7.1 Columns created with tabs. Notice the tab settings on the ruler bar.

Columns Created with Tabs

Current and Past Officers

President	Vice President	Secretary
Wallace Nietzell	Evelyn Weldy	Douglas Crone
Steven Holtz	Jeffrey Martens	Joann Schult
Denise Olberg	Myron Borg	Dan Blue

Figure 7.2 Columns created as a table. Notice the nonprinting gridlines.

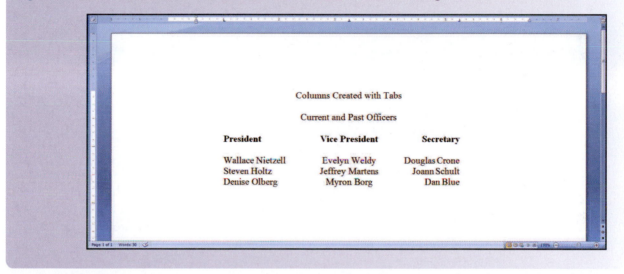

Columns Created as a Table (showing nonprinting gridlines)

Current and Past Officers		
President	Vice President	Secretary
Wallace Nietzel	Evelyn Weldy	Douglas Crone
Steve Holt	Jeffrey Martins	Joan Schult
Denise Olberg	Myron Borg	Dan Blue

Figure 7.3 Columns created as a table. Notice no gridlines and column markers on ruler bar.

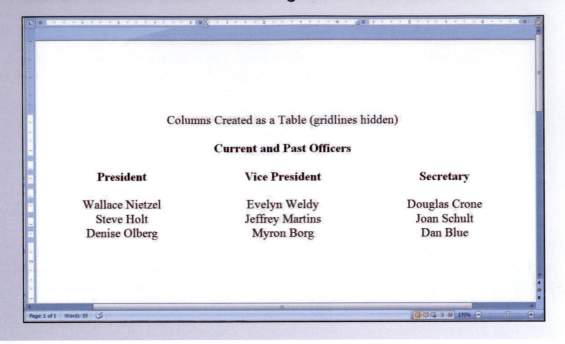

Columns Created as a Table (gridlines hidden)

Current and Past Officers

President	Vice President	Secretary
Wallace Nietzel	Evelyn Weldy	Douglas Crone
Steve Holt	Jeffrey Martins	Joan Schult
Denise Olberg	Myron Borg	Dan Blue

Automatic Line Wrapping

Sentences and paragraphs created in a word processing program should be allowed to automatically wrap to the next line. Do not press the Enter key when you get close to the right margin unless you intend for the paragraph to end and for a new one to start. By pressing the Enter key you are making what is referred to as a hard enter or a hard return. If you use a hard enter at the end of the line and later add additional words, paragraphs, or figures, the hard enter will move to an unwanted place in the middle of a line.

When you proofread a document and have the formatting key selected, verify that the hard enter/new paragraph symbol (¶) does not appear within what should be a consistent paragraph. Always question the appearance of this symbol or remove this formatting error within the document.

Spaces after Periods

What habit have you formed in spacing after a period? It probably depends on when you were learning to type. Years ago it was correct to put two spaces after the period at the end of a sentence to make the text more readable, because typewriters used monospace fonts, meaning that each letter used the same amount of space. Because proportional font is more readable and computers have proportional font size readily available, one space is more appropriate today with end-of-sentence punctuation or after a colon. *Proportional font* means that each letter takes up a different amount of space. For example, an "m" takes up more space than an "i."

Monospace font: `Courier New`

Proportional font: Times New Roman

Check whether your law office's style follows single or double spacing after punctuation and proofread for these spaces in every document. The original writer may have included inconsistencies as he or she attempted to adhere to the office style.

Lines between Items in Numbered or Bulleted Lists

Letters are usually singled spaced with double spacing (one blank line made by pressing the enter key twice) between paragraphs. Documents are generally double spaced. In double spacing, indent paragraphs to show the difference between one paragraph and another.

If you are using numbered or bulleted paragraphs in a singled spaced letter, use a double space (one blank line) between the enumerated items. See Figure 7.4 on the following page.

If you are using numbered or bulleted paragraphs in a double spaced document, you will simply enter once (spacing set on double spacing). If you are using automatic numbering or bullets, the word processing program will most likely indent the first line ½ inch. See Figure 7.5 on the following page.

The important part of all of this discussion of editing and proofreading rules is to be consistent. Make a great effort, however, to be consistently correct.

Proofreading Exercises

Use the information you learned in the previous section to complete the following exercises.

Exercise 7.10 Complete the following exercise to examine the effects of a hard enter within a document.

1. Open **C07_Ex7.10_HardEnter**.
2. Click on the "show/hide" button (¶) if it is not already selected.
3. Notice the paragraph mark (¶) at the end of each line. The person who typed this did not allow the program to automatically wrap at the right margin.
4. Insert your cursor after the end parenthesis and the period in the second line.
5. Type in this sentence:

   An organizer of a limited liability company may become but is not required to become either a member or a manager of the company.

6. Note what happened when you inserted a sentence into text previously typed where the typist "entered" at the right margin.
7. Insert your cursor after the period to the right of "holiday" in the fourth line of the third paragraph.
8. Type in this sentence:

   If it is determined that the proposed name of the new company is available and that the Articles of Organization otherwise comply with statute, you will be notified of the approval by email and provided with a link to a "filed" copy of the Articles.

9. Notice the result.
10. Correct the mistakes that allowed the inappropriate line formatting.
11. Save the corrected paragraphs as **LastName_C07_Ex7.10_HardEnter** and submit the file to your instructor.

Figure 7.4 **Example of spacing between numbered paragraphs in a letter.**

Current Date

Mr. Arnold McDougal
ABC Law
6574 Money Road
Fort Worth, TX 76052

Dear Mr. McDougal:

Re: Writing a Demand Letter

Below is a list of what we discussed during our lunch meeting on Friday. I hope our talk about writing productive demand letters will be helpful in your office.

1. Date your letter the day you write it, and send it the same day. Undated letters are difficult to reply to. I usually reply to them by saying, "This is in reply to your undated letter that I received in the mail on 24 June 20xx."

    If you are sending a fax or email, then type the time next to the date. While letters "cross in the mail" in days, faxes and emails "cross in the wires" in hours and minutes.

2. Remind your client to preserve attorney-client confidentiality. Sometimes clients show your letters to others without realizing they can lose the attorney-client privilege of that communication. Add this phrase at the top of the letter to remind them not to do this:

    CONFIDENTIAL ATTORNEY-CLIENT COMMUNICATION

    If the letter is written during or in anticipation of litigation, the following phrase can be used: DO NOT COPY OR DISCLOSE TO ANYONE ELSECONFIDENTIAL ATTORNEY-CLIENT COMMUNICATION

3. Be sure to use the recipient's correct legal name and address. Your letter may be relied upon for its accuracy, so be accurate. Verification of names can be obtained from the public records, the phone book, or the Texas Division of Corporations Web site at http://ccfcorp.dos.state.tx.us/index.html. And when it comes to middle initials, never rely on your memory or guess at it because most of the time you'll be wrong.

Please call my office if I can be of further assistance. Our legal assistant could be of help to you as well.

Sincerely,

Iris Roma
IRoma@Lotton.com

IR:yi

B. Term of Employment—At Will Employee.

1. Employer shall employ employee in the capacity set forth above commencing on 10–1–2004 (or such other date as the parties may agree to) and continuing, with no fixed termination date, until either party shall give proper notice of termination of this employment agreement to the other.

2. **No fixed contract period.** There shall be no fixed date for termination of this employment agreement and it shall continue indefinitely until either party gives proper notice to the other as required in this paragraph. Furthermore, employee specifically waives any rights he or she may or may not have under state law (such as the Model Employment Termination Act or like legislation) requiring that any and all termination of employment be "for good cause." This is an "at will" employment arrangement and, as such, no cause is required by either party for termination hereof.

3. **Notice Period.** Any party wishing to give notice of termination of this agreement, or of an intention not to renew at the end of a contract period, shall give the other party ten days advance notice. The notice period does not commence until actually received by the other party. Should state or federal law require a longer notice period, the longer notice period so required under the law shall be applicable to this contract.

4. **Method of Notice**. Notice of termination or an intention not to renew this contract shall be given in writing delivered by any method.

Exercise 7.11 Before you begin this exercise, open your word processing program and make sure the show/hide option (¶) is *not* selected. As you begin this exercise you should not be able to see the formatting or hidden symbols within the document.

1. Open **C07_Ex7.11_Spaces** and deselect the show/hide option if you have not already done so.
2. Resave the file as **LastName_C07_Ex7.11_Spaces**.
3. Put the cursor one space before "Amount" and type "Gross."
4. Put the cursor one space after the "4" in "376,399.14" and type "including interest."
5. Put the cursor one space after the final "7" in "871,026.47" and type "including interest."
6. Save the file again.
7. Look at the results.
8. Now, select the show/hide button or reveal codes (¶) to see how this paragraph was originally set up.
9. Summarize how the paragraph was originally set up and what happened when you added new material.

_____

_____

_____

_____

10. Discuss with your classmates.
11. Correct the formatting errors so that adding words does not change the format of the columns.

Exercise 7.12 Before you begin this exercise, open your word processing program and make sure the show/hide option (¶) is *not* selected. As you begin this exercise, you should not be able to see the formatting or hidden symbols within the document.

1. Open **C07_Ex7.12_Tabs**.
2. Save this file as **LastName_C07_Ex7.12_Tabs**
3. Put the cursor one space before "Amount" and type "Gross."
4. Put the cursor one space after the "4" in "376,399.14" and type "including interest."
5. Put the cursor one space after the final "7" in "871,026.47" and type "including interest."
6. Save the file again.
7. Look at the results.
8. Now, click on the show/hide button or reveal codes to see how this paragraph was set up.

9. Summarize how the paragraph was set up and what happened when you added material on the following lines.

_____

_____

_____

_____

10. Discuss with your class. Does this exercise look similar to how you corrected the file in 7.11? Write notes from your class discussion on the lines provided below.

_____

_____

_____

_____

11. Correct the formatting errors so that adding additional words does not change the format of the columns.

12. Resave the file and submit it to the instructor, if requested.

Business, Corporate, and Employment How-To Guide

When a person needs legal advice and assistance with starting a new company, he or she will typically consult an attorney who practices in the area of business law. After discussing the client's business goals, the attorney advises the client to set up the business as a specific type of company (such as a limited liability company [LLC]). The attorney and the attorney's staff will assist their new client with registering the business name; preparing and filing/recording the organizational documents required by the secretary of state or department of commerce (hereafter referred to simply as state); preparing an operating agreement, bank resolution, bylaws, actions in writing, and other resolutions of the company; as well as preparing and maintaining the company's record/minute book.

At the direction of the attorney, a legal support person will verify the availability of the business name with the state, locate the appropriate form, complete a certificate of formation or articles of organization, and file that form with the state. The legal support person may also be asked to use premade forms within the office or to create drafts of other organizational documents that the new business will need. The attorney will review the drafts of those additional documents and secure the client's signature. In addition, the client may ask the attorney to apply for and secure the necessary tax identification numbers from the state and the Internal Revenue Service.

After all documents have been completed and signed, the legal support person will assemble them in a minute or record book.

When a company or employee decides an attorney is needed to assist with business organization or employment problems, he or she will contact a lawyer, just as others do in areas such as litigation, family situations, criminal issues, and real estate matters. The legal support staff starts the relationship with a business or employment client by scheduling an appointment and completing a fact-gathering form, such as an information for new business entity sheet. Remember that these information-gathering forms can have a variety of names depending on the practice in your office. The name of the form is not important, but its purpose *is* important since the office needs to gather detailed information to assist the client.

The attorney will discuss with the client the facts needed to complete the necessary legal work. As a legal support person, you would obtain information from the office file, the attorney, and the client to create and file the initial documents. You must be organized, pay attention to the smallest details, and be analytical in your thinking so that you will be able to identify the facts needed to complete the legal documents. In addition to using forms and templates to create organizational documents for businesses, you might also prepare employment policy handbooks and employment contracts, following instructions from the attorney and client.

A legal support person assists the attorney by performing duties such as:

- Doing the online research needed to determine the availability of a business name for a new client
- Completing online forms to secure or register a business name
- Gathering information from the client and the office file to prepare initial organizational documents
- Assisting clients with maintaining company records and stock ledgers
- Scheduling and sending notices to shareholders for annual meetings
- Preparing minutes of meetings for shareholders and directors for placement in the minute book
- Drafting resolutions, waivers, minutes, approvals of actions, and related documents
- Preparing drafts of buy-sell agreements, employment agreements, promissory notes, leases, and so on
- Obtaining information and file documentation necessary to qualify a company to transact business in foreign countries

The secretary of state or department of commerce in your state regulates business creation, and commercial and financial transactions. The **secretary of state** in some states is responsible for the administration of the election laws, the Uniform Commercial Code records, and business filings. Some states have a **department of commerce**, which is an agency established within a state to regulate commercial and financial transactions. As a legal support person, you will be filing certain business documents with these offices. You will need to determine the correct location for filing documents and whether a fee is involved. The state will have an official website where you can find the information you need.

Best Practice Tip

FINDING YOUR STATE'S OFFICIAL BUSINESS WEBSITE

When you are certain that you have found the correct official business website for your state, bookmark it and any specific pages you frequently use, such as forms or fee schedules, to make your work more efficient.

Prepare Selected Documents for a Limited Liability Company

Even though multiple business organization options are available, the limited liability company (LLC) is most commonly chosen because it is inexpensive to set up and offers the owners personal protection from the company's debts and liabilities. The following discussion and projects focus on the process of creating an LLC, since that business type is so often chosen.

In starting a new business, the company must create a set of organizational documents, some of which will be provided to the state and the company's bank.

Business Name Availability The state regulates the names of businesses to avoid duplication, confusion, and unfair competition. The first step in starting a new company is to check the availability of the business name and then to register it with the state. To avoid duplication of a business name, the law office must search its official availability.

Initial Organizational Document The company must also file **articles of organization** (known in some states as a **certificate of formation**) with the state, indicating the name and address of the person or persons organizing the business and the business's legal address. This document establishes legal recognition of a limited liability company (LLC).

Local Focus 7.2

Tax Identification Numbers Applications for state and federal **tax identification numbers** will be made by the client, attorney, or client's accountant. Tax identification numbers will be used to identify the business when taxes are being paid, quarterly reports are being filed, and annual tax returns are being submitted to state and federal taxing authorities.

Operating Agreement The attorney will also prepare an **operating agreement** outlining how the business will function. The operating agreement will state the rights and duties of each member and manager, the company's period of existence, and the nature of the business.

Bank Designation The business will designate a banking institution, and the attorney will prepare a **bank resolution** indicating the name of the bank to be used for deposits and withdrawals and who has authority to make financial transactions for the business. The bank resolution will be provided to the bank.

Bylaws The business will adopt bylaws at its first official meeting. **Bylaws** are rules and regulations adopted by a corporation that govern the business's internal affairs. Bylaws are not filed with the state. They are more flexible than the articles of organization because they are easier to amend.

Actions in Writing The official decisions made by the business will be recorded in a document known as an **action in writing**. There are two types of actions in writing. One type is made by the organizer of the business and identifies the members of the business's initial board of governors. The other type is a joint action in writing, which summarizes the actions or decisions/resolutions adopted by the governing body of the business. The governing body in an LLC is known as the **members and board of governors**.

Resolutions A **resolution** is a formal business decision made by a company that is recorded in a written document describing the decision. Any time a formal business decision is made, a separate resolution document is created. Resolutions may be made, for example, for:

- Adopting a fiscal year
- Adopting a trade name
- Authorizing a contract
- Defending a legal suit
- Purchasing or leasing equipment
- Purchasing or selling real estate
- Purchasing or selling business assets

Figure 7.6 is an example of how a resolution would be formatted. The wording and formatting of a resolution depends on a particular office's style. Resolutions usually begin with the word RESOLVED followed by a description of the decision made. Additional related decisions may follow starting with the words FURTHER RESOLVED.

If several decisions are made, a business may include them all in one resolution document. These additional decisions also start with the word RESOLVED.

Business Minute/Record Book All registered businesses are required to summarize the actions taken by a corporation's board of directors or shareholders—such as information about major purchases by the corporation, hiring/firing, acquisitions, and so on—in the form of **corporate minutes**. These minutes are maintained in a **minute/record book** along with permanent and detailed records of the resolutions adopted at the official meetings of the business as well as all organizational documents. This book should be accessible to all members of the business at its registered office or legal address. The attorney and client should agree on who will be responsible for maintaining the official minute/record book. Sometimes the attorney will maintain the official record book with documents that contain original signatures and records of information. In addition, the office may also create a copy of the book for the client. When documents are created and inserted into the official record book, the legal support staff will send copies to the client.

Minute/record books are available from legal office suppliers and are generally rather expensive. As an alternative, some law offices will use a simple three-ring binder to file business documents.

Prepare an Employment Agreement with Attached Riders

Often, when a company has policies that are given to employees or has agreements that employees will sign, the company will include a section at the bottom of every page with a place for the employee's initials, a place for the initials of the company representative, and the date the policy is received by the employee or date the document is signed. This is usually placed in the footer area of the page at either the right or left margin; it may be in a smaller font size and may look like the examples in Figures 7.7 and 7.8. Add this provision to documents if instructed to do so.

If a company is involved in a competitive area of business or offers a unique service, it may enter into an employment agreement with certain types of employees, such as those hired as managers, marketing personnel, salespeople, or engineers, for example. The **employment agreement** will state the terms of employment, compensation, benefits, and termination of employment. It will also contain a rider or attachment that

Figure 7.6 **Resolution.**

FARM BUSINESS WOMEN, LIMITED LIABILITY COMPANY
RESOLUTION AUTHORIZING LAND RECLAMATION APPLICATION

I, Annie N. Schleicher, President of Farm Business Women, Limited Liability Company

(hereinafter referred to as LLC), organized and existing under the laws of Nebraska and having

its principal place of business at 8826 Trenton Avenue, Omaha, NE 76334, hereby certify that

this resolution was adopted by the Farm Business Women, LLC, Board of Directors at a meeting

held on June 13, 20xx, at which a voting quorum existed and was maintained throughout and that

the resolution adopted at that meeting was voted, recorded, and is now in full effect, according to

the charter, provisions, and bylaws of the Farm Business Women, LLC.

RESOLVED: That the Farm Business Women, LLC, approves the Land Reclamation
Application as submitted, or to be submitted, to the office of Omaha City Services;

RESOLVED: That the Treasurer of the Farm Business Women, LLC, is hereby
empowered to sign any forms or contracts on behalf of the LLC for the Land
Reclamation Application;

RESOLVED: That the Farm Business Women, LLC, Board of Directors are hereby
directed to certify that this resolution has been duly voted, approved, and adopted, is in
full force, and is in compliance with the charter and bylaws of the Farm Business
Women, LLC.

I further attest that this Limited Liability Company is legally registered and that it is

empowered by and through bylaws to take such actions as are called for by this stated resolution.

DIRECTORS:

_____	_____
President	Date
_____	_____
Vice President	Date
_____	_____
Secretary	Date
_____	_____
Treasurer	Date

Witness my application of the seal of this LLC on this

_____ day of _____, _____.

details the duties and responsibilities of the employee. A **rider** is an attachment to a
document stating additional terms or conditions related to the document.

Another rider would be a **noncompetition agreement** that restricts the
employee's work activities after termination of employment with the company and
protects the company's trade secrets, client lists, and other confidential matters

Figure 7.7 **Example of left margin placement.**

Employee's initials: _____
Company's initials: _____
Date: _____

Figure 7.8 **Example of right margin placement.**

Employee's initials: _____
Company's initials: _____
Date: _____

pertaining to the company. After termination of employment, the employee may be restricted in the type of business he or she may work in for a certain period and within the geographic area in which the company does business. Additional compensation must be provided to the employee in exchange for these restrictions.

Legal support staff make revisions in documents such as employment policy handbooks. Clients will sometimes ask the attorney to suggest different options to be considered in setting company policy. Commonly, you will be asked several times to make changes as the attorney and the client discuss the wording of these policies. They may also want to save each version so that they can easily be compared and the similarities and difference among the ideas can readily be seen.

Employment Policy Handbook Changes and Paid Time Off Calculations

For businesses to operate efficiently, they need to have guidelines for their administrators and employees that explain the policies and procedures of the company. This is accomplished by the use of an employment policy handbook. Some topics covered in

It is important that you understand and carefully follow directions and requests from your employer and clients. In situations where multiple revisions will be made to a document, focus only on the version on which you are working at the moment. Make sure you are revising the correct document. Clearly name the revised document so that you can easily identify it later and distinguish it from previous versions. Keep the many documents you work on organized in your word processing program by using subfolders with names you will easily recognize.

this handbook would be **paid time off (PTO)**, which might include vacation time and sick days, personal leave days, holidays, working hours, and overtime. Some businesses provide separate amounts of time off for vacation time, sick leave, and personal leave. Other businesses may group these items into one category called paid time off, or PTO.

When a business creates company policies regarding PTO, its managers may not know what type of calculation best suits the company's goals. Also, businesses sometimes reevaluate their policies and may want to change a PTO policy. The company may want to see different calculations before deciding which method to use for its PTO policy. It is important that a legal support person understand how to calculate PTO in different ways. The legal support person may be asked to create several scenarios of PTO for a company to review.

PTO can be calculated in different ways, such as a certain number of hours per pay period or a certain number of days or weeks per year. A business may decide to change how it calculates PTO after its current policy has been in place for some time. A standard workday is 8 hours long; a standard work week is 5 days, so a typical worker will put in 40 hours of work each week. The following examples present PTO calculations for various scenarios.

PTO Example 1 If an employee receives 80 hours of PTO, the equivalent number of days of PTO would be 10 days.

> 80 hours of PTO/8 hours per day = 10 days of PTO

Calculate an answer to the following situation based on Example 1. Write your answer on the line provided.

> If an employee receives 24 hours of PTO, the equivalent number of days of PTO would be _____ days.

PTO Example 2 If an employee receives 90 hours of PTO, the equivalent number of days of PTO would be 11 days plus 2 hours.

> 90/8 = 11 days plus 2 hours
>
> Math: 90 PTO hours divided by 8 hours per day = 11 days with a remainder of 2 hours.

Calculate an answer to the following situation based on Example 2. Write your answer on the line provided.

> If an employee receives 39 hours of PTO, the equivalent number of days of PTO would be _____ days.

PTO Example 3 If an employee receives one PTO day for each full calendar month worked, and the employee starts working for the company on March 15, the employee would receive 9 days of PTO for the remainder of the year (April through December = 9 months). The equivalent hours for 9 days is 72 hours. (9 × 8 = 72)

Calculate an answer to the following situation based on Example 3. Write your answer on the line provided.

> If an employee receives two PTO days for each full calendar month worked and the employee starts working for the company on September 8, how many days of PTO will the employee receive and what is the equivalent number of hours for those days? _____

Answer for PTO Example 1: 24/8 = 3 days

Answer for PTO Example 2: 39/8 = 4 days plus 7 hours

Answer for PTO Example 3: 6 days. Equivalent hours = 48. Explanation: No PTO for September. PTO given for October, November, and December. 2 days × 3 months = 6 days × 8 hours a day = 48 hours

---

BASIC EQUATIONS

Here are two basic equations that can be applied to any PTO calculation. Keep these formulas handy in your computer in a reference folder or on piece of paper posted in a convenient location near your work area.

Days to Hours:
Days × hours in a workday = number of total hours of PTO available

Hours to Days:
PTO hours / hours in a workday = number of PTO days available

How-To Guide Exercises

Use the information you learned in the previous section to complete the following exercises.

Exercise 7.13 Practice applying for a business name by completing the following activity. You will need to locate your secretary of state or department of commerce official website before you begin this activity. Write the URL that you locate on the following line.

_____

1. Assume that you are considering starting your own business in your state.
2. Make up a name that you might consider using.
3. Research the name on your secretary of state or department of commerce official website. Be sure to check inactive records. Find out if other companies are using that name.
4. If there are other companies, change the name a bit until you find one that is not being used.

5. Summarize your process and results in a document and save the document as **LastName_C07_Ex7.13_BusNameResearch**.

6. Discuss the process with your classmates and submit your work to the instructor.

Exercise 7.14 Now that you have experience with PTO conversions, answer the following questions. Write your answers on the lines provided. Share your answers with your class and discuss how you arrived at each answer.

1. How many hours are equivalent to 17 days? _____

2. How many days are equivalent to 256 hours? _____

3. How many hours are equivalent to 6 ½ days? _____

4. How many days are equivalent to 184 hours? _____

Critical Thinking: Professional Communications

Professional communication is important when you working in a legal office or business setting. Generally, law offices are formal. Communication can be written and spoken. This textbook focuses on written communication. However, a legal support person should also be aware of and practice professional oral communication in addressing attorneys, clients, judges, other court personnel, and business contacts in general.

Addressing People

Regardless of whether you would address the attorney by his or her first name in other settings, when you are speaking to others outside the office, always refer to attorneys using Mr., Mrs., Ms., or Attorney with his or her last name.

> Attorney Smith has asked me to call and reschedule your appointment.

> Ms. Smith would like to meet with Attorney Simpson on Friday to discuss settlement.

Best Practice Tip

COMMUNICATING EFFECTIVELY

Consider the following tips to be a more professional speaker while on the job:
- If necessary, think about and organize your thoughts before speaking with another person. Make notes if necessary.
- Enunciate clearly and avoid speaking too fast.
- Before speaking with someone or answering the telephone, put a smile on your face. Even if you are not feeling cheerful, a smile will be reflected in the tone of your voice.
- Always answer the phone by greeting the caller and introducing yourself.
- When leaving voicemail messages, state who you are, include why you are calling, and leave a contact number.
- Do not eat or chew gum when you are speaking on the phone or in person.
- Keep social conversations with other employees to a minimum to avoid distracting and annoying your coworkers.
- Know your office policies regarding the use of personal cell phones and office email.

In speaking to court personnel, you will usually become familiar enough with them to address them by their first names. However, judges are always addressed as Your Honor or referred to as Judge and his or her last name.

Good morning, Your Honor.

May I speak with Judge Goldstein's clerk?

In speaking to attorneys (both internal and external), address them using Mr., Mrs., or Ms. with his or her last name. Diverge from this only if the attorney asks that you address him or her by a different title or by his or her first name.

Address a client using Mr., Mrs., or Ms. with his or her last name. Diverge from this only if the client asks that you to refer to him or her by first name.

Although it may vary from office to office, it is typical for peers within the office to address each other by first names.

Communicating by Email

Email is the common informal means of communication in offices of any kind. Although email is informal, it is still necessary to write complete sentences with proper grammar, punctuation, and spelling. Do not use the abbreviations commonly employed in texting.

Even though email is not yet an acceptable method of delivering court documents for filing purposes, it is acceptable in some instances and at the request of the court to provide proposed orders or other documents that the court may use parts of in issuing an order. Remember to check your local preferences and court rules before assuming that email is an acceptable method of delivering/filing documents.

In addition, many court personnel do not feel that email is confidential enough to be used for correspondence. Legal support staff and court personnel generally communicate by telephone, fax, or written communications.

Email Etiquette Be certain that you know to whom your email will be sent before sending the message. It is not uncommon for unintended recipients to receive messages that were sent by the "Reply All" button. Most offices do not want

---

Best Practice Tip

SEND A TEXT MESSAGE BY EMAIL

The support person may be asked to send brief messages to the clients, attorneys, and others who may be away from their computers. Although you can send text messages using a cell phone, most legal support staff work at their desks throughout the day and have quicker access to the computer. To send text messages from a computer, you will need to know the recipient's 10-digit cell phone number and the cell service carrier's email format. The email format is easily found by searching the Internet for "How to send a text message by email." Here is an example:

- Your customer's cell phone number is 999-555-1092.
- The customer's cell carrier is Cellphone Wireless, as an example.
- A search of the Internet shows that Cellphone Wireless's carrier email is @cwire.emcp.net.
- In your email program, send a message to 9995551092@cwire.emcp.net.

Try this yourself by sending an email message to your own cell phone or the phone of a friend by locating the carrier email format for the wireless carrier on the Internet. Because there is usually a 160-character limit, this method works well for short messages.

employees replying to all in an extended email conversation. For example, the human resources department may send an employment policy email to all employees. Do not use "Reply All" when you are asking a question about the policy.

Forwarding messages can also be a concern in the office. Although many people would not question forwarding information in a personal email account, emails sent in an office setting can be confidential. It is important to know the company's policy on forwarding messages and to obtain the original sender's permission to forward an email to other recipients. Other issues to consider in using email for professional reasons include these:

- Always check that necessary attachments are included before you send the message.
- Avoid using all capital letters (all caps) in the message of an email. All caps may be interpreted as shouting. The use of all caps in a message should be done only when it is deemed appropriate and necessary.

Be certain that you also know your company's policy regarding the use of office email for personal reasons. Remember that your email at work is not private. It belongs to the company for company business.

Prompt Responses People tend to expect instant responses when texting; however, it is unrealistic to assume that an email message sent to others will be read soon after you have sent it. The recipient may be in a meeting or not able to read the message immediately. If you need a quick response to your email, it is a good practice to phone the other person or his or her office and mention that you sent a time-sensitive email. By making that call, you will alert the recipient or office staff of the fact that a prompt response is requested.

When you receive emails, do your best to respond promptly to any request. If you are unable to respond when you receive a request, consider flagging the email so that you will not overlook it once you do have time.

Make an appropriate automatic "out-of-office" reply in your email program if you know you will be unable to reply or will be out of the office for a period of time.

> I will be out of the office until Thursday, April 15, 20xx. I will respond to your message when I return. If you need immediate assistance, please contact Janice Miller at JMiller@jlslaw.emcp.com or 555-555-1111.

or

> I have received your email. I am currently working against a deadline and will respond to your message this afternoon or tomorrow by 3 p.m. If you need immediate assistant, please contact Janice Miller at JMiller@jlslaw.emcp.com or 555-555-1111.

Diversity and Biases

Attorneys and support staff working in any area of law must have good people skills to establish relationships of trust and confidence with their clients. Many different people will seek the services of your law office or business for various reasons. Whether you are working in a law office or in another type of business, it is crucial that you be mindful of diversity. It is wise for you to educate yourself about the differences and various customs among others to which you may not normally be exposed.

Cultural diversity is an area that can cause communication difficulties. Some things you should be aware of are the amount of physical space to maintain between yourself and the person with whom you are speaking, the amount of eye contact that is appropriate, whether it is permissible to shake hands, and the role that gender can play in communication. For example, a male from some cultures may not be able or willing to answer questions presented by a woman, or a woman may not be allowed in a room alone with a man who is not her relative.

Diversity includes not only cultural customs but also variety in many other human characteristics. Sometimes we are not aware of biases that we may have formed throughout our lives. Bias against others can be found in many areas, including

- gender
- race
- religion
- age
- sexual orientation

Be consistent in how you treat others. Everyone appreciates being treated with respect and as an individual. Keep an open mind and do not form an opinion about an individual because of his or her race or culture.

Critical Thinking Exercises

Complete the following exercises to practice the skills discussed in the previous section.

Exercise 7.15 Choose a culture that is different from your own and research its business and social communication customs and rules. Use these websites to begin your research, but locate other websites, if necessary.

 http://lep.emcp.net/worldbusiness
 http://lep.emcp.net/cyborlink
 Discuss your findings with your classmates.

Exercise 7.16 Review the email shown in Figure 7.9 and highlight on the page any potential problems you find. When you are finished, rewrite the email using professional communication and save it as **LastName_C07_Ex7.16_EmailRevision**. Submit the file to your instructor.

Exercise 7.17 Review the email shown in Figure 7.10 and highlight on the page any potential problems you find. When you are finished, rewrite the email using professional communication and save it as **LastName_C07_Ex7.17_EmailRevision**. Submit the file to your instructor.

Figure 7.9 **Email example.**

To: Jim Parson (client)
From: Legal Support Person
Re: Inquiry for Attorney Barbara Michaels

Hey Jim!
I hear that you had asked Barbie if she was available to work with you on creating an LLC. That's great news! Making your company an LLC will really help your checkbook! She asked me to get some information from you so she could prepare for the meeting (you know, like your current address, your full name, etc.). Shoot me an email when you have a sec and I'll send you the required paperwork to fill out.

Take care!
xoxo,
Legal Support

Figure 7.10 **Email example.**

To: Jordan, Leone & Sanchez (company)
From: Legal Support Person
Re:Re:Re:Re: FW: RE: EMPLOYMENT POLICY

DEAR HUMAN RESOURCES,
WHY ARE WE CHANGING SECTION 2 (THE VACATION SECTION) OF THE EMPLOYMENT POLICY? HAS ANYONE DONE ANYTHING TO VIOLATE THIS RULE? PLEASE LET ME KNOW ASAP AS I'M PLANNING A VACTION FOR NEXT MONTH.
THANKS,
LEGAL SUPPORT

Chapter Summary and Projects

Summary

You have now reviewed procedures that are important to legal support staff in assisting the attorney with client communications and gathering information from clients necessary to prepare, file, and maintain documents for the client's business.

You have also reviewed and practiced applying language, editing, proofreading, and critical thinking skills to legal documents; learned new legal terms; practiced finding official websites for the secretary of state or department of commerce; and worked with document forms and templates to create business documents. You have learned new ways to carry out professional communications with clients, coworkers, and other legal professionals as well as the importance of understanding cultural differences in the workplace.

Remember that as a legal support person, it will likely be your responsibility in a business, corporate, or employment law case to complete the following tasks:

- find and bookmark the appropriate state business website
- prepare business organization documents
- edit and proofread business organization documents
- communicate professionally with clients, coworkers, and other legal professionals

Key Terms

action in writing, 225
adjectives, 205
adverbs, 207
articles of organization, 225
bank resolution, 225
business entity, 202
business law, 201
buzzwords, 212
bylaws, 225
certificate of formation, 225
colloquialisms, 213
comparative form, 206
corporate law, 202
corporate minutes, 226
corporation, 203
department of commerce, 224
employment agreement, 226
employment law, 205

idioms, 212
limited liability company (LLC), 203
limited liability partnership (LLP), 203
members and board of governors, 225
minute/record book, 226
noncompetition agreement, 227
operating agreement, 225
paid time off (PTO), 229
partnership, 203
positive form, 206
redundancies, 212
resolution, 226
rider, 227
secretary of state, 224
sole proprietorship, 202
superlative form, 206
tax identification numbers, 225

Local Focus Research

Locate the Chapter 7 folder in your electronic storage medium and open the local focus file **C07_LocalFocus_BusinessCorporateEmployment**. Resave the file as **LastName_C07_LocalFocus_BusinessCorporateEmployment**. Research the following topics and record your research in the file that you just created. Use this information as a reference tool as you start and continue your career as a legal support staff member. Your instructor may ask you to submit a copy as homework.

Local Focus 7.1   On page 224, you learned that it is often the legal support person's job to look up and obtain information from the state's official business website. You are familiar with locating official court websites on the Internet from your research work in previous chapters. The following exercise will aid you in finding information you will need to file documents. Remember that filing requirements may differ from state to state.

1. Find your state's official business website to determine where to file business documents and what fees are required. For future reference, bookmark the URL and document it here. _____

2. Research and record the following information for your state.
   A. Name of your state. _____
   B. What is the official website address for your state's secretary of state or department of commerce?
   _____
   C. Where are business documents filed when starting a new business?
   _____
   D. What fees are due for the filing of documents?
   _____

3. Research and record the following information for a bordering state. Discuss with your classmates the differences in requirements compared to those in your own state.
   A. Name of state. _____
   B. What is the official website address for the state's secretary of state or department of commerce?
   _____
   C. Where are business documents filed when a new business is being started? _____
   D. What fees are due for the filing of documents?
   _____

Local Focus 7.2 Page 225 discusses articles of organization and certificate of formation. These names differ from state to state. Return to your state's official business website and determine whether your state requires articles of organization or a certificate of formation. Write the name that is used on the line provided:

_____

Local Focus 7.3 Identify the three most prevalent ethnic cultures in your local area. List these prevalent cultures on the following lines.

_____

_____

Choose a culture that is not your own and research its communication customs and rules. Discuss your findings with your classmates.

Scenario

You have made a career change from working in a law office to working in the legal department of a large corporation. You have relocated from the law office of Jordan, Leone & Sanchez, PLLP, and now work for the legal department of Lotton Corporation in its home office at 21B Highway 87, Galveston, TX 77658. Lotton Corporation is opening a new subsidiary, Luxury Limo LLC, which will be located in Crystal Beach, Texas. Luxury Limo will manage the leasing of vehicles to serve the transportation needs of Lotton Corporation's many executives and large sales force. Your supervising attorney, Iris Roma, will be out of the office for two weeks at a trade convention. Ms. Roma left you the following memo with instructions for completing your assignments.

Project 1   Task List

Read the memo in Figure 7.11 and make a list of the tasks you have been asked to complete. Save your task list as **LastName_C07_P1_TaskList** and submit your list to the instructor.

Project 2   New Business Entity

In her memo to you, Attorney Roma instructed you to review the information for a new business entity form, which is in the forms for new business entity folder within the Luxury Limo folder (C07_P2_P3_P4_InfoForNewBusEntity), and to prepare the following documents for a limited liability company. The Luxury Limo folder referenced in her email can be found in the Chapter 07 folder on your storage medium.

Figure 7.11 **Memo from Attorney Roma**

INTEROFFICE MEMO

TO: LEGAL SUPPORT
FROM: ATTORNEY IRIS ROMA
RE: NEW BUSINESS ENTITY

Hello,

Welcome to your new job at Lotton's home office. I hope you are getting settled in your new home after moving here from Michigan. If you need any help finding your way around town or finding local resources, please talk to Joe in our Human Resources Department.

I am sorry I am not here for your first day with our company. I will be out of town for two weeks at a trade convention. While I am gone, I would like you to work on a few things so that they will be ready for my review when I return to the office.

Lotton Corp. is starting a new business entity which will be located at 2800 West Fourth Avenue, Crystal Beach, Texas 77650. The name of the new company will be Luxury Limo LLC. This new company will manage the leasing of vehicles for our executives and sales force. I have already completed the form containing information for the new business entity.

Open the client folder entitled "Luxury Limo." There are subfolders within that main folder entitled "New entity setup forms" and "Employment policies." The fillable form documents you will need are saved in those subfolders.

Review the document that contains the info for new business entities within the Luxury Limo folder (C07_P2_P3_P4_InfoForNewBusEntity). Using the forms provided, prepare the following: (1) Certificate of Formation, (2) Action in Writing by Sole Organizer, (3) Joint Action in Writing of Members and Board of Governors, and (3) Bank Resolution. You can find fillable forms for those documents on your computer in the folder entitled "forms for new business entity."

We will eventually create an employment policy handbook for Luxury Limo LLC. On your computer, you will also find a document entitled "C07_Bus_EmplPol_Sec2,3_original." Use that file when working on the employment policies.

George Sanchez is the contact person at the new company. I have already sent him my original draft of Section 2 (Working Hours) and Section 3 (Benefits). He is going to review those sections and contact you with suggested changes. He may make multiple suggestions or change his mind. You can make the changes he suggests but save each new revision with an added "update 1, update 2," etc., at the end of each new file and add your last name to the start of each file so I will know which documents to review. When I return, I will review these files, discuss his ideas with him, and we will decide on a final policy.

Please save the drafts of all the documents you create in the subfolder entitled "Drafts Of Documents Prepared by Assistant."

Here is what I have set up and what you will see on your computer:

Main folder: LUXURY LIMO

        Subfolder: FORMS FOR NEW BUSINESS ENTITY
            Form documents: Certificate of Formation
                               Action in Writing by Sole Organizer
                               Joint Action in Writing
                               Bank Resolution
                               Information for New Business Entity

        Subfolder: EMPLOYMENT POLICIES AND DOCUMENTS
            Document: Employment Policies_Sections 2,3_original
                               Employment Agreement with attached Riders

        Subfolder: DRAFTS OF DOCUMENTS PREPARED BY ASSISTANT

Thanks for your help. I will see you in a couple of weeks and we can review the work you have done in my absence.

Iris Roma

Part A Using the available resources, create a certificate of formation for Luxury Limo.

1. Locate and open the certificate of formation file called **C07_P2A_CertForm** from the Luxury Limo folder.
2. Resave the file as **LastName_C07_P2A_CertForm**.
3. Review the information for a new business entity form and complete the certificate.
4. Resave the file and place it in the appropriate folder.
5. Submit the file to the instructor.

Part B Using the available resources, create an action in writing by the sole organizers of an LLC for Luxury Limo.

1. Locate and open the action in writing by the sole organizer of an LLC file named **C07_P2B_ActionInWritingOrg**.
2. Resave the file as **LastName_C07_P2B_ActionInWritingOrg**.
3. Review the information for a new business entity form and complete the document.
4. Resave the file and place it in the appropriate folder.
5. Submit the file to the instructor.

Part C Using the available resources, create a joint action in writing of the members and board of governors of an LLC for the Luxury Limo company.

1. Locate and open the joint action in writing of the members and board of governors of an LLC saved as **C07_P2C_JointActionMembers**.
2. Resave the file as **LastName_C07_P2C_JointActionMembers**.
3. Review the information for a new business entity form and complete the joint action in writing of the members document.
4. Resave the file and place it in the appropriate folder.
5. Submit the file to the instructor.

Part D Using the available resources, create a bank resolution for Luxury Limo.

1. Locate and open the bank resolution named **C07_P2D_BankRes**.
2. Resave the file as **LastName_C07_P2D_BankRes**.
3. Review the information for new business entity form and complete the document.
4. Resave the file and place it in the appropriate folder.
5. Submit the file to the instructor.

Project 3   Revising Employment Policy Documents

Iris Roma previously sent sections of an employment policy handbook to George Sanchez, chief manager/president of Luxury Limo, for his review and comment.

Part A Mr. Sanchez has asked you to make changes to the benefits section of the employment policy handbook. His first email to you is shown in Figure 7.12.

Figure 7.12 **First email from George Sanchez regarding the original draft of the employment policy handbook.**

Email

TO: LEGAL SUPPORT
FROM: GEORGE SANCHEZ, CHIEF MANAGER/PRESIDENT
RE: ORIGINAL DRAFT OF BENEFITS POLICY

Hello,

I reviewed the original draft of the benefits section of the employment policy you sent. Please make the following changes and send it back to me for further review. Rather than using track changes for the revisions, I would like revisions to be saved as new documents so I can review each draft separately.

- Add this language at the end of the first sentence on 3.A. Policy: "Every employee has a 'fund' of time to use for vacation, sick, and personal reasons based on eligible years of service with Luxury Limo LLC. This fund is referred to as 'Paid Time Off' or PTO. PTO does not include designated paid holidays. Holiday benefit time is given to employees in addition to PTO."

- Change "Vacation" to "Paid Time Off" in 3A; 3.A.1; 3.A.2; 3.A.3; 3.A.4; 3.A.5;

- 3.A.1.a.: Change the terminology referring to week(s) to read ___ hours / ___ days. Please do the conversion of weeks to hours/days.

- 3.A.4.: after half-day, add (4 hours); after full-day add (8 hours).

Thanks,
George

---

1. Locate and open **C07_P3_EmplPol_Sec2,3_orig**.
2. Resave the document as **LastName_C07_P3A_EmplPol_Sec2,3_update1**.
3. Review the email from Mr. Sanchez in Figure 7.12 and make the requested changes to the specific parts of the benefits section within the employment policy.
4. Resave the file and place it in the appropriate folder.
5. Submit the file to the instructor.

Part B After you completed the first update to the benefits section of the employee policy handbook, Mr. Sanchez sends you another email with further requests for sections 2 and 3. Read the email in Figure 7.13.

1. Open **LastName_C07_P3A_EmplPol_Sec2,3_update1**, which you created in Part A.

Figure 7.13 Second email to you from George Sanchez regarding update #1.

TO:	LEGAL SUPPORT
FROM:	GEORGE SANCHEZ, CHIEF MANAGER/PRESIDENT
RE:	EMPLOYMENT POLICY: REVIEW OF UPDATE 1

Hello,

I reviewed the first update of the benefits policy you sent. I would like to make a different PTO schedule for 3.A.1.a. The revised policy should read as follows:

Procedure

During an employee's first calendar year of employment, the employee is eligible for one PTO day for each *full calendar month* worked for the remainder of the year. For example, employees hired in January will receive eleven (11) days of PTO while those hired in August will receive four (4) days of PTO. For the second through fourth calendar years of employment, employees are eligible for seventeen (17) days each year. In January of their fifth calendar year, employee balances are increased to twenty-two (22) days per year. Balances continue to be increased at various intervals of service, as shown in the chart below.

Years of Service	PTO Days
First calendar year	Prorated (one day for each full month worked)
Years 2 through 4	17 days
Years 5 through 14	22 days
Years 15 through 24	27 days
Year 25	32 days

Everything else in the document can stay the same. Please make the changes and send it back to me for further review.

Thanks,
George

2. Resave the file as **LastName_C07_P3B_EmplPol_Sec2,3_update2**.

3. Review the email from Mr. Sanchez in Figure 7.13 and make the changes to the specific parts of the benefits policy.

4. Resave the file and place it in the appropriate folder.

5. Submit the file to the instructor.

Part C After you have completed the second update to the benefits section of the employee policy handbook, Mr. Sanchez sends you another email with further requests for sections 2 and 3. Review the requests from the email in Figure 7.14.

1. Open **C07_P3B_EmplPol_Sec2,3_update2,** which you created in Part B.

Figure 7.14 Third email message to you from George Sanchez regarding Update #2.

TO: LEGAL SUPPORT
FROM: GEORGE SANCHEZ, CHIEF MANAGER/PRESIDENT
RE: EMPLOYMENT POLICY: REVIEW OF UPDATE 2

I reviewed the second update of the benefits policy you sent. I apologize for changing my mind so often. We are trying to create a policy that will be convenient for the employees and easy for us to manage.

We want to change the language to allow the employees to use PTO in one-hour increments.

Please keep the same PTO chart as in version 3, but add to each category the number of hours that are equivalent to the days.

Please make the changes and send it back to me.

I think this is the last change we will make. The partners will discuss all versions of the PTO policy and meet with Iris when she gets back from the convention.

I think we better add some paid holidays. Please insert that as the next section of the handbook.

6   Holidays

The following days are observed as paid holidays by full-time employees: New Year's Day, Memorial Day, Independence Day, Labor Day, Thanksgiving, and Christmas.

Thanks for all your help.

2. Resave as **LastName_C07_P3C_EmplPol_Sec2,3_update3**.

3. Review the following email from Mr. Sanchez and make the required changes to the specific parts of the benefits policy.

4. Resave the file and place it in the appropriate folder.

5. Submit the file to the instructor.

Project 4   Employment Agreement with Job Description and Noncompetition Agreement Riders

Read the email message in Figure 7.15 to you from George Sanchez of Luxury Limo LLC asking you to prepare a draft of an employment agreement with job description and noncompetition agreement riders for a future employee so he can review it with Attorney Iris Roma when she returns from the trade convention.

1. Locate and open **C07_P4_EmplAg**.

2. Resave the file as **LastName_C07_P4_EmplAg**.

3. Review the email from Mr. Sanchez and create the document.

4. Resave the file and place it in the appropriate folder.

5. Submit the file to the instructor.

Project 5   Probationary Letter

Attorney Roma is the chairperson of the personnel committee at Lotton Corporation. The committee reviews employee performance and makes recommendations for improving work efficiency. Employee Alton Schmidt was reprimanded last week for excessive personal use of company computer equipment. The personnel committee met and decided on probationary terms for Mr. Schmidt. You typed a letter to him stating the probationary terms.

1. Open **C07_P5_ProbLtr**.

2. Resave the file as **LastName_C07_P5_ProbLtr**.

3. Proofread and edit the letter correcting the errors on the computer screen.

4. Resave your corrections and submit the file to the instructor.

Discuss the Projects

Consider the projects you have just completed. Commonly, forms provided by courts or governmental agencies do contain instructions for completion and further handling of the actual form. However, once you have successfully completed this form, you have much more to do to finalize the task, such as getting signatures, photocopying, and mailing. Discuss with your classmates other tasks you must do related to the projects you just completed.

TO: LEGAL SUPPORT
FROM: GEORGE SANCHEZ, CHIEF MANAGER/PRESIDENT
RE: EMPLOYMENT AGREEMENT

Hello,

Thanks for all your help in making changes to the employment policies.

Would you have time to create an employment agreement (and the two riders that are attached to it) that I can use for someone I will be hiring soon? I know Iris has a form someplace that she uses. I will give you the pertinent information in this message, and all other provisions in the form can remain as they are. Please draft this so I can review it with Iris when she returns from the convention.

Here is some of the information you will need:

Terms of employment:
Employee: John Street.
Effective date: February 15, 2011.
Job title: Senior leasing manager.
Annual compensation: $68,000, payable monthly.
Noncompete: $1,000 per year, paid in January.
Holidays: I don't recall exactly what we decided; please look back at the last version we did of the employment handbook.
Retirement plan: We need to address this policy later.
Transportation: He will be provided with a new vehicle every two years and all expenses of insurance, gas, and repairs will be paid by the company.
Termination notice: Four weeks written notice by either party.
Notices: All notices should be sent by mail to the residence address of the employee and to the Crystal Beach office.
Arbitration: We can get a judge from Galveston to appoint an arbitrator if we can't agree on one.

Rider 1: Complete as much as you can with the information I gave you. I still need to create a job description. I will give that to you when I meet with Iris in a few weeks.

Rider 2: Noncompetition Agreement
Luxury Limo LLC provides vehicle leasing and limousine services.
Compensation: $1,000 per year.
Term of noncompete after leaving employment and for trade secrets: for two years.
Radius: within 100 miles of Galveston or Crystal Beach.
I will sign on behalf of the company.
I would like one witness for the signatures.
Please make a small line at the bottom right corner of each page for the initials of each person signing the agreement, plus a line under that for the date of the agreement.

Thanks,
George Sanchez

Estate Planning and Probate

Chapter Objectives

- Compare estate planning options available
- Review requirements of wills and codicils
- Review requirements of trusts
- Review requirements of health care directives
- Review probate procedures
- Edit and proofread wills, codicils, trusts, health care directives, and probate documents

Dirk Meising has worked for three years as a legal support person in the estate planning and probate division of the Westveer, Pate, Walsh & Hamilton Law Office in Billings, Montana. Dirk's double major in legal assisting and accounting has prepared him for an interesting and challenging career. Working at Westveer, Pate, Walsh & Hamilton has allowed him to combine his knowledge of accounting and his desire to help people. This week he and Mr. Westveer are meeting with the parents of two young children who would like to finalize their own wills. Another client, Tobias Hobson, is coming to the office this afternoon to review his brother's will and start the probate process. Tomorrow morning Mr. Westveer has an appointment with Leon LeDoux, who is contesting his father's will because Leon believes that his stepbrothers are receiving more than their share of their father's estate.

Estate Planning

Estate planning is a set of procedures intended to manage an individual's assets in the event of incapacitation or death, including the giving of assets to heirs and the settlement of estate taxes. **Heirs** are the persons who are entitled by law to the estate if the decedent died without a valid will; they may include a surviving spouse, children, and possibly more remote descendants. Most estate plans are set up with the help of an attorney experienced in estate planning law. The reasons for estate planning include protecting assets from taxes, making sure that survivors are properly cared for, and establishing a wealth-management plan.

Estate planning procedures include:

- Creating a will
- Setting up trust accounts in the name of beneficiaries
- Establishing a guardian for living dependents
- Naming an executor or personal representative of the estate
- Creating plans such as life insurance, IRAs, and 401(k)s
- Updating beneficiaries on plans when life circumstances change
- Planning funeral arrangements
- Establishing annual gifting to reduce the taxable estate
- Setting up durable power of attorney (POA) to direct other assets and investments

Wills

A **will** (or **last will and testament**) is a document spelling out what is to be done with a person's assets after he or she has died. This document has no force while the person is alive and may be altered or revoked at any time. The will becomes applicable at the time of the person's death and applies to the estate as it is at the time of death. *Last will and testament* is a fancy and redundant way of saying "will." Attorneys continue to use *last will and testament* because they and clients like the formal sound of the words. The words *will* and *testament* mean the same thing. A document will be the "last" will if the maker of it dies before writing another one. Creating or making a will usually does not cross young people's minds until they are married and/or have children. If parents were to die with minor children and no will, the court would decide where the children would live and who would care for them. Parents usually want to be the ones who decide these important details, and a will is the legal document through which to make those decisions.

When a person dies and has completed a valid will, he or she is said to have died **testate**. The term **intestate** describes a situation where a person dies without a will. As mentioned previously, this can cause problems if the decedent has children and there is no other surviving parent. Dying without a will can also cause issues if the decedent has considerable assets. When a person dies intestate, the courts will apply statutes intended to pass property and other assets on to legal heirs. The court will also appoint a guardian for minor children. This may be a problem when the legal heirs or appointed guardians are not those whom the decedent would have chosen.

Best Practice Tip

CAPITALIZATION

"Last Will and testament" may be the title used on the official document; however, in other estate planning documents and legal communications, the term *will* (used as a noun) is used as a shortened form of "last will and testament." Because the English language also uses *will* as a helping verb, this shortened term for Last Will and Testament can cause confusion when reading. To avoid the confusion, some legal support persons capitalize the word *will* when it means last will and testament. ("Will" is not capitalized in this text because of the number of times it is used.)

Historically, a man referred to in a will has been called the **testator** and a woman referred to in a will has been called the **testatrix**. Since modern legal writers have accepted the use of testator as referring to either a man or a woman, the word *testatrix* has become obsolete. However, you will still see this term in some places.

The testator of a will also chooses an executor or personal representative. An **executor** is the person responsible for carrying out the directions in a will. In some states this person is called the **personal representative**, who has the same responsibilities as the executor. Traditionally, the term *executor* has referred to a man and *executrix* to a woman. Similar to the use of the term *testator*, modern legal writers are moving toward using *executor* to refer to either a man or a woman chosen to carry out the directions of a will. The executor/personal representative is a fiduciary in the management of an estate. A **fiduciary** is a person who has been chosen by another to make financial decisions on behalf of that person.

Wills can be prepared by an attorney in a typewritten format, meaning that the testator signs in front of the attorney, witnesses, and in many states, a notary public. Some states recognize **handwritten wills** (also called **holographic wills**), which are written in the testator's handwriting. Handwritten wills are not prepared by attorneys and are simply signed by the testator and witnesses if required by the state. Even though handwritten wills may not meet the guidelines of a standard will, most states do allow a person's wishes to be considered when this type of will is the only one available. If the will is in handwriting and can be verified, it is admissible in a court of law. Two requirements are necessary for a handwritten will to be considered valid: a clear mental state (being of sound mind) and the intent to make a will.

A variety of wills are available depending upon the situation, such as simple wills, oral wills, joint wills, and conditional wills.

Simple Will A **simple will** leaves the entire estate (the testator's property covered by the will) to one or more named beneficiaries.

Oral Will An **oral will** is a will spoken at the time of imminent death, but it is recognized only in certain states. This type of will usually requires a presence of fear of death. An oral will applies only to personal property, leaving any real property (real estate) to be taken care of by heirs.

Joint Will/Mutual Will A **joint will** (also called a **mutual will**) distributes the property of two or more people. A joint will is a single document signed by each testator and leaving all assets to the other. It also stipulates what will happen with the assets when the second person dies. This type of will is essentially a contract between the two testators and requires the consent of both for it to be revoked. A joint will is designed to prevent the surviving person, usually the spouse, from changing his or her mind about the distribution of the property after the first person dies.

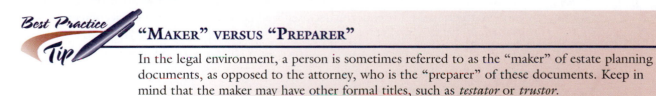

"MAKER" VERSUS "PREPARER"

In the legal environment, a person is sometimes referred to as the "maker" of estate planning documents, as opposed to the attorney, who is the "preparer" of these documents. Keep in mind that the maker may have other formal titles, such as *testator* or *trustor*.

Reciprocal Will A **reciprocal will** is a mirror image of a will made by another person—usually a spouse. Two wills are made, each one signed by an individual. Reciprocal wills generally have wording such as the following: "If I die first, everything goes to my spouse. If my spouse has already died, my descendants take in equal shares." Reciprocal wills can be changed at any time during a testator's lifetime and after a spouse dies. A reciprocal will may not be the right choice for all couples. Complex relationships are almost the norm today, including second marriages. People marry later in life, and both spouses may have a financial history and assets coming into a marriage. Individuals might not have children together; the beneficiaries of one spouse's estate may be different from the beneficiaries of the other. All these factors add up to unique wills, even between spouses who may spend many happy years together.

Conditional Will The terms of a **conditional will** go into effect only when a certain future act or condition happens, not including the testator's death. Examples of conditions in a will might be that a beneficiary may obtain an asset if he or she:

- Turns a certain age
- Marries or does not marry a certain person
- Completes or doesn't complete a certain action, such as losing weight, cutting (or not cutting) hair, or learning (or not learning) to speak a certain language

Some states do not allow conditional wills.

Statutory Will A **statutory will** is one that contains standard terms provided by state law to simplify the process of creating a will. This will is normally made by using a form that provides the basic terms of a will and allows a person to fill in the blanks or check off the specifics. A few states have mandatory provisions considered part of the statutory will. In these states, the standard terms are implied even if they were not explicitly written in the will.

Codicil A **codicil** is an addition to a will made sometime after the signing of the original will. Usually another document, a codicil is used if the testator does not want to write a completely new will or a major life change occurs. A major life change may include a birth, adoption, marriage, divorce, death of an heir, or the loss of property in the will. The codicil must be witnessed and signed just like the original will. Many attorneys advise clients to make a new will when a major life change occurs so that the terms of the will are absolutely clear to everyone involved.

Marriage is considered a major life change. When a person gets married after a will has already been signed, the new spouse in some states is called an after-acquired spouse. Most legal professionals recommend that a new will should be written rather than just adding a codicil to ensure that the spouse is included in the will.

Under the general laws of wills, a surviving spouse who is left out of a will is protected by law and is said to have an elective share. An **elective share** allows a surviving spouse to claim a portion of the deceased's estate regardless of the will's contents. The portion of the estate to which the spouse is entitled depends on the laws of the state.

Another way to plan an estate is to create a trust to pass on assets and properties to the intended beneficiaries.

Trusts

A **trust** is a legal entity that holds assets for the benefit of another. The person who provides property and creates a trust is called a **trustor**, sometimes referred to as a trust maker, grantor, donor, or settlor. The trustor appoints a **trustee**, who holds legal title to property or money and has broad powers over its maintenance and investment. Sometimes the trustee is a person or corporation (such as a bank) or a combination of both. A **beneficiary** to a trust is the person who receives the benefits or advantages (such as income) of a trust either during the lifetime or after the death of the trustor.

Trusts can be either revocable or irrevocable. A revocable trust is sometimes called a living trust or an *inter vivos* trust. A **revocable trust** is one that can be changed after the trust is created. Life circumstances change and a revocable trust gives the maker the ability to make changes to the trust as necessary. On the other hand, an **irrevocable trust** is one that, once made, cannot be changed.

In a revocable trust, the trustor fulfills the roles of trustee and beneficiary during his or her lifetime. In other words, a person may decide to set up a trust to help the family avoid probate in the event of his or her death. That person would be called the trustor. Because this person would want to be in control of the assets of the estate, he or she would also be the trustee and have total control over the current estate while living. Upon death, an alternate trustee manages the assets of the trust for the other named beneficiaries.

Wills are subject to the probate process, depending upon the value of the estate. A trust is different from a will in that a trust is not subject to probate after the maker dies. Basically, a trust holds money or property. Almost any kind of asset can be included in a trust, including cash, stocks, bonds, insurance policies, real estate, and artwork. The assets placed in a trust depend largely on the client's goals. For example, if it is desired that the trust generate income for the beneficiaries, then income-producing securities, such as bonds, may be placed in the trust. If the trust is meant to create cash that may be accessible to pay any estate taxes due upon the client's death or to provide for the surviving family, the trust might be funded with a life insurance policy.

A will is a different option from a trust. However, both wills and trusts are legal tools a person can use to distribute an estate after death. A client may consult with an attorney, who will assist the client in evaluating the advantages and disadvantages of each option before deciding on one form or the other. Table 8.1 summarizes the differences between a will and a trust with regard to probate, tax savings, management of assets, and costs.

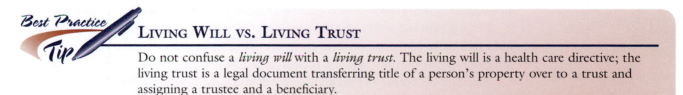

Best Practice Tip

LIVING WILL VS. LIVING TRUST

Do not confuse a *living will* with a *living trust*. The living will is a health care directive; the living trust is a legal document transferring title of a person's property over to a trust and assigning a trustee and a beneficiary.

Table 8.1 Comparison of Wills and Trusts

	Will	Trust
Probate	Subject to probate proceedings. Out-of-state property requires probate proceedings in that state as well. Provides court supervision for handling beneficiary challenges and creditor disputes. Becomes public record at the time of the maker's death.	Not subject to probate proceedings. Avoids the cost of a second-state probate proceeding where there is out-of-state property. No automatic court supervision to deal with disputes. Remains private.
Tax savings	Same tax-saving provisions as are available in a trust.	Same tax saving provisions as are available in a will.
Management of assets	In addition to the will, must use a power of attorney or conservatorship to manage assets.	Allows the trustor to manage the trust assets as long as the trustor is willing and able. Makes provisions for a successor trustee to take over in place of the trustor when necessary.
Costs	Costs less to prepare than a trust. Cost to probate a will can be substantial.	Costs more to prepare, fund, and manage than to prepare a will. Avoids probate costs if all assets are held by the trust.

Health Care Directives

Estate planning may also include health care directives such as a living will and a durable power of attorney. A **health care directive** provides advance instructions regarding care should the person be incapacitated and unable to communicate these decisions directly. The maker of a health care directive will name one or more persons, known as agents, to be responsible for carrying out his or her health care wishes or directives. Health care directives can include a medical power of attorney, a "do not resuscitate" (DNR) order, a living will, and a durable power of attorney.

A **medical (or health care) power of attorney** gives an agent the power to make health care decisions on behalf of the maker. These decisions may include "do not resuscitate" (DNR) orders. A **DNR order** directs medical staff not to utilize mechanical means such as heart support or a breathing machine to keep an individual alive.

A **living will** is a written health care directive outlining an individual's wishes; it is addressed to health care providers concerning health care decisions. It can be detailed and extensive or may just address certain situations.

The main difference between a living will and a medical or health care power of attorney is that the latter document gives a specific person the power to make health care decisions and the living will gives the health care providers the power to make health care decisions.

A durable power of attorney document can relate to any legal situation, including a person's health care. A durable power of attorney can be related to either finances or health care. A **durable power of attorney** is a document that gives decision-making power to another; it remains effective even if the maker of the document becomes mentally incompetent or disabled. The person named in the power of attorney may be called an agent, attorney-in-fact, health care proxy, patient advocate, or something similar, depending on where the maker lives.

You have now reviewed information about estate planning documents that can be used during a person's lifetime—documents defining the management of a person's assets. The following discussion focuses on the process required to distribute a person's assets after death.

Probate

Probate is a legal process needed for the orderly transfer of possession of and/or title to a decedent's property to his or her heirs. After a person dies, he or she is referred to as the **decedent**. Within three to four months of his or her death, the decedent's assets must be transferred to the heirs. The assets must be transferred as the decedent directed in a will and through the probate process, or, if the decedent died intestate (without a will), the court will apply statutes intended to pass property on to the legal heirs. It will also appoint a guardian for minor children, if any.

The process of transferring title of the decedent's assets to heirs is called **estate administration**. The federal government allows each state to administer its own probate laws. However, the process becomes complex when a decedent owns property in multiple states. Some states have adopted the Uniform Probate Code to make the administration of an estate uniform from one state to another. The **Uniform Probate Code (UPC)** is a standard comprehensive set of federal laws, adopted in whole or in part by various states, that regulate the administration of estates, including wills and trusts.

The attorney is responsible for the accuracy of the probate process. Since the probate process includes gathering facts and inserting information into forms, legal support staff are sometimes given the responsibility of gathering the details required to complete the required forms.

Local Focus 8.6

Remember that a personal representative/executor is the person appointed by the testator to carry out the terms of a will. Through the probate process, the personal representative is given authority by the court to "step into the shoes" of the decedent, take control of the decedent's assets, and distribute them to the beneficiaries. Personal representatives usually hire an attorney to advise and guide them through the probate process. This can be a long, laborious, expensive process. Before discussing the details of probate administration, it is important to review

Best Practice Tip

"PROBATE" AS DIFFERENT PARTS OF SPEECH

The term *probate* tends to have several meanings in the law office because it can be used as an adjective, noun, or verb.

Adjective:	The decedent owns *probate property*.
Noun:	An estate must *go through probate* and a personal representative must be appointed to distribute the decedent's property.
Verb:	We have to *probate the will* in order for the assets to be distributed.

inheritance laws and how they affect the distribution of an estate depending on its location. An **estate** is the property and debt left by a person upon death.

Inheritance law governs the rights of a decedent's survivors to inherit property. Depending on the type of inheritance law your state has, a surviving spouse may be able to claim an inheritance regardless of what the decedent's written will states. This statutory right of a surviving spouse hinges on whether a state follows the community property approach or the common law approach.

Community property is property acquired by either spouse during the marriage. This may include income received from work, property bought during the marriage with income from employment, and separate property that a spouse gives to the community. The two people in a marriage are sometimes referred to as a **community**. A spouse retains a separate interest in property acquired through the following methods:

- Inheritance or gift
- Acquisition of property prior to marriage
- An agreement between the spouses to keep the property separate from the marriage community

In a **community property state**, each spouse owns a half interest of the marital property and has the right to dispose of his or her half interest in whatever way desired. The following are currently community property states: Alaska, Arizona, California, Idaho, Louisiana, Nevada, New Mexico, Texas, Washington, and Wisconsin. The remaining states follow common law.

Some states are **common law states**, meaning that a surviving spouse is not automatically entitled to a half interest in all property acquired during the marriage. A state following common law rules is sometimes referred to as an **equity state**, meaning that spouses retain the value of their respective premarital property. Both spouses do not necessarily own the property acquired during marriage. Ownership is determined by the name on the title or, if the title is irrelevant, by ascertaining which spouse's income purchased the property. However, a spouse in a common law state has protection from complete disinheritance. Every common law state has different guidelines, but most common law states' inheritance laws allow the surviving spouse to claim one-third of the deceased spouse's property. A deceased spouse can choose to leave less than a state's mandated inheritance right, but the surviving spouse may make a claim with the court to inherit the predetermined amount. The will is carried out according to the decedent's wishes if the surviving spouse agreed in writing to accept less than the statutory amount or the surviving spouse never goes to court to claim the legal share.

An asset given by will is called a **bequest**. The act of giving an asset by will is to **bequeath**. Another name given to an asset given by will is a devise. Traditionally, a devise has been real estate given by will. Over the years and to this date, the word **devise** means any asset, including real estate, given by will. The person giving the asset can be called the **devisor**. The person receiving the asset is called the **devisee**.

Probate is required if the net value of the probate assets of the decedent exceeds a certain amount. For instance, in some states, a probate proceeding may be avoided entirely if the net value of the probate assets does not exceed $50,000. In that case, the assets may be collected by the person entitled to obtain them by simply furnishing an appropriate affidavit to the property possessor. Figure 8.1 shows a collection of personal property by affidavit in the state of Colorado. Notice that it is signed by the successor. A **successor** is the person who officially takes over or fills in for another after death. The decedent may or may not have a will. This document is used to collect a decedent's assets if the estate's value is less than a certain amount of money.

STATE OF COLORADO
COUNTY OF _____

COLLECTION OF PERSONAL PROPERTY
BY AFFIDAVIT PURSUANT TO §15-12-1201, C.R.S.

1. I, _____, am a Successor and swear/affirm under oath that the following statements are true and correct and that I am 18 years of age or older:

2. At least ten days have elapsed since the death of _____(Decedent).

3. The Decedent did not own any real property. The total fair market value of all property owned by the Decedent and subject to disposition by Will or intestate succession at the time of the Decedent's death, wherever that property is located, less liens and encumbrances, does not exceed $50,000.00.

4. No Application or Petition for the appointment of a personal representative is pending or has been granted in any jurisdiction. I understand that I am answerable and accountable to any subsequently appointed personal representative of the estate or any other person having a superior right to the estate.

5. The Successor(s), listed below, is/are entitled to the payment of any sums of money due and owing to the Decedent, and to the delivery of all tangible personal property belonging to the Decedent and in the possession of another, and to the delivery of all instruments evidencing a debt, obligation, stock or chose in action (right to bring legal action) belonging to the Decedent. Identify the proportion/percentage that each Successor will receive for each asset listed below:

Description of Asset	Name of Successor	Proportion or Percentage

_____
Signature of Successor   Date

Subscribed and affirmed, or sworn before me   in   the
County of _____, State of _____,
this _____day of _____, 20___, by the Successor.

My Commission Expires: _____

_____
Notary Public

BEQUEST, BEQUEATH, DEVISE, DEVISOR, AND DEVISEE DEFINED

As with any new vocabulary word, knowing the word's part of speech will help you use it properly. The words *bequest, bequeath, devise, devisor,* and *devisee* can be confusing. Refer to the following table to better understand them.

Word	Part of Speech	Definition	Example
Bequest or devise	Noun	The actual asset given by will	Joseph Hiller left a bequest to his grandchild. The devise was referred to in Mr. Hiller's will.
Bequeath	Verb	The act of giving an asset by will	Mr. Hiller will bequeath his antique motorcycle to Brandon, his grandchild.
Devisor	Noun	The person giving assets to another by will	The devisor, Mr. Hiller, met with his attorney to discuss the distribution of his assets.
Devisee	Noun	The person receiving an asset by will	Brandon Hiller, as the devisee of his grandfather's will, received an antique motorcycle.

Initiating a Probate Procedure: Formal or Informal, Supervised or Unsupervised

If a probate procedure is required, the next step is determining whether a "formal" or "informal" probate proceeding should be initiated.

In most states, one can take two different tracks when an estate needs to go through the probate process: formal and informal. The **informal probate** of an estate is a nonjudicial process conducted by a judge, registrar, or other designated person. This process is used when assets are straightforward and parties are amicable. The informal probate process is initiated by submitting an application to court administration personnel instead of a judge to approve the estate and proceed informally. Court administration personnel are not involved in the process between when the estate is approved and when the final accounting of the estate's assets and liabilities is due. The personal representative and his or her attorney proceed through the steps of distributing assets. The court is involved in closing the estate. The informal probate process has less oversight by the court and is less expensive than the formal probate process. However, other situations exist where formal probate is strongly recommended or even required.

Formal probate is a judicial process required when a judge must review the legality of the will, the heirs are not known, the will is missing, one or more heirs are minors, known heirs are not on good terms, or problems are expected with the administration of the will. The formal probate process is also required when the estate is **insolvent** (meaning that the estate has more debts than it does assets).

The formal process is initiated by the filing of a petition and a subsequent hearing in front of a judge. The court reviews the paperwork and approves the personal representative. The personal representative is the person selected by the testator in his or her will to carry out the testator's wishes regarding the estate. A personal representative is usually appointed by the court within the first 30 days after a decedent's death.

To assist in the proceedings, the personal representative usually contacts an attorney who specializes in probate. Official probate documents use the phrase "the personal representative will...." This phrase indicates that the personal representative will probably sign certain documents and perform certain duties. However, the attorney and support staff will complete certain tasks on behalf of the personal representative, such as completing documents, attending hearings, sending notices to heirs, inventorying assets, and completing the final accounting of assets.

Once the personal representative has been approved by the court, he or she works to resolve all outstanding issues in the estate. The formal probate process includes the option for the estate to be either **supervised**, meaning that the court must approve any distributions to heirs before they are made, or **unsupervised**, meaning that the court does not have to approve distributions before closing the estate. An informal probate has very little court involvement once the personal representative is appointed, and he or she is usually unsupervised. Consultation with an experienced probate attorney can help the personal representative decide whether or not the court should supervise the probate process.

A formal probate can be either supervised or unsupervised. A formal *supervised* probate is required if an estate is insolvent or if an attorney who is unrelated to the decedent acts as the personal representative. A formal *unsupervised* probate may be used if there are beneficiaries who are minor children, problems with devisees or heirs, problems with the will, etc. See Figure 8.2 to review formal, informal, supervised, and unsupervised probate administration.

Figure 8.2 **Characteristics of formal, informal, supervised, and unsupervised probate procedures.**

Formal Probate	Supervised Probate
• Judicial process initiated by a petition • Presented at a hearing before a judge • Problems with the will • Heirs may be unknown • Will may be missing • Heirs may be minors • Heirs may not get along • Unexpected problems may come up • Estate is insolvent (has more debts than assets)	The personal representative must have the court approve all documents and distributions to heirs before they are made.
Informal Probate	**Unsupervised**
• Nonjudicial process initiated by an application submitted to court personnel instead of to a judge • Assets are straightforward • All heirs are getting along • Less court oversight • Less expensive	The personal representative does not need the court's approval for anything before closing the estate.

The probate process can start out formal and supervised and, if the judge thinks that all is going well, the process can be shifted to informal and unsupervised.

Once the attorney has decided whether the probate process is to be informal or formal and supervised or unsupervised, the next step is preparing the documents that officially start the process with the court. The *application* **for appointment as personal representative** is the document prepared if the estate is to be administered *informally*. The *petition* **for appointment as personal representative** is the document (signed by the nominated personal representative under penalties of perjury) that is filed with the court to initiate a *formal* probate proceeding.

Information such as place and date of birth, decedent's address, and list of interested persons and their addresses will be needed to complete the application or petition. **Interested persons** are all those who are named in the will as beneficiaries and heirs as well as personal representatives or trustees.

Other items necessary to complete either the application or the petition include:

- The decedent's death certificate
- The estimated value of assets summary
- The decedent's original will

A certified death certificate or other proof of death is required to initiate a probate proceeding. A summary of the estimated value of assets is also required. This summary notes all of the assets owned by the decedent at the date of death as well as his or her debts. This estimate notifies the court about the solvency of the decedent's estate. If the decedent dies testate, meaning "with a will," the court requires that the original will be filed. Most of the time, the decedent's original will is either in the possession of the attorney who drafted it or is among the decedent's important papers. If only a copy of the will is available, it may be possible to petition the court to admit the copy to probate.

The probate application or petition should be filed in the county where the decedent was domiciled at his or her death. Essentially, **domicile** means where the decedent was living at the time of death. If domicile is unclear (for example, if the decedent spent half the year in one state and half the year in another), probate can be filed in any jurisdiction where the decedent owned property. Determining where to file can be a complex decision that the personal representative will make with the advice of an attorney.

Sometimes the court and/or the testator requires the personal representative to file a bond. A **bond** is insurance that protects the assets of the estate from possible misconduct by a personal representative.

Once the court appoints the personal representative, a document called letters testamentary or letters of general administration is issued. **Letters testamentary** (for decedents dying with a valid will) and **letters of general administration** (for decedents dying without a valid will) give authority to the personal representative to gather the decedent's assets and pay the expenses of the estate. The personal representative is required to give notice of the probate and his or her appointment to all interested persons listed in the application or petition and to all known creditors. Letters testamentary also gives the personal representative authority to present the letters to holders of the decedent's property. Property holders can rely on the letters testamentary as proof that the decedent has died and that the personal representative has authority to manage and/or receive the decedent's property. In addition to the letters testamentary, the personal representative must publish notice of the probate in the legal newspaper for the county so that creditors have an opportunity to file

claims against the estate. The **legal newspaper** is one that has been designated by the county to publish legal notices. Legal notices will not be published in any other newspaper in the county.

If there is no will, state law dictates who has priority to serve as personal representative, since the decedent did not specify one. Priority in the appointment of a personal representative means that the law has specified the order in which relatives of the decedent may be appointed as personal representative. Language in probate laws identifies who this person should be according to how closely he or she is related, such as surviving spouse or other heirs.

Identifying and Collecting Assets of the Probate Estate

When a person dies, the survivors, of course, need time to grieve, but they also need to know the deadlines within the probate process. Within the first two to three months from the date of death, the personal representative must start the process of identifying and collecting the decedent's assets. The personal representative and/or closest relative will generally contact a lawyer within several weeks of the death.

Probate Assets **Probate assets** include property titled in the decedent's name alone, without a "payable on death" or other beneficiary designation listed. The phrase "payable on death" would be seen in insurance documents and other documents that pay the value to a named beneficiary. Examples of probate assets include bank accounts, cars, securities, or real estate in the decedent's name only. If the decedent's interest in property is titled as "tenants in common," it is considered a probate asset. Remember that tenants in common is a type of ownership whereby the decedent owned an undivided half interest in real property. If the decedent had owned property with a spouse as tenants in common, probate is required to transfer the decedent's half interest in the property. The decedent's portion of the property is the only part that must go through the probate process. Property owned as joint tenants is not a probate asset in the estate. The other owner owns the property individually after the death of the joint owner. Owning property as joint tenants is a type of ownership in which the decedent owned property with a spouse or other person. Upon the death of one owner, title passes entirely to the other. The other person is said to have rights of survivorship.

Additional probate assets may include life insurance or retirement accounts payable to "the estate." When no beneficiary is listed other than the decedent's estate, the insurance or retirement account will be a probate asset subject to a probate proceeding.

Nonprobate Assets **Non-probate assets** include real property owned with a spouse or another person as joint tenants with rights of survivorship (or with a spouse as "tenants by the entirety" in some states). If the joint tenant survives the decedent, the decedent's interest passes to the joint tenant by operation of law. The surviving joint tenant will have to record an affidavit of survivorship (and death certificate) with the county recorder or registrar of titles; property held in a trust, revocable or irrevocable; property that identifies a beneficiary other than "the estate," such as life insurance, IRAs, etc.; and property that includes a "pay on death" or "transfer on death" designation, such as a bank account or brokerage account.

Determining and Collecting the Decedent's Assets The personal representative is officially responsible for determining and collecting the decedent's assets. The probate process requires that the decedent's assets be inventoried, accounted for to the court, and distributed. The attorney and legal support staff hired by the personal representative usually assist in the task of inventorying by looking for assets in the following places:

- Check the decedent's mail. The personal representative should have the decedent's mail forwarded to the personal representative or the attorney. Mail should be monitored for evidence of assets such as account statements, shareholder mailings, tax documents, and for evidence of debts or potential claims.
- Safe deposit box. If the decedent owned a safe deposit box, the personal representative should look at the contents (using the letters testamentary for authority). If the personal representative suspects that the decedent's original will may be in the safe deposit box, a procedure is in place for gaining access to the safe deposit box to determine whether the will is located there.
- Home safe. People often hold asset information, including stock certificates, in home safes.
- Decedent's income tax returns. Income tax returns include information about banks and brokerage accounts, rental properties, farm interests, interests in partnerships or corporations, and beneficial interests in trusts.
- Personal files of the decedent. Most people have some type of "important paper" filing system. Documents may be organized and well labeled, or they could simply be tossed into a box in no order at all. The important documents needed for the probate process include bank statements, investment statements, recurring bills, documents validating personal debts, titles to and insurance on vehicles, etc. The legal support person must organize this documentation by year and payment status.

Transferring the Assets to the "Estate"

To transfer the decedent's assets to the estate, the personal representative, with the assistance of the attorney, will obtain a taxpayer identification number for the estate from the Internal Revenue Service (IRS). This number is similar to a social security number. It is needed to establish estate accounts at brokerages and banks.

Best Practice Tip

FUTURE DIGITAL INVENTORY

Finding personal files of a decedent will change in the years to come, considering the tech-savvy world in which we live. In the near future, you will be planning for and administering digital property at death, including emails, photos, videos, music, medical records, legal or financial records, websites, blogs, or other social media accounts that may hold little or no monetary value but that undoubtedly holds significant monetary value to the surviving descendants of the decedent.

In addition, the personal representative will open an estate account at a bank and transfer the decedent's checking, savings, brokerage, and/or investment accounts to the estate account.

The personal representative will provide the broker or brokers with a letters testamentary, a death certificate, and a letter instructing them to transfer the contents of the account to a separate estate account. This letter can instruct the broker either to keep the securities in their current form or to liquidate them before placing them in the estate account. The decision to retain assets or liquidate them will be determined by market conditions, the wishes of the beneficiaries, the need for liquidity in the estate to pay bills, and other considerations.

Once the assets of the estate have been determined, gathered, and transferred to the estate, those assets must be officially inventoried and an official final accounting must be completed and filed with the appropriate probate court.

The following are fundamental steps to estate administration:

A. Preparing the Inventory The **inventory** includes all probate assets listed together with the assets' fair market value on the date of death. Fair market value is determined by the type of asset. For marketable securities, the fair market value of an asset is not the closing price of the security on the date of death. Rather, it is the average of the high and the low on the date of death. Cash is included on the inventory at its face value. Other assets may require an appraisal to establish fair market value. The inventory should be prepared within six months after death or nine months if an estate tax return is required. The inventory is needed because the personal representative, acting in a fiduciary capacity, must account to the beneficiaries of the estate. The inventory is also the "starting point" for the final account. Figure 8.3 shows just the first page of the document called the inventory. Notice the inventory summary showing asset categories. Each of the asset categories is summarized within additional pages called schedules. The remainder of the inventory document includes each of these schedules.

Within three months after appointment, a personal representative shall prepare an inventory of property owned by the decedent that is subject to disposition by will or intestate succession. The inventory must list the property with reasonable detail, indicate the decedent's interest in the property, and include the fair market value as of the decedent's date of death. The type and amount of any liens and encumbrances on the property must also be listed. If additional property is discovered after the initial inventory has been completed, a supplemental inventory listing the newly discovered property shall be completed.

If additional space is needed, separate sheets may be used. The inventory shall be sent to interested persons who request it or it may be filed with the court.

B. Managing the Estate "When will I get my inheritance?" is a common question from beneficiaries who may push to get distributions from the estate. They may not understand that the probate process involves many different parties (creditors, government entities, and beneficiaries), and that the personal representative must wait for a variety of information to complete the process. The following are situations that cause the probate process to progress more slowly than beneficiaries might prefer:

- Distributions generally should not be made until bills and other claims have been paid, estate tax issues have been resolved, and tax payments have been made or provided for. Be aware that partial distributions are possible.

Figure 8.3 **The first page of the document called the inventory.**

District Court	Denver Probate Court	

District Court   Denver Probate Court
_____ County, Colorado

Court Address:

_____

In the Matter of the Estate of:

_____

Deceased

COURT USE ONLY

Attorney or Party Without Attorney (Name and Address):

_____

_____

_____

Phone Number: _____ E-mail: _____

FAX Number: _____ Atty. Reg. #: _____

Case Number:

_____

Division _____ Courtroom _____

DECEDENT'S ESTATE INVENTORY

Within 3 months after appointment, a personal representative shall prepare an Inventory of property owned by the Decedent that is subject to disposition by will or intestate succession. The Inventory must list the property with reasonable detail, indicate the Decedent's interest in the property, and include the fair market value as of the Decedent's date of death. The type and amount of any liens and encumbrances on the property must also be listed. If additional property is discovered after the initial inventory has been completed, a supplemental inventory listing the newly discovered property shall be completed.

If additional space is needed, separate sheets may be used. The Inventory shall be sent to interested persons who request it or it may be filed with the Court.

INVENTORY SUMMARY		
Schedule	Asset Category	Value
1	Real estate	0.00
2	Stocks, bonds, mutual funds, securities and investment accounts	0.00
3	Mortgages, notes, and cash	0.00
4	Life insurance	0.00
5	Pensions, profit-sharing plans, annuities, and retirement funds	0.00
6	Motor and recreational vehicles	0.00
7	Other assets	0.00
Total gross value		0.00
8	Liens and encumbrances on inventoried assets	0.00
Total net value		0.00

- The personal representative must consider alternate valuation of the assets to calculate taxes in a taxable estate to the best financial advantage of the beneficiaries. The **alternate valuation date** is the date six months after the date of death *or* the date the asset is sold (if earlier). The estate tax value of an asset is either the date-of-death value of the asset or the value of the asset on the alternate valuation date. The alternate valuation date should be used if the resulting estate tax will be reduced if the value is set by that date. Therefore, it is important to consider *when* assets should be sold if alternate valuation is a consideration. Various tax considerations should be taken into account depending on the size of the estate. The personal representative and his or her attorney may consult an accountant or financial advisor to determine the tax advantages that may apply and might help to preserve as much of the estate as possible for the beneficiaries. The personal representative can retain professionals to help with the management and investment of assets. This all takes additional time, but it is for the financial advantage of the beneficiaries of an estate.
- The personal representative may have to wait if the estate has assets that may not be suitable for immediate distribution, such as a house, apartment building, or cabin, especially when there are multiple beneficiaries. Unless the beneficiaries can agree amicably on who gets which property, the assets may have to be sold and the profits distributed among the beneficiaries.
- Selling of real estate can slow the distribution process as well. In some instances, the personal representative can sell real estate as soon as 30 days after the issuance of the letters testamentary. It is important for an attorney to review the purchase agreement. A personal representative should not sign a purchase agreement that promises delivery of a warranty deed. The purchase agreement should indicate that the deed will be a "personal representative's deed." The personal representative will have to provide proof of authority to sell the decedent's property. Therefore, probate "sale papers" will be needed. These papers are a packet of certified documents issued by the probate court, including a certified copy of the will, a certified letters testamentary, and a certified order for probate.
- The personal representative must decide whether to liquidate assets (sell for cash) or maintain the assets in the estate. In determining whether to retain assets or liquidate them, two key points are considered to preserve the estate for the beneficiaries:
  1. One of the personal representative's obligations to the heirs is to retain the value of the estate's assets. Because there may be real estate to sell, the personal representative and attorney may want to determine the current real estate sales values.
  2. Because cash may be needed to pay claims or taxes, the personal representative may have to wait until certain portions of the estate have been sold.

C. Paying Claims, Debts, and Expenses Paying claims, debts, and expenses should be done six to 12 months after the date of death.

Soon after the attorney for the personal representative prepares and files the application or petition, he or she will prepare and publish a notice to creditors in the local legal newspaper. In general, creditors have four months after the date of the notice to file claims against the estate, which is referred to as the **creditors' claim period**. Claims are liabilities of the decedent that arose during the decedent's life and liabilities of the estate that arise after death. Claims include medical expenses, funeral expenses, costs of nursing care, costs and expenses of estate administration, and other debts of the decedent.

The claimant (person or entity making a financial claim against an estate) may mail or deliver a written statement of the claim to the personal representative or file a written statement of the claim with the court administrator.

The personal representative does have the right to object to a claim if the claim is not valid. For example, if a claimant files a claim alleging that the decedent had contracted for services but no proof of the contract exists or the service was provided, the personal representative should object to the claim and send a notice of disallowance to the claimant. Notice of disallowance or objections to claims should be filed with the court within two months after the time for original presentation of claims has expired.

In general, expenses of administration, claims, and debts should not be paid before the 4-month creditors' claim period has expired, since some states have laws setting forth the priority for payment of claims. The reason for waiting to pay expenses of administration, etc., is that this allows the personal representative to make sure that all creditors have had time to make their claims and the estate has enough money to pay all creditors.

D. Tax Considerations Income Tax Returns: The personal representative is responsible for filing the decedent's individual income tax returns. The personal representative may be required to file two returns, as follows:

Date of Death 10/29/2011:

- 2011 tax return due 4/15/12 for January 1, 2011, through October 29, 2011
- 2012 return not required

Date of Death 2/1/2012:

- 2011 tax return due 4/15/12 for January 1, 2011, through December 31, 2011
- 2012 tax return due 4/15/13 for January 1, 2012, through February 1, 2012

If there is a surviving spouse, a joint return may be filed for the year of death.

Estate Tax Returns: The personal representative is required to file *estate* tax returns for the decedent if the value of the decedent's estate exceeds the amount of the state's current estate tax exemption. In general, the estate tax return identifies every asset, probate and nonprobate, owned by the decedent and indicates its value (either date of death or alternate value). The returns are due nine months after the date of death, although automatic 6-month extensions are permitted.

Estate and Trust Income Tax Returns. Estates frequently earn income after a decedent's death, in which case a personal representative may be required to file a fiduciary income tax return. The fiduciary income tax return must be filed if an estate earns more than $600 in income. This dollar amount may vary from state to state and year to year. The attorney will always be aware of the current amount. The due date for an estate income tax return is April 15 of the year following death unless the estate chooses a fiscal year. A **fiscal year** is a period of 12 consecutive months without regard to the calendar year. The attorney will advise the personal representative whether or not to use a fiscal year. This choice should be made after an analysis of income and deductions has been completed.

Trusts may also earn income after a decedent's death. If a trust earns more than $100 in income, an income tax return must be filed. Except in limited circumstances, a trust must use a calendar year as its tax year. Therefore, a trust's income tax return for a year will be due on April 15 of the following year.

E. Distribution of the Estate Before distributions are made from an estate, the law office assisting the personal representative must prepare a final accounting for the beneficiaries' review. The beneficiaries must sign a consent to the proposal for distribution of the assets. Beneficiaries of the estate are entitled to an accounting of all assets and any gain or loss on those assets since the decedent's death.

The first step in preparing a final accounting is to make sure that the inventory is accurate. Increases and decreases in the value of assets since the decedent's death must be recorded in the final accounting. Then administration and funeral expenses must also be deducted. Expenses of administration include the following:

- Attorney fees
- Accountant fees
- Personal representative fees
- Copy and publication fees
- Probate filing fees

Once written consents of the distribution plan are received, the personal representative will issue checks to the beneficiaries for their shares of the estate. Beneficiaries may also receive the actual assets, such as stocks or real estate, depending on the circumstances. Once assets have been distributed to the beneficiaries, the court may require signed receipts from the beneficiaries verifying that they have received the distributions.

F. Closing the Estate If an estate tax return is not required, the personal representative can generally officially close an estate shortly after the claims and expenses have been paid, distributions made, and receipts received. However, if an estate tax return is required, the personal representative will be advised to keep the estate open until after the IRS or state department of revenue issues a closing letter.

Recall that estates can be handled either formally or informally and either supervised or unsupervised. Refer to Figure 8.2 for a review on formal, informal, supervised, and unsupervised probate procedures. If the estate is relatively uncomplicated and the beneficiaries agree about the plan of distribution and composition of their respective shares, an informal closing is possible. In that case, the attorney for the personal representative will prepare and file a closing statement and receipts (if required). The estate is then closed after a closing statement is filed with the court.

Even though the estate is closed upon filing of the closing statement, the personal representative may continue to act for a year after the estate is closed. This can be helpful if additional probate assets are discovered after the closing statement is filed.

A formal closing would occur if there was a disagreement among the beneficiaries or if the personal representative wanted to be formally discharged from his or her duties and/or relieved of liability. In this situation, the attorney for the personal representative files a final account; the inventory (if not previously filed); a petition to allow final account, settle, and distribute estate; and a petition to discharge the personal representative.

In this formal closing, the court will set a date for a hearing on the petition. Notice of the hearing must be sent to all interested persons. The personal representative will attend the hearing, testify about the estate, and ask the court to settle the estate and discharge the personal representative. After the hearing, if the court is satisfied that the estate has been properly handled, the court will issue an order settling the estate and discharging the personal representative. This concludes the probate process.

Language Focus: Commas, Semicolons, and Colons

Wills and probate documents must be handled with care, and punctuation is especially important when dealing with finances. The article in Figure 8.4 illustrates how one mark of punctuation can seriously change the meaning of a sentence in a legal document.

The story in Figure 8.4 shows just how important proofreading for punctuation really is. Legal writing tends to include long, grammatically complex sentences. The legal office worker must be able to analyze sentence structure in both legal documents and correspondence to convey clear and understandable messages.

The following are examples of incorrect punctuation that drastically changes the intended meaning.

Incorrect: Say NO to Drugs from the Police D.A.R.E. Officers.

Correct: Say NO to Drugs. Presentation by Police D.A.R.E. Officers on Friday at 2 p.m.

(Oops! That one missing comma turned police officers into drug dealers.)

Incorrect: Let's eat mommy. (Mommy sandwiches?)

Correct: Let's eat, mommy.

Incorrect: Giant moving, sale Friday (Get clothing from the giant!)

Correct: Giant moving sale Friday

To understand the rules governing punctuation, one must understand clauses. Remember the two types of clauses: independent and dependent. Both have subjects and predicates (verbs). The *independent* clause can stand alone because it makes sense on its own. The *dependent* clause also has a subject and predicate, but it cannot stand alone because it does not make sense by itself. Do your best to identify independent and dependent clauses as you proceed through the following rules.

Commas

Including a comma in a sentence should always be justified by a rule. Writers sometimes insert commas and other punctuation whenever they take a breath or want the reader to pause within a sentence. The news story of "The $2-million Comma" in Figure 8.4 illustrates why each and every mark of punctuation should have a purpose and should function in the manner intended. Some basic rules for the use of commas are discussed on the following pages.

Figure 8.4 **The $2-million Comma**

The Globe and Mail

The $2-million Comma

GRANT ROBERTSON
Toronto Globe and Mail, July 8, 2006

It could be the most costly piece of punctuation in Canada. A grammatical blunder may force Rogers Communications Inc. to pay an extra $2.13-million to use utility poles in the Maritimes after the placement of a comma in a contract permitted the deal's cancellation.

The controversial comma sent lawyers and telecommunications regulators scrambling for their English textbooks in a bitter 18-month dispute that serves as an expensive reminder of the importance of punctuation.

Rogers thought it had a five-year deal with Aliant Inc. to string Rogers' cable lines across thousands of utility poles in the Maritimes for an annual fee of $9.60 per pole. But early last year, Rogers was informed that the contract was being cancelled and the rates were going up. Impossible, Rogers thought, since its contract was iron-clad until the spring of 2007 and could potentially be renewed for another five years.

Armed with the rules of grammar and punctuation, Aliant disagreed. The construction of a single sentence in the 14-page contract allowed the entire deal to be scrapped with only one year's notice, the company argued.

Language buffs take note — Page 7 of the contract states: The agreement "shall continue in force for a period of five years from the date it is made, and thereafter for successive five-year terms, unless and until terminated by one year prior notice in writing by either party."

Rogers' intent in 2002 was to lock into a long-term deal of at least five years. But when regulators with the Canadian Radio-television and Telecommunications Commission (CRTC) parsed the wording, they reached another conclusion.

The validity of the contract and the millions of dollars at stake all came down to one point — the second comma in the sentence.

Had it not been there, the right to cancel wouldn't have applied to the first five years of the contract and Rogers would be protected from the higher rates it now faces.

"Based on the rules of punctuation," the comma in question "allows for the termination of the [contract] at any time, without cause, upon one-year's written notice," the regulator said.

Rogers was dumbfounded. The company said it never would have signed a contract to use roughly 91,000 utility poles that could be cancelled on such short notice. Its lawyers tried in vain to argue the intent of the deal trumped the significance of a comma. "This is clearly not what the parties intended," Rogers said in a letter to the CRTC.

But the CRTC disagreed. And the consequences are significant. The contract would have shielded Rogers from rate increases that will see its costs jump as high as $28.05 per pole. Instead, the company will likely end up paying about $2.13-million more than expected, based on rough calculations.

Despite the victory, Aliant won't reap the bulk of the proceeds. The poles are mostly owned by Fredericton-based utility NB Power, which contracted out the administration of the business to Aliant at the time the contract was signed.

Neither Rogers nor Aliant could be reached for comment on the ruling. In one of several letters to the CRTC, Aliant called the matter "a basic rule of punctuation," taking a swipe at Rogers' assertion that the comma could be ignored.

"This is a classic case of where the placement of a comma has great importance," Aliant said.

Taken from *The Globe and Mail*, 444 Front St. W., Toronto, ON Canada M5V 2S9, Phillip Crawley, Publisher.

MNEMONIC "FANBOYS" TO REMEMBER COORDINATING CONJUNCTIONS

If you forget what the coordinating conjunctions are, use the mnemonic *fanboys* to remember them:

For
And
Nor
But
Or
Yet
So

Commas and Coordinating Conjunctions

Use commas to separate two *independent* clauses when they are joined by any of these coordinating conjunctions: *for, and, nor, but, or, yet,* and *so.*

> Snow was coming down hard, but we left for the hearing anyway.

> We saw the snow coming down hard but left for the hearing anyway.

No comma is after the coordinating conjunction "but" because no subject is on the right side of the conjunction. This is a simple sentence with a compound verb: We saw...and left....

Commas and Introductory Clauses

Use a comma after an *introductory* clause that comes before the main clause. Introductory clauses introduce or "set the stage" for main clauses.

Introductory dependent clauses are introduced by subordinate conjunctions such as those listed in Table 8.2. An example follows the table.

Table 8.2 Subordinate Conjunctions

after	even though	that
although	how	though
As	if	till (or 'til)
as if	inasmuch	unless
as long as	in order that	until
as much as	lest	when
as soon as	now that	whenever
as though	provided (that)	where
because	since	wherever
before	so that	while
even if	than	

Because Mr. Urness created a trust before his death, his heirs avoided paying excessive taxes.

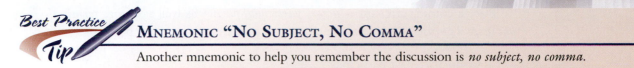

MNEMONIC "NO SUBJECT, NO COMMA"

Another mnemonic to help you remember the discussion is *no subject, no comma.*

Use a comma before a coordinating conjunction if an independent clause both on the left and right of the conjunction. However, the sentence has a compound verb if no subject is on the right of the conjunction.

The clause "Because Mr. Urness created a trust before his death" is an introductory dependent clause and must be attached to an independent clause to make sense. A comma goes between the introductory dependent clause and the independent clause. Note that the introductory clause begins with a subordinate conjunction.

> His heirs avoided paying excessive taxes because Mr. Urness created a trust before his death.

This sentence does not have a comma between the independent and dependent clauses because the dependent clause ("because Mr. Urness created a trust before his death") is no longer introductory. This type of clause is sometimes called a terminal dependent clause.

Introductory Phrases Remember that *phrases* are groups of words without a subject or a predicate. The phrase may have nouns alone or verbs alone, but none of them will be the subject or the predicate of the sentence. A comma is used only when these phrases are introductory. If they are found anywhere else in the sentence, they usually do not have commas around them—even if you pause or take a breath! Use a comma after the following introductory phrases:

- Prepositional phrases
- Infinitive phrases
- Participial phrases
- Appositive phrases

Place a comma after introductory prepositional phrases.

> After the adjustment for measurement errors, the distance was decreased by 1.5 centimeters.

A comma should be placed after *infinitive phrases* of any length. Remember that an infinitive is the word "to" plus any verb.

To agree	To advise	To contemplate
To bequeath	To analyze	

> To stay within the requirements of the will, the personal representative had to sell all personal property and divide the money among the heirs.

Place a comma after *introductory participial phrases* as well as before *terminal participial phrases*. Participles are either past participles or present participles.

Introductory past participle:
Attached to the end of the booklet, the exhibit did not make an impact on the reader.

Terminal past participle:
The courier approached the desk timidly, scared that she would interrupt the attorney's conversation.

Introductory present participle:
Crying constantly, the child got us all to pay attention to him.

Place a comma after an *appositive phrase*. An appositive is a phrase that renames the words directly following it.

A popular and well-dressed attorney, Allen was the clear favorite in the campaign for governor.

Introductory Words Words like *however, still, furthermore,* and *meanwhile* create continuity from one sentence to the next. Use a comma after these words when they are introductory.

The judge reviewed the motion. *Meanwhile,* the attorney and the executor discussed the strategy needed in the will contest.

Most of the evidence seemed convincing. *Still,* the credibility of the witness was in question.

Commas and Nonessential and Essential Clauses

Use a pair of commas in the middle of a sentence to set off a clause that is not essential for the remainder of the sentence to make sense. Use just one comma if the nonessential information is the final part of a sentence. In some reference books *nonessential* and *essential* clauses are referred to as *nonrestrictive* and *restrictive* clauses.
  • Use commas before and after nonessential information.
  • Do not use commas before or after essential information.
Think of the commas as walls or fences that contain information. When you put commas before and after nonessential information, you signal that information is not needed for the remainder of the sentence to make sense. It also indicates that the remainder of the sentence makes sense without the contained information.

Even if information is nonessential within a sentence, it does not mean that the information is unimportant. Nonessential information, though not strictly necessary, is included to elaborate on the topic or to present additional "nice-to-know" information. If you encounter information that is unimportant, it is best to remove it to create clear and concise documents.

The opposite is true for essential information. Do not use commas before and after essential information because the information must remain open if the remainder of the sentence is to make sense. It must not be kept behind commas.

Who or *Whom* Clauses

Nonessential:
Oliver Winters, whom I met on a flight from New York, is the CEO of Winters Engineering.

The clause "whom I met on a flight from New York" is interesting information but nonessential because the sentence "Oliver Winters is the CEO of Winters Engineering" makes sense without the clause. Notice the commas before and after the clause.

Essential:
All employees who work overtime will get a bonus.

Commas are not inserted before or after the clause "who work overtime" because that clause is essential for the remainder of the sentence to make sense. The sentence "All employees will get a bonus" is not what the writer intended to communicate.

Consider the following sentence:
The teacher helped the students, who had fallen behind.

With the comma included in the sentence, the sentence indicates that every student in the class had fallen behind. Removing the comma would indicate that only a few students had fallen behind and the teacher was helping those specific students.

That and *Which* Clauses
Do not use commas before or after essential elements of the sentence, such as clauses beginning with *that*. A *that* clause following a noun is always essential. A *that* clause following a verb expressing mental action is also always essential.

Always insert commas before and after *which* clauses. When the word *which* is included at the start of a clause, it indicates that the clause is nonessential.

Please bring me the will that is in the safe.

This sentence indicates that multiple wills are found in different locations within the decedent's house. The sentence also indicates that a particular will (the one from the safe) is required. The clause "that is in the safe" is an essential clause.

Please bring me the will, which is in the safe.

This sentence indicates only one will is within the decedent's house, and it is located in the safe. The clause "which is in the safe" provides additional information but is a nonessential clause.

Students were asked to make a list of books that had inspired them.

The list that the students create should consist of inspiring books.

Students were asked to make a list of books, which inspired them.

The sentence indicates that the students were inspired when the teacher asked them to create a list of books.

WHICH HUNT

As a writer or editor, watch for *that* or *which* to assure that they are used properly. You should immediately determine whether *that* is used with an essential clause and whether *which* is used with a nonessential clause. Editors sometimes say that they are going on a "which hunt" to verify that the writer did not mix up using *that* for *which* and vice versa. Many writers make the mistake of confusing these words.

Serial Commas

Use commas to separate three or more words, phrases, or clauses written in a series. The current trend is to include a comma after the item immediately preceding the conjunction. A comma is not required if just two items are listed in the sentence.
Examples:

You will have to be present at the office meeting, the hearing, and the trial.

Would you prefer that your relative receive the cabin, the boat, or the car?

You will have to be present at the office meeting and the trial.

Commas and Coordinate Adjectives

Coordinate adjectives are two adjectives that independently describe the same noun. Use commas to separate coordinate adjectives. Never put a comma between the last adjective and the noun that it describes or use commas with noncoordinate adjectives.

Did you know that the man who signed the document was an ill, confused patient at the hospital?

You can determine if two adjectives in a row are coordinate by asking the following questions:
• Does the sentence make sense if the adjectives are written in reverse order?
• Does the sentence make sense if the adjectives are written with *and* between them?
If you answer yes to these questions, then the adjectives are coordinate and independent of each other and should be separated by a comma. The following are some examples of coordinate and noncoordinate adjectives.

Our 2 p.m. appointment proved to be a difficult, demanding man.

Test the comma by reversing the adjectives (demanding, difficult man) or inserting *and* between the adjectives (difficult and demanding man). Both of these tests make sense, so the adjectives are coordinate and should have a comma between them. Notice no comma is between the last adjective (demanding) and the noun (man).

They lived in a white frame house.

Test where you should put a comma between *white* and *frame* by reversing the them (...in a frame white house) or inserting *and* between the adjectives (...in a white and frame house). The tests do not make sense, so the adjectives are noncoordinate and do not have a comma between them.

Don't confuse compound adjectives with coordinate adjectives. Compound adjectives are hyphenated and function as a unit in modifying the noun.

The two-page will was dictated and printed for the client.

"Two-page" is a two-word but one-idea adjective and should be hyphenated instead of including a comma.

Commas within Geographical Names, Dates, Addresses, and Titles

Use commas to set off all geographical names, items in dates (except the month and day), addresses (except the street number and name), and titles in names.

The decedent has been domiciled in Denver, Colorado, for the last five years.

The decedent died on Thursday, July 29, 2011, at 5:15 p.m.

The last time the heirs were together was in June 2010.

The sole beneficiary is Arleta Thompson, 449 First Avenue, Littleton, Colorado.

Peter James Johnson III, is the sole heir of the decedent.

Commas for Clarity

Use commas wherever necessary to prevent possible confusion or misreading. Words and phrases can be either essential or nonessential. Be aware that the treatment of the clauses can change the meaning of a sentence. The following examples show how a sentence changes when the clause is treated as essential and nonessential.

Evan's brother, Finn, has a degree in psychology.

This sentence indicates that Evan has only one brother.

Evan's brother Finn has a degree in psychology.

This sentence allows Evan to have more than one brother.

Finn, Evan's brother, has a degree in psychology.

This sentence indicates that Finn is Evan's brother but has no reference to whether he has other brothers.

What it was, was a big mistake.

Outside, the lawn was scattered with dry leaves. (outside the window)

Outside the lawn was scattered with dry leaves. (somewhere outside the lawn but not on the lawn!)

Semicolons

The semicolon is often described as being stronger than a comma but weaker than a colon or period. When you reach a semicolon in a sentence, it demands a pause in that same way (longer than a comma and shorter than a colon). Use a semicolon in the following situations:

- Between two independent clauses not joined by a conjunction
- In a series that contains other types of punctuation
- Before an adverb
- Before a conjunction
- Before expressions

Semicolons to Separate Two Independent Clauses Connecting two independent clauses with a semicolon makes it unnecessary to include a conjunction, as you would in using a comma.

Make three copies of the application; include a copy of the will with each copy.

Remember that the topics of the two independent clauses must be closely related. For example, the following example is not correct and should be rewritten:

Incorrect: The personal representative requested that the attorney secure an appraiser; the decedent died on May 8.

The following independent clauses go together more appropriately:

The personal representative requested that the attorney secure an appraiser; the decedent's antiques must be appraised within 30 days. The decedent died on May 8.

Semicolons in a Series with Other Punctuation Semicolons assist with sentence clarity when used in series that contain other punctuation. Compare the following two examples.

Incorrect: The decedent was survived by four children: Adam, 17, Bryan, 13, Catherine, 10, and Donald, 7.

Correct: The decedent was survived by four children: Adam, 17; Bryan, 13; Catherine, 10; and Donald, 7.

Semicolons between Two Independent Clauses Linked with an Adverb When two independent clauses are linked by an adverb, a semicolon should be used prior to the adverb. Adverbs include:

- However
- Therefore
- Consequently
- Moreover

These words help transition the reader from one thought to the next.

> We retained an appraiser; however, we will not be able to appraise the antiques until a week from Friday.

Semicolons before a Conjunction A semicolon can also be used before a conjunction, although the use of a comma is more common. One might choose a semicolon when the connecting independent clause contains additional punctuation.

> We will arrive at your office to sign the will on Friday, May 15, 20xx, at 3 p.m.; and we will bring our daughter.

Notice that if the first independent clause didn't have commas in it already, the semicolon before "and" would have been a comma.

Semicolons before Expressions Expressions such as *that is to say*, *to wit*, *namely*, or *clearly* may be preceded by a semicolon.

> The attorney requested information from the beneficiaries; namely, the beneficiaries' addresses and how they would prefer to be contacted.

> The probate process was highly unusual; that is to say, we had never assisted in one so complicated.

Colons

Aside from the period, the colon demands the longest pause when a sentence is read. Colons are typically used only to introduce specific elements that serve as examples for the initial part of the sentence.

Colons to Introduce a List Use a colon after independent clauses that lead you to believe that a list will follow. The list may be in line with the clause, or the list may start on the next line with bullets or numbers. These independent clauses usually have "leader words" such as the following:

- As follows
- The following
- For example

Do *not* use a colon after verbs or prepositions.

Incorrect:	The heirs to Ms. Hollingsworth's estate are: Alesha Wisch, Travis Hollingsworth, and Bonnie Hiller.
Correct:	The heirs to Ms. Hollingsworth's estate are Alesha Wisch, Travis Hollingsworth, and Bonnie Hiller.

Incorrect:	The assets consisted of: automobiles, farm equipment, household goods, and jewelry.
Correct:	The assets consisted of automobiles, farm equipment, household goods, and jewelry.

Colons vs. Periods A colon should not end a sentence but should connect the initial part of the sentence immediately to a list. If a sentence interrupts between the "leader word" and list and the list does not immediately follow the colon, use a period. Do not use a colon at the end of either sentence.

Incorrect
Gather all of the following by Friday afternoon: Keep them in the office instead of taking them to the warehouse.
• Household goods
• Personal clothing
• Jewelry
• Sporting goods

Correct
Gather all of the following by Friday afternoon. Keep them in the office instead of taking them to the warehouse.
• Household goods
• Personal clothing
• Jewelry
• Sporting goods

To avoid having the leader word in the first sentence, another option is this:

Gather all of the following items by Friday afternoon, and keep them in the office instead of taking them to the warehouse:
• Household goods
• Personal clothing
• Jewelry
• Sporting goods

Language Focus Exercises

Complete the following exercises using what you learned in the Language Focus section.

Exercise 8.1 Circle the letter for the correctly punctuated sentence.

1.

 a. Attorneys whose clients are planning their estates will receive a special bonus at the seminar.

 b. Attorneys, whose clients are planning their estates, will receive a special bonus at the seminar.

2.
   a. After signing the will in all required locations, the man who was wearing a red shirt wished he had called his wife.
   b. After signing the will in all required locations, Mr. Guerber who was wearing a red shirt wished he had called his wife.

3.
   a. Mr. Franklin who is a well-respected estate law lawyer is retiring at the end of January.
   b. Mr. Franklin, who is a well-respected estate law lawyer, is retiring at the end of January.

Exercise 8.2 Read the following sentences and cross out incorrect punctuation, insert and circle needed punctuation, or write a "C" for "Correct" in the left margin.

1. The attorney wore a gray, wool suit to the probate hearing.

2. Eleanor, his wife of 30 years died suddenly on Sunday evening.

3. The decedent's cousin will receive the green old rusty 1962 Chevy.

4. Eventually the personal representative got around to gathering all assets.

5. The relentless, powerful, summer sun beat down on them as they cleared the warehouse of the decedent's assets.

6. With tears streaming down her face the decedent's daughter read the will.

7. As the personal representative cleaned out the garage he found green, blue and brown paint.

8. Pausing for just a 15-minute recess the judge continued the hearing.

9. The personal representative was unable to continue the inventory this afternoon, because he needed to meet with the attorney about the next steps in the probate process.

10. The old rusty hot water heater in the decedent's home was due to be replaced.

11. Although I was tired I finished the work by the 5:00 p.m. deadline on Monday.

12. The man who attempted to save the decedent's life is a retired teacher.

13. The woman, who was dressed in a bright red coat walked into the hearing late.

14. Judge Zima a district court judge postponed the hearing until tomorrow at 2:00 p.m.

15. The decedent's brother who is a dentist left Portland Monday to attend his brother's funeral on Wednesday. (The decedent has one brother.)

16. The decedent's brother who is a dentist left Portland Monday to attend his brother's funeral on Wednesday. (The decedent has 4 brothers.)

17. Finally, after much hesitation the personal representative came to the point.

18. Underneath the desk was taped a separate list of assets written by the decedent before she died.

19. Underneath the desk the will was found in an envelope.

20. The bequests which included a range of charitable organizations were given by Mr. and Mrs. Pfau.

Exercise 8.3 Read the following sentences and cross out incorrect punctuation, insert and circle needed punctuation, or write a "C" for "Correct" in the left margin.

1. The judge asked for the following documents by Friday notice of hearing and affidavit of personal representative.

2. The judge asked for documents by Friday namely notice of hearing and affidavit of personal representative.

3. The personal representative will be working all day on Saturday, the inventory is due by Wednesday.

4. The heirs were unhappy with the details of the will; therefore they all visited the attorney's office.

Editing: Active and Passive Voice

While editing estate planning and probate documents and correspondence, watch for active- and passive-voice verbs. Active voice has been called the "voice of business" because it projects a clear and positive tone to the reader.

The subject of an active voice verb is the "doer" of the action, and this voice should be used to convey positive or neutral news. Passive voice in a sentence focuses more on the action instead of on the person who performed the action. In most forms of writing, an active voice is preferred. In professional writing, it is acceptable to use passive verbs when tone must convey negative or bad news and when it does not matter who is performing the action.

In the following active-voice examples, notice that the subject is doing the action and the subject is an important part of the sentence.

> The judge signed the letters testamentary.
>
> The heirs approved the distribution plan.
>
> The heirs listened as the attorney discussed the requirements of distribution.

In the following passive-voice examples, the subject is not doing the action. It seems that the action is being done to the subject. You can recognize a passive-voice verb because it has a "being" verb helper (such as *be*, *am*, and *was*) and a past participle.

> The affidavit for collection of property has been prepared and is ready to be picked up.

The subject (affidavit) is more important in this sentence than who is preparing the affidavit.

> When we drove by the property, we noticed that the lawn had been mowed and the garage door had been closed.

We is the main subject and *noticed* is the main verb. This part of the sentence is in the active voice. The subordinate or dependent clause "that the lawn had been mowed and the garage door had been closed" has two passive-voice verbs: "had been mowed" and "had been closed." In this part of the sentence, the actions of *mowed* and *closed* are more important than who completed those actions.

Sometimes people get the idea that passive voice is *bad*. It isn't. It is important to use it appropriately, however. The following examples show instances when passive voice is the best choice in conveying bad news or when the performer of the action isn't important:

Active:	We misplaced the original of your last will and testament.
Passive:	The original of your last will and testament has been misplaced.
Active:	Mandy may have misfiled the will.
Passive:	The will may have been misfiled.

Exercise 8.4 Read the following sentences and determine if the verb is active or passive. Circle "Active" or "Passive" to the right of the sentence. Then, rewrite the sentence so that it is the opposite of what is shown. For example, if the sentence is currently passive, rewrite it so that it is active.

1. The client postponed the meeting regarding estate planning.   Active   Passive

_____

2. The assets will be distributed to all heirs by the end of January.   Active   Passive

_____

3. The heirs will be informed of the lack of funds available for distribution.   Active   Passive

_____

4. The client signed the will yesterday at the hospital three hours before he died.   Active   Passive

_____

5. On Friday, the final accounting will be reviewed by the judge.   Active   Passive

_____

Exercise 8.5

1. Open **C08_Ex8.5_ActivePassive**.
2. Edit the document for the following:
   a. Appropriate use of active and passive voice verbs
   b. Correct punctuation
   c. Misspelled or misused words

Proofreading: Check Punctuation

Until you use punctuation correctly all the time, you should be prepared to justify the reason for the punctuation you allow in a document. As has been mentioned before, legal writing can be complicated with legal jargon, long clauses and sentences, and many

Best Practice Tip

PROOFREADING PUNCTUATION

A common trick of proofreading for punctuation is to print out the document and circle each punctuation mark. The proofreader does this so that punctuation will not be missed and each mark can be addressed individually—in this way one is really looking to make sure that each is the right punctuation mark for the sentence.

interruptions. Read sentences carefully looking for independent clauses. Notice where two or more independent clauses are joined with either a comma and a coordinating conjunction (fanboys) or a semicolon. Then, work with each individual independent clause punctuating interrupting words and phrases along with other punctuation rules.

Proofreading Exercises

Use the information you have learned in the previous sections to complete the following proofreading exercises.

Exercise 8.6 Some of the punctuation in the letter in Figure 8.5 is incorrect. Read the letter and circle each mark of punctuation. Write a rule on the line provided justifying the correctness of the mark. Use this textbook and/or any style guide of your preference to find the rules.

Figure 8.5 Letter with Punctuation Errors

(Current Date) _____

Ms. Josephine Dell _____
9634 Parkway Avenue _____
Evergreen, CO 76312 _____

Dear Josephine: _____

Re: Health Care Decisions for Wilbur Ziffler _____

Enclosed is a copy of Wilbur Ziffler's Health Care Directive. You will note under _____
Paragraph 6 and Paragraph 9(a) you have the power to consent for him to receive _____
medical treatment or care it appears that the power is quite broad. _____

I understand you wish to move Wilbur from Colorado to Sunny Hills Cancer _____
Center 4977 Bayside Drive Naples, FL 32762 for specialized treatment. It would _____
seem to me that if Wilbur's health clearly has reached a level where life support _____
decisions could be made, and you have some idea as to his feelings regarding this, _____
I think you could make those decisions. In addition, there is case law stating that _____
if it will benefit him, you may move him. In Wilbur's situation I would continue _____
to take the position that he remains a citizen of Colorado, and he has been _____
moved to Florida only for health care reasons. _____

Please let me know by Friday May 30, 20xx, what you have decided to do. _____

Sincerely _____

Jeremy Smithfield _____
jsmithfield@jlslaw.emcp.com _____

JS:xx _____
Enclosure _____

BRAINSTORM PROOFREADING ACCURACY

Find a coworker as interested in proofreading accuracy as you are and share your insights, examples, and questions about punctuation as well as grammar and spelling.

Exercise 8.7 Proofread the Living Will in Figure 8.6 for punctuation errors. Use an X to cross out incorrect punctuation. Insert and circle punctuation that needs to be added. Correct your paper in class with your instructor.

Figure 8.6 **Living Will with Punctuation Errors**

Living Will
DECLARATION AS TO MEDICAL OR SURGICAL TREATMENT

I, Evan Pottenger being of sound mind and at least eighteen years of age, direct that my life shall not be artificially prolonged under the circumstances set forth below and hereby declare that:

1.   If at any time my attending physician, and one other physician certify in writing that:

a. I have an injury, disease or illness that is not curable or reversible and that, in their judgment, is a terminal condition; and

b. For a period of ten (10) consecutive days or more, I have been unconscious, comatose, or otherwise incompetent so as to be unable to make or communicate responsible decisions concerning my person; then I direct that, in accordance with Colorado law life-sustaining procedures shall be withdrawn and withheld pursuant to the terms of this declaration; it being understood that life-sustaining procedures shall not include any medical procedure or intervention for nourishment considered necessary by the attending physician to proved comfort or alleviate pain. However I may specifically direct, in accordance with Colorado law, that artificial nourishment be withdrawn or withheld pursuant to the terms of this declaration.

2. In the event that the only procedure I am being provided is artificial nourishment, I direct that one of the following actions be taken;

_____(initials of declarant) a. Artificial nourishment shall not be continued when it is the only procedure being provided; or
_____(initials of declarant) b. Artificial nourishment shall be continued for five (5) days when it is the only procedure being provided, or
_____(initials of declarant) c. Artificial nourishment shall be continued when it is the only procedure being provided.

3. I execute this declaration as my free and voluntary act this 2nd day of May in this year of 20xx.
                                    By_____

The foregoing instrument was signed and declared by Evan Pottenger to be his declaration in the presence of us, who, in his presence, in the presence of each other, and at his request have signed our names below as witnesses, and we declare that, at the time of the execution of this instrument the declarant, according to our best knowledge and belief was of sound mind and under no constraint or undue influence. We further declare that neither of us is: (1) a physician; (2) the declarant's physician or an employee of his physician (3) an employee or a patient of the health care facility in which the declarant is a patient; or (4) a beneficiary or creditor of the estate of the declarant.

Dated at_____ Colorado, this_____ day of _____, in the year_____.

_____   _____
        (Signature of Witness)   (Signature of Witness)

Exercise 8.8 The document **C08_Ex8.8_SheareRevTrust** represents part of the Sheare Family revocable trust. Remember that a revocable trust means that it can be changed after the trust is created. Complete the following activity to practice proofreading a trust.

1. Open the document and print a copy to proofread as a hard-copy document.
2. Proofread the document for misused and misspelled words as well as punctuation errors.
3. Circle punctuation that you insert and cross out any that is in the incorrect place.
5. If the instructor requires, open the electronic file **C08_Ex8.8_SheareRevTrust** again and make the corrections directly in the file. Save as **LastName_C08_Ex8.8_SheareRevTrust**.
6. Submit the requested document(s) to the instructor.

Estate Planning and Probate How-To Guide

Legal support staff play a substantial role in assisting the attorney and client through the probate process to make it as efficient as possible. The following text describes the various parts of wills and probate documents as well as procedures to follow in completing them.

A will is a very important document to the person creating it. The testator, understandably, should be confident that everything in the will is exactly as he or she wishes it to be. As the legal support person involved in preparing a client's will, it is important to spend the time needed to guarantee that the will is exactly what the client is expecting.

The Will

Being familiar with the basic content of a will helps the legal support person be more confident that the will is correct and that the testator's requests are included. Open and print the electronic file **C08_WillWithCallouts**. This document shows a basic will with trust provisions. The callouts point out significant parts to a will that every legal support person should know or learn. The paragraph following discusses specific details in the construction of any will. Refer to the will with callouts file as you continue.

By now you know several types of wills are available, including simple wills, joint or mutual wills, reciprocal wills, conditional wills, and statutory wills. Regardless of the type of will being used, they all have similar characteristics.

Wills are intended to be around a long time, so they are usually printed on high-quality bond paper. Sometimes that paper is engraved (preprinted) with the words "Last Will and Testament of ..." centered at the top in formal lettering. Beneath the printed heading, the name of the testator and the rest of the will requirements are typed; for example:

Last Will and Testament

of

Jane Greathurst

As you continue to read, refer to the numbered callouts on the will as shown in file **C08_WillWithCallouts**. The first nine numbers are in order. Ten and beyond appear throughout the document.

1. Two-Inch Top Margin Because most wills include a protective back cover (or legal back), the first page of a will has a 2-inch top margin, allowing the legal back to be stapled onto the will. A legal back to a will is usually made of thicker paper and placed behind the last page. The legal back is placed 1 inch above the top of the will and folded over to the front of the will, then stapled twice at the top. Remember that people are hoping that this document will be around for many, many years after it is created!

2. Spacing A will is always double-spaced for ease of reading unless the attorney prefers to single space it.

3. Introductory Paragraph The introductory paragraph indicates the testator's domicile. Recall that *domicile* indicates the place where the probate court proceedings will take place and the state that will collect death taxes. A person may have several residences but only one domicile. The testator decides which of several residences will be the domicile, and it is then written into the will.

The introductory paragraph also includes wording that the testator is of sound mind and is declaring that this is his or her valid last will and testament.

4. Payment of Debts Clause Debts and funeral expenses are always paid before heirs are given any money or assets. Sometimes people think they are getting something from a decedent's estate while not being aware of how many debts the decedent's estate must settle.

5. Residuary Bequest Clause A will always has a clause indicating the disposition of property. This property may be "preresiduary gifts" or "residuary bequests." **Preresiduary gifts** are assets or money given to heirs or beneficiaries as stated in the will and distributed after all debts of the estate are paid but before the payment of **residuary bequests**, which are bequests that give money or assets to heirs after the debts are paid and preresiduary gifts are distributed.

6. Appointment of Personal Representative In a will, the testator names an individual who should carry out the testator's wishes. Every estate requires that someone be chosen for this role. Some states call this person the personal representative; other states, the executor. This person may be a spouse, other family member, unrelated friend, attorney, accountant, or any person of the testator's choice.

7. Testator's Signature Line The testator's signature is the most important part of the will. The will *must* be signed for it to be valid. Notice that the signature line starts at the center of the page and goes to the right margin. Since the will is double spaced, at this point the spacing of the document is changed to single spacing so that the testator's name is typed directly below the signature line. Then the will changes back to double spacing as it continues.

8. Attestation Clause A will must be witnessed for it to be valid. After the testator signs a will, the witnesses also sign what is called the attestation clause. **Attestation clause** means a clause at the end of a will in which the witnesses state that the will was signed and witnessed with all the formalities required by law. Witnesses can be anyone who will not benefit from the will that they are signing. In some states, if a beneficiary to a will signs as a witness, he or she forfeits his or her right to receive distributions from the will.

As a legal support person, you may be asked to sign as a witness to the will. All you are looking for is that the testator seems to be of sound mind and that no one is forcing him or her to sign the will.

9. Self-Proving Affidavit On the last page of the will, you may also find a self-proving affidavit. Some states may require a will to include this affidavit. In other states, adding the affidavit is an attorney preference. A self-proving affidavit is added to a will at the time of the execution (signing). The testator and witnesses sign under oath (acknowledged by a notary public) and swear that the testator is at least 18 years of age, of sound mind, and under no undue influence or pressure by anyone to sign the will. Self-proving affidavits are added to wills so that a witness will not have to be called many years in the future to verify that he or she witnessed the execution of a particular will. Recalling a witness to a will would happen only if someone contests or argues about the validity of a will after the testator's death. With the self-proving affidavit added to the will, the notary signs the acknowledgment. The notary's signature would then be adequate proof years after the signing of the will.

10. Separate Written List Clause Paragraph III in the will is called the "separate written list clause." Some state laws allow a separate written list, which is a handwritten or typed list separate from the will indicating that certain items are to be given to certain people. If you are given such a list, follow the instructions of the attorney about where the list is to be kept.

11. Common Disaster Clause Paragraph IV of this will is the "common disaster clause." It is used in reciprocal wills only. The will shown is a reciprocal will in which the testator (the husband) gives everything to his wife. Although the parties do not have to be legally married, users of a reciprocal will usually are. The wife then makes a will giving everything to her husband. The common disaster clause in a reciprocal will says that if this is the husband's will and he dies in a car accident and his wife dies in the same accident, then everything that he says that he gives to his wife should actually pass to their children.

12. Appointment of Guardians Included in the common disaster clause is the wording for identifying the guardians of the surviving children, since guardians would be needed if both parents died.

13. Simple Trust in the Event That Both Parties Die The testator can choose to include paragraphs describing trust provisions in a will; however, not all wills include these paragraphs. If the testator has minor children, the will must include wording to appoint a guardian or guardians, and money will typically be provided from the estate. These paragraphs may also set up a trust fund for the care of the minor children to be accessed by the guardian. The trust provisions included in the will provide for the health, care, comfort, and education of the beneficiary of each trust. The testator can choose any age for the beneficiaries to receive funds from the trust. Notice that the beneficiaries of this trust do not receive the funds until they are 25 years old.

14. Revocation Clause The words in the revocation clause revoke any previous wills. Remember that heirs may find several signed wills after a person dies. If two wills are found, the most recently dated one is the valid will.

15. Appointment of Alternate Personal Representative A will should always appoint an alternate personal representative. The original personal representative may not be willing or able to carry out the wishes of the testator after the testator's death. In that event, the alternate personal representative would be required. If neither personal representative can perform the duties, the court will appoint someone who can.

16. Requirement of a Bond The law requires that the will indicate whether the personal representative has to be bonded. Recall that when a personal representative is bonded, an insurance policy that protects against dishonesty on the part of the personal representative is required. The testator can choose in the will whether the personal representative is to be bonded or not.

17. Testimonium Clause The testimonium is the final clause in a document; it restates the purpose of the document and includes the date on which the document is signed.

You will see similar paragraphs in many legal documents, such as contracts and deeds. This clause always appears right before the signature line. The testimonium clause also always starts with the phrase IN TESTIMONY WHEREOF, in all capital letters.

Page Numbering and Footers in Wills In the legal office, multipage documents are usually paginated (page-numbered) at the bottom center of the page with no page number on the first page. Pagination would begin on the second page starting with "2." Wills, however, generally use page numbers in footers on *every* page *including* the first. The page numbering also includes *the total number of pages* and notes that page out of the total number the reader is viewing.

The footer in wills includes pagination but also the testator's signature line on every page *except* pages that already provide a signature line for the testator. Notice in Figure 8.7 that page 5 of 6 has a signature line in the footer (because the testator does not sign on this page). In addition, the bottom of page 6 of 6 does not have a signature in the footer because the testator already signed in the body of the will.

This type of footer can be tricky to create since it means changing the content of the footer in the middle of the will. When you insert a footer into a document, you would expect that the footer would automatically appear on every page of the document. To make the footer different on some pages, you will need to insert a section break so that you will be able to include a different footer on certain pages.

Because office styles vary, the page number/testator signature footer can be formatted in a variety of ways. The important part is that the footer must have the current page number of total pages and the testator's signature on those pages that do not have a place in the will for the testator's signature. Follow the preferences of your office.

CREATING HEADERS AND FOOTERS IN WILLS

Until you are proficient in inserting headers and/or footers, always type and save a will (or any document that has complicated headers and/or footers) without inserting the header or footer. Then save it again with another name. Use the second file to insert the headers and/or footers. If you have trouble getting them right, delete the one you have been working in, resave the original another time with a different name, and work in it until you have the headers and/or footers right. It is easier to start over in a document that has not been worked in.

Figure 8.7 **Will Pages That Require Testator's Signature in the Footer**

have custody of my minor children, and shall serve without bond. If he does not qualify or for

any reason ceases to serve as guardian, I appoint as successor guardian my cousin Kevin Moon.

I have signed this will this _____ day of _____, 20___ .

_____
Tessa Tatterall

SIGNED AND DECLARED by Tess Tatteral on_____, 20_____, to be her will, in our

presence, who at her request, in her presence and in the presence of each other, all being present

at the same time, have signed our names as witnesses.

Witness

_____
(signature)

_____
_____
_____
Address

Witness

_____
(signature)

_____
_____
_____
Address

Sworn to before me this_____ day of _____,
20_____.

_____
Notary Public

Official Seal

Page 6 of 6

r is unable or unwilling to act, the survivor shall serve

e powers allowable to executors under the laws of this

any kind shall be required of any executor.

ou could name the trustees in this clause as well. The

ave the estate money.

I: Simultaneous Death Clause

r such circumstances that the order of our deaths cannot

e deemed to have predeceased me. No person, other

survived me if such person dies within 30 days after my

s of this will accordingly.

This clause helps avoid the sometimes time-consuming problems that occur if you and

your spouse die together in an accident. Your spouse's will should contain an identical clause;

even though it seems contradictory to have two wills each directing that the other spouse died

first, since each will is probated by itself, this allows the estate plan set up in each will to go

forward as you planned. The second sentence exists to prevent the awkward legal complications

that can ensue if someone dies between the time you die and the time the estate is divided up.

Instead of passing through two probate processes, your gift to a beneficiary who dies shortly

after you do would go to whomever you would have wanted it to go had the intended beneficiary

died before you did. Most such gifts go into the residuary estate.

ARTICLE IX: Guardian

If my husband does not survive me and I leave minor children surviving me, I appoint as

guardian of the person and property of my minor children my uncle Ernest Entwistle. He shall

Page 5 of 6

_____
Tessa Tatterall

The Signing or Execution of the Will

The signing of a formal, typewritten will is an important point in the process of completing it.

After the will has been drafted by the attorney and prepared by the legal support person, it will be given to the client to review before signing. If the client is satisfied with the contents of the will, the legal support person will be asked to set up an appointment between the attorney, the client, and witnesses to sign or execute the will. Generally, prior to the actual signing of the will, the attorney will:

- Verify that the testator is of appropriate age and of sound mind and mental capacity to sign the will
- Verify that the testator understands the contents of the will and made it of his or her own free will
- Ask the witnesses if they believe the testator is of sound mind and mental capacity to sign the will and that the testator is signing of his/her own free will

The testator must be present as well as the witnesses and the attorney. Some states require a notary public be present to verify signatures as well. The testator may invite his or her own witnesses to the signing of the will as long as they are not beneficiaries or heirs of the will. Often the witnesses are staff members of the law office. The witnesses are not required to read the last will and testament. Witness duties focus on the individual signing the will and not the terms of the will. From the witnesses' perspective, the testator should appear sober, competent, and aware of what he or she is doing in regard to executing the will.

The notary public is present to officially verify that the people signing the will as testator and witnesses are truly who they say they are.

Each page of the will must be signed by the testator. The witnesses sign on the last pages following the testator's signature. The notary public signs at the very end.

A testator can have just one valid will—the most recently dated will with the original signatures. Older versions of wills or copies of wills will not be deemed valid by the probate court. The original will must be kept in a secure place, such as the testator's safe. Some attorneys keep original valid wills in their offices in fireproof safes. Other attorneys do not want the responsibility of other people's valid wills in their possession. Some people put their valid wills in their safe deposit boxes, which can cause problems, since some states do not allow anyone but the owner of the box to open it. As a result, extra court procedures are required to officially open the safe deposit box. In addition, some people also file their wills with the court administrator so that they will be available when needed.

Preparing Probate Documents

A law office that works with clients needing assistance with probate will have access to the appropriate forms. The probate courts in most states have information and

Best Practice Tip

CHECK FONT SIZE AND STYLE IN PAGE NUMBERS AND OTHER FOOTERS

When you are inserting the page number in the footer, check that it is the same font style and size as the body of the will. Some word processing programs make the page numbers bold. You may want to unbold the numbers so that the entire footer is the same. Remember, however, to always follow your office's current style.

NATIONAL CENTER FOR STATE COURTS WEBSITE

You will be using this website in this chapter to find probate information. However, continue to use it for all the areas of law you may find yourself working in. Feel free to explore the website so that you will know what it contains.

forms readily available on the Internet. The National Center for State Courts has a large amount of information available on its website at http://lep.emcp.net/ncsc/. The website contains links to each state's official court website at which information associated with probate procedure, rules and forms are available.

The forms provided by the National Center for State Courts website come in several formats:

- Microsoft Word fill-in template: Created and protected so that a user can fill in the fields but cannot change anything else in the form. This type of document can be saved.
- Microsoft Word document: Created so that the user can change anything in the document along with filling in needed information. This document can be saved.
- PDF form: Created as a pdf. Users cannot change the form but can fill in the needed information and print the document. This form cannot be saved.

The Microsoft Word fill-in template is the most flexible for the needs of the law office. The templates have not been password protected, which allows you to change the form, if necessary. Note, however, that the court would probably prefer that you simply fill in the correct information without making changes.

How-To Guide Exercises

Complete the following activities using the information discussed in the previous section.

Exercise 8.9

1. Research your own word processing program to determine how to successfully insert section breaks and footers so that some pages have page numbers and signature lines and other pages have page numbers and no signature lines.

2. Write the steps on the lines below. You will be using these steps in Exercise 8.10.

_____

_____

_____

_____

_____

_____

_____

Exercise 8.10

1. Open **C08_Ex8.10_FooterSignaturePractice**.
2. Resave as **LastName_C08_Ex8.10_FooterSignaturePractice**.
3. Using the information you discovered in your research in Exercise 8.8, insert a footer showing the current page number and the total number of pages.
4. Also include a signature line for the testator within the footer on the pages that do not already have a place for the testator's signature.
5. Resave the document and submit it to the instructor.

Exercise 8.11 Practice navigating the National Center for State Courts website by locating files that you will need for the end-of-chapter projects.

1. Create a folder within the Chapter 8 folder of your storage device called "Colorado Probate Forms."
2. Go to the National Center for State Courts website and search for probate courts.
3. Find the website for Colorado state courts.
4. Find and select the link to probate forms.
5. Locate and save the following Word template forms into the folder you just created.
   - Petition for formal probate of will and formal appointment of personal representative. Save this document as **LastName_C08_P3A_PetitionFormalProbate**.
   - Letters testamentary/of administration (this document can be used as letters testamentary or letters of administration). Save the document as **LastName_C08_P3B_LettersTestamentary**.
   - Notice to creditors by publication. Save this file as **LastName_C08_P3C_NoticeCreditorsPub**.

Exercise 8.12

1. Open the following documents:
   a. **C08_Ex8.12_IDWillParts**
   b. **C08_WillWithCallouts**
2. Compare the will in file A to the will in file B.
3. In file A select sections of the will and insert a comment identifying the part of the will using file B as a guide.
4. After inserting comments into File A identifying the parts, save it as **LastName_C08_Ex8.12_IDWillParts**.

Critical Thinking: Efficiency in the Office

Efficiency in the office contributes to the profits of your firm. Use your critical thinking skills to examine your current work procedures and determine if they could be restructured or standardized to avoid repetition and missed deadlines. Standardizing work processes in a legal setting means being aware of routine tasks and noticing steps that are repetitive or unnecessary. Repetitive tasks can sometimes be done to several similar items at the same time.

EFFICIENT USE OF TIME

If you encounter tasks that appear unnecessary, check with your office manager or supervisor to determine if the task is a good use of your time.

File Maintenance

Maintaining orderly files allows the attorney to make good decisions with current information. You will not be saving time if the attorney drafts a letter to a client suggesting solutions to a legal problem only to learn that the client left a phone message or sent a letter saying the problem had been solved, but the information had not been filed yet.

File maintenance means keeping up with the filing required on a daily or weekly basis as well as reviewing the work in active files. Watch for the following while maintaining files to ensure that tasks and deadlines have not been overlooked:

- Look for immediate work to be done.
- Remind the attorney of the work to be done.
- Make reminder dates of when to look at the file again.
- Make reminder dates on items that are due back to you, due from you, or when you are to report back to the client.

Clients will be assured that the firm is focusing on their cases if contact is made periodically. Some attorneys prefer to contact the client every four to six weeks, whether there is work to do or not. This contact does not have to be a long communication. A recap of what work has been done recently and what work is in progress lets a client know that the case is important to the office. If all current work is completed, this contact can be simply a short email asking if all is well. It could even be a flier introducing a new attorney in the office or an office newsletter. Any communication will be useful that lets the client know the office is there if assistance is needed in the future.

Procedure Checklists

Procedure checklists are helpful in determining what you can do without the assistance of the attorney and when to remind the attorney of the next step he or she must do. In the office, if you do not have a procedure checklist prepared, put a blank sheet of paper on top of the file. As you work through the file with the attorney, create your checklist. When you are satisfied that this checklist includes all necessary steps to complete a probate procedure, type it and make the document a standardized checklist to be used in all probate files.

Figures 8.8 and 8.9 are examples of two different checklists that a legal office support person might use. Figure 8.8 is a checklist to verify that all informal probate documents have been completed, sent, and filed. Figure 8.9 shows a checklist with reminder information to complete probate forms more efficiently. Remember in your own lists to change or add information depending upon the procedures in your local area.

Figure 8.8 **Probate Document Checklist**

CHECK LIST FOR INFORMAL PROBATE

ITEM	COMPLETED	SENT	FILED
Application	____	____	____
Application and Oath	____	____	____
Notice of Informal Probate	____	____	____
Letters Testamentary	____	____	____
Statement of Informal Probate	____	____	____
Aff. of Service of Notice of Appointment/ Hearing	____	____	____
Spousal Notice/Children	____	____	____
Aff. of Service of Spousal/Children	____	____	____
Notice	____	____	____
Aff. of Publication	____	____	____
SS-4 for Estate	____	____	____
SS-4 for Trust	____	____	____
PR's Duties Letter	____	____	____
PR's Tax Obligations	____	____	____
Retainer Signed	____	____	____
Notice to Judge	____	____	____
Notice to Atty. General	____	____	____
Inventory	____	____	____
Service of Inventory	____	____	____
Aff. of Service of Inventory	____	____	____
Information Statement to Close Estate	____	____	____
Service of Informal Statement	____	____	____
Aff. of Mailing/Informal	____	____	____

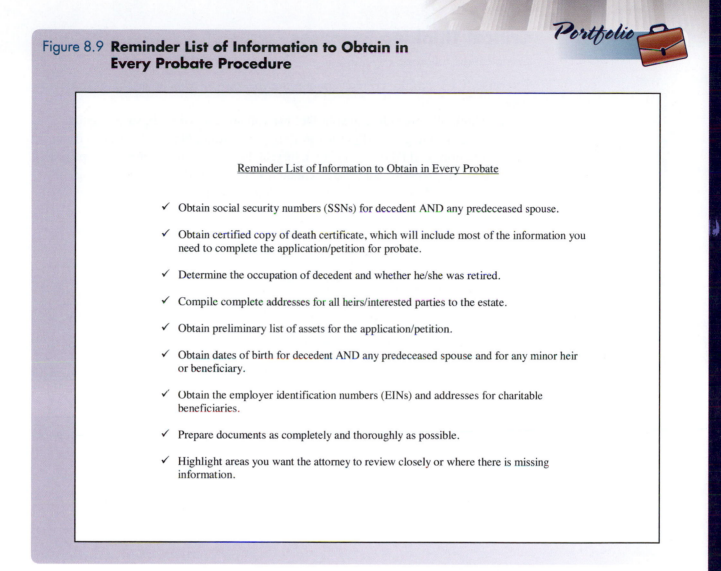

Reminder List of Information to Obtain in Every Probate

✓ Obtain social security numbers (SSNs) for decedent AND any predeceased spouse.

✓ Obtain certified copy of death certificate, which will include most of the information you need to complete the application/petition for probate.

✓ Determine the occupation of decedent and whether he/she was retired.

✓ Compile complete addresses for all heirs/interested parties to the estate.

✓ Obtain preliminary list of assets for the application/petition.

✓ Obtain dates of birth for decedent AND any predeceased spouse and for any minor heir or beneficiary.

✓ Obtain the employer identification numbers (EINs) and addresses for charitable beneficiaries.

✓ Prepare documents as completely and thoroughly as possible.

✓ Highlight areas you want the attorney to review closely or where there is missing information.

Critical Thinking Exercises

Complete the following exercises using the information provided in the previous section.

Exercise 8.13 Practice creating a procedure checklist by completing the following steps.

1. Think of a procedure in your life that you are familiar with, such as child care, changing the oil in the car, things you would like a babysitter to do in addition to child care, tune up a bicycle, housecleaning, preparing to plant a garden, preparing for a party, children's chores, studying and preparing for a test, etc. Write the procedure on the lines provided:

_____

_____

_____

_____

_____

_____

_____

_____

_____

_____

2. Write a procedure checklist for the tasks you listed in step 1. Be specific enough in your checklist that another person would be able to complete the tasks with very little assistance. Be creative in using check boxes or lines for check marks. Make the document usable.

3. Save the document as **LastName_C08_Ex8.13_ProcedureChecklist**.

4. Email your procedure checklist to three other students in your class. Ask them to read the checklist and add any steps that they feel are missing or would make it better.

5. Submit the list to the instructor.

Chapter Summary and Projects

Summary

You have now read an overview of estate planning and probate and should have an understanding of what tasks you might perform in a legal office that practices in these areas of law. You have also reviewed procedures that are important to legal support staff in assisting the attorney and client prepare a will. You have reviewed and practiced applying language, editing, and proofreading skills to legal documents, and have also practiced methods to help your future office create procedures and checklists to be more efficient.

Remember that as a legal support person, it will be your responsibility in a probate procedure to complete the following tasks:

- Verify that the client has supplied all the information requested on the estate planning information form.
- Prepare and print estate planning documents as the attorney requests.
- Obtain additional information from the client, if needed.
- Obtain and prepare forms necessary to complete a probate procedure using instructions from the attorney.
- Assist the attorney and the client with the execution of estate planning documents.
- Prepare and use checklists when needed.
- Assist the personal representative to perform the necessary tasks in officially closing an estate.

Key Terms

alternate valuation date, 263

application for appointment as personal representative, 258

beneficiary, 251

bequeath, 254

bequest, 254

bond, 258

codicil, 250

common law states, 254

community property, 254

community property state, 254

community, 254

conditional will, 250

creditors claim period, 264

decedent, 253

devise, 254

devisee, 254

devisor, 254

DNR order, 252

domicile, 258

durable power of attorney, 253

elective share, 250

equity state, 254

estate administration, 253

estate planning, 247

estate, 254

executor, 249

fiduciary, 249

fiscal year, 264

formal probate, 256

handwritten wills, 249

health care directive, 252

heirs, 247

holographic wills, 249

informal probate, 256

inheritance law, 254

insolvent, 256

interested persons, 258

intestate, 248

inventory, 261

irrevocable trust, 251

joint will, see also mutual will, 249

last will and testament, 248

legal newspaper, 259

Local Focus Research

The Local Focus icons that appear in the chapter indicate that your local court may have different rules, due dates, terminology, and/or procedures than what has been discussed. The following Local Focus assignments will help you acknowledge these differences. Locate the Chapter 08 folder in your electronic storage medium and open the local focus file **C08_LocalFocus_EstatePlanning&Probate**. Resave the file as **LastName_C08_LocalFocus_EstatePlanning&Probate**. Research the following topics described and record your research in the file you just created. Use this information as a reference tool as you start and continue your career as a legal support person. Your instructor may ask you to submit a copy as homework.

Local Focus 8.1   Research the Internet to determine whether your state recognizes handwritten/holographic wills. If it does, write the requirements on the lines provided. If not, research a nearby state until you find one that does recognize handwritten or holographic wills. Write the answer on the following line.

_____

Local Focus 8.2   Research the Internet to find whether your state allows oral wills, and if it does, whether any special requirements make them allowable. Write the answers below:

_____

_____

Local Focus 8.3 Research the Internet to find whether your state allows conditional wills, and if it does, whether any special requirements make them allowable. Write the answers on the lines provided:

_____

_____

Local Focus 8.4 Research the Internet to find the statutory requirements of a will in your state. List the requirements on the lines below:

_____

_____

_____

Local Focus 8.5 Research the Internet to find out whether your state's laws include a law regarding elective shares, and if it does, whether specific procedures must be followed in enforcing an elective share. Write the answers on the lines provided:

_____

_____

_____

Local Focus 8.6 Research the Internet to determine whether your state has adopted all or parts of the Uniform Probate Code. In addition, choose another state and determine its UPC status. Write the information on the lines provided, indicating whether the state has adopted the UPC in its entirety or only in part.

_____

_____

_____

_____

Local Focus 8.7   Determine which newspaper is the official newspaper for the publication of legal notices in your area. You can find this information in a number of ways:

1. Look in the Yellow Pages or do an Internet search for the names of local newspapers.
2. Call a newspaper's business office and ask if it is the official newspaper.
3. Look in your local newspaper to see if it includes legal notices. This paper will probably be the official newspaper for publishing them.

Write the name of the official newspaper in your area on the line provided.

_____

Local Focus 8.8   Page 289 discusses the National Center for State Courts website. Go to the website and find your own state's website. Type "probate court" into the search box. Search for and bookmark (or favorite) areas of your state's court website that you feel will help you through the probate process, including rules, deadlines, and official court forms. On the lines provided, list two websites that you bookmarked.

_____

_____

Scenario

You work for Jeremy Smithfield in the Golden, Colorado, office of Jordan, Leone & Sanchez, whose address is 3966 Bitter Root Concourse, Golden, CO 67203. The office telephone number is 691-555-9765 and the fax number is 691-555-5230. Mr. Smithfield's attorney identification number is 082546. Three weeks ago, Kenneth Cross contacted Jeremy Smithfield about writing a will. Mr. Cross had a two-hour appointment and discussed his estate situation. During the appointment, you sat with Mr. Cross, asking him the necessary questions to complete the estate planning information form. Mr. Cross took the form home to look up additional information for questions to which he did not readily know the answers. After finding the needed information, Mr. Cross mailed the completed form back to the office. Attorney Smithfield then dictated and you transcribed Mr. Cross's will.

Another client, Timothy Wickstade, visited with Attorney Jeremy Smithfield last week about the probate of Harold Wickstade's estate. Timothy's father, Harold Wayne Wickstade, died recently. Eight years ago Jordan, Leone & Sanchez had prepared Harold Wickstade's last will and testament, which named Timothy as the personal representative of the estate.

Project 1   Edit a Will

Use the completed estate planning information form to verify details, edit, and proofread the recently prepared will.

1. Open and print **C08_P1_CrossInfoForm**.
2. Open the file **C08_P1_LastWillCross** and display it on the computer screen. This is the will that you and Attorney Smithfield prepared for Mr. Cross.
3. Resave the file as **LastName_C08_P1_LastWillCrossCorrected**.
4. Use the printed copy of the information form to check the information in the prepared will. Make corrections directly into the file as you go.
5. Read the will for content first, checking facts and details that may be incorrect or missing.
6. Read the will once more for errors in spelling, grammar, and punctuation.
7. Resave the corrected file.
8. Submit the file to the instructor.

Project 2 Proofread Letters

Yesterday you transcribed several letters for Attorney Smithfield, but you did not have time to proofread them before you left for the day. After proofreading Mr. Cross's last will and testament, you find the time to proofread the letters for Mr. Smithfield's signature.

1. Open the following letters:

   C08_P2_Letter1

   C08_P2_Letter2

2. Proofread each letter on the computer screen, making corrections directly into the files.

3. Resave each letter as

   LastName_C08_Letter1Corrected

   LastName_C08_Letter2Corrected.

4. Submit the letters to the instructor.

Project 3 Petition for Formal Probate of Will and Formal Appointment of Personal Representative

After their meeting last week, Attorney Smithfield asked Timothy Wickstade to complete the estate information form regarding his father's estate. You and Attorney Smithfield have worked with Timothy Wickstade, the personal representative, to complete the following documents:

- Petition for formal probate of will and formal appointment of personal representative
- Letters testamentary
- Notice to creditors by publication

Part A Petition for formal probate of will and formal appointment of personal representative.

1. Open and print **C08_P3_WickstadeEstateInfoForm**.

2. Locate and open the **LastName_C08_P3A_PetitionFormalProbate** file that you found saved during your research in Exercise 8.11.

3. Using the Wickstade estate information form, complete the template for a petition for formal probate of will and formal appointment of personal representative. Use this additional information in completing the Petition for Formal Probate caption: Denver Probate Court of Douglas County at 3867 Fifth Street, Golden, CO 67203. The Case Number is Pro4963-221 and the hearing will be held in Probate Division in Courtroom 19A.

4. Save the petition as **LastName_C08_P3A_PetitionWickstade**.

5. In addition to completing the form, type a list of missing information.

6. Save the list as **LastName_C08_P3A_MissingInfoList**.

7. Submit both the petition and the list to the instructor.

Part B Letters Testamentary

1. Using the Wickstade estate information form, complete a letters testamentary for Harold Wayne Wickstade's appointed personal representative.

2. Locate and open the **LastName_C08_P3B_LettersTestamentary** file that you saved during your research in Exercise 8.11.

3. Save as **LastName_C08_P3B_LettersWickstade**.

4. If you find that information is missing for you to complete the letters testamentary, add the questions to the list that you started in Part A.

5. Submit these documents to the instructor.

Part C Notice to creditors by publication

Timothy Wickstade, as personal representative of his father's estate, must give notice to creditors by publication with the following information:

- Notice must be published on or before October 15, 20xx.
- Notice is to be published in The High Country Journal, 115 South Ranch Road, Highlands Ranch, CO 65771.
- Instructions to the newspaper: Publish this notice once a week for three consecutive calendar weeks. Send an invoice to Jeremy Smithfield at the preceding address.

As the legal support person for Attorney Smithfield, you will have to help Timothy Wickstade to obtain and complete this form.

1. Using the Wickstade estate information form, complete a notice to creditors by publication.

2. Locate and open **LastName_C08_P3C_NoticeCreditorsPub** that you found during your research in Exercise 8.11.

3. Save as **LastName_C08_P3C_NoticeCreditorsPub**.

4. Submit the file to the instructor.

Discuss the Projects

Recall that the critical thinking section of this chapter discusses efficiency in the office, file maintenance and procedure checklists. Think of the "important paper files" in your personal life and how you have them organized. Some of us are more organized than others. Share with your classmates how you organize your important paper files at home. You may learn more efficient ways to organize your files. In addition, discuss with the instructor and your classmates how your electronic files are organized for school and home.

Bankruptcy

Chapter Objectives

- Review terminology specific to bankruptcy
- Perform Internet research to locate information about federal and state bankruptcy codes
- Review the various types of bankruptcy relief
- Use critical thinking skills to find solutions to problems
- Use the editing skills you have developed in previous chapters to convert information to the correct format required by your project
- Use the proofreading skills you have developed in previous chapters to check information for accuracy and completeness

Before beginning the exercises for this chapter, copy to your storage medium the Chapter 09 folder from the Student Resources disc that accompanies this textbook. Do this for each chapter before starting the chapter's exercises.

In 2010, Diana Baker decided to pursue her lifelong dream and opened her own restaurant. To accomplish this endeavor, she had to obtain a small-business loan from a local bank, use most of her savings, and accept a personal loan from a friend. After two bad reviews in the local paper, a failed health inspection, and numerous customer complaints, Diana realized that her restaurant was not going to be a success. To cover her debts, she attempted to sell the building and the materials she had purchased. But she owed more than $140,000 to the bank, her friend, and a number of credit card companies. She was now receiving angry letters and phone calls daily, demanding that she send money. Having no other options, she decided to meet with an attorney at the law offices of Nelson & Klug to discuss whether bankruptcy was a viable solution.

The employees at Nelson & Klug spend their work days helping clients through personal and business legal procedures. Herman Nelson's legal support staff research, draft, and finalize business contracts including litigation documents, sales contracts, and employment agreements. Marilyn Klug's team handles both personal and business bankruptcy. Whether an individual or business is succeeding or reorganizing, the staff at Nelson & Klug work together to meet or exceed the expectations of their clients.

You may know of someone whose life has been touched by bankruptcy. **Bankruptcy** is a legal procedure governed by federal statute that enables individuals and businesses to resolve debt problems. This typically means that the person or entity filing for bankruptcy will lose non-exempt assets but will be able to stop any financial claims that creditors might make. Individuals and businesses file for bankruptcy for various reasons, including unemployment, high medical bills, harassment by creditors, fraudulent claims by creditors, foreclosure, divorce, and poor business practices. The need to file bankruptcy can happen to anyone if the right circumstances arise. Although it can be a highly emotional experience, it gives people an opportunity to make a fresh financial start. The bankruptcy code gives debtors the protection of the federal government and helps them to either repay or eliminate their debts. The **bankruptcy code** is a federal bankruptcy law known as Title 11 of the U.S. Code (11 U.S.C. §§ 101–1330). The bankruptcy code contains all of the laws pertaining to the different types of bankruptcy, time limitations, and standards that must be met for filing. In addition, each state has its own local bankruptcy rules. These rules must be reviewed by the attorney in conjunction with the federal rules in preparing bankruptcy filings.

The Bankruptcy Process

Bankruptcy protection is available to individuals as well as businesses. People live their daily lives or conduct business and for various reasons (such as home mortgages, unexpected medical bills, excessive spending, job loss, loss of business income, and/or mismanagement of money) may not be able to pay their bills. If bills are not being paid, then creditors begin collection efforts. A person or business may start receiving late payment notices or phone calls from creditors, or property may be repossessed. As part of the collection process, creditors may obtain judgments to seize a portion of the debtor's wages. A **debtor** is a person or entity who owes money or a legal obligation to creditors. A **creditor** is a person or organization to which the debtor owes money or legal obligation. A **debt** (sometimes referred to as a legal obligation) is money owed to another.

If a debtor has not been able to manage repayment, the debtor will consult an attorney for assistance. The debtor will attend prebankruptcy credit counseling, in the course of which the credit counseling service determines whether the debtor is eligible to file for bankruptcy. The debtor will be given a credit counseling certificate that is later filed with the bankruptcy court.

The attorney will ask the client to complete a client questionnaire, which the attorney will review to determine the type of bankruptcy for which the debtor may file (chapter 7 or 13 bankruptcy, etc.). The attorney and legal support staff will then begin the process of preparing and filing the bankruptcy documents, such as a bankruptcy petition and related bankruptcy schedules. A **bankruptcy petition** is the initial document filed with the bankruptcy court giving information needed to start the bankruptcy process.

After the bankruptcy petition is filed with the bankruptcy court, the court will set a date for a **meeting of creditors**, at which the debtor is questioned under oath about assets and liabilities. If creditors do not raise objections, the bankruptcy judge will allow or disallow the bankruptcy and either discharge allowable debts or make a repayment plan.

The debtor must attend additional debtor education sessions and is given information designed to help the debtor manage his or her finances more successfully in the future. However, a debtor who is granted bankruptcy protection is not automatically immune from future financial hardship, and some debtors have been known to file bankruptcy several times. Restrictions, however, are in place on how often a debtor can file for bankruptcy. For instance, after filing a chapter 7 bankruptcy, a debtor must wait eight years before filing for bankruptcy relief under chapter 7 again. If a debtor files under chapter 7, the debtor cannot file under chapter 13 for four years. Because the bankruptcy code is occasionally amended, the attorney must be familiar with the changes in the law.

When debtors decide to file for bankruptcy, they usually consult an experienced attorney. The attorney will complete a **disposable income test** and **means test**, which are tests used to determine the type of bankruptcy for which a debtor may file and whether the debtor will have income available after paying necessary monthly expenses to pay off at least part of his or her unsecured debt. **Unsecured debts** are debts for which credit was given without security or collateral. **Secured debt** is debt that is protected by a tangible asset such as a home or vehicle. The home and/or vehicle(s) are referred to as **secured property**.

Types of Bankruptcy

Because the clients who desire bankruptcy protection are so diverse, there types of bankruptcy are available, each with a specific purpose.

A debtor may be relieved of most or all financial obligations or may be required to repay a percentage of some debts. If the debtor is ordered to repay some debt, the bankruptcy trustee will work out a repayment plan with the debtor that is agreed to by the creditor. A **bankruptcy trustee** is an officer of the court who reviews the bankruptcy documents and represents the interests of the creditors. The trustee may also be known as the **bankruptcy administrator** in other states. The role of the bankruptcy trustee varies under different chapters or types of bankruptcy. The types of bankruptcy protection available are summarized in the following paragraph:

Chapter 9 is a reorganization of debt for cities, towns, villages, counties, taxing districts, municipal utilities, and school districts. Chapters 9, 12, 13, and 15 involve debtor reorganization. **Chapter 11** is a reorganization plan under which a debtor may remain in possession of assets and operate a business under the supervision of the court for the benefit of the creditors. **Chapter 12** allows family farmers and fishermen to repay debts over time from future earnings. It is similar to chapter 13 but has restrictive eligibility requirements. **Chapter 13** is a consolidation of debt with repayment of all or part of the debt over a period of time. **Chapter 15** deals with cases that cross state borders. **Chapter 7** is the most common type of bankruptcy because all unsecured debt is traditionally discharged. Debtors can keep exempt assets and the case is completed in a very short time. Chapter 7 does not involve payments to creditors over time.

Upon review of a debtor's particular situation and a conference with the debtor, an attorney will perform a means test and determine which chapter to file under. Once the bankruptcy type is determined, the attorney will give the client detailed instructions about the many items of documentation the client is required to produce so that the bankruptcy petition can be prepared correctly and completely. The court will set deadlines after the petition for bankruptcy has been filed, so the attorney must make sure that all documentation is in place before filing. The attorney will rely on the legal support person to help keep track of the various deadlines and documents the client has provided.

Disclosing Debt, Income, and Assets

When a debtor files a petition for bankruptcy, the debtor must disclose on the petition and bankruptcy schedules all income, assets, and debts in addition to answering detailed questions concerning the history of the debtor's financial affairs. The attorney will use this information to perform the means test calculation to determine whether the debtor is eligible to file for bankruptcy protection and under which chapter the debtor may file. The list of assets is used to determine what property or assets are exempt versus nonexempt for liquidation purposes. **Non-exempt assets** are property of a debtor that can be liquidated to satisfy claims of creditors. The trustee will make an effort to pay the creditors an equitable distribution of the assets and will, in most cases, stop any one creditor from taking all the assets. **Exempt assets** are property that a debtor is allowed to retain free from the claims of creditors who do not have liens (official claims) on the property.

The history of the debtor's financial affairs is necessary to assure that the debtor acted in accordance with the laws during the period prior to filing.

Debts When filing for bankruptcy, a list of all debts must be provided to the attorney to be listed in the bankruptcy petition, because if the bankruptcy is allowed, only the debts listed will be eliminated. **Dischargeable debts** are personal liabilities of the debtor that may be eliminated through bankruptcy. The individual debtor will be granted a discharge that releases the debtor from personal liability for certain debts. This gives the debtor a fresh financial start. Not all debts are dischargeable in bankruptcy. **Non-dischargeable debts** are liabilities of the debtor that may not be eliminated in bankruptcy and remain legally enforceable. Non-dischargeable debts include the following:

- certain types of tax claims
- debts not named on the lists and schedules the debtor must file with the court
- debts for spousal or child support or alimony
- debts for willful and malicious injuries to person or property
- debts to governmental units for fines and penalties
- debts for most government-funded or guaranteed educational loans or benefit overpayments
- debts for personal injury caused by the debtor's operation of a motor vehicle while intoxicated
- debts owed to certain tax-advantaged retirement plans
- debts for certain condominium or cooperative housing fees

Each state follows the rules of the federal bankruptcy code but must also follow local bankruptcy rules. A client will file for bankruptcy protection in the state in which he or she resides. Updated bankruptcy rules and regulations can be found at the following website: http://lep.emcp.net/FederalCourts/Bankruptcy/BankruptcyBasics. Attorneys and legal support staff use this website to verify information related to their cases, such as the bankruptcy process, glossary of terms, and bankruptcy forms.

After the filing of the bankruptcy petition is completed, an **automatic stay** goes into effect that protects the debtor from collection efforts by creditors. All lawsuits, foreclosures, garnishments, and collections against the debtor are stopped for the remainder of the proceeding unless a lifting of the automatic stay is granted upon motion by a creditor. Also, all phone calls and letters from creditors to the debtor are stopped if the debtor files for bankruptcy. This stay remains in place until the bankruptcy is dismissed or discharged unless a creditor is granted relief from the automatic stay.

Income **Income** is the sum of all the forms of earnings received during a certain period, including wages, interest income, business income, royalties, etc. Financial information, including income and deductions, must be reported as average gross monthly amounts. **Average gross monthly amount** means an average of income and deductions over the six calendar months before filing for bankruptcy. The income must be calculated in this manner because the attorney must use average amounts in completing the required means test to determine the type of bankruptcy filing a debtor is allowed to use.

Assets **Assets** are every form of property owned by a debtor. All assets must be disclosed in the various bankruptcy documents. All of the debtor's legal and equitable interests in assets and debts at the time of filing bankruptcy become known as the **bankruptcy estate**. Recall that the bankruptcy estate will be managed by the bankruptcy trustee or administrator, who is an officer of the court who reviews the debtor's schedules and represents the interests of the creditors. If the debtor has no assets to liquidate, the matter is known as a **no-asset case**. The attorney must still perform the means test and make sure the debtor has made full disclosure of assets and debts. Likewise, the legal support person must still input information into all bankruptcy schedules when completing the petition. A bankruptcy trustee or administrator will manage the **liquidation** or sale of a debtor's non-exempt assets and pay the proceeds to creditors. Recall that an asset may be nonexempt or exempt.

Exemptions The federal bankruptcy code contains certain exemptions. An **exemption** is property that the debtor gets to keep after the bankruptcy because it is legally excluded from the bankruptcy estate. Because states also have local bankruptcy rules, exemptions may vary from state to state and are determined by both state and federal statutes. Some states have different exemptions that a debtor may use, and some states allow the debtor to use the state exemptions *in addition to* the federal exemptions. With the assistance of an attorney, the debtor will choose which exemption laws to follow in filing for bankruptcy. Federal exemptions are uniform and apply to all bankruptcy filings. In addition, each individual state has its own local bankruptcy rules that may contain additional instructions or requirements for debtors filing for bankruptcy relief. Federal exemptions are defined in the federal bankruptcy code at 11 U.S.C. § 522. This citation means Title 11 of the U.S. Code, Section 522, which can be found at http://lep.emcp.net/uscode.

Some federal exemptions include the following:
- The debtor's aggregate interest* in real property or personal property that the debtor or a dependent of the debtor uses as a residence, in a cooperative that owns property that the debtor or a dependent of the debtor uses as a residence, or in a burial plot for the debtor or a dependent of the debtor

Local Focus 9.1

COURT UPDATES

You will be of great assistance to the attorney if you are able to find information on court websites. Throughout this textbook, you have been instructed to find information regarding many areas of law. The Internet is a wonderful tool for the courts to share changes in rules and regulations and for you to find the changes. Some courts have a link on their court websites where you can sign up for email updates whenever the court makes changes.

- The debtor's interest* in one motor vehicle
- The debtor's interest* in aggregate value in household furnishings, household goods, wearing apparel, appliances, books, animals, crops, or musical instruments, that are held primarily for the personal, family, or household use of the debtor or a dependent of the debtor
- The debtor's aggregate interest* in jewelry held primarily for the personal, family, or household use of the debtor or a dependent of the debtor
- Implements, professional books, or tools, of the trade of the debtor or the trade of a dependent of the debtor; or professionally prescribed health aids for the debtor or a dependent of the debtor

---

* Not to exceed a maximum value established by the bankruptcy code and updated from time to time based on inflation.

If the debtors are filing a joint petition (husband and wife), most exemptions are doubled or at least are greater than for an individual debtor. This amount will be defined in the individual state's bankruptcy statutes.

The term *household goods* means clothing, furniture, appliances, one radio, one television, one VCR/DVD, linens, china, crockery, kitchenware, educational materials and educational equipment primarily for the use of minor dependent children of the debtor, medical equipment and supplies, furniture exclusively for the use of minor children or elderly/disabled dependents of the debtor, personal effects (including toys and hobby equipment of minor dependent children and wedding rings) of the debtor and the dependents of the debtor, and one personal computer and related equipment.

The term *household goods* does *not* include works of art (unless by or of the debtor or any relative of the debtor); electronic entertainment equipment not to exceed a fair market value as defined by current law (except one television, one radio, and one VCR); items acquired as antiques not to exceed a fair market as defined by current law; jewelry not to exceed an amount as defined by current law (except wedding rings); and a computer (except as otherwise provided for in this section), motor vehicle (including a tractor or lawn tractor), boat, or a motorized recreational device, vehicle, watercraft, or aircraft.

People filing bankruptcy in all states are allowed to take federal exemptions. People in a few states are also allowed to use certain state exemptions along with federal exemptions. Figure 9.1 shows the federal exemptions supplementing Indiana exemptions.

Individual states also have local rules providing guidelines regarding exemptions. The exemptions shown in Figure 9.1 may be used *in conjunction* (in combination) with Indiana's state exemptions. Most states allow a debtor to claim *either:*

- The state exemptions *or* the federal exemptions

  or
- Certain federal exemptions *in addition to the state exemptions*

Indiana is one state that allows both. For example, Figure 9.2 shows the exemptions allowed by the state of Indiana. These exemptions are posted on the court's website at http://lep.emcp.net/indianabankruptcy. Go to this website if you

Figure 9.1 **Federal exemptions supplementing Indiana exemptions**

ASSET	EXEMPTION DESCRIPTION
retirement benefits	CIA employees, civil service employees, foreign service employees, military honor roll pensions, military service employees, railroad workers, Social Security, veteran's benefits, veteran's medal of honor benefits
survivor's benefits	Judges, U.S. court directors, judicial center directors, Supreme Court chief justice administrators, lighthouse workers, military service
death & disability benefits	Government employees, longshoremen and harbor workers, war risk hazard death or injury compensation
miscellaneous	Klamath Indian tribe benefits for Indians residing in Oregon, military deposits in savings accounts while on permanent duty outside the continental United States, military group life insurance, railroad workers' unemployment insurance, seamen's clothing, seamen's wages (while at sea) pursuant to a written contract, 75 percent of earned but unpaid wages (bankruptcy judge may authorize more for low-income debtors)

Source: http://www.indianabankruptcy.com/fedstate.html

would like to read more about Indiana exemptions. The website will indicate whether these exemptions may be used *in addition to* certain federal exemptions. A state's bankruptcy website will explain the allowed exemptions that a debtor may claim.

Note the differences between the state exemptions allowed by Indiana in Figure 9.2 and the federal exemptions shown in Figure 9.1.

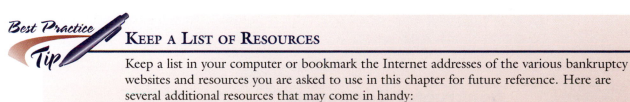

Best Practice Tip

KEEP A LIST OF RESOURCES

Keep a list in your computer or bookmark the Internet addresses of the various bankruptcy websites and resources you are asked to use in this chapter for future reference. Here are several additional resources that may come in handy:

- NADA.com or Kelley Blue Book (kbb.com) for valuing automobiles, boats, motorcycles, and all-terrain vehicles
- State tax assessor websites for real estate values
- Court websites for judgment searches

Figure 9.2 **Indiana state exemptions allowed in addition to certain federal exemptions. Note that the values listed in this table may change periodically.**

ASSET	EXEMPTION DESCRIPTION
homestead (also see wild card)	Real or personal property used as residence to $7,500 (homestead plus personal property—except health aids can't exceed $10,000); property held as tenancy by the entirety may be exempt against debts incurred by only one spouse
insurance	Fraternal benefit society benefits, group life insurance policy, life insurance policy; proceeds, cash value or avails if beneficiary is insured's spouse or dependent, life insurance proceeds if clause prohibits proceeds to be used to pay beneficiary's creditors, mutual life or accident proceeds
miscellaneous	Property of business partnership
pensions	Firefighters, police officers (only benefits building up), public employees, public or private employee retirement benefits, sheriffs (only benefits building up), state teachers
personal property (also see wild card)	Health aids; $100 on any intangible personal property except money owed to you
public benefits	Crime victims' compensation unless seeking to discharge debt for treatment of injury incurred during the crime; unemployment or worker's compensation
tools of trade	National guard uniforms, arms and equipment
wages	Minimum 75 percent of earned but unpaid wages (bankruptcy judge may authorize more for low-income debtors)
wild card	$4,000 of any real estate or tangible personal property

Source: http://www.indianabankruptcy.com/exemptions.html

9.2

Bankruptcy Documents

After the attorney has collected the appropriate information from the client (debtor), the bankruptcy petition and supporting documents will be prepared. Supporting documents consist of various bankruptcy schedules. **Schedules** are forms that list assets, liabilities, financial information, and names of creditors. Schedules A through J are official bankruptcy forms. The following is a list of documents common to all bankruptcy filings:

- Petition
- Notice to Debtors
- Summary of Schedules
- Verification of Creditor Counseling (prefiling)
- Schedule A: Real Property
- Schedule B: Personal Property
- Schedule C: Property Claimed as Exempt
- Schedule D: Secured Claims
- Schedule E: Unsecured Priority Claims
- Schedule F: Unsecured Claims
- Schedule G: Executory Contracts and Unexpired Lease
- Schedule H: Codebtors
- Schedule I: Statement of Income
- Schedule J: Expenses
- Statement of Intention
- Declaration of Schedules Signed by Debtor
- Statement of Financial Affairs
- Verification of Creditor Matrix
- Creditor Matrix
- Certification of Debtor Education
- Declaration of Payment Advices (pay stubs)

A creditor matrix must also be filed with the court, along with the petition and schedules. The **creditor matrix** is a list of the names and addresses of all creditors to whom the debtor owes money. This matrix is simply typed in columns using a word processing program. No actual form is used. However, the official forms for the petition and schedules can be found on the bankruptcy court's website. The legal support person will input the information into schedules and prepare the creditor matrix.

Accurate and complete creditor names, addresses, and account numbers must be provided on the creditor matrix. Sometimes a client will have several credit cards from the same company but the addresses will be different. In entering account numbers on the creditor matrix, use only the last four digits of the account number. This information is transmitted electronically and is then available online to the public; therefore, using only the last four digits of an account number provides protection and privacy to the debtor. Enter an "x" for each digit of the account number preceding the last four digits (e.g., xxxxxx5632). Occasionally there may be a creditor for whom no account number exists, such as a relative who has made a personal loan.

A debtor may have to file a **face sheet filing** (an emergency petition) for the purpose of delaying an eviction or foreclosure or to stop the garnishment of wages. The face sheet filing consists of the petition, credit counseling certificate, verification of signature and social security number, creditor matrix, and payment of the filing fee. A petition in a face sheet filing may be filed with incomplete schedules. Within 15 days after filing the emergency petition, the debtor must file all additional required schedules with the court.

As mentioned earlier, to ensure that the debtor does not repeat financial mistakes, he or she is required to attend two types of credit counseling as part of the bankruptcy proceeding. **Credit counseling** is instruction from a nonprofit agency that individual debtors must undergo before filing a bankruptcy petition. One type is **pre-bankruptcy counseling** to determine the debtor's financial status prior to filing the bankruptcy petition. The debtor must provide proof of attendance at the time of filing the petition. The debtor must also attend **debtor education instruction** to be educated about good personal financial management practices to avoid similar situations in the future. This instruction must be provided by an approved non-profit agency a minimum of 45 days after the *first* date set for the meeting of creditors. The court provides a list of the approved credit counseling agencies. If the date for the meeting of creditors is extended, the education must still take place based on the *first* meeting date that was scheduled.

Most bankruptcy courts require that the petition and supporting documentation be filed electronically using a program on the court's website. The court usually sends notices electronically to debtors and creditors in the form of an email with a link to the case on the court's website. A few days after a petition is filed, the court will send a **notice of commencement of case** (notice of chapter 7 bankruptcy case, meeting of creditors, and deadlines) to the debtor or debtor's attorney and to all the creditors listed in the creditor matrix filed with the bankruptcy petition. This notice will contain:

- the date set by the court for the meeting of creditors (also referred to as a 341 meeting)
- the deadlines for creditors to object to the case and file their claims against the debtor
- other deadlines with which the debtor must comply

The court will set a date for the 341 meeting. The **341 meeting** is known as the meeting of creditors. The debtor must attend the 341 meeting and answer questions about assets and debts and the ability to repay those debts.

The court will also set a date by which the debtor is required to file a **statement of intention** in which the debtor informs the court if he or she intends to keep any secured property that serves as collateral for secured debts or if the debtor plans to surrender the property. A debtor can **reaffirm** the debts, which allows him or her to continue to make payments on those debts if he or she wishes to keep the property, or the property can be sold at fair market value. If the debtor chooses to reaffirm a debt, he or she will be required to file a **reaffirmation agreement** with the court, which is an agreement to continue paying a dischargeable debt. Within 45 days after the statement of intention is filed, the debtor must surrender or keep the property as indicated in the statement of intention.

Seven days before the 341 meeting, the debtor must provide to the bankruptcy trustee a copy of the debtor's federal income tax return for the most recent tax year ending immediately before the commencement of the case and for which a return

Best Practice Tip

FORM NAMES

The court rules refer to a "notice of commencement of case." However, when you receive this form from the court, you will notice that it is actually labeled as "notice of chapter 7 bankruptcy case, meeting of creditors, and deadlines." You will sometimes find that the court rules refer to a form by a shorter name but that the actual name on the form is slightly different.

CREATE A CHECKLIST

To prepare for the 341 meeting, maintain a checklist of documents requested from the client and what you have already received so you will know if anything is missing. To see an example of a checklist, open **C09_BPTip_341MeetingChecklist** from the student data disc. Keep a copy of this checklist for future use.

was filed including any attachments, or a transcript of the tax return or a written statement that the documentation does not exist. Some bankruptcy trustees may also require copies of bank statements for the 90 days prior to and including the date of filing and copies of all pay stubs or other evidence of income for the date of filing.

Language Focus: Numbers, Dates, and Time

Bankruptcy, as well as other areas of law, requires office staff to be sharp with numbers and basic math skills. If several people review the numbers, accuracy will be improved. Even though formal rules regarding numbers exist and how they should be formatted, most rules apply to written documents and correspondence. Bankruptcy procedures utilize forms that require the legal support person to use numerals (2) as opposed to spelling out numbers (two); however, both methods are used in regular correspondence and in other legal documents. You will use the following rules in preparing correspondence to the client or others regarding the bankruptcy. These rules apply to all other areas of law as well.

If you look at different style manuals and search the Internet, you will find a variety of rules—some of them contradictory! The most important rule to follow is to *be consistent*! If your office does not have a set rule on numerals, dates, percentages, and time, you must choose a set of rules and stick with them. Inconsistency in this regard reflects poorly on any legal support member and office.

Using Numbers

One of the most prominent mistakes made in regard to numbers is whether the writer has chosen to spell the number out (eight) or write it as a numeral (8). *Three, 3*, and *III* all represent the same amount (or the concept of "threeness"). The important thing to know is which style you should use in your writing and when you should change someone else's writing.

Spell Out Numbers 1 through 10 One common style for numbers is to spell out one through ten. All numbers over ten should be written as numerals. Many offices will also choose to spell out estimated or round numbers.

The attorneys have four assistants.

The attorney found hundreds of credit card receipts in the box.

Our law firm currently has 124 active clients.

Numbers That Begin a Sentence Always write out the number if it starts a sentence. However, if it is a long number and/or seems cumbersome, rewrite the sentence so that the number is not the first word.

Incorrect:	94,900,000 people and businesses filed for bankruptcy in the United States last year.
Correct:	Nine hundred forty-nine thousand people and businesses filed for bankruptcy in the United States last year.
Improved:	In the United States, 949,000 people and businesses filed for bankruptcy last year.

Simplify Large Numbers The simplest way to express large numbers is best. Be careful to be consistent within a sentence.

Incorrect:	Before the bankruptcy the firm earned from one million to $5,000,000. (Inconsistent)
Correct:	Before the bankruptcy the firm earned from one million to five million dollars.
Incorrect:	The firm earned from $5 to $10 million before the bankruptcy. (Confusing because the writer intended $5 million to $10 million.)

Two (or More) Numbers in a Row Because two numbers next to each other can be confusing, write one of them numerically and spell out the other one. Choose the number that has the fewest letters to spell out.

Incorrect:	12 13-year-olds
Correct:	twelve 13-year-olds

Consistency of Use Be consistent within the same sentence as to how you write numbers when the numbers refer to similar items. For example, if two or more numbers in a sentence reference items purchased and one is more than ten and one is less than ten, then use numerals for both numbers if one is over ten. If the numbers refer to different types of items, write in words the numbers ten or less. Remember to use numerals for double-digit numbers.

Correct:	The plaintiff, World Wide Online Education, had 7 beginning students and 43 advanced students. (related items)
Correct:	The plaintiff answered 43 questions from seven reviewers during the administrative proceeding. (unrelated items)

Percentages In business and legal writing, percentages should be expressed as numerals with the word *percent* spelled out.

I have completed 40 percent of the petition. (used in legal context)

Only 45 percent of the clients responded to the invitation to the bankruptcy seminar.

We have received 90–95 percent of the client's supporting documents have been received.

There is a 75 percent likelihood that the creditors will appear at the 341 meeting.

Use the symbol for percent (%) only when writing in a technical context. A technical context might include assembly or installation instructions, scientific manuals or results, or industrial and mechanical documents. The court system frequently analyzes the types of cases filed, how quickly cases are closed, or where the concentration of cases are handled, for example. This type of data would be considered technical context within the legal setting.

> The court's statistical analysis showed that 20% of the bankruptcy petitions filed in one year were rejected because the petitioners were not properly qualified.

> The requirement for debtor education resulted in a 10%–15% reduction in repeat bankruptcy filings.

When using the word *percent* alone, always spell out the word.

> What percent of the bankruptcy petition has been completed?

Fractions and Decimals A mixed fraction can be expressed in numerals unless it is the first word in the sentence. Spell out simple fractions and use a hyphen between words.

Correct: The corporation expected a 5½ percent increase in profits.

Correct: One-half of the jurors were released.

Put a zero in front of a decimal unless the decimal itself starts with a zero.

Correct: The plant grew 0.79 of a foot in one year.

Correct: The plant grew only .07 of a foot this year because of the drought.

Shorten long numbers by using decimals, if possible.

> The judge approved the $4.3 million bankruptcy. ($4,300,000)

> The CEO of the company filed personal bankruptcy after making $14.6 million over five years. ($14,600,000)

Best Practice Tip

TYPES OF DOCUMENTS

Writing styles vary among types of business and industry. Writing styles may include conversational, legal, business, and technical types.
- Conversational: informal; letters and personal emails
- Business: formal; company correspondence and documents
- Legal: formal; legal documents, legal briefs, legal research and writing, and legal correspondence
- Technical: formal; mechanical, industrial, electronic, scientific manuals, assembly or installation instructions, specifications, computer hardware and software, chemistry, aerospace, robotics, finance, consumer electronics, and biotechnology

For example, a legal support person would work with technical data in the legal department of a manufacturing company, a company that writes technical manuals for industry, in intellectual property law firms, or within the court system.

Monetary Amounts Legal support staff working in bankruptcy law will need to discuss financial information and know how to communicate dollar amounts in legal documents. As noted earlier, spell out round numbers, use decimals to clarify large numbers, and be consistent in how you treat these amounts within a document. If an amount is less than $1, use a numeral and the word *cent* or *cents*.

Black-and-white copies cost 15 cents each.

Do not use the word *cent* or *cents* when a full dollar or more is before the decimal.

Color copies are $1.01 per copy.

Writing Numbers as Both Words and Numerals Writing numbers and dollar amounts as both spelled out words and as numerals has been a common practice in the writing of legal documents and correspondence. This particular style can be cumbersome and is not recommended for non-legal writing. Consider the following examples:

Mr. Ide was ordered by the bankruptcy judge to pay one of his creditors nine thousand four hundred sixty-seven and 22/100 dollars ($9,467.22) by June 8, 20xx.

The farmer contracted to sell one thousand three hundred sixty-two (1,362) head of cattle before filing for bankruptcy.

This style may seem contradictory to the earlier rules regarding when to write numbers in words or numerals, but in legal writing the writers want to be assured that the reader is completely aware of the exact amount described. Writing amounts in this manner ensures that the transposition of numerals will be noticed in the proofreading process. Legal writers write certain numbers in both words and numerals to prevent confusion. Situations where this style of writing numbers would occur might include the following:

- The exact dollar amount a debtor agrees to pay a creditor in exchange for the creditor's agreement not to initiate a lawsuit to recover the amount
- The exact dollar amount that a defendant agrees to pay the plaintiff in a settlement of a contract dispute or personal injury claim
- The exact number of days a judge sentences a defendant to spend in jail

Not all numbers are spelled out in both words and numerals because words and numerals are difficult to read. Using this more difficult format forces the reader to slow down so that he or she acknowledges that the number is correct. This method is similar to writing the dollar amount on a check both in numerals and in words to verify that the amount is correct.

Best Practice Tip

USING BOTH NUMERALS AND WORDS

Write numbers as words and numerals sparingly, since this is difficult to read. Write numbers in words and numerals only when the number is a very important, final number. Numbers used while negotiating or suggesting should be in numerals alone. You will have to use your discretion in determining this or follow your office's style.

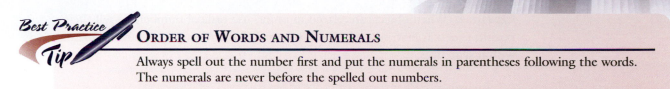

ORDER OF WORDS AND NUMERALS

Always spell out the number first and put the numerals in parentheses following the words. The numerals are never before the spelled out numbers.

The business owner is obligated to pay fifteen thousand, seven hundred sixty-eight dollars and thirteen cents ($15, 768.13) to the creditor.

The invoice showed that the replacement window in the home cost the owner one thousand, fifty-four and 21/100 dollars ($1,054.21).

When spelling out numbers, except for numbers from one thousand to nine thousand nine hundred ninety-nine, use a comma in the words just as it would appear in the numeral format.

19,093.65 = nineteen thousand, ninety-three and 65/100 dollars ($19,093.65)

Notice the comma after *nineteen thousand*.

6,592.11 = six thousand five hundred nine-two and 11/100 dollars ($6,592.11)

Notice that no comma is after *six thousand*.

Use the word *and* where the decimal point appears in the numeral format. Notice in the examples that the word *and* is typed before the fraction indicating cents.

Depending on your office's style, it is acceptable to use the word *cents* or *##/100* when a dollar amount should be written in words.

$428,170.37 = four hundred twenty-eight thousand, one hundred seventy and 37 cents

or

four hundred twenty-eight thousand, one hundred seventy and 37/100.

Compound Numbers Hyphenate all compound numbers from twenty-one through ninety-nine when they appear as the first word in a sentence or when writing numbers in both words and numerals.

The debtor is obligated to repay 32 percent of his debt to the bank or sixty-three thousand, two hundred forty-six and 59/100 dollars ($63,246.59).

Forty-three creditors appeared at the 341 meeting.
Twenty-three of them were represented by counsel.

CAPITALIZING DOLLAR AMOUNTS

You may find some legal style guides that say that when written in both words and numerals, dollar amounts should have initial capital letters (e.g., One Thousand Fifty-four and 21/100 Dollars [$1,054,21]). These guides may also say that numbers referring to any items other than money should start with lowercase letters (twenty-six thousand, five hundred twenty-nine steers). Follow the style of your office and always *be consistent!*

Ordinals When objects are placed in order, use ordinal numbers to tell their position such as first, second, third (1st, 2nd, 3rd). Always spell out ordinal numbers within sentences.

    Incorrect: He was our 1st client of the day.

    Correct: He was our first client of the day.

At times, the legal support person will be required to type legal citations, which are references to law books where examples of previously decided law (precedent) can be found. These citations usually include a reference to a law book in its second or third edition. The citations are also highly abbreviated. In correspondence, documents, and forms, use either words (second, third, fifth, etc.) or ordinals (2nd, 3rd, 5th, etc.) In legal citations, *second* and *third* are abbreviated as *2d* and *3d*, as shown in this example:

Henderson v. Gaylord, 142 NW3d 892, 37 Minn. 88 (2011)

Dates Even though you say the "st," "nd," "rd," and "th" sounds when you say the number in a date, you do not type these endings when you write a date in a document unless the date is inverted. The following examples apply in using dates:

Correct:

The meeting is scheduled for Friday, June 30, 20xx.

The hearing will be held on the 16th day of December, 20xx. (inverted date)

This document is signed on this 30th day of June, 20xx. (inverted date)

The document will be reviewed on the 2nd of November, 20xx. (inverted date)

Because we have to be in court on Tuesday, April 1, 20xx, we will not attend the training in Columbus.

The 1st of April puts some people on edge.

Incorrect:

The hearing will be on Thursday, December 16th, 20xx.

APPOINTMENTS

When making appointments or relaying information about important dates in the future, always include the day of the week as well as the date. It is easy to make a mistake with either the day of the week or the date, so including the day and date will allow the recipient to catch any discrepancies. For example, it is possible that someone would question the accuracy of *We will meet with you on Monday* or *We will meet you on the 14th*. However, when both the day of the week and the date are given, the other person can cross check with a calendar and contact you to confirm the correct date if the day and date do not match up. For example, if Monday is the 14th of May and you have written *We will meet you on Tuesday, May 14*, the recipient will likely contact you to ask whether you are planning to meet on Monday or Tuesday.

Also, at the end of December and in early January, remember to pay close attention to the year as you type, since the calendar changes over to the new year.

Time Use figures for exact times. Use *a.m.* for times before noon and *p.m.* for times after noon. Notice that both are lowercase and use periods. Do not include spaces after the periods in either *a.m.* or *p.m.* Always spell out the number when using *o'clock* and use the words *noon* and *midnight* rather than 12:00 p.m. and 12:00 a.m.

> The meeting of creditors is scheduled for 9:30 a.m.
>
> Please meet with Attorney Jones and the bankruptcy trustee at three o'clock this afternoon.
>
> Please arrive by 12:30 p.m. sharp for the bankruptcy hearing.
>
> She had a 7:00 p.m. deadline for filing the bankruptcy petition.
>
> The client stopped by the office at noon.

Language Focus Exercises

Complete the following exercises using the information in the previous section.

Exercise 9.1 Circle all errors in number style and write the correct form on the line provided. Write "C" on the line if the sentence is correct.

1. The managing attorney will be leaving in 3 days for a trip to Washington, D.C.

   _____

2. The new building overran the budget between $2 and $3 million, causing the owner to file for bankruptcy.

   _____

3. I found a supplier who will sell preprinted bankruptcy forms for 98 cents each.

   _____

4. The bankruptcy rules committee consists of 11 legislators, eight senators, and one bankruptcy judge.

   _____

5. We will arrive in Phoenix on January 19th, 20xx for the audit.

   _____

6. Last year's sales were recorded as $2,456,912; this year's, $3 million.

   _____

7. The bankruptcy forms have been revised two times in the last fifteen years.

   _____

8. Why haven't we reviewed the Maxwell file for 6 months?

   _____

9. This is the 2nd time he has called with additional information for the bankruptcy schedules right before 5 o'clock p.m.

_____

10. The meeting of creditors is set for Wednesday, March 3, 20xx, at 12 p.m.

_____

Exercise 9.2

1. Open **C09_Ex9.2_NumberLetter**.
2. Save the file as **LastName_Ex9.2_NumberLetter**.
3. Edit and proofread the document, making corrections directly in the file.
4. Resave and submit the file to the instructor.

Editing: Helpful Information and Editing for Tone

Editing will allow the legal support person an opportunity to examine a document for professional tone, which is necessary in all legal writing. Tone indicates the emotional attitude toward the reader and toward the subject of the work. One simple yet important rule in editing is to be conscious of how the document will be interpreted by the recipient. Is the intent of the document to make a firm request? Writing in a firm tone in bankruptcy and other areas of law is common, since attorneys are asked to solve problems and must adhere to deadlines. If you must make a firm request in correspondence, make certain that the documents leaving your office are polite and mannerly. In an office, it is just as necessary to use your manners when you are writing as it is when you are speaking. The words *please* and *thank you* in correspondence are expected inclusions, but other acts of politeness when you are corresponding in a professional setting should not be overlooked. These include providing helpful information, including clear instructions and requests, and understanding the intended tone of the document. Editing a document for these specific inclusions will guarantee that the work you produce is effective.

Provide Information

Letters should remind the reader of the topic of the communication with a short summary, a clear subject line, and file and case numbers. These inclusions show respect for the recipient's time, since the recipient is not required to hunt down information or previous correspondence to recall the subject at hand.

Also, provide the recipient with file details and clear instructions as to how to complete a task or where to locate information. This saves time and energy for both the sender and the recipient, since the information helps to avoid any miscommunication that could otherwise occur.

Request Information and/or Actions

Be pleasant in requesting information or actions from other people. Remember that a command and a request are different, and the words you include will set the tone of the document.

In a command, the subject of the sentence is implied. Commands may sound demanding or unreasonable if you are not careful.

> Send the information to our office as soon as you complete the document. (*You* is the subject and *send* is the verb.)

> Please send the information to our office as soon as you complete the document.

Including the word please not only softens the tone of the command but can make requests clearer. Instead of writing a question that could be answered with a yes or no or could be read as a mere suggestion, revise your requests so that they are not posed as questions. Each should be presented as a specific request that requires action.

> Could you send me the requested information this afternoon?

> Please send me the requested information this afternoon.

Note, however, that sometimes a more commanding tone is necessary.

> Send me the requested information this afternoon.

Editing Correspondence for Tone

As a legal support person, you may be asked to assist other attorneys and legal support staff to edit correspondence for tone. It is not uncommon for attorneys and legal support staff to use each other as sounding boards in writing correspondence that could convey angry or emotional undertones. Editing for tone can prevent a number of problems from arising, such as upsetting a client by writing with an excessively stern tone or failing to obtain necessary materials because of an ineffective request. A successful editor will be able to rewrite a problematic sentence without altering the sentence's purpose.

The easiest way to edit for tone is to consider word choices and connotations. Words have the ability to convey negative, positive, and neutral connotations. When emotionally difficult issues such as bankruptcy, divorce, personal injury, or any other legal matters are involved, it is important to be sensitive in communicating with the client. Table 9.1 shows words of negative and more moderate tones.

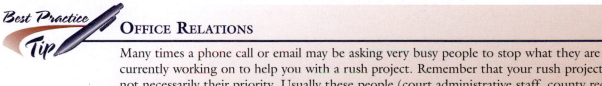

OFFICE RELATIONS

Many times a phone call or email may be asking very busy people to stop what they are currently working on to help you with a rush project. Remember that your rush project is not necessarily their priority. Usually these people (court administrative staff, county recorder staff, other law office staff, etc.) will accommodate you. Be helpful in return.

Table 9.1 Connotation Examples

Negative	Moderate
bitter, resentful	divided
insult	provoke, underestimate
enrage	anger, irritate
belligerent	argumentative, quarrelsome
cheap	frugal, thrifty

Some situations are truly difficult and cannot be addressed in a positive manner. In that case, the writer and editor must strive to use words with more moderate or neutral tones and replace words that have negative connotations. The legal support person can help the attorney by being aware of the attorney's mood and intent while the attorney is composing. By making suggestions to the attorney about the tone, the legal support person will be able to temper the client's reaction to the communication. Consider the following sentences:

Negative Tone: I cannot believe that you wasted my time!

Moderate Tone: I am surprised that you are not more responsive.

Negative Tone: George thought his brother was being cheap by asking the attorney to reduce his hourly rate.

Moderate Tone: George thought his brother was being thrifty by asking the attorney to reduce his hourly rate.

Editing Exercises

Apply what you have learned to the following exercises.

Exercise 9.3 Using some of the suggestions from this edition, retype the following angry letter using a more professional tone.

1. Rewrite the letter in the appropriate tone.
2. Save your letter as **LastName_C09_Ex9.3_AngryLetter**.
3. Share letters with classmates to see alternate ways to communicate more politely.
4. Submit the file to the instructor.

Best Practice Tip

ANGRY EMAILS

One must avoid communicating while feeling angry or upset. Allowing your emotions to determine how you communicate can be a professional disaster. It is likely that you have regretted things you have said when you were angry or irritated. Everyone has! It is much easier to control anger in your writing than it is in speaking since, if you take advantage of it, you have time to cool off before sending the written communication. If you are not sure about the tone of your message, ask a coworker to review the message and give you his or her impression. Others will have an unbiased viewpoint and help you to moderate your message.

As a suggestion, go ahead and write while you are angry. Once you have written your response, put the letter or email aside to give yourself a moment to regroup; then address the matter once you are less upset. Rewrite the correspondence in a professional tone. *However*, if you are conversing by email, *always* remove the recipient's name prior to typing your message to avoid accidently sending the angry message before you have revised it.

Figure 9.3 **Angry Letter Sample**

(Current Date)

Ms. Janis Jamplain
333 South Visner Avenue
Grand Meadow, MI 11110

Dear Ms. Jamplain:

Re: Bankruptcy Claim #8888
    Our File No. 12991-001

I have asked you 4 times to bring this information to my office so that we can
provide it to the bankruptcy trustee by the deadline. I'm frustrated and upset
with you for not responding to my requests. If you don't have these documents
to my office in 3 days, you can go to the meeting by yourself. You are on your
own. Don't count on me to explain. I won't be yelled at by this trustee again.

Cynthia McCormick

Exercise 9.4 Examine a letter using the information you learned in the section on editing.

1. Open **C09_Ex9.4_UnclearLetter**.
2. Read the letter and work with your classmates to brainstorm any missing information and errors within the letter.
3. Write your ideas on the lines provided.

_____

_____

_____

_____

_____

_____

_____

_____

_____

Exercise 9.5 Practice editing a letter using the information you learned in the section on editing.

1. Open **C09_Ex9.4_UnclearLetter** again if it is not open already.
2. Resave the file as **LastName_C09_Ex9.5_RevisedUnclearLetter**.
3. Revise the letter using the list of missing information and errors you noted in Exercise 9.4.
4. Resave the file and submit it to the instructor.

Exercise 9.6 Practice writing in moderate tones using information you learned in the section on editing. Use a thesaurus to find more moderate word choices for the following negative words. Write the moderate words on the corresponding line. When you are finished, create sentences that utilize the moderate terms you identified. Write these sentences on the lines provided.

1. badger, bully, harass _____

2. obnoxious _____

3. arrogant _____

4. threatening, ominous _____

5. uncaring, apathetic _____

_____

_____

_____

_____

_____

_____

Proofreading: Checking for Accuracy in Dates and Numbers

The most common mistakes made in completing and proofreading bankruptcy forms are missing dates; wrong account numbers; transposing numbers; entering data in the wrong area of the forms; incomplete addresses for creditors; failing to properly list income, expenses, and deductions as average gross monthly amounts; and incorrectly counting the number of pay periods. The editing and proofreading skills you will utilize in bankruptcy law will focus on these areas as well as mathematical conversions of dollar amounts to average gross monthly amounts.

To find these types of errors, you must pay close attention to the details of the file. Bankruptcy forms include many lines and columns similar to the HUD Closing Statement you worked on in Chapter 6. Until you are comfortable with bankruptcy forms and if your office permits, proofread from hard copy. Use a straight edge when you are reviewing and comparing lines of numbers. It is easy to transpose or get off by a line when you are referring back and forth between client information and what is entered into the form. Put a check mark by the input information as well as the source information to indicate that you have verified that item. This process will help you to return to the correct location if you are interrupted.

When you are proofreading complicated forms involving numbers, it helps to work with a partner; however, in a busy law office, you would also have to be able to proofread these documents by yourself.

Recognizing Common Mistakes in Proofreading Completed Bankruptcy Forms

Nobody is perfect in creating or proofreading a complicated legal document for the first time. Documents can be created by a number of people from within or outside the office, and the legal support person will then be required to proofread them. What is important is to be able to recognize the *types* of errors you often make or that are commonly made by others and to make a point of searching for those specific errors in your final proofread. Pay attention to the kinds of errors you make as well as to each individual error. Make a list of the errors you commonly make and review for those. The following tips can be applied when you create or proofread bankruptcy forms:

❑ Proofread text as well as numbers.

❑ Read the directions on the forms to make sure subtotals and totals are entered in the appropriate fields on the form.

❑ Recheck totals in columns of numbers, especially after numbers have been revised. Also, check to see if subtotals are needed.

❑ Look for transposed numbers. Team proofread the numbers, since it is very easy to transpose them. It is easy to see what you want to see when you are proofreading on your own.

❑ Verify that numbers are on the correct line and in the correct category.

❑ Insert zeros if no other number goes on a line within the form because it assures you and the reader that the item has not been overlooked.

❑ Watch for the words *yes* and *no* and think about how they apply to the form, so that the remainder of the form is completed correctly. For example, a question may require a yes or no answer. The next part of the question may say, "If you answer no, skip numbers 55 through 75 and answer the remainder of the questions to 100."

❑ Pay close attention to the checkboxes on the forms. Notice the checkbox on the form in Figure 9.4. Missing this box would make the form rather confusing. The reader is not sure which to trust, the unchecked box or the information written on the form.

Figure 9.4 **Schedule G showing checkbox that is checked incorrectly**

B 6G (Official Form 6G) (12/07)

In re __Joseph Wayne Sample_____ ,   Case No._____
         Debtor   **(if known)**

SCHEDULE G - EXECUTORY CONTRACTS AND UNEXPIRED LEASES

Describe all executory contracts of any nature and all unexpired leases of real or personal property. Include any timeshare interests. State nature of debtor's interest in contract, i.e., "Purchaser," "Agent," etc. State whether debtor is the lessor or lessee of a lease. Provide the names and complete mailing addresses of all other parties to each lease or contract described. If a minor child is a party to one of the leases or contracts, state the child's initials and the name and address of the child's parent or guardian, such as "A.B., a minor child, by John Doe, guardian." Do not disclose the child's name. See, 11 U.S.C. §112 and Fed. R. Bankr. P. 1007(m).

☑ Check this box if debtor has no executory contracts or unexpired leases.

NAME AND MAILING ADDRESS, INCLUDING ZIP CODE, OF OTHER PARTIES TO LEASE OR CONTRACT.	DESCRIPTION OF CONTRACT OR LEASE AND NATURE OF DEBTOR'S INTEREST. STATE WHETHER LEASE IS FOR NONRESIDENTIAL REAL PROPERTY. STATE CONTRACT NUMBER OF ANY GOVERNMENT CONTRACT.
Don's Lawns 1340 Greenbay Road, Suite 963 Kenosha MI 67896	take care of yard and landscaping at Lakeshore Drive residence; contracted at $450 per month for next six months

- Ask questions whenever you do not understand a request.
- Pay close attention to two-letter abbreviations for states. Many are similar, such as Missouri (MO) and Michigan (MI) and Alaska (AK) and Arkansas (AR). Concentrate on these abbreviations, because the forms that you will be sending to creditors and others will not get to their destinations if the state abbreviations are typed incorrectly.
- Proof zip codes against the source from which you are copying.

Most bankruptcy forms will automatically repeat information typed in certain areas of the form (usually at the top of the page, such as case and debtor identification information). Always proofread these numbers carefully, since any errors made in headers and footers will likely transfer to all pages.

It is important to verify details because if an error is discovered after the petition and schedules are filed, the attorney will be required to file an amendment. An error could be costly, depending on whether the amended forms have to be sent to everyone involved or just to one or two parties. The law office will not be able to recover the expenses of postage, paper, and time spent because of an error made by the office. For example, a debtor may have 30 or more creditors. If an error is in an asset or debt schedule, an amended copy must be mailed to all creditors and their representatives. Another example is an error in a real estate description. If that occurs, the attorney must file amended information regarding the legal description.

Remember: Once a bankruptcy is filed with the court, the attorney may amend the forms to correct errors. Errors may be discovered by the bankruptcy trustee, the creditors, or the law office. Once the bankruptcy judge makes a ruling either allowing or denying a discharge, the attorney can no longer amend forms and the case is closed. Also, if a debt is not included in the bankruptcy filing, it will not be discharged and the client will remain responsible for the debt.

Proofreading Exercises

The following exercises are intended to simulate the following situation: In the law office, a legal support person will be given many documents, bills, bank statements, etc., from the client. These items will contain pertinent information that will have to be inserted into the bankruptcy petition as well as various schedules to be filed with the bankruptcy court. After the legal support person has entered the data in the bankruptcy forms, he or she would proofread the document by comparing what was entered into the form with the original documents provided by the client. For the following exercises, you will have to proofread bankruptcy forms that have been completed against the client's original documents. Compare what was entered on the forms with the "original to proofread from" file.

In addition to the petition, other documents are common to all bankruptcy filings. In the following exercises, you will proofread a bankruptcy petition, various schedules, and a creditor matrix.

Exercise 9.7 While working through Exercise 9.7, do not be concerned about missing information. For this exercise, assume that the client may have failed to provide complete information for some areas on the client questionnaire. For the purposes of this exercise, you will proofread only the information that was entered on the sample petition and schedules.

1. Open and print the following three documents from your electronic storage medium.
   a. **C09_Ex9.7_SchedulesCreditorMatrix**
   b. **C09_Ex9.7_ClientQuestionnaire**
   c. **C09_Ex9.7_VoluntaryPetition**
2. Proofread the voluntary petition and bankruptcy schedules by comparing them to the information provided by the client on the bankruptcy client questionnaire.
3. Compare the completed creditor matrix with the list of creditors provided by client.
4. Proofread the name and address at the top of the voluntary petition and verify that it is correct by comparing it with the information provided by the client. If any information on the petition form is incorrect or incomplete, highlight it in yellow and write the correct information next to it in the margin.
5. All schedules are included in the **C09_Ex9.7_SchedulesCreditorMatrix** file you opened in step 1. Proofread Schedule D—creditors holding secured claims. Types of secured claims are home mortgage loans and automobile loans. Review the information the client provided for Section 2, Parts A and B, and Section 3—debts on the client questionnaire—and compare it with the information on schedule D. If any information on schedule D is incorrect or incomplete, highlight it in yellow and write the correct information next to it in the margin.
6. Also, proofread Schedule D by comparing its contents to the description of the home, its value, the creditor, and the mortgage amount on the client questionnaire. If any information on Schedule D is incorrect or incomplete, highlight it in yellow and write the correct information next to it in the margin.

7. Proofread Schedule F—creditors holding unsecured nonpriority claims. Types of unsecured claims are debts owed to credit card companies. Review the information the client provided for Section 3—debts—on the client questionnaire. Compare it with the information on schedule F. If any information on schedule F is incorrect or incomplete, highlight it in yellow and write the correct information next to it in the margin.

8. Proofread Schedule I—current income of individual debtor(s). Review the information the client provided for Section 5—current income. Compare it with the information on schedule I. If any information on schedule I is incorrect or incomplete, highlight it in yellow and write the correct information next to it in the margin.

9. Proofread the creditor matrix. Review the creditors listed on Schedules D and F. Compare the creditor information with the information entered on the creditor matrix. If any information on the matrix is incorrect or incomplete, highlight it in yellow and write the correct information next to it in the margin.

10. Submit your corrected hard copies to the instructor unless directed otherwise.

Exercise 9.8 Open the file **C09_Ex9.8_TwoLetterAbbrev** and use it to identify the correct two-letter abbreviation in the following questions. Circle the correct answer.

1. Which of the following is the two-letter abbreviation for Alaska?
   a. AL
   b. AK
   c. AR
   d. None of the above

2. MI stands for
   a. Minnesota
   b. Missouri
   c. Michigan
   d. None of the above

3. MS stands for
   a. Missouri
   b. Mississippi
   c. Marshall Islands
   d. None of the above

4. NE stands for
   a. Nebraska
   b. Nevada
   c. New Hampshire
   d. None of the above

5. MR stands for
   a. Marshall Islands
   b. Northern Mariana Islands
   c. Armed Forces Middle East
   d. None of the above

Bankruptcy How-To Guide

The bankruptcy attorney must be familiar with the bankruptcy code and the federal and state exemptions while also keeping up to date on changes in the law. If the attorney works with business clients, some knowledge of business law, employment law, and transactional law is also necessary. If he or she is working with an individual, it is necessary to have knowledge of family law and real estate. The legal support person working with a bankruptcy attorney must have exceptional organization skills and sharp analytical skills to assist the attorney in analyzing a multitude of very detailed bankruptcy documents.

Both the attorney and the legal support person must be able to perform well under last-minute pressure, be comfortable working with numbers, be comfortable with extensive client contact, and have good proofreading skills. Bankruptcy is fast-paced, and every case is different.

The legal support person and attorney will take a team approach to handling the client's bankruptcy matter. A busy bankruptcy attorney will rely heavily on legal support staff to assist in gathering and analyzing information from the client and preparing drafts of the forms required to file the bankruptcy petition. After the attorney's initial meeting with the client, the legal support person may be asked to complete the following tasks independently:

- Meet with the client to obtain and organize documents and information
- Assist the client in completing the office questionnaire
- Request additional information from the client

The legal support staff will work with the attorney to:

- Track and meet deadlines for the case
- Review the client's information
- Complete bankruptcy forms
- Perform electronic filing of documents

A self-confident, detail-oriented legal support person who enjoys personal contact with clients and working with numbers in a fast-paced area of law such as bankruptcy will quickly become a valued member of the legal team.

Electronic Filing

All bankruptcy documents must be filed electronically on the court's website. The court offers training in electronic filing. The court also provides all the forms necessary to file for bankruptcy; however, most law firms have specialty document-preparation programs to make the process more efficient. The program requires that all personal and financial client information be initially inputted so the program can automatically insert the information where it is needed on the various forms and schedules. The forms and schedules will be in fillable format allowing you to tab from one field to the next to complete them quickly. In addition, all client private personal identifiers must be redacted prior to electronic filing.

Best Practice Tip

REDACTED INFORMATION

Bankruptcy law requires that social security numbers be redacted from the bankruptcy forms before filing the petition electronically and be shown as xxx-xx-xxxx or just show the last four digits. This requirement protects the client's information, since these files will be available to the public.

Calculating Average Gross Monthly Amounts

Bankruptcy forms indicate if an item on the form is to be reported as an aggregate amount over a set time frame or as an average amount (usually an average monthly amount). An example of an aggregate amount is when one must provide the total wages earned during the prior calendar year.

Average monthly amounts are commonly derived from the usual expenses of living, such as the cost of groceries, gasoline, telephone, television, utilities (heat, water, and electricity), wage deductions (taxes), and wages earned.

Since the remaining months of the year have not occurred, an average monthly amount is required and calculated using a formula estimating the monthly amounts of expenses, deductions, and wages based upon the past history of those amounts. If possible, you should use at least six months' worth of historical data to calculate the average monthly amounts.

Debts such as credit card bills, mortgage payments, car payments, or student loan payments are not averaged. They are entered onto the bankruptcy forms in the exact current amount due.

People are not always paid at the same intervals; therefore, the legal support person would have to know and understand the various pay intervals to calculate average gross monthly amounts. At least six different pay intervals or pay types are available:

- Weekly
- Biweekly
- Semimonthly
- Monthly
- Yearly
- Commission

The most common types of pay periods are weekly, biweekly (meaning every other week), and semimonthly (meaning twice a month on specified days, such as the 1st and 15th of each month). Table 9.2 shows abbreviations for the various types of pay periods. The abbreviations are used in the formulas you will use later in this chapter when you practice converting wages to average gross monthly amounts. This table is also provided on the student data disc for your convenience (**C09_PayPeriodIntervalAbbreviations**).

GROSS AND NET

Many people get confused between the terms *gross pay* and *net pay*. The two are different. Here are the definitions:

Gross pay: The total amount of pay earned by an employee *before* withholding deductions
Net pay: The amount of pay an employee takes home *after* deductions are made from gross pay

Try to remember that *gross* means "large" and gross pay is the larger amount of pay before deductions are made. Another way to remember the definitions is that *G* comes *before* *N* in the alphabet. Gross pay is what you get *before* net pay.

Table 9.2 Pay Type Abbreviations

Pay Period Interval Abbreviations	
W:	weekly (once every week) 52 pay periods in a year
BW:	biweekly (every other week) 26 pay periods in a year
SM:	semimonthly (twice a month on set days) 24 pay periods in a year
M:	monthly (once every month) 12 pay periods in a year
Wage Abbreviations	
YTDG:	year-to-date gross wage
AWW:	average weekly wage
ABWW:	average biweekly wage
ASMW:	average semimonthly wage
AYW:	average yearly wage
AGMW:	average gross monthly wage

The legal support person must understand the various pay intervals and abbreviations as well as how to calculate average gross monthly amounts, because some bankruptcy document preparation software programs do not perform calculations. Formulas have been written to aid in calculating average gross monthly amounts for wages. The formulas can be applied to other items that need to be averaged, such as taxes, utilities, or anything the bankruptcy form asks for in an average amount. These formulas are provided to you in the Chapter 9 folder on your storage medium (**C09_ConversionFormulasAverageAmounts**) for use in future projects in this chapter, but they are also discussed in the following text.

The attorney will obtain six months' worth of pay stubs from the client and determine how often the client is paid. Some attorneys will do the calculations to convert the income and deductions to average gross monthly amounts and ask the legal support person to double check the calculations. Other attorneys may ask the legal support person to do the calculations for the attorney's later review. In either case, a legal support person must understand the pay period that applies to the client and count the weeks on a calendar to determine the number of pay periods that apply to the client's situation. After the number of pay periods has been determined, the legal support person can do the calculation to determine the average gross monthly amounts of wages and deductions.

Because businesses are able to choose pay-period types that are most convenient to them, the legal support person will be presented with various pay periods in calculating average gross monthly amounts for different clients. A perpetual calendar is a helpful tool. A **perpetual calendar** is a type of calendar used to find what day of the week certain dates are on in certain years. You can go backward in time or forward. A perpetual calendar is provided on the student data disc along with directions for use.

Wages and deductions are converted to *average gross monthly amounts* by using the year-to-date gross totals shown on the client's pay stub.

Expenses such as school or athletic expenses, tuition, school lunches, medical expenses, insurance premiums, groceries, gasoline, telephone, television, and utilities (heat, water, electricity) must also be averaged. The bankruptcy schedules require these amounts to be entered as *average gross monthly expenses.*

The legal support person will be using information from pay stubs to calculate average gross monthly wages. Most pay stubs will contain additional categories for the number of hours worked and rate of pay; they may include other categories of pay or deductions; and they may be configured differently. The following section will explain three common formulas for calculating average gross monthly amounts using sample pay stubs.

Calculating Average Gross Monthly Wage from Weekly Payment Interval

To begin, review Figure 9.5, which is an example of a *weekly* pay stub. Open **C09_PerpetualCalendars** from the Chapter 9 folder on your electronic storage medium and scroll to calendar number 6.

Next, use the information from the pay stub in Figure 9.5 and the following formula to convert the gross weekly wage to an average gross monthly amount.

Formula:

$$\underset{1,\,2}{\frac{\text{(YTDG)}}{\text{(number of pay periods)}}} = \underset{3,\,4}{\text{(AWW x pay periods per year)}} = \underset{5}{\frac{\text{(AYW)}}{\text{(12 months per year)}}} = \underset{6}{\text{AGMW}}$$

1. First, locate the amount on the current pay stub for year-to-date gross wage (YTDG).
2. To determine the *number of pay periods* the client has been paid in the last six months (or since the client started work), first determine how often the client is paid by examining the pay-period dates on the pay stub (for this example,

Figure 9.5 **Weekly pay stub, example 1.**

Check date: 05/18/xx								
For period: 05/09/xx to 05/14/xx								

Pay This Check (gross)	YTD Gross Pay	Tax Type	Tax	YTD Tax	Deduction Type	Deducted	YTD Deductions
316.15		Federal			Christmas		
			8.35	569.81	savings	37.93	360.00
		FICA					
			19.60	445.95			
		Medicare					
			4.58	104.29			
		State					
			12.70	334.20			
Totals	9,207.00					37.93	451.88
			45.23	1,454.25			

Net pay this check: 232.94								

the client is paid weekly). This client started employment on January 4, 2010, and is paid every Friday. Next, on the appropriate perpetual calendar, start at the end of the most recent pay period (May 14, 2010) and go back six months (or, in this situation, to the client's first date of employment) and count the number of pay periods, stopping at the most recent one. You will discover that there were 19 pay periods through May 14. This number is the *number of pay periods* in the formula.

3. Divide the YTDG by 19 (*pay periods*) to get the average weekly wage (AWW).

4. Use calendar number 6 to count the number of pay periods per year. Since the pay stub in Figure 9.5 is a *weekly* pay stub, you would count all of the weeks in the calendar to determine the number of pay periods in the year. The number of pay periods in a year for a weekly pay interval is 52.

5. Multiply the AWW amount by 52 (pay periods per year) to get the average yearly wage (AYW).

6. Divide the AYW by 12 (months per year) to get the average gross monthly wage (AGMW).

The calculation that follows shows the conversion of the gross weekly wage to the average gross monthly wage using the data from Figure 9.5.

Calculation:

$$\frac{(\$9,207)}{(19)} = (\$484.57 \times 52) = \frac{(\$25,198.10)}{(12)} = \$2,099.84$$

Calculating Average Gross Monthly Wage from Biweekly Payment Interval

Now that you have calculated average gross monthly wages from weekly pay periods, the following exercise will explain calculating average gross monthly wages from a *biweekly (every other week)* pay stub.

Use the information from the pay stub in Figure 9.6 and the following formula to convert the gross biweekly (every other week) wage to average gross monthly wage.

Formula:

1	2	3	4	5	6

YTDG / number of pay periods = ABWW x pay periods per year = AYW / 12 (months per year) = AGMW

KEYBOARD SHORTCUTS

It is customary to use a forward slash (/) for the division symbol when writing mathematical formulas. However, sometimes you will have to use the division symbol (÷). No division symbol is on an actual keyboard, but certain word processing programs have shortcuts to insert symbols that are not on the keyboard. Try this using your keyboard: hold down your Alt key and at the same time, using your number keypad, key the number 0247. When you release the keys the ÷ symbol will appear. Look in MS Word symbols to find a keyboard shortcut for different characters and symbols. The slash is used as the division symbol in this book. Keep in mind that not all versions of software support these keyboard shortcuts.

Figure 9.6 **Biweekly pay stub example 1.**

Check date: 05/10/xx
For period: 04/26/xx to 05/07/xx

Pay This Check (gross)	YTD Gross Pay	Tax Type	Tax	YTD Tax	Deduction Type	Deducted	YTD Deductions
316.15		Federal	8.35	569.81	Christmas savings	37.93	360.00
		FICA	19.60	445.95			
		Medicare	4.58	104.29			
		State	12.70	334.20			
Totals	9,207.00		45.23	1,454.25		37.93	451.88

Net pay this check: 232.94

1. First, locate the amount on the current pay stub for year-to-date gross wages (YTDG).
2. To determine the *number of pay periods* the client has been paid in the last six months (or since he started work), first determine how often the client is paid (for this example—biweekly). This client started employment on January 4, 2010, and is paid every other week (in this case, on Friday, because the pay period ends on May 7, 2010, a Friday). Next, on the appropriate perpetual calendar, start at the end of the most recent pay period (May 7, 2010) and go back six months (or, in this situation, to the client's first date of employment) and count the number of pay periods, stopping with the most recent one. After counting every other Friday from January 15 through May 7 in the perpetual calendar, you will discover that there were 9 pay periods through May 7. This number is the *number of pay periods* in the formula.
3. Divide the YTDG by 9 (*pay periods*) to get the average bi-weekly wage (ABWW).
4. Using the perpetual calendar (**C09_PerpetualCalendars**), count the number of pay periods in a year based on a biweekly payment interval. Remember that *biweekly* means "every other week." To determine the number of pay periods in a year for a biweekly payment interval, count every other week of the year. The number of pay periods in a year for a biweekly pay interval is 26.
5. Multiply the *ABWW* amount by 26 (*pay periods per year*) to get the average yearly wage (*AYW*).
6. Divide the AYW by 12 (*months per year*) to get the average gross monthly wage (*AGMW*).

The calculation that follows shows the conversion of the gross biweekly wage to average gross monthly wage using the data from Figure 9.6.

Calculation:

$$\frac{(\$9,207)}{(9)} = (\$1,023 \times 26) = \frac{(\$26,598)}{(12)} = \$2,216.50$$

Compare the biweekly calculation with the weekly calculation. Notice that the differences are the number of pay periods and the number of pay periods per year.

Calculating Average Gross Monthly Wage from a Semimonthly (twice a month) Payment Interval

Finally, the following will explain how to calculate average gross monthly wages for a semimonthly (twice a month on set days) pay-period interval.

Use the information from the pay stub in Figure 9.7 and the following formula to convert the gross semimonthly wage to an average gross monthly amount.

Formula:

$$\underset{1,\,2}{\frac{(\text{YTDG})}{(\text{number of pay periods})}} = \underset{3,\,4}{(\text{ASMW} \times \text{pay periods per year})} = \underset{5}{\frac{(\text{AYW})}{(12 \text{ months per year})}} = \underset{6}{\text{AGMW}}$$

1. First, locate the amount on the current pay stub for the year-to-date gross wage (*YTDG*).
2. To determine the *number of pay periods* the client has been paid in the last six months (or since he started work), determine how often the client is paid

Figure 9.7 **Semimonthly pay stub, example 1.**

Check date: 05/21/xx
For period: 05/01/10 to 05/14/xx

Pay This Check (gross)	YTD Gross Pay	Tax Type	Tax	YTD Tax	Deduction Type	Deducted	YTD Deductions
316.15		Federal	8.35	569.81	Christmas savings	37.93	360.00
		FICA	19.60	445.95			
		Medicare	4.58	104.29			
		State	12.70	334.20			
Totals	9,207.00		45.23	1,454.25		37.93	451.88
Net pay this check: 232.94							

(for this example—semimonthly). This client started employment on January 4, 2010, and is paid twice a month on the 15th and the last day of the month (in this case, the attorney asked the client who said this is when he gets paid). Next, on the appropriate perpetual calendar, start at the end of the most recent pay period (May 14, 2010) and go back 6 months (or, in this situation, to the client's first date of employment) and count each 15th day and each last day of the month to determine the number of pay periods in the year. The *number of pay periods* in this situation for a semimonthly payment interval is 9.

3. Divide the *YTDG* by 9 (*pay periods*) to get the average semimonthly wage (*ASMW*).

4. Use Calendar #6 to count the number of pay periods per year. Since the pay stub in Figure 9.7 is a semimonthly pay stub, count each 15th day and each last day of the month to determine the number of pay periods in the year. The number of pay periods in a year for a semimonthly pay interval is 24.

5. Multiply the *ASMW* amount by 24 (pay periods per year) to get the average yearly wage (*AYW*).

6. Divide the *AYW* by 12 (*months per year*) to get the average gross monthly wage (*AGMW*).

The calculation that follows shows the conversion of the gross semimonthly wage to average gross monthly wage using the data from Figure 9.7.

Calculation:

$$\frac{(\$9,207)}{(9)} = (\$1,023 \times 24) = \frac{(\$24,552)}{(12)} = \$2,046$$

How-to Guide Exercises

Complete the following exercises using the information in the How-To Guide.

Exercise 9.9 Page 306 discusses dischargeable debts. The following exercise will explain how to find information on court websites and is also an overview of which debts may be discharged in bankruptcy.

1. Go to the following Internet address:
   http://lep.emcp.net/FederalCourts/Bankruptcy/BankruptcyBasics

2. Click on "Are all of the debtor's debts discharged or only some?"

3. Read the information and discuss with your classmates the types of debts that are *not* dischargeable in bankruptcy. All the various types of debts are listed in this chapter on page 305. Leave this website page open on your computer, because you will use it in the next exercise.

Exercise 9.10 Page 305 discusses waiting periods to refile for different types of bankruptcy. Complete the following exercise to practice finding information on the Internet, such as whether the waiting period to file a future bankruptcy petition has changed.

1. With the "Discharge in Bankruptcy" web page open, click on "Can a debtor receive a second discharge in a later chapter 7 case?"

2. Read the paragraph and compare it with the information provided in this book. If the law has changed since this book was published, the change will appear on this website.

3. Share what you find with your classmates.

Exercise 9.11 Complete the following activity to practice converting wages to average gross monthly amounts. Review the formulas and explanations presented earlier on converting wages paid to an average gross monthly amount for a weekly pay stub. Practice the conversion you studied using the YTD gross pay ($7,192.80) from the following Figure 9.8.

1. On the line provided, write the generic formula for the conversion that pertains to converting bi-weekly pay to average amounts.

_____

2. Using the formula from step 1 and calendar number 6, calculate the average gross monthly wage using the information in Figure 9.8. Write the calculation on the lines provided.

_____

_____

_____

_____

Figure 9.8 **Weekly pay stub, example 2.**

Check date: 05/18/xx
For period: 05/09/xx to 05/14/xx

Pay This Check (gross)	YTD Gross Pay	Tax Type	Tax	YTD Tax	Deduction Type	Deducted	YTD Deductions
316.15		Federal	8.35	569.81	Christmas savings	37.93	360.00
		FICA	19.60	445.95			
		Medicare	4.58	104.29			
		State	12.70	334.20			
Totals	7,192.80		45.23	1,454.25		37.93	451.88

Net pay this check: 232.94

Exercise 9.12 Practice the conversion you just studied again using the YTD gross pay ($7,192.80) from the following Figure 9.9.

1. On the line provided, write the generic formula for the conversion that pertains to converting weekly pay to average amounts.

   _____

2. Using the formula from step 1 and calendar number 6, calculate the average gross monthly wage using the information in Figure 9.9. Write the calculation on the lines provided.

   _____

   _____

   _____

   _____

   _____

Figure 9.9 **Biweekly pay stub, example 2.**

Check date: 05/10/xx							
For period: 04/26/xx to 05/07/xx							

Pay This Check (gross)	YTD Gross Pay	Tax Type	Tax	YTD Tax	Deduction Type	Deducted	YTD Deductions
316.15		Federal	8.35	569.81	Christmas savings	37.93	360.00
		FICA	19.60	445.95			
		Medicare	4.58	104.29			
		State	12.70	334.20			
Totals	7,192.80		45.23	1,454.25		37.93	451.88
Net pay this check: 232.94							

Exercise 9.13 Practice the conversion you just studied again using the YTD gross pay ($7,192.80) from the following Figure 9.10.

1. On the line provided, write the generic formula for the conversion that pertains to converting semi-monthly pay to average amounts.

_____

2. Using the formula from step 1 and calendar number 6, calculate the average gross monthly wage using the information in Figure 9.10. Write the calculation on the lines provided.

_____

_____

_____

_____

_____

Figure 9.10 **Semimonthly pay stub, example 2.**

Check date: 05/21/xx
For period: 05/01/xx to 05/14/xx

Pay This Check (gross)	YTD Gross Pay	Tax Type	Tax	YTD Tax	Deduction Type	Deducted	YTD Deductions
316.15		Federal	8.35	569.81	Christmas savings	37.93	360.00
		FICA	19.60	445.95			
		Medicare	4.58	104.29			
		State	12.70	334.20			
Totals	7,192.80		45.23	1,454.25		37.93	451.88

Net pay this check: 232.94

Critical Thinking: Checklists and Organization

A legal support person must be organized and efficient to remain employed. Fortunately, these are qualities that one may learn by applying critical thinking skills. Skills such as determining the best way to organize files, keeping track of deadlines, and making helpful checklists will ensure the efficient and organized handling of tasks.

File Organization

The following items are examples of the main categories of information that you would encounter in a bankruptcy case. Law offices maintain client documents within a paper file folder (sometimes referred to as a physical file). This file will include subfolders for each main category of information shown in the following list. Following each category heading are examples of items that may be included within that category. Keep in mind that because other types of information may be presented during a case, you may have to create additional folders for those items. The attorney you work with may already have a file organization system in place; but if not, the following example is a good place to start. The documents and information in the client's physical file will be kept in the office and eventually returned to the client at the end of the case. Data from the physical file will be used to complete the bankruptcy forms and assist the attorney throughout the case.

Main Categories of Information in the Physical File
Notices from Court
341 meeting notice
Notice of chapter 7 bankruptcy case
Income-generating documentation
Commission statements
Interest earned on savings account
Investments
Pay stubs
Statement of child support income received
Assets
Bank statement showing checking account balance
Bank statement showing savings account balance
Certificates of deposit
College tuition savings accounts
Financing agreements for vehicle loans
Life insurance policies
Proof of insurance for automobiles that are financed
Statement of child support arrearages owed
Statements for retirement accounts, 401k plan, pension plan, IRA
Stock certificates and statements regarding stock accounts
Titles for automobiles, boats, recreational vehicles, etc.

Real estate

Appraisal or market analysis done by a realtor showing current market value

Loan applications

Monthly mortgage statement

Mortgage document, note, and settlement statement

Property tax statement

Record of transfers of property (refinancing, real estate, vehicles, boats)

Warranty deed to property or owned home

Creditor documentation

Contact information for each company to which the client owes money, including company name, address, telephone number, and account number

Correspondence from creditors

Debt documentation

Bank loans

Credit cards

Medical bills

Mortgage

Student loan

Utility bills

Credit report and authorization

Tax returns and W-2 Forms

Original signed documents

Proof of attendance at credit counseling and debtor education classes

Attorney's notes and research

Correspondence

Representation agreement

Bankruptcy petition and schedules

Business documents (for people who own a business)

Business loan documents

Business tax returns

Corporate stock/share certificates

Current balance sheet

Incorporation papers

List of company assets

List of company debts

List of names and addresses of all company employees

Profit and loss statements

Records of transfers of assets to and from the company

Miscellaneous

Divorce decrees

Judgment papers either in or against the creditor's favor

Lawsuit papers for any pending lawsuit

Name and address of person (wife/husband) who receives support

Papers from any prior bankruptcies

State court orders for child support or spousal maintenance received or paid

Assisting with Deadlines

You can help the attorney meet deadlines and prepare for meetings by using a reminder checklist similar to the following. Use this checklist to create a list of deadline dates once you have received the notice scheduling the date of the meeting of creditors. This checklist (as **C09_BankruptcyReminderChecklist**) can be found in the Chapter 09 folder on your electronic storage medium.

> **Bankruptcy Reminder Checklist for the Attorney**
>
> ❑ Send a copy of the debtor's most recently filed tax return or a transcript of that tax return to the trustee at least seven days before the meeting of creditors. If the debtor has not filed returns in recent years, prepare and provide an affidavit to that effect.
>
> ❑ Remind client to gather the following information to present at the meeting of creditors:
>
>   ❑ Picture identification (A picture I.D. may include a driver's license, government I.D., state picture I.D., student I.D., passport, military I.D., or resident alien card.)
>
>   ❑ Proof of social security number (proof of social security may include social security card, pay stub, W-2, IRS 1099 form, SSA report, or other government-produced document that has the full social security number.)
>
>   ❑ Wage verification, such as a recent payroll stub; and
>
>   ❑ Statements for *all* deposit or investment accounts (including checking, savings, money market accounts, mutual funds and brokerage accounts) for the time period that includes the date of filing.
>
> ❑ Determine, verify, and disclose the debtor's involvement in any business enterprise and/or self-employment as called for in the statement of financial affairs.
>
> ❑ Determine if any tax refunds are applicable to the date of the filing of bankruptcy, are an asset, and are property of the bankruptcy estate. List these amounts even if it is unknown exactly how much will be received. If the debtor wants to avoid having the refunds taken by the trustee, then the refunds should be exempted, if possible.
>
> ❑ Obtain the amount of bank account deposits that constitute property of the estate and the actual balance as of the filing date and verify by the statement, not the debtor's "check register" balance. Having written a check that has not cleared as of the filing date does not reduce the size of the asset.

Color Coding

Not all bankruptcy clients have their paperwork and documentation in a neatly organized package. Some clients will bring all their information (such as bank statements, bills, letters from creditors, pay stubs, real estate information, and business records) mixed up in a box, bag, and/or envelope. It will be somebody's job within the office to sort through the material, organize it, and then analyze it. The attorney may ask for your help with this task. You may receive guidance about how to organize the material or you may be allowed to use your own organizational methods.

One organizational method is to use color coding. Using various colors of highlighters, highlight the different categories of information (such as assets/income, liabilities/debts, real property, etc.) in the client information form. Make a key that you can refer to so you know what color information goes into which bankruptcy schedule. An example of the key is shown in Figure 9.11. For example, the color green might mean assets, red might mean liabilities or debt, orange could represent real property, and bright yellow might mean income. Simply make a colored mark at the top of the paper with the appropriate colored highlighter. Then, sort the documentation from the client into these various categories. Place a color coded note on top of each category using one color for each category of information.

Another option is to sort all of the client's documentation into different stacks representing the various categories. Then, place each stack into the correct file folder within the client's physical file.

If you are given the responsibility of entering information into the bankruptcy schedules, use a pencil to make a check mark by the data on the client questionnaire after you *enter* it into a schedule. Place an X by the client's data after you have *compared* it with the information that was entered on the schedules. Using two different types of marks will help you to determine if you have completed both tasks of entering and comparing.

Highlight, flag, or use sticky notes on the client questionnaire for items that require more information or that denotes questions for the attorney or client.

Critical Thinking Exercises

You learned earlier from reviewing court rules and from this book that many deadlines needs to be met in bankruptcy practice. You also learned in the chapter on civil litigation how to calculate reminder dates. The attorney you work with may already have a method of keeping track of deadlines and reminder dates. The following exercise will refresh your memory about this.

Figure 9.11 **An example of a key used for color coding documents.**

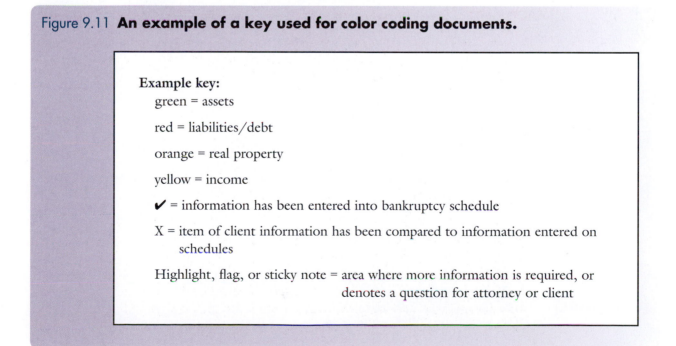

Example key:
green = assets

red = liabilities/debt

orange = real property

yellow = income

✔ = information has been entered into bankruptcy schedule

X = item of client information has been compared to information entered on schedules

Highlight, flag, or sticky note = area where more information is required, or denotes a question for attorney or client

Exercise 9.14 This exercise will help you become familiar with identifying the deadline dates set by the court and determining reminder dates to help the attorney to keep the file on track and meet those deadlines. Identifying and meeting deadlines are important tasks you will be likely to do. It is better to have too many reminders than not enough. The attorney or office may have a guideline for reminder dates in place. This exercise should refresh your memory and stress the importance of making sure that reminder dates are made so deadlines are met. Identifying and meeting deadlines is one of the most important tasks on the job.

1. Open the file **C09_Ex9.14_NoticeOfChapter7** from your electronic storage medium. Review that example of a notice of chapter 7 case.

2. Refer to Figure 9.12. The deadline dates from the sample notice of chapter 7 case have already been entered on the deadline reminder list form in Figure 9.12 along with other deadlines. Some deadlines are set by the court, and some are deadlines set by your office. Other deadline dates are prescribed by the bankruptcy rules as you learned earlier in this chapter.

3. Find the deadlines set out on the sample notice of the chapter 7 case you opened in step 1 and double check that those dates have been entered correctly on the deadline reminder list form.

4. Using perpetual calendar number 6, determine reminder dates that you think would be appropriate for the attorney to review the file and follow up on each item.

5. Determine reminder dates for all items on the list in Figure 9.12.

6. Write your answers in the third column on the deadline reminder list form.

7. Discuss your list with your instructor and classmates and update your list.

Figure 9.12 Example of Deadline Reminder List

DEADLINE REMINDER LIST FORM

Client Name: John Sample
Bankruptcy File Number: 10-xxxx-GFK
Date Filed: June 24, 2010
Trustee Name: Carrie Jones
Date for Meeting of Creditors: July 21, 2010 at 10:00 a.m.

Deadline	Item	Reminder Dates and Work to be Done
06/30/10	Notify client of date for meeting of creditors.	
07/12/10	Debtor's federal income tax return and bank statements due to trustee seven days prior to 341 meeting.	
07/21/10	341 meeting of creditors at 10:00 a.m.	
	Statement of intention	
08/20/10	Deadline to object to exemptions. (This is done by the creditors)	
09/07/10	Certificate of completion of debtor education or financial management class due.	
09/20/10	Deadline to file complaint objecting to discharge of the debtor or to determine dischargeability of certain debts. (This is done by the creditors)	

Chapter Summary and Projects

Summary

You have now read an overview of bankruptcy and have an understanding of what tasks you might perform working in a legal office that specializes in bankruptcy. You have also reviewed procedures that are important to legal support staff in helping the attorney manage client data and prepare the client's bankruptcy filing. You reviewed and practiced applying language, editing, and proofreading skills to legal documents and practiced methods to help your future office meet deadlines in the progression of the client's bankruptcy case.

Remember that as a legal support person, it will be your responsibility in a bankruptcy case to complete the following tasks:

* Find and access official bankruptcy court forms and court rules
* Find the various types of information available on court websites
* Become familiar with the details of the client's file
* Proofread information that has been entered into official bankruptcy forms
* Determine if the information was entered in the correct areas of the forms
* Double check the addition of numbers
* Perform calculations using mathematical formulas to convert wages and expenses to average gross monthly amounts
* Identify information on an official court notice
* Prepare a deadline reminder list
* Think critically and independently to prove yourself a valued legal support person in the bankruptcy process

Your education about the interesting and complicated bankruptcy process will not end with your work here. While the bankruptcy attorney may perform multiple functions in the bankruptcy proceeding, you will learn many more tasks and be asked to perform them after you acquire experience on the job.

Key Terms

assets, 307
automatic stay, 306
average gross monthly amounts, 307
bankruptcy, 304
bankruptcy administrator, 305
bankruptcy code, 304
bankruptcy estate, 307
bankruptcy petition, 304
bankruptcy trustee (see also U.S.
   Bankruptcy Trustee), 305
chapter 7 bankruptcy, 305
chapter 9 bankruptcy, 305
chapter 11 bankruptcy, 305
chapter 12 bankruptcy, 305
chapter 13 bankruptcy, 305
chapter 15 bankruptcy, 305
creditor, 304
creditor matrix, 311

credit counseling, 312
debt, 304
debtor, 304
debtor education instruction, 312
dischargeable debt, 306
disposable income test, 305
exempt asset, 306
exemption (see also exempt asset,
   non-exempt asset), 307
face sheet filing (or emergency filing), 311
gross pay, 330
income, 307
liquidation, 307
means test, 305
meeting of creditors (see also 341
   meeting), 304
net pay, 330
no-asset case, 307

Local Focus Research

The Local Focus icons that appear in this chapter indicate that your local court may have rules, due dates, terminology, and/or procedures that differ from what has been discussed. The following Local Focus assignments will help you to acknowledge these differences. Locate the Chapter 09 folder in your electronic storage medium and open the local focus file **C09_LocalFocus_Bankruptcy**. Resave the file as **LastName_C09_LocalFocus_Bankrutpcy**. Research the following topics described and record your research in the file you just created. Use this information as a reference tool as you start and continue your career as a legal support person. Your instructor may ask you to submit a copy as homework.

Local Focus 9.1 Page 307 discusses the need to locate state websites and to determine if they contain an updated service. This service will alert you to the latest changes in bankruptcy rules and regulations. Search your state's court website to determine if the court has an update service. If it does, record the location of this service (URL) in the space provided.

_____

_____

Local Focus 9.2 Review Figures 9.1 and 9.2 in the main text which show the state and federal bankruptcy exemptions allowed in the state of Indiana. Knowing where to locate your own state's bankruptcy exemptions is essential in working on bankruptcy cases.

1. Perform Internet research for the state in which you reside and find your state's bankruptcy exemptions. Identify the URL on the line provided.

_____

_____

_____

2. Compare the exemptions allowed by your state with those allowed by Indiana. Does your state allow any *state* exemptions to be used *in addition to* the federal exemptions, or must you choose between using the state *or* federal exemptions? Write your answers on the lines below:

_____

_____

_____

3. Bookmark your state's bankruptcy website address for future reference.

Scenario

Your office has been hired by Mr. and Mrs. Sample to help them with their financial problems. Joseph Wayne Sample and Sarah Lynn Sample are in deep financial trouble. They owe more money to creditors than they will be able to repay. They are being harassed by phone calls and letters from debt collectors, owe back taxes to the federal government, and have large balances due on their credit cards. Mr. and Mrs. Sample contacted Attorney James Wong in the Detroit, Michigan, office of Jordan, Leone & Sanchez to help them file for bankruptcy relief. Attorney Wong met with the Samples and determined that they were qualified to file a chapter 7 voluntary petition. He gave the Samples a client bankruptcy questionnaire to complete and return to his office. After receiving the completed questionnaire from the clients, Attorney Wong started to complete the voluntary petition and the creditor matrix by using the official bankruptcy forms provided on the website of the U.S. Bankruptcy Court for the Eastern District of Michigan. Attorney Wong knows it is best to have another person review the client's information and make sure the information was entered correctly on the court forms. He, therefore, printed the client questionnaire, the voluntary petition, and the creditor matrix and left you an email asking you to review the documents, also giving you additional details that might or might not be on the client questionnaire. He wants you to use the copies that he printed, highlight areas in yellow that are not correct, and write the correct information on the document next to the error. It is also your task to review the client's pay stubs and convert the data into average gross monthly amounts to be used in the petition. Follow the instructions to complete these tasks.

Project 1 Conversion of Pay and Deductions to Average Gross Monthly Amounts and Calculating Pay Periods.

Part A

1. Use the year-to-date totals on the check stub provided in the file. **C09_P1A_PayStubForConversions** on your electronic storage medium to calculate the conversion of gross pay and deductions to average gross monthly amounts.

2. Open **C09_P1A_DataForm** from the same location.

3. On the lines in numbers 1 to 5 in the **C09_P1A_DataForm** file, write in the amounts for the YTD wage, federal tax, FICA tax, Medicare tax, and state tax from the pay stub you opened in step 1. These are the amounts that you will use to perform the calculations.

4. Identify and write out what the following abbreviations mean.

   a. W to M = _____

   b. BW to M = _____

   c. SM to M = _____

5. Find the correct formula for each of the conversions in 4a, 4b, and 4c from the How-To Guide.

6. Using the correct formula, perform the calculation for each type of pay period for each of the categories of wages and taxes.

7. Enter your answers on the data form and resave the form as **LastName_C09_P1A_DataForm**.

Part B

1. Locate within the Chapter 09 folder of your electronic storage medium the number of the perpetual calendar you will use for the year 2014.

2. Open **C09_P1B_DataForm** from your electronic storage medium.

3. Using the calendar, determine the number of pay periods in each method of pay based on the last pay date listed on the data form.

4. Write your answers on the data form.

5. Resave the file as **LastName_C09_P1B_DataForm**.

Project 2   Proofread Bankruptcy Documents

Attorney Wong has asked you to proofread a completed voluntary petition and the creditor matrix by comparing the information within the documents to the information originally provided by the client.

1. Open and print **C09_P2_ClientQuestionnaire**.

2. Open and print **C09_P2_VoluntaryPetition**.

3. Open and print **C09_P2_CreditorMatrix**.

4. Open and print the following schedules for the project:

   - **C09_P2_B6SumSched**
   - **C09_P2_B6ASchedA_RealProp**
   - **C09_P2_B6BSchedB_PersProp**
   - **C09_P2_B6CSchedC_PropClaimedExempt**
   - **C09_P2_B6DSchedD_CreditorsHoldingSecClaims**
   - **C09_P2_B6ESchedE_CreditorsHoldingUnsecPriorityClaims**
   - **C09_P2_B6FSchedF_CreditorsHoldingUnsecNonpriorityClaims**
   - **C09_P2_B6GSchedG_ExecutoryContractsUnexpiredLeases**
   - **C09_P2_B6HSchedH_Codebtors**
   - **C09_P2_B6ISchedI_CurrentIncomeIndDebtor(s)**
   - **C09_P2_B6JSchedJ_CurrentExpendituresIndDebtor(s)**

5. Compare the information entered on the petition, schedules, and creditor matrix with the information on the client questionnaire.

6. If any information is incorrect or incomplete, highlight it in yellow and write the correct information in the margin.

7. Review the following email from the attorney and use the information where needed during your proofreading tasks.

8. When you have addressed the requests in Figure 9.13, submit your handwritten corrections to the instructor.

Figure 9.13 email

To: legalsupportperson@jlslaw.emcp.net
From: wong@jlslaw.emcp.net
Date: April 15
Subject: Additional Information for Documents

Hello!

Regarding the documents you are working on:

1. There is no case number because the petition has not yet been filed with the court.

2. At the bottom of some of the pages, you will see a blank and the words "continuation sheets attached." You would normally fill in the number of additional sheets you have added to the document. Ignore that blank for this task since this is not a complete set of schedules.

3. As you proofread the petition, check that the following were completed correctly:

   - Petition:
     - see that the full filing fee has been check marked.
     - In the four rows of statistical administration information there should be check marks in the following areas::
       - Row 1: Check second box
       - Row 2: Check first box (1-49)
       - Row 3: Check third box ($100,001 to $500,000)
       - Row 4: Check same box as third row
   - On page 2 of the petition, make sure that:
     - Exhibit A is blank
     - Exhibit C has "no" checked
     - Exhibit D has both boxes checked
     - The section called "Information Regarding Debtor Venue" has the first box checked
     - The certification to a debtor who resides as a tenant of residential property is left blank

4. I have already verified the citations in the second column on schedule C. Be sure to proofread all the other columns.

Thanks for your help!
Sincerely,
Attorney Wong

Discuss the Projects

Now that you have completed this chapter on bankruptcy, think about and discuss the following questions with your classmates. Write your ideas on the lines provided.

1. Name one item that you learned about the bankruptcy procedure that you found of particular interest.

    _____

    _____

2. What, in your opinion, are the skills you should develop to be successful in a law firm that practices bankruptcy law?

    _____

    _____

3. What skills do you currently have that would be helpful to you in the area of bankruptcy law?

    _____

    _____

4. What skills do you need to attain or improve upon?

    _____

    _____

5. Can you think of any other methods for organizing client documents from which data must be extracted to complete the bankruptcy forms?

    _____

    _____

Special Topics

Chapter Objectives

- Consider tasks that apply to many areas of law
- Prepare typed documents from handwritten notes
- Proofread items printed in newspapers and draft corrections
- Prepare affidavits of service
- Perform Internet research to locate information on official websites
- Complete projects related to critical thinking and time management
- Prepare a typed medical record resume from dictation
- Learn about metadata
- Learn about legal specialty certification

Before beginning the exercises for this chapter, copy to your storage medium the Chapter 10 folder from the Student Resources disc that accompanies this textbook. Do this for each chapter before starting the chapter's exercises.

As a legal support person, you will be required to think independently and critically and to adapt to the variety of tasks and projects assigned to you by your supervisor or other attorneys. This includes adapting quickly to new concepts and changes within the office—for example, computer software upgrades and special assignments, such as making changes to the office website and assisting with marketing and the office newsletter. The ability to address the needs of your office with little or no instruction is a skill that is sought by many employers.

This chapter addresses key topics that do not pertain to one specific area of law. To complete this chapter and its projects, you will have to recall information that you learned in previous chapters. You will also have to apply your own critical thinking skills to navigate through the chapter successfully.

The practices and projects you completed earlier helped you to hone your skills in grammar, editing, proofreading, and critical thinking. You now have the knowledge and confidence to do more difficult work on your own, just as you will be expected to do at your future job. This "special topics" chapter covers a broad range of assignments and activities and does not contain a section on law review. Unlike previous chapters, the Chapter 10 projects will contain new information and instructions prior to each project. Use this information as a starting point to complete each project.

Language Focus: Complete Sentences, Sentence Fragments, Run-on Sentences, and Comma Splices

It is not uncommon to use incomplete sentences when one is speaking. A speaker has the luxury of connecting directly with the listener, and the listener can fill in any implied information that may have been left out of a sentence. Writers, on the other hand, do not have the luxury of connecting directly with the reader. Incomplete sentences and ideas are quickly misinterpreted, and the writer does not have the ability to repeat things in the same manner that a speaker does. Clear communication is essential in all professionally written materials, so professionals must always use complete sentences in their writing.

Unlike the spoken word, written communication is more or less permanent. Mistakes or inaccuracies made in a document can cause confusion and frustration for each and every person who reads it. Once it is delivered, an unclear piece of writing will continue to cause confusion as others read it. Professionally written communications are expected to be completely clear, since the business typically has time to edit and revise the work prior to delivering it to the intended recipients. As a legal support person, you will have to ensure that your office produces clear and understandable work by watching for incomplete and fragmented sentences, run-on sentences, and comma splices.

Complete Sentences

Complete sentences have a subject and a predicate *and* make sense! The subject in a sentence is the main noun or pronoun. The predicate is the main verb phrase in a sentence.

To verify that a sentence is complete, follow these steps:

1. Identify prepositional phrases. Nouns in phrases will never be the subject, so eliminate the noun in the prepositional phrase as the subject.

2. Identify the main verb or verb phrase. The main verb will be either a linking verb or an action verb. The verb may also have a helping verb.

3. Ask yourself this question to find the subject: Who/what + verb = subject

4. Then, ask yourself if the sentence makes sense. If so, the sentence is complete.

Apply these steps to the following example.

If this contract is breached by the purchasers, the purchasers shall pay damages to the seller.

The first part of the sentence, "If this contract is breached by the purchasers," is a dependent clause; therefore, although this group of words has a subject (*contract*) and a verb (*is breached*), they are not the main subject and verb of the sentence. Remember that the word *if* acts as a subordinating conjunction, which indicates that the clause is dependent. You can also tell that this clause is dependent because it does not make sense on its own.

The second part of the sentence, "the purchasers shall pay damages to the sellers" is the independent clause. This group of words can stand alone and contains a subject (*purchasers*) and a verb (*shall pay*). The group of words *does* make sense alone because it is an independent clause, and it also contains a complete thought.

In composing written materials, many attorneys simply record their ideas without thought to structure or logical order. They will either return to the page and edit it after they are finished or turn it over to someone else for editing. Other writers will edit and proofread as they go and take care to organize the work logically. In any of these scenarios, the legal support person must watch for errors in sentence structure and provide corrections that resolve them. See the explanations and examples in each of the following sections.

Sentence Fragments

A **sentence** always contains a subject and a verb and expresses a complete thought. A **sentence fragment**, in contrast, is a group of words that may contain a subject and a verb and may be punctuated like a complete sentence but does *not* contain a complete thought.

The attorney contacted. (fragment)

Our neighbor's more-than-qualified attorney. (fragment)

Since the client called. (fragment)

versus

The attorney contacted the client. (complete)

Our neighbor's more-than-qualified attorney was very affordable. (complete)

Since the client called, we have been able to draft the necessary documents to initiate the lawsuit. (complete)

Best Practice Tip

SUBORDINATING CONJUNCTIONS

Remember that dependent clauses are sometimes referred to as subordinate clauses, since they must be attached to independent clauses. Dependent clauses usually start with subordinating conjunctions. If you know the most common subordinating conjunctions, you will be able to quickly identify dependent clauses. Subordinating conjunctions include the following:

• if	• since	• although	• whenever	• even though
• when	• because	• until	• even if	• inasmuch

A sentence fragment will often not include a subject and predicate together. A fragment could also be a dependent clause.

Here are examples of fragments:

1. Even though he had the best argument of all the attorneys.

2. Ms. Petrich brought an entire suitcase full of insurance documents. Such as receipts, invoices, and collection letters.

3. Working into the night to research her response for the next day.

4. FOR AND IN CONSIDERATION of the sum of Eighty-four Thousand Dollars ($84,000) cash.

5. Going to court today to appear with our client at the omnibus hearing.

To correct these fragments, decide if the sentence needs to be rewritten to add a subject and verb or added to another complete sentence. Here are ways in which the previous fragments might be corrected.

1. Even though he had the best argument of all the attorneys, **Mr. Randall spent additional hours reviewing the file for details.**

2. Ms. Petrich brought an entire suitcase full of insurance documents, such as receipts, invoices, and collection letters.

3. Working into the night to research her response for the next day, **Ms. Coughlin was well prepared but tired.**

4. FOR AND IN CONSIDERATION of the sum of Eighty-four Thousand Dollars ($84,000) cash, **the grantor hereby transfers title to the grantee.**

5. I am going to court today to appear with our client at the omnibus hearing.

Run-on Sentences

A **run-on sentence** is a term used to describe what happens when two sentences are run together without punctuation between them. To correct a run-on sentence, insert the correct punctuation or divide the sentences, then punctuate and capitalize them correctly. Here are examples of run-on sentences:

1. A contract is a legally binding agreement not all agreements are contracts because they lack one or more of the legal requirements.

2. The distinction no longer has practical significance it has been eliminated.

3. Medical benefits are also paid to disabled employees these provide for the payment of charges made by physicians and hospitals.

Correcting run-ons is fairly simple once you have identified them. However, writers and editors sometimes have trouble recognizing run-ons. Rei R. Noguchi, in his book *Grammar and the Teaching of Writing*, suggests that you test your sentences by two methods:

- Turn them into yes/no questions.
- Turn them into tag questions (sentences that end with a questioning phrase, such as *isn't it, doesn't it,* or *aren't they*).

If the sentence you are testing is not a run-on, you will easily be able to adapt it to these tests. But if the sentence being tested *is* a run-on, the revised question will either be clumsy or will lose the original meaning.

Consider the following sentence:

The typical workers' compensation claim begins with the filing of a report of industrial injury.

Test whether the sentence is correct or a run-on by turning it into a question or adding *isn't it* to the end to create a tag question.

Does the typical workers' compensation claim begin with the filing of a report of industrial injury?

The typical workers' compensation claim begins with the filing of a report of industrial injury, doesn't it?

By using the testing methods noted here, you can confirm that the sentence is complete and not a run-on. Now apply the test to the following run-on sentence.

A contract is a legally binding agreement not all agreements are contracts because they lack one or more of the legal requirements.

The yes/no question can only be made with each separate thought. The run-on sentence cannot be made into a single question.

Incorrect   Is a contract a legally binding agreement are all agreements contracts because they lack one or more of the legal requirements?

Correct   Is a contract a legally binding agreement? Are all agreements contracts because they lack one or more of the legal requirements?

Isn't it cannot be added to the example sentence either.

Incorrect   A contract is a legally binding agreement not all agreements are contracts because they lack one or more of the legal requirements, *isn't it?*

Correct   A contract is a legally binding agreement, *isn't it?* Not all agreements are contracts because they lack one or more of the legal requirements, *aren't they?*

Neither test works, does it? You should see that you have more than one complete concept in that sentence, and you cannot make the whole thing turn into one question. Make sure you try both tests with each of your problem sentences. Sometimes one test will sound right, but the other will make it obvious that there are two sentences.

Sentences in legal writing tend to be long. You may think that these long sentences are run-on sentences, but they often are not. Care should be taken to determine whether the sentence has to be altered. Use the tests mentioned in this section to identify and fix any run-on sentences you encounter on the job.

Comma Splices

A **comma splice** occurs when a writer attempts to combine two independent clauses without a coordinating conjunction between them.

> Tender of payment by the buyer is a condition to the seller's duty to tender and complete any delivery, tender of payment by check in the usual course of business is permissible unless the seller demands legal tender and allows the buyer a reasonable time in which to obtain it.

This example is actually two independent clauses that have been *spliced* with a simple comma. A comma alone is not strong enough to separate two independent clauses. A legal support person could fix this problem in several ways.

> Tender of payment by the buyer is a condition to the seller's duty to tender and complete any **delivery; tender** of payment by check in the usual course of business is permissible unless the seller demands legal tender and allows the buyer a reasonable time in which to obtain it.

> Tender of payment by the buyer is a condition to the seller's duty to tender and complete any **delivery. Tender** of payment by check in the usual course of business is permissible unless the seller demands legal tender and allows the buyer a reasonable time in which to obtain it.

> Tender of payment by the buyer is a condition to the seller's duty to tender and complete any **delivery, but** tender of payment by check in the usual course of business is permissible unless the seller demands legal tender and allows the buyer a reasonable time in which to obtain it.

> Tender of payment by the buyer is a condition to the seller's duty to tender and complete any **delivery; however, tender** of payment by check in the usual course of business is permissible unless the seller demands legal tender and allows the buyer a reasonable time in which to obtain it.

The corrections shown previously are all acceptable. Because the writer should be cautious not to have too many simple sentences and no transitions from one sentence to another, some solutions are better than others. Just remember that a single comma between two independent clauses is not enough to separate them.

Language Focus Exercises

Complete the following exercises using the information presented in the Language Focus section.

Exercise 10.1   Using the suggestions found on page 357, test the following sentences to determine whether they are run-ons. Write your test questions on the lines provided. After you have completed the tests, identify the sentence as a "Run-on" or "Correct as is" by circling the corresponding notation. If the sentence is a run-on, rewrite the sentence so that it is correct.

1. The distinction no longer has practical significance it has been eliminated.

   a. Can you make a question out of the sentence as it is written? Write your question on the lines provided.

   _____

   _____

   _____

   b. Can you make the sentence a question by adding a tag-on question at the end of the sentence? Write your tag-on question(s) on the lines provided.

   _____

   _____

   _____

   c. Is the sentence correct as it is or is it a run-on sentence? Write "Correct" on the following line if the sentence is correct or rewrite the sentence if it is a run-on sentence.

   _____

   _____

   _____

2. Medical benefits are also paid to disabled employees these provide for the payment of charges made by physicians and hospitals.

   a. Can you make a question out of the sentence as it is written? Write your question on the lines provided.

   _____

   _____

   _____

   b. Can you make the sentence a question by adding a tag-on question at the end of the sentence? Write your tag-on question(s) on the lines provided.

   _____

   _____

   _____

c. Is the sentence correct as it is, or is it a run-on sentence? Write "Correct" on the following line if the sentence is correct or rewrite the sentence if it is a run-on sentence.

_____

_____

_____

3. After jurors have taken their oath, the judge admonishes them that it is their duty not to converse with or permit any other person to address them on any subject of the trial, and it is their duty not to form or express an opinion on the case until it is finally submitted to them for their verdict.

a. Can you make a question out of the sentence as it is written? Write your question on the lines provided.

_____

_____

_____

b. Can you make the sentence a question by adding a tag-on question at the end of the sentence? Write your tag-on question(s) on the lines provided.

_____

_____

_____

c. Is the sentence correct as it is or is it a run-on sentence? Write "Correct" on the following line if the sentence is correct or rewrite the sentence if it is a run-on sentence.

_____

_____

_____

4. This certificate must be filed or recorded in the office of the designated public official in the county in which the principal office of the limited partnership is located additional requirements are needed in some states.

a. Can you make a question out of the sentence as it is written? Write your question on the lines provided.

_____

_____

_____

b. Can you make the sentence a question by adding a tag-on question at the end of the sentence? Write your tag-on question(s) on the lines provided.

_____

_____

_____

c. Is the sentence correct as it is, or is it a run-on sentence? Write "Correct" on the following line if the sentence is correct or rewrite the sentence if it is a run-on sentence.

_____

_____

_____

5. Basically, a letter of credit is an agreement in which one party, usually a bank, agrees in advance with a prospective buyer of goods to honor a draft drawn upon it by the seller of the goods upon compliance with the conditions stated in the agreement a financing technique substitutes the financial responsibility of a bank for that of the buyer of the goods.

a. Can you make a question out of the sentence as it is written? Write your question on the lines provided.

_____

_____

_____

b. Can you make the sentence a question by adding a tag-on question at the end of the sentence? Write your tag-on question(s) on the lines provided.

_____

_____

_____

c. Is the sentence correct as it is, or is it a run-on sentence? Write "Correct" on the following line if the sentence is correct or rewrite the sentence if it is a run-on sentence.

_____

_____

_____

Exercise 10.2 Identify if the following sentences are fragments, run-ons, comma splices, or correct as they are written. Circle the answer. If necessary, correct the sentence on the lines provided.

1. In a criminal prosecution and on the day of the trial.

    fragment   run-on   comma splice   correct

    Correction, if necessary:

_____

_____

2. Statutes are laws enacted by the Congress of the United States or by the legislatures of each of the states in the union.

fragment   run-on   comma splice   correct

Correction, if necessary:

_____

_____

3. Evidence of a fact or a series of facts from which the existence of the fact to be determined may reasonably be inferred.

fragment   run-on   comma splice   correct

Correction, if necessary:

_____

_____

4. Wishing he'd brought his computer and worrying about the deadline for the answers to interrogatories. John waited for the bus all morning last Tuesday because his car was in the shop.

fragment   run-on   comma splice   correct

Correction, if necessary:

_____

_____

5. The second requirement of a contract is reality of consent this means that both parties must give unqualified approval to the terms of the agreement.

fragment   run-on   comma splice   correct

Correction, if necessary:

_____

_____

6. Disputes sometimes arise between owners of conflicting interests in property as to whether the property involved is real property or personal property, these differences may arise between a landlord and a tenant or seller and buyer.

   fragment   run-on   comma splice   correct

   Correction, if necessary:

   _____

   _____

7. Because the proper court may be one of general jurisdiction or a specialized court. The choice must be well considered.

   fragment   run-on   comma splice   correct

   Correction, if necessary:

   _____

   _____

8. Once it is determined that a child is eligible for adoption by someone either because the appropriate person has consented or because parental rights have been terminated, the next step in the process is the establishment of a relationship with the adoptive parents.

   fragment   run-on   comma splice   correct

   Correction, if necessary:

   _____

   _____

9. All witnesses have been examined and all evidence has been introduced each attorney makes a closing statement or summation in which he or she summarizes what has been proven and attempts to convince the jury that it should decide the case in favor of the client.

   fragment   run-on   comma splice   correct

   Correction, if necessary:

   _____

   _____

10. The most important right of a defendant in the courts in the United States is the presumption of innocence, the prosecution must prove beyond a reasonable doubt that the defendant is guilty of the crime of which he or she is accused.

fragment   run-on   comma splice   correct

Correction, if necessary:

_____

_____

Editing for Conciseness

The expression "time is money" is accurate in any office. When you **edit for conciseness**, you are checking to make sure that the document or correspondence communicates clearly and efficiently. The recipient will take longer to understand and respond to a request that rambles than he or she would take to respond to a request that is clear and to the point. A clear and concise document is always preferable to a long-winded one. In a legal office, clients are billed for the time the attorney spends working on the case, including drafting documents and correspondence, consulting with the client and other attorneys, and talking with witnesses related to the file. Some offices bill just for attorney time, whereas others bill the client for legal support staff time in situations where documents are being drafted for the client at the direction of the attorney. The legal support person must use time efficiently and respect the time of others.

In editing for conciseness, you will have to keep the following two questions in mind:
- What is the purpose of the sentence?
- What can be removed without losing information or meaning?

Use the following suggestions to edit your communications so they are clear and orderly:
- Replace or remove wordy phrases
- Remove unnecessary passive voice occurrences
- Remove outdated language
- Remove unneeded introductory words or phrases
- Delete unnecessary modifiers

Best Practice Tip

TIME IS MONEY

The longer you take to perform your duties, including correcting errors, the less time you will have to work on clients' projects. The attorney can charge a client only so much for a document or procedure. The more revisions that need to be made because of your errors, the less profit the office will make. Therefore, all office communications must be clear, concise, and correct. Poor communicators require more time and space to convey their ideas. In a legal office, everyone must be able to communicate effectively in all matters (in both written and verbal form). In addition to the time it takes to communicate clearly, an office must also consider the expense of printing documents several times because of errors.

REMOVE REDUNDANCIES

Chapter 7 discussed the need to avoid redundancies in professional writing. In editing a document for conciseness, consider whether a phrase is redundant and can be replaced with a single word.

close proximity (change to "close")

end result (change to "result")

written down (change to "written" or "recorded")

Refer to Table 7.3 to review other common redundant phrases.

Replace Wordy Phrases

Wordy phrases can typically be replaced with one-word alternatives. In Table 10.1, compare the phrases listed on the left with the alternatives on the right.

Table 10.1 Common Wordy Phrases

at all times	always
due to the fact that	because/since
in most instances	usually
in the event that	if
on an everyday basis	routinely
the reason is because	because
I am of the opinion that	I believe

Some wordy phrases can be left out completely without changing the meaning or purpose of a sentence.

As a matter of fact

To all intents and purposes

It is clear that

It seems that

As far as I'm concerned

Replace Passive Language

The appropriate use of active and passive voice is explained in Chapter 8. Although passive voice does have a purpose within a business environment, in most cases it should be replaced with active language. When you encounter passive language, determine whether the sentence can be rewritten with a more active verb. Consider the following two sentences.

It was decided that your case would be accepted by the attorney.

The attorney decided to accept your case.

The second sentence is shorter yet communicates the intended message more effectively.

Remove Outdated Language

In an office, it is easy to use older, previously written letters as examples. The problem with this practice is that writers often pick up and reuse outdated language and phrases. The following is a list of outdated language that should be removed from your writing:

Attached herewith

As per your request

Enclosed please find

This is to advise you

I am writing to you because

Pursuant to your phone call of May 15

Heretofore

Herewith

Whereas

In regards to

As regards

Do not perpetuate outdated language. Trimming the previous wording from your work will make the document much easier to understand. The sooner a message is understood, the sooner the work can be done.

Remove Unneeded Introductory Words and Phrases

A number of words and phrases are repeatedly used to introduce a sentence. Although some of these words may be needed, they can often be removed without affecting the intent or purpose of the sentence. Consider the following sentences and the more concise options that follow:

There are a number of attorneys at the office who prefer working in hard copy.

A number of attorneys at the office prefer working in hard copy.

It is true that the client has not been available.

The client has not been available.

These examples illustrate that unneeded introductory words and phrases can be removed without changing the meaning of the sentence. The resulting sentences are more effective.

Delete Unnecessary Modifiers

Analyze each sentence and remove any unnecessary modifiers (or qualifiers). Modifiers are used to provide additional detail but are often unnecessary. In legal writing, modifiers are seldom needed within documents or correspondence.

Best Practice Tip

TRANSITIONAL PHRASES

Chapter 4 discussed the use of transitions to add clarity to a document and show relationships between ideas. When you edit for conciseness, be certain you do not delete words or phrases that clarify relationships or lead the reader from one topic to the next. Remove only the words and phrases that are superficial and unnecessary within the sentence.

Editing Exercises

Complete the following exercises using the information from the editing section.

Exercise 10.3 Identify a one-word alternative to the following wordy expressions. Write the alternative on the corresponding line.

1. Beyond the shadow of a doubt. _____

2. In connection with. _____

3. In order to. _____

4. In spite of the fact. _____

5. On a daily basis. _____

Exercise 10.4 Practice editing a letter for conciseness.

1. Open and review the file **C10_Ex10.4_WordyLtr** from your electronic storage medium. The letter was created by Ms. Amie Roberts, the attorney for Sally Snow. Attorney Roberts will be sending the letter to Mr. Harrison Bussard, 1163 Bird Place, San Diego, CA 99111. Mr. Bussard is the attorney for Kari, Eric, and Tim, who are mentioned in the letter.

2. Save the file as **LastName_C10_Ex10.4_WordyLtr**.

3. Edit the letter to make it clear and concise. Keep in mind that you must convey the same idea as is in this letter; however, you may select alternative wording to convey the information.

4. When you have edited the document, take a moment to proofread the letter for sentence structure, spelling, and punctuation. Make corrections as needed directly in the file.

5. Format the letter according to the Appendix: Style Guide for this textbook provided in your electronic storage medium.

6. Resave the file and submit it to the instructor.

Proofreading: Promissory Notes and Commonly Misused Words

When you work in a legal office, you will rarely know what types of documents (perhaps even what area of law) you will be working on each day. While you may become familiar with forms and documents that you use regularly, you will learn something new every day! Laws and procedures constantly change, and you will consistently find that you do not understand parts of documents. That is understandable. Legal documents are intended to be read by lawyers and other legal professionals, such as judges and court personnel. Your job is to learn how to format, edit, and proofread the correspondence and documents according to your office style and court specifications.

Non-court Documents

In previous chapters, the format of court documents as well as wills and trusts were discussed in detail. This section discusses the formatting of noncourt documents, such as promissory notes, leases, and contracts. **Non-court documents** differ from court documents in that promissory notes, leases, contracts, etc., do not have court captions and are generally not signed by an attorney.

A good example of a noncourt document used frequently in a law office is a promissory note. Much of what you have learned previously can be applied to noncourt documents. Figure 10.1 is an example of a short promissory note. Following the example are discussion points referring to the formatting and content of the promissory note that a legal support person must be aware of.

Figure 10.1 **Promissory Note Example**

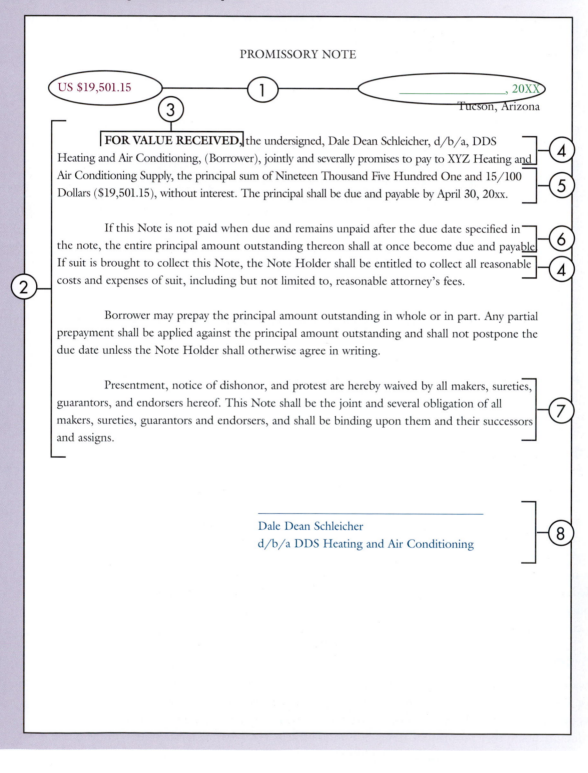

SUBJECT/VERB AGREEMENT

Promissory notes generally indicate the amount of the note under the title and to the left of the date line. Unlike most legal documents, the date in a promissory note is usually right aligned at the top instead of the customary bottom left near the signature line. The location of signing is generally right under the date [1].

In previous chapters it was mentioned that legal documents are almost always double spaced. In general, notes, contracts, and leases, are single-spaced because certain documents, such as contracts, can be quite lengthy. [2].

These types of documents may also start with traditional legal words or phrases [3], for example, FOR VALUE RECEIVED, IN CONSIDERATION OF, KNOW ALL BY THESE PRESENCE, and COMES NOW, among others. They are generally typed in all capital letters, and some require punctuation following while others do not. These phrases may or may not be bolded. Follow your office style. These traditional phrases continue to be used and do have meaning. However, a trend in the legal system encourages legal writers to use plain language. While experts on legal writing suggest leaving these phrases out, you will most likely continue to use them in noncourt documents if that is the style in your office.

Because these phrases are used only in legal writing, the legal support person may find it difficult to know how to punctuate them. The following examples show how these phrases should be punctuated:

- FOR VALUE RECEIVED,
- KNOW ALL (MEN is sometimes used here) BY THESE PRESENCE,
- COMES NOW the (followed by a singular noun)
- COME NOW the (followed by a plural noun)
- IN CONSIDERATION OF

Consider the first sentence of the note in Figure 10.1. In proofreading a promissory note, the proofreader must always verify to whom the note is directed. The subject in this sentence is *undersigned*. The verb is *promises*. You must determine whether *undersigned* is singular or plural. In this case, *undersigned* could be either singular or plural, depending on who is actually signing the promissory note. In Figure 10.1, Dale Dean Schleicher is signing so *undersigned* is singular. The verb *promises* is the correct choice to make the subject agree in number.

Pay attention that titles are used correctly throughout the document [4]. When people involved in legal situations are assigned titles, such as "Borrower" and "Note Holder" (lines 7 and 9) in this example, pay close attention that you continue to use the correct titles throughout the document.

Recall that whenever a dollar amount or other number is especially important, it is generally written in both words (first) and numerals (second)[5]. The purpose of a promissory note is to identify how much the borrower is promising to repay under certain terms. The dollar amount referred to in the example promissory note is Nineteen Thousand Five Hundred One and 15/100 Dollars ($19,501.15).

PRINCIPAL VS. PRINCIPLE

Make sure that you thoroughly understand the difference between *principal* and *principle*. The word *principal* is often used in monetary situations because it can mean the main amount of money borrowed or lent. A *principle*, however, broadly means "a rule of action or conduct."

His overriding principle is greed.

The adjective *principal* means "most important, chief, first, or foremost."

My principal objection is the cost of the project.

The noun *principal* can also mean "the head or director of a school" as well as "a sum of money other than interest."

The faculty supported the principal in her negotiations with the board.

The monthly payments go mostly for interest, leaving the principal practically untouched.

References in the promissory note such as *thereon* are commonly used to refer to some previously mentioned document or situation [6]. In the third sentence of the note, *thereon* refers to the note mentioned earlier in the same sentence.

Another common reference is *therefor*, which means "for that or this." Notice that this word is similar to *therefore*, which means "as a result" or "consequently."

We are ordering five computers and are including payment therefor.

The borrower is delinquent three months in payments; therefore, we are starting collection proceedings.

The fourth paragraph in Figure 10.1 is necessary legal language included by the attorney to meet all legal requirements [7]. As long as all words dictated or written by the attorney are spelled correctly and punctuated properly, you have done your job. You will become familiar with legal verbiage and be able to accept it as correct.

The signature line should always start somewhere near the center and continue to the right margin [8]. Leaving sufficient white space and balancing parts of the document allow it to be easily read. Notice that d/b/a (doing business as) and the name of the business are included in the signature block, since the business is equally responsible for this note as the individual.

UNKNOWN LEGAL JARGON

Do not change any of the legal wording in documents just because you are unfamiliar with it. Type the wording exactly as you hear it in dictation or see it on the original. When you wonder whether you should change wording in a legal document, the following is the best advice: When in doubt, DON'T. Always ask the attorney before changing any legal wording.

Commonly Misused and Confused Words

Note the best practice tip regarding the differences between the words *principal* and *principle*. In the English language many instances of misused and confused words exist. It is the proofreader's job to verify that words are used accurately within a document or correspondence.

Sound-alike words are the most common types of words that give writers trouble. **Homonyms** are words that sound alike and are spelled alike but have different meanings, such as:

club (a place to dance)

club (a bat to hit with)

bore (drill a hole)

bore (to be dull)

While proofreaders do not need to worry about homonyms for the sake of spelling (since these words share the same spelling), a proofreader should know the intended meaning for any homonym encountered within a document.

A proofreader should know common homophones. **Homophones** are words that sound alike but are spelled differently and have different meanings. These include:

accept, except

affect, effect

carrot, caret, carat

piece, peace

sent, cent, scent

then, than

to, two, too

weather, whether

A proofreader must verify that all of the words used within a document are as intended in terms of spelling and meaning.

What about words professionals misuse that are not homophones or homonyms but just commonly misused words?

Toward (not towards)

Used/supposed to (not use to or suppose to)

Bimonthly (every two months) vs. semimonthly (every other month)

Farther/further

Nonplussed (meaning bewildered, not calm)

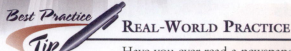
Have you ever read a newspaper and noticed errors in spelling, grammar, and composition in headlines and stories? A legal support person who seeks to gain experience proofreading can practice by proofreading published materials such as news articles, real estate listings, or other publications to hone his or her skills.

Proofreading Exercises

Complete the following exercises using the information from the proofreading section.

Exercise 10.5 Practice proofreading published material, such as real estate advertisements, to gain experience. Real estate advertisements are expensive, so they are typically written using as few words as possible. The following text represents a real estate listing, printed in a newspaper, that describes property for sale.

> 3 same floor bedrooms plus an 12x10 office all on the main floor of this well cared for rambler on hilltop. The 1,200 sq. ft. on the main floor is in immaculate condition with all the word done for you! Recent updates include but not limited to the following: windows & steel siding w/transferable warranties, roof, front and back doors, water heater, water softener, concrete driveway, new street as well as water & sewer to home and roof. Call now & make this home yours.

1. Rewrite this description without adding additional words.
2. Correct any grammatical or spelling errors and rearrange the text if it does not read well.
3. Save your work as **LastName_C10_Ex10.5**.
4. After discussing your changes with others in your class, make any additional changes you would like and resave your corrected work.
5. Submit the file to the instructor.

Exercise 10.6 Sometimes errors are overlooked by the proofreaders at a newspaper office.

1. Read the material in the following paragraph. It represents a news article printed in a newspaper.

> A 43-year-old man is in fair condition today after crashing his motorcycle into a fence in rural Faribault County Tuesday. He was airlifted to the hospital after the crash, which occurred at about 5:30 p.m. on County Road 6. He had just passed another vehicle when his motorcycle veered off the road, according to the State Patrol. General Growth Properties plans to continue to operate its six malls while it works through bankruptcy reorganization. The bankruptcy plan for the

SPELLING

Proofread carefully for the word *statute*, since it is very common to type *statue*. Of course, the spell checker will allow this substitution. Only manual proofreading can find this error. Another similar error is typing *trail* instead of *trial*.

country's second largest mall owner splits the company in two and restructures about $15 billion in secured debt.

2. Write your observations and comments about this article on the lines provided.

_____

_____

_____

_____

_____

3. Share your observations with your instructor and classmates.

Exercise 10.7 Sometimes it appears that no proofreading is done at all by the newspaper office, or it may be that the newspaper just prints the submission as received without making any changes.

1. Rewrite the public service announcement shown in the paragraph that follows these instructions.
2. Use correct grammar and punctuation.
3. Save your work as **LastName_C10_Ex10.7**.
4. Submit the file to the instructor.

MCI, Inc., make a fresh-baked lunch each weakday for senors. Meals can also be delivered or brought home and freezed. Meal cards are also available for purchase and can be used at local Diner's Clubs or restaurants that are partnered with MCI, Inc.

Exercise 10.8 Practice proofreading for misused or confused words by completing this exercise. Open **C10_Ex10.8_SoundAlikeList** to find a comprehensive list of misused, confused, and sound-alike words and use the list to complete the following exercise.

1. Open and print **C10_Ex10.8_AppellateBriefWithErrors**, which is an appellate brief containing many sound-alike word errors in addition to misspelled words. Each line of this brief has been numbered for your convenience in finding and discussing the errors. Appellate briefs are not normally line numbered.
2. Proofread the appellate brief writing the corrections previous to the errors.
3. Compare your corrections with another student's and update your brief.
4. Submit your corrected brief printout to the instructor.

Exercise 10.9 Complete the following exercises using what you have learned about proofreading promissory notes.

1. Open **C10_Ex10.9_PromissoryNote** from your electronic storage medium.
2. Save the file as **LastName_C10_Ex10.9_PromissoryNote**.
3. After reviewing the previous comments regarding the items in the example promissory note of Figure 10.1, proofread the promissory note that you just opened on the computer screen.
4. Make all necessary changes.
5. Resave the file and submit it to the instructor.

Critical Thinking:
Prioritizing and Scheduling Tasks

It is essential to your productivity in the office to prioritize your tasks. Legal support staff may be assigned to work with multiple attorneys and may have several tasks assigned from each one. Your job is to prioritize the tasks that you have been given based on which tasks must be completed first (including new tasks suddenly added to your list). As you prioritize, you will also have to estimate the time it will take to complete each task. It is important to determine whether you can complete them all in one day.

Prioritizing Tasks

A legal office must be able to make time for clients who have urgent needs. For example, you may have clients who are leaving the country in a matter of days and it only just occurred to them to update their wills. Both you and the attorney would need to adjust your work schedules to assist the client and have the work finished on time. You may have other tasks that need to be completed on the same day. If you work in a larger office, you may be able to find someone else who can complete your previously scheduled tasks. If not, the tasks will need to be prioritized. If you work for more than one person, your supervisors may need to discuss which of their projects take priority over others. If you work in a small office where you are the only support staff member, discuss the conflicts with the attorney and create a manageable solution. In any size office, be certain that the attorneys or supervisors involved understand how you are prioritizing your work.

Stay organized by knowing what tasks need to be completed and how long each task will take. Knowing these details will help you prioritize your work. At the end of each day, review your workload and make an outline of what needs to be done on the following day.

PRIORITIZING CONFLICTING TASKS

Alert the people you work for when you must prioritize multiple urgent tasks. The attorneys may have scheduled additional review/lead time without having informed you. Attorneys schedule the additional review or lead time to give themselves flexibility if an emergency project should present itself, such as clients having to update their wills at the last minute. The attorneys will take all of this into consideration in deciding which task should be done first.

Scheduling Tasks

Schedule additional time between tasks, because there will inevitably be interruptions, such as phone calls, clients needing to have items photocopied, voice mails and emails to which to respond, personal needs, and errors to correct. Even the most experienced legal support person will encounter unforeseen errors. Every office will be different in its approach to allowing additional time for the correction of errors; however, at the start of your career, it is best to err on the side of allowing more time rather than less time.

SCHEDULING COMMON TASKS

Be conscious of common tasks that you do at the end of every day, such as mail, cleanup, making the reminder/task list for the next day, and checking the email outbox to verify that everything was actually sent. Avoid scheduling complicated tasks near the end of the day, especially if they must be completed that day.

DETERMINING TIME NEEDED TO COMPLETE TASKS

Keep a running list of the various tasks that you complete during the day. Make a note of how long it takes you to complete each task. Use this as a reference to help you schedule time for future tasks.

Consider the following scenario:

> You have a summons and complaint that should be served on a person by the sheriff. You look up the address of the person to be served on the postal service website or another resource and see that the address is designated to be in County A. You send the documents and service fee to the sheriff of County A for service, but that sheriff returns the documents and fee to you saying that the address is actually located in County B. In that case, you must prepare another service fee and letter, sending the documents to the sheriff of County B for service.

Local Focus **10.1**

This type of error would cause considerable delay in the service of documents. While this does not happen frequently, you may not always be aware that a question of identifying the correct county could occur.

CONTACTING THE SHERIFF'S OFFICE REGARDING COUNTY BOUNDARIES

The sheriff has the last word on the boundaries of the county and in which county an address is located. If you have any question that an address is near a boundary line, it is accepted practice to call the sheriff's office to clarify the correct county before sending out papers for service. This county boundary issue pertains to service by a sheriff or law enforcement official. An independent process server may serve documents in any county.

Critical Thinking Exercises

Practice prioritizing and planning your tasks list by completing the following exercise.

Exercise 10.10. Prioritizing Tasks

Assume that your 8-hour workday is 8 a.m. to 12 noon with a 1-hour lunch, and 1 p.m. to 5 p.m. with two 15-minute paid breaks during the day. The 1-hour lunch can be adjusted 30 minutes earlier or later depending upon the work to be done. Figure 10.2 contains a random task list of work to be done today, including the estimated time needed to complete each task. Assume that you are to attend the 4 p.m. meeting for 30 minutes. It is your job to prioritize the list to have more urgent work completed first.

1. Prioritize the list of random tasks in Figure 10.2 and indicate in what order you would do these tasks by writing the number on the corresponding line to the left of each task.

   _1_ Punch in, get coffee, turn on computer. <u>(done before official workday starts at 8 a.m.)</u>

   _2_ Check and answer email. <u>(10 minutes) 8:10 a.m.</u>

2. After addressing each task, write the approximate time of day at which you would be completing that task.

3. Add up all of the times for the tasks you are to complete.

4. Write the total number of hours and minutes these tasks will require on this line:

   _____

5a. Does the total time for the tasks fit into an 8-hour day? Yes/No

5b. If not, write what tasks you would leave until tomorrow on the following lines and place an asterisk before the corresponding item in the list in Figure 10.2.

   _____

   _____

   _____

   _____

6. What personal tasks or interruptions have to be allowed for? Write them on the following line.

   _____

7. If more than 8 hours of work are required, consider how you would get work done that has to be done today. Write your ideas on the following lines.

   _____

   _____

   _____

   _____

   _____

Figure 10.2

_____ 4 p.m. meeting. (30 minutes)

_____ Afternoon break.

_____ Check and answer email. (10 minutes)

_____ Check and answer voice mails. (15 minutes)

_____ Filing. (30 minutes)

_____ Filing and file maintenance. (1.5 hour)

_____ Final mail for the day. (15 minutes)

_____ Finalize changes to estate planning documents to be signed at 2 p.m. today. (30 minutes)

_____ Finalize real estate documents for closing scheduled for noon today. (1 hour)

_____ Lunch 12:30 to 1:30.

_____ Make to-do list for tomorrow. (15 minutes)

_____ Morning break.

_____ Print three bankruptcy schedules and add signature "sign here" tabs for appointment with client at 10 a.m. tomorrow. (30 minutes)

_____ Punch in, get coffee, turn on computer (done before official work day starts at 8 a.m.)

_____ Relieve receptionist for his or her afternoon break. (15 minutes)

_____ Research federal court electronic filing rules for your meeting with attorney at 4 p.m. today. (research takes about 30 minutes)

_____ Research procedures for appeal brief due in two weeks. (30 minutes)

_____ See what remains from the day before, organize work area, determine what you did not finish yesterday, and ask attorney what he or she anticipates doing today. _____ (20 minutes)

_____ Transcribe 20-page contract to be signed tomorrow at 10 a.m. (2 hours transcribing, 45 minutes proofreading)

Chapter Summary and Projects

Summary

You have now read about a few special tasks you may encounter in the legal office and how you can prioritize your work to more efficiently assist your attorney. You reviewed and practiced applying language, editing, and proofreading skills to noncourt legal documents such as promissory notes, reviewed the need to identify incorrect word usage and sentence structures, and also practiced prioritizing daily tasks. The projects that you will encounter in the following section will require you to apply what you learned in this and previous chapters as well as to review and apply additional information to the following projects.

Remember that as a legal support person, it will be your responsibility in most legal offices to complete the following tasks:

- Prioritize tasks for the day
- Edit and proofread court and non-court documents
- Proofread for misused words
- Identify, edit, and proofread for proper sentence structure punctuation
- Identify wordy and outdated phrases
- Edit previously drafted material into concise text

Key Terms

affidavit of service, 386

certificate of service, 386

comma splice, 358

copy typing, 380

edit for conciseness, 364

fax transmission report, 387

homonyms, 371

homophones, 371

legal specialty certification, 398

medical records summary, 395

metadata, 397

non-court document, 367

proof of service, 386

run-on sentence, 356

sentence, 355

sentence fragment, 355

transcription, 380

wordy phrases, 365

Your local court will have rules and due dates specific to your jurisdiction. Locate the Chapter 10 folder in your electronic storage medium and open the local focus file **C10_LocalFocus_SpecialTopics**. Resave the file as **LastName_C10_LocalFocus_SpecialTopics**. Research the following topics and record your research in the file you just created. Use this information as a reference tool as you start and continue your career as a legal support person. Your instructor may ask you to submit a copy as homework.

Local Focus 10.1   Look up your county on a local map and see if any cities are on the boundaries. If there are, determine the correct county for each city and write the notes on the lines provided.

_____

_____

Local Focus 10.2   Page 387 discusses the differences between a certificate of service and an affidavit of service. Research your local county and state court to see if it is customary to use a general certificate of service or a sworn affidavit of service in serving legal documents on other attorneys. Record your findings on the lines provided.

_____

_____

_____

_____

_____

_____

_____

Scenario

You have accepted a position as a legal support person in a busy law office. You will be working as a floater, a title given to those who fill in for absent personnel or in departments that might need extra help. As a floater, you never know where your skills and services will be needed in the office from day to day. You may work all or part of a day in one area or department and then move to another area. Your assignments will vary. Some tasks you receive will have short instructions but may take all day to complete; some may take several days or longer to complete; and other projects may take a short time so that you may be able to complete many in a day. A person who works as a floater is always appreciated for his or her willingness to be flexible and learn new things.

Project 1   Type From Handwritten Material

When you arrived at work today, your supervisor gave you a number of handwritten documents that had to be typed into electronic files. A number of these documents contain abbreviations and many are difficult to read. Your supervisor trusts that you will be able to type them accurately.

Copy Typing

Copy typing is the act of typing from previously printed or handwritten copy. You may be familiar with transcription. **Transcription** is a different skill and is generally done by a typist while listening to an audiotape, videotape, DVD, or digital recording. Copy typing does not involve audio recordings, but it does require the legal support person to be able to interpret handwriting accurately.

Although it seems as though unlimited technology is available at our fingertips, at times we are forced to live without the convenience of technology. A person might also make handwritten notes in editing a document, doing research, or attending a meeting. Sometimes a person might choose several paragraphs from various documents and put them together with additional material to make a new piece of work. In many cases, a legal support person will be given handwritten documents (such as client questionnaires, meeting transcripts, letters from clients, or notes from the attorney) and will have to type the documents as electronic files.

WORKING WITHOUT TECHNOLOGY

During a power outage or equipment failure, employers expect their office workers to do what they can during the outage, such as filing, file maintenance, desk organization, or handwriting basic parts to documents or correspondence to be typed later. Many people may struggle to continue working if they do not have access to electronic technology. However, it is possible to draft handwritten, shorter pieces of work and type them when things are back to normal. This may seem like a waste of time or duplicative effort, but it allows employees to make productive use of time.

Legal support staff will be expected to type a variety of documents from handwritten copy. Some handwriting is precise and easy to read, while other samples may look like foreign languages or may have been written in the writer's personal style of shorthand. It can be challenging to decipher handwritten documents if they are not legible. It is helpful if one has an idea of the topic, knows the intent of the writer, or has a list of terms available for the topic. Because of the difficulty of deciphering some handwritten copy, remember that you are probably creating a draft. All legal writing must be accurate, so always have the author review the draft until you are confident of your deciphering skills.

Here are several steps you can follow in preparing a document from handwritten material:

- Read the material to get an idea of the topic.
- Read the material again to become familiar with the handwriting patterns, abbreviations, and punctuation.
- If the creator of the handwritten material is available, ask questions about the content or topic of the material and verify any confusing notations.
- Create a typewritten document of the handwritten material.
- Proofread the newly created document for spelling, grammar, and punctuation errors and edit, if needed.
- Give the typed document to the author to review for accuracy.

Make sure that you proofread for spelling, grammar, and punctuation errors after you have finished typing the document. If you cannot decipher a word, leave an underlined blank space in your document so you can fill in the correct word later or highlight the area in yellow to remind yourself that you should add information.

Part A The first document you are asked to type is displayed in Figure 10.3. It is from Attorney Sam Smith regarding resolution of a construction dispute. Your supervisor would like the copy typed as soon as possible.

1. Type the material you see in Figure 10.3.
2. Save your work as **LastName_C10_P1A**.
3. Compare your work against the answer key file provided by your instructor. Correct any errors you made, fill in blank areas, and resave your corrected work as **LastName_C10_P1A_corrected**.
4. Submit the document to the instructor.

Part B The second handwritten document, shown in Figure 10.4, is from the human resources department regarding employment law material.

1. Type the material you see in Figure 10.4.
2. Save your work as **LastName_C10_P1B**.
3. Compare your work against the answer key file provided by your instructor. Correct any errors you made, fill in blank areas, and resave your corrected work as **LastName_C10_P1B_corrected**.
4. Submit the document to the instructor.

Figure 10.3 **Project 1A handwritten note.**

Enclosed is a ltr from Atty Sam Smith. As you can see, he suggests a meeting at the property b/twn the attys and the parties in order to attempt to find a resolution. I am not sure how helpful that would be at this point in time. In my opinion, we need a professional tile contractor to take a look at the situation and to come up with a solution for the drainage issue. Then it will be up to the parties, thru their attys, to determine how to pay for the fix. Is there anybody in particular that ewe want to work with that I cld suggest to Mr. Smith? Please let me know b/cse I think they are anxious to proceed with this and will eventually take away the indefinite extension of time too answer the complaint if no progress is being made.

Figure 10.4 **Project 1B handwritten note.**

Weather you are working in employment law, bizness, or any other area of law, it is crucial that you be mindful of cultural diversity. Many people will seek the services of your law office or business for many different reasons. It is wise for you to educate yourself about the cultural differences and customs of your various clients to which you are not normally exposed. You can do research using the public library or Internet and reviewing two or three sources of information for the culture you wish to learn about. Some things you shld no are the amount of physical space to maintain btwn yourself and the person w/ whom you are speaking; the amount of eyes contact that are appropriate; and the roll that gender can play in communication (for example, a mail from a certain culture may not be able to answer questions presented by a woman, or a women may not be allowed in a room alone w/ a man). Above all else, be consistent in how you treat all clients, regardless of their culture. Everyone appreciates being with respect and as an individual. Keep an open mind and due not form an opinion about an individual because of their appearance, race, or culture.

Part C The third handwritten document, shown in Figure 10.5, is a note from an attorney to the file regarding probate assets.

1. Type the material you see in Figure 10.5. The handwriting in this project is very difficult to read.
2. Save your work as **LastName_C10_P1C**.
3. Compare your work against the answer key file provided by your instructor. Correct any errors you made, fill in blank areas, and resave your corrected work as **LastName_C10_P1C_corrected**.
4. Submit the document to the instructor.

Part D The fourth handwritten document, shown in Figure 10.6, is a legal notice that contains the writer's personal style of abbreviating.

1. Type the written text of the legal notice indicated by formatting locations and notes shown in Figure 10.6.
2. Save your work as **LastName_C10_P1D**.
3. Compare your work against the answer key file provided by your instructor. Correct any errors you made, fill in blank areas, and resave your corrected work as **LastName_C10_P1D_corrected**.
4. Submit the documents to the instructor.

Figure 10.5 **Project 1C handwritten note.**

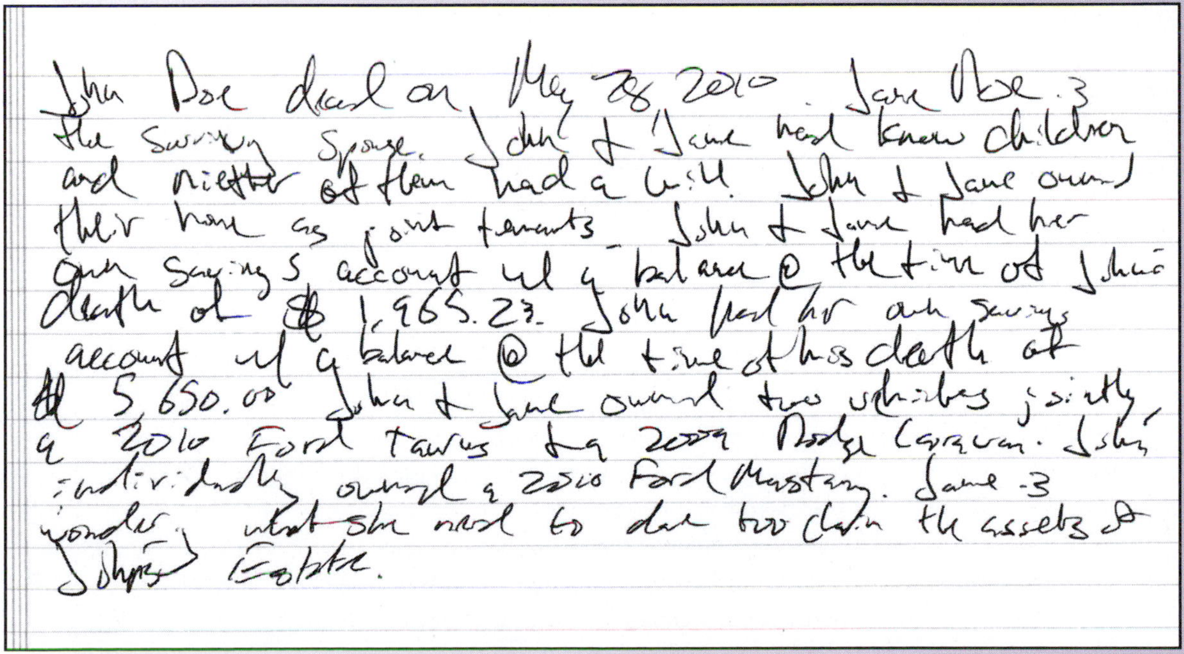
John Doe died on May 28 2010. Jane Doe is the surviving spouse. John & Jane had know children and neither of them had a will. John & Jane owned their home as joint tenants. John & Jane had her own savings account w/ a balance @ the time of John's death of $1,965.23. John had his own savings account w/ a balance @ the time of his death of $5,650.00. John & Jane owned two vehicles jointly, a 2010 Ford Taurus & a 2009 Dodge Caravan. John individually owned a 2010 Ford Mustang. Jane is wondering what she need to do to claim the assets of John's Estate.

Figure 10.6 **Project 1D handwritten note.**

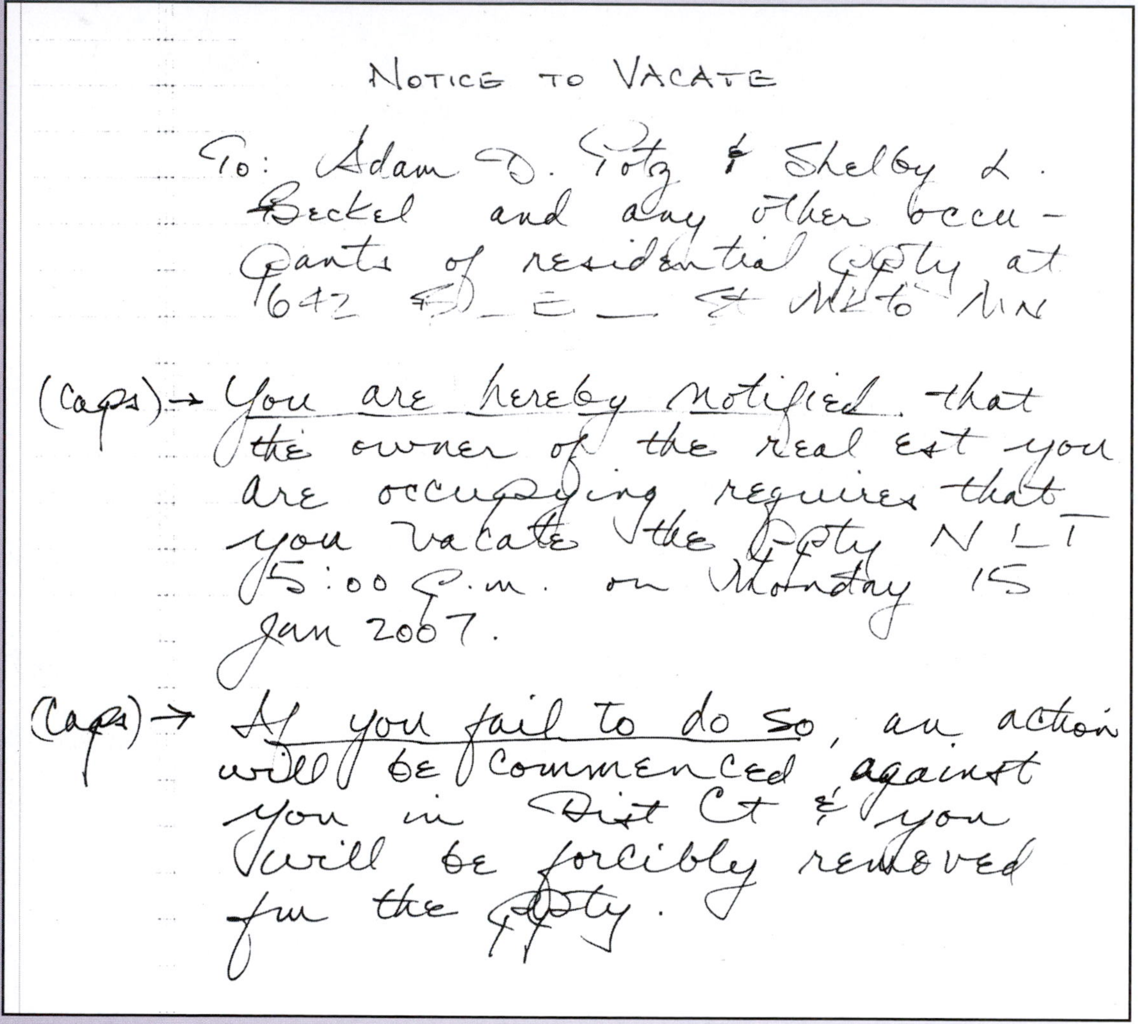

NOTICE TO VACATE

To: Adam D. Getz & Shelby L. Beckel and any other occupants of residential pty at 642 ___ ___ ___ & ___ MN

(caps) → You are hereby notified that the owner of the real est you are occupying requires that you vacate the pty NLT 5:00 p.m. on Monday 15 Jan 2007.

(caps) → If you fail to do so, an action will be commenced against you in Dist Ct & you will be forcibly removed fm the pty.

Part E The handwritten document, shown in Figure 10.7, is a note whose author abbreviated words. The topic is not clear and it may include abbreviations that you do not understand. Remember to leave an underlined blank in the document whenever you cannot decipher a word.

1. Type this handwritten material as a flush left letter to Ms. Fiona Fabiano, Butler and Fabiano, 101 East Main Street, Jacksonville, FL 55881. Use your own name as the person signing the letter.
2. Save your work as **LastName_C10_P1E**.
3. Compare your work against the answer key file provided by your instructor. Correct any errors you made, fill in blank areas, and resave your corrected work as **LastName_C10_P1E_corrected**.
4. Submit the documents to the instructor.

Figure 10.7 **Project 1E handwritten note.**

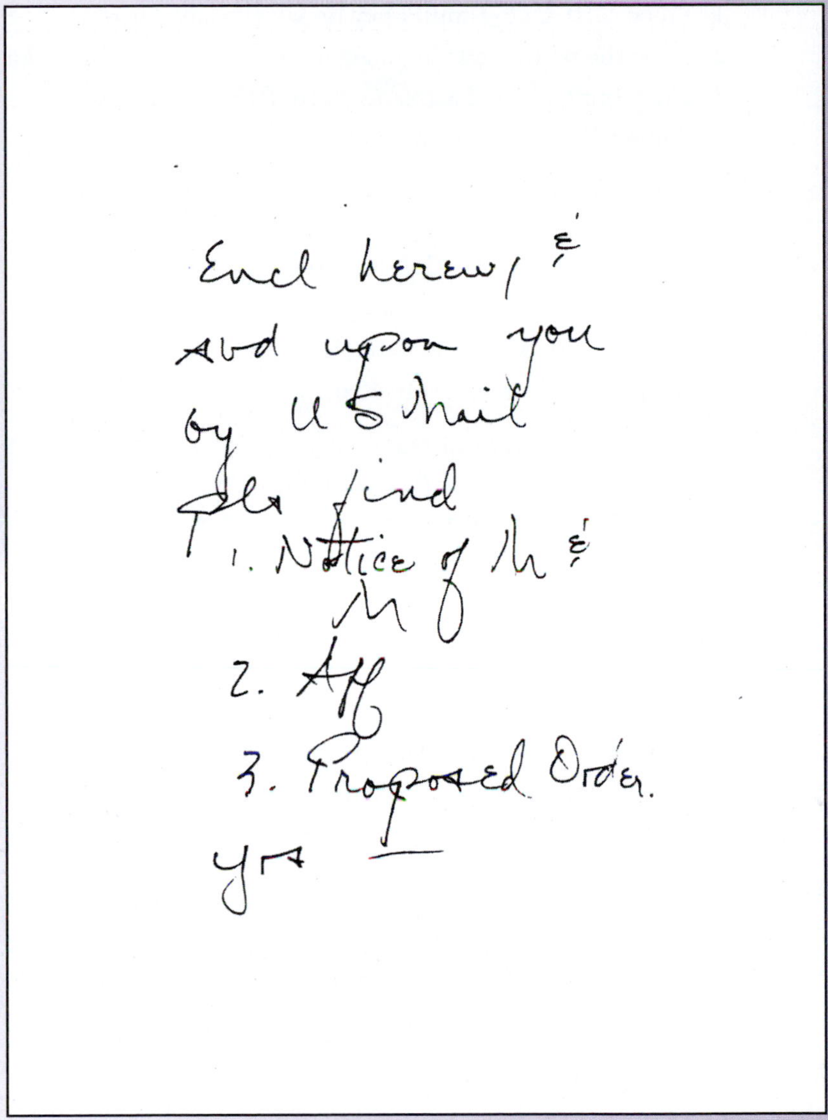
Encl herew/ ē
srvd upon you
by US Mail
Pls find
1. Notice of M ē
M O
2. Aff
3. Proposed Order.
yrs

Part F Next, you need to locate and copy type a scanned file containing the text for the draft of an employment policy handbook.

1. Open **C10_P1F_EmplPolicy** on your storage medium.
2. Type the written text in paragraph format within a new document.
3. Save your work as **LastName_C10_P1F_EmplPolicy**.
4. Submit the file to the instructor.

Part G The next document requires you to copy type a handwritten notice from an insurance company.

1. Open **C10_P1G_InsCoNotice** on your storage medium.
2. Type the written text in paragraph format.
3. Save your work as **LastName_C10_P1G_InsCoNotice**.
4. Submit the file to the instructor.

Part H The final document that you are asked to copy type is a handwritten summary of law regarding probate administration.

1. Open **C10_P1H_ProbLawSum** on your storage medium.
2. Type the written text in paragraph format.
3. Save your work as **LastName_C10_P1H_ProbLawSum**.
4. Submit to the instructor.

Project 2   Affidavit of Service and Certificate of Service

In your position as a floater in the law office, you are asked to complete a project started by another legal support person who had to leave the office for a family emergency. This legal support person had prepared a motion and supporting memorandum that had to be served today by mail. The only task remaining was the preparation of the proof of service document.

Affidavit of Service

Recall from your work in previous chapters that you created letters by which you served several types of pleadings on the opposing attorney. You must create one additional document in serving pleadings that will show **proof of service**, including the name of the person serving the document (you), the date the document was served, the name of the document served, the method of service, and the name and address to which the document was sent. This additional document will be either a certificate of service or an affidavit of service. The difference between these two documents is that the **affidavit of service** is a sworn statement that must be notarized. A **certificate of service** is not notarized. Court rules in most states allow pleadings to be served by mail, by facsimile (fax) transmission, or by hand delivery. In all methods used, proof of service is required. The rules of court will specify whether to use an affidavit or a certificate of service. Most states require that you complete an affidavit of service, and some provide an example form within the state's rules of court. If you are not sure which method is required by a particular state, you can look it up in the rules of court or ask someone in your office what the accepted practice is for proof of service of pleadings in your state

A certificate of service is typically used when doing electronic filing of documents in federal court or other court that allows electronic filing. The federal court provides a specific format for the certificate of service, so you will know exactly what information you are required to provide on the form.

Examples of both types of forms are provided in the Chapter 10 folder on your storage medium. The actual format of the forms may vary among states, but the information required is similar.

Serving Documents by Fax Attach the fax transmission report and your fax cover page to the affidavit or certificate of service. All three documents are then attached to the document being served. The **fax transmission report** will show the fax number of the person served, the date and time of the transmission, and the number of pages transmitted. Sometimes a party to whom the documents are faxed might claim they did not receive the transmission. If you have the transmission report, at least you have proof that the transmission was successfully completed by your office. File the report in the appropriate part of the physical or electronic file.

Serving Documents by Mail or Personal Delivery Sometimes a party to whom the documents are mailed might claim he or she did not receive the document. Your signed affidavit of service is proof that the document was actually mailed from your office and shows the address to which it was mailed. Attach your signed affidavit of service to the document that was served so that it follows the last page of the document and file it in the appropriate part of the physical or electronic file.

Refer to the letter you prepared in Project 1, Part E, serving documents on an attorney.

Assume you are employed by ABC Law Office, 123 Alpha Court, Jacksonville, FL 558811. Using the affidavit of service form provided in the Chapter 10 folder of your storage medium, and information from the letter you prepared in Project 1, Part E, prepare an affidavit of service for the documents that you served on the attorney. Sign the affidavit of service and have a classmate act as the notary public who witnesses your signature. Remember, when working in the law office, you must sign the affidavit *in the presence of a notary public,* and the notary public should insert the date on which he or she witnessed your signing the document.

1. Open **C10_P2_AffofServiceForm**.
2. Prepare an affidavit of service for the documents that were served in Project 1, Part E.
3. Save your work as **LastName_C10_P2**.

Project 3 Determining a Correct County of Residence

Earlier in the week one of your associates at the office sent a summons and complaint to a sheriff for service on a resident of the sheriff's county. Unfortunately, the documents and fee were returned, having been delivered to the wrong county's sheriff's office. You know from experience that if a person resides at or near the boundary line of two counties it is possible that the city, town, or village may be divided by a county line with part of the city in one county and the other in a different county.

This problem can cause considerable delay in the service of documents. It does not happen frequently, and you may not always know question of identifying the correct county will occur unless the documents are returned to you.

Because of your colleague's experience, your office created the following procedure to use in determining the correct county of residence.

Practice using the instructions from your attorney by locating the address of the publisher of this book. Following the steps in the bulleted list, look up the zip code

Figure 10.8 Instructions for finding county of residence.

To: All Legal Support Staff
From: Attorney Michael Forrest
Re: Steps to Determine County of Residence

Follow the steps in the bulleted list below to verify the zip code and county of a needed address. Even though you may eventually phone the sheriff to clarify the county of residence, most of the time the correct address information can be found on the postal service's website.

- Open website "usps.com"
- Click on the Find a Zip Code tab
- Enter a street address, city, and state
- Click Submit
- Zip code + 4 results will be shown
- Click on "mailing industry information" link
- A new window will open that shows the county for the address that was entered as well as other postal service information.

Note: This county boundary issue pertains mainly to service by a sheriff or law enforcement official. An independent process server may serve documents in any county.

Thank you.

and county for the publisher of this book. Write the publisher's address, zip code, and county on the lines provided.

Street address: _____

City, state, and zip: _____

Zip code shown on postal service website: _____

County shown on postal service website: _____

Project 4 Find Answers to Questions on the Internet

As a floater in your new office, you know many occasions on the job will occur when you will need to find answers to questions. Official court websites contain much detailed information that may include answers to your questions. When you arrived at work today, you realized that you had time to research the answers to questions that had come up during your first few weeks on the job. Review the following questions and use the Internet to locate the answers.

Part A

1. Refer to the federal bankruptcy court website that you worked with in Chapter 9: Bankruptcy Law. Questions 1–10 are shown in Figure 10.9. The answers can be found on the court's website under the various categories of information.

2. Open **C10_P4A_ResearchQuestions** from your electronic storage medium. Key your answers to questions 1–10 on the form. Include the URL for each answer and any other search steps you took to find your answer.

3. Save your answers as **LastName_P4A_ResearchQuestions**.

Figure 10.9 **Research questions 1 to 10.**

1. What are the three branches of federal government?
2. What is the URL for the official website of the U.S. Supreme Court?
3. Which entity hears appeals of bankruptcy court decisions?
4. What are the three main chapters of the bankruptcy code?
5. Which three types of federal courts accept electronic case filings?
6. What is the number of the federal court form for a substitution of attorney?
7. What is the number of the federal court form for a transcript order?
8. What are six types of cases heard by the federal court system?
9. What are the five types of cases heard by the state court system?
10. What is the first term in the Glossary of Legal Terms?

Part B Give some thought to the topic of a question you have and where you would be likely to find the answer. For example, if you need to find a zip code, you would associate a zip code with the U.S. Postal Service and look for its website to find zip codes.

1. Answer questions 11 to 29 in Figure 10.10 by performing general research on the Internet.
2. Continue to record your answers on the file named **LastName_P4A_ ResearchQuestions**. Include the website address for each answer and any other search steps you took to find your answer.
3. Resave and submit your answers to the instructor.

Figure 10.10 **Research questions 11 to 29.**

11. What is the zip code + 4 and county for the following street address? 247 Main St., Newport, VT.
12. What is the state abbreviation for American Samoa?
13. What is the official website address for the White House?
14. How does a person get a tour of the White House?
15. In Mariposa County, California, what is the court fee for filing a request for change of venue?
16. In Mariposa County, California, what is the court fee for filing a petition or other first paper in a family law matter?
17. In the Arizona Court of Appeals, Division One, what is the initial case filing fee?
18. In the Arizona Court of Appeals, Division One, what is the fee for a certificate of good standing?
19. In what Florida city and county is Disney World located?
20. What city is the county seat for Mason County, West Virginia?
21. What is the URL for the official website of the Minnesota Judicial Branch?
22. Using links on the website of the Minnesota Judicial Branch, find and list the definition of the legal term *perjure*.
23. Using links on the website of the Minnesota Judicial Branch, find and list the number of judicial districts in Minnesota.
24. Find the application form to become a notary public in the state of New Mexico.
25. Find the process for applying to become a notary public in the state of Louisiana.
26. Find the location on the website for the Iowa Secretary of State on which you would do a business corporation search.
27. Find the form for Inventory and Appraisement of Estate on the website for the Kentucky Court of Justice.
28. Find the web page for the Court Interpreter Program for the California courts.
29. Find the website for the National Board of Trial Advocacy.
    a. On that site, find the page for How to Apply for Board Certification. Bookmark this page for future reference.
    b. Find the principles for certification. Bookmark this page for future reference.
    c. On that site, find the page for Civil Trial Law Itemization of Substantial Active Trial involvement. Bookmark this page for future reference.
    d. On that site, find the page for Civil Contested Matters. Bookmark this page for future reference.

Project 5 Critical Thinking in the Office

As a floater, you receive instructions in various forms such as dictation, email, written notes, or spoken in person. Sometimes the instructions are quite detailed, so you will know exactly what to do. Other times the instructions are more of an outline of the attorney's thoughts and lack detail. In both situations, and especially when detail is lacking, you know you must use critical thinking to analyze the situation and anticipate the needs of the attorney and other members of the legal team.

Before beginning your work in any situation, you know it is wise for you to analyze the instructions, read between the lines, make a list of what you believe is required to complete the instructions, and then discuss any questions you may have with the attorney.

Part A The instructions in Figure 10.11 were given to you by Attorney Corbin Locke in an email. The instructions do not provide much detail. The attorney has a big trial coming up, and you have been asked (vaguely) to help the attorney make certain arrangements before trial. In this project, you know that you must anticipate the needs of the attorney.

1. Open the file named **C10_P5A**.
2. Save the file as **LastName_C10_P5A**.
3. Analyze each item shown in Figure 10.11 and list under each item what you think you should do to accomplish that item.
4. Put yourself in the position of the attorney and think about what else you might do to be of further assistance and add those ideas to your list under each item.
5. Insert all answers below each item using an italicized font.
6. Resave the file and submit to the instructor.

Part B You received the instructions in Figure 10.12 by Attorney Colleen Behrens. Compared to project 5A, these instructions provide more detail. In addition to the attorney's comments in regular font, the statements following each comment in *italics* are the actual instruction from the attorney telling you what tasks to perform. This example contains much detail and very specific instructions, but it still requires you to use critical thinking skills to determine if you could perform additional tasks.

ANTICIPATING NEEDS OF THE ATTORNEY

Anticipating needs is a skill that is appreciated by the attorney, whether the directions are complete and detailed or not. This anticipation and independent thought will help both you and the attorney to be more organized.

It may sometimes seem that what is required to complete certain tasks will be quite personal, and some people may consider this outside the scope of their job duties. However, a busy attorney will appreciate the extra thought given by the assistant. The attorney may ask the assistant to follow through on some or all of those items or may indicate it is not necessary or the attorney will handle the matter. However, it never hurts to offer additional assistance.

Figure 10.11 **Project 5A Vague Email Instructions from Attorney**

MEMO
To: Legal Support Person
From: Attorney Corbin Locke
Re: Johnson v. Smith

The trial of the Johnson v. Smith matter is set for 15 days starting Monday, October 1. We do not have trial on Mondays after the first week of trial. I have to be at the courthouse at 8:30 a.m. each day for conferences in chambers.

I want to meet with the clients at their home on Sunday afternoon, the day before trial, at 2:00 to prepare them for trial. It is a 3-hour drive to their house and they live somewhere out in the countryside. A 2:00 meeting should allow me enough time to get to their house without leaving too early.

I will work in my hotel room in the evening after each day of trial to prepare my notes for the next day and do any additional legal research that might become necessary.

You know, I will really miss getting my bike ride every day with this long trial.

We are going to have about a dozen large poster exhibits for display at trial.

This file has gotten so large. It has grown to require eight file boxes.

I intend to call four people to testify in addition to our clients. We have already taken their depositions. I will call them the week before trial to tell them what day and time they should appear at trial.

Since this is a long trial, my wife and children want to come and visit the city where the trial will be held. They think there might be something fun going on that we can all do together some weekend.

Thanks

Figure 10.12 **Project 5B: detailed instructions from attorney.**

MEMO
To: Legal Support Person
From: Attorney Colleen Behrens
Re: Johnson v. Smith

The trial of the Johnson v. Smith matter is set for 15 days starting Monday, October 1. We do not have trial on Mondays in the second and third week of trial. I have to be at the courthouse at 8:30 a.m. each day for conferences in chambers. I don't want any appointments on those Mondays when there is no trial time.

Please put the trial dates and starting times on the appropriate office calendars.

I want to meet with the clients at their home on Sunday afternoon, the day before trial, at 2:00 to prepare them for trial. It is a three-hour drive to their house and they live somewhere out in the countryside. A 2:00 meeting should allow me enough time to get to their house without leaving my home too early.

Call the clients and tell them the date and time I want to meet with them at their home. I want you to call the clients the week before trial to remind them of the meeting. Ask the clients for driving directions to their home from the south.

I will do further preparation in the evenings after each day of trial to prepare my notes for the next day and do any additional legal research that might become necessary.

The courthouse is in Jackson. I am not exactly sure where the new facility is located.

Check the Internet or call the Visitor Bureau in that town to get a list of hotels. Check the websites for two or three hotels, or call them, and give me an idea of prices for a room and what amenities are available in the hotel. Ask if they will give me a discount for an extended stay. I would like a small suite where the bedroom is separate. I want a separate work area that has a small table where I can work on my computer. I need Internet access. See if the hotel has an in-house restaurant or continental breakfast. If not, where is the nearest restaurant to the hotel? After I have decided on the hotel I will give you the dates I need to stay and my credit card. Please call and make the reservation.

Talk to our office administrator and arrange for me to take a small printer so I can print my notes each night. I will need a small box of supplies such as pens, pencils, notepads, printer paper, printer ink, paper clips, and sticky notes. Let me know if you think I will need anything else.

continues

Figure 10.12 **Project 5B: detailed instructions from attorney.** *Continued*

You know, I will really miss getting my bike ride every day with this long trial.

Ask if the hotel has an exercise facility available for guests or if there is a gym near the hotel.

We are going to have about a dozen large poster exhibits for display at trial.

Find a way for me to display these exhibits at trial.

A month before trial we are going to prepare the exhibits. Please have our office messenger take those to the copying service. They should copy each exhibit onto 3' x 5' paper and mount them onto foam board. Remind me when it is time to do the exhibits.

This file has gotten so large. It has grown to require eight file boxes.

The office has a portable luggage cart. Please find it and see that it is in good working order. Reserve that for me to use during the trial for moving all the boxes.

I intend to call four people to testify in addition to our clients. We have already taken their depositions. I will call them the week before trial to tell them what day and time they should appear at trial.

We will need to subpoena these witnesses and I need their contact information. Six weeks before trial I would like you to obtain and prepare subpoenas, request the appropriate witness fee, and arrange for the subpoenas to be served upon or delivered to the witnesses in accordance with our local rules.

Since this is a long trial, my spouse and children want to come and visit the city where the trial will be held. They think there might be something fun going on that we can all do together some weekend.

When you collect information on hotel rooms, request a room with a sleeper sofa for the children.

1. Open the file named **C10_P5B**.
2. Save the file as **LastName_C10_P5B**.
3. Read each instruction given in Figure 10.12.
4. Think about what additional tasks you could perform.
5. Record your answers on the document you opened in item 1 of these instructions.

6. Insert and underline the additional tasks you could do under the italicized instructions from the attorney.

7. Resave the file and submit to the instructor.

Project 6   Preparing a Summary of Medical Records

Opportunities will occur for you to work with medical records in many areas of law. In both the prosecution and defense of personal injury matters, the attorneys or legal support staff will collect some or all medical records of the injured person, summarize and analyze the records, and use the information to prove or defend the claims made. Medical records may also be used in criminal matters relating to charges of chemical or alcohol use or assault. In a will contest matter, medical records may be reviewed to determine a person's mental capacity at the time of making or signing a will. Medical records, mental health records, school records, and counseling records are sometimes collected during family law matters.

It will be somebody's duty to prepare a **medical record summary**, which may also be called a résumé of the medical records. The summary will itemize each date of treatment, the treatment facility or doctor, and the type of treatment received by an individual. Some attorneys prefer to do this summary themselves, or they may ask a paralegal or law clerk to prepare the summary. They may dictate the summary for you to transcribe or they may highlight certain parts of the records and ask you to put the highlighted information into a summary document. After you have more experience working with medical records, the attorney may ask that you review the records and prepare your own summary.

Creating a Medical Summary   If you have been assigned the task of preparing a summary of medical records, you will first have to organize the records. One suggested way of doing this is to separate the records by medical provider, and then arrange the records from each provider in chronological order with the oldest record being on top, followed by later records. Some attorneys prefer that lab and x-ray reports be grouped together, and some prefer that all records be put in chronological order regardless of their type. You could three-hole punch the records and put them into a ring binder with numbered dividers between each provider and create a table of contents listing the number tab followed by the name of the provider. You should also create a cover page for the binder identifying the person the records relate to, the person's date of birth, the date of loss/incident, and a list of complaints or injuries made by the person. Organizing the records in this fashion makes it easier to page through while creating the summary. It also keeps the records together in the event that someone would drop them on the floor and keeps them from getting mixed up with other papers that might be on your desk.

Some attorneys may also want the medical records scanned and saved in electronic format in the client's computer file. Whichever method your office or attorney uses for organizing medical records, be sure to follow that method consistently.

Different methods are available to use in preparing medical summaries. Some people use a spreadsheet or merely type the information in paragraph form. A more manageable method is to create the summary using a table format with the number of columns depending on the types of information to be included in the summary. You may be familiar with working in tables from other classes you have taken. After the medical summary is prepared, the attorney may want you to sort the table by date or medical provider. The following are tips to use when working with information in tables.

Sorting a Table When you are sorting information in a medical summary created in a table, select the *entire* table. Then, using the table "sort" feature, choose the information you wish to sort (field, paragraph, numbers) and whether you want to sort in ascending (low to high) or descending (high to low) order. If you select only one column of the table, that is the only information that will be sorted. Selecting the entire table will keep all the information together properly. Of course, it is helpful to review the sorting process by reading about this topic in the help menu of your word processing program.

Medical Abbreviations, Symbols, and Terms Spelling medical terms and understanding the meanings of abbreviations and symbols used in medical records can be challenging. In the office, search online for "medical abbreviations and symbols" and "medical terminology." Print the list and/or bookmark the website address for future reference on the job. Sometimes it is more convenient to keep a printed list of certain things because website addresses may change or become disabled. A printed list of abbreviations will not be overly lengthy, and it is convenient to have all the abbreviations handy if you are working with medical records. It will save you time if you do not have to stop to find a working website and keep clicking around to find the term you need.

One of the attorneys in the litigation department has asked for your assistance in creating a summary of his client's medical records.

1. Open the file entitled **C10_P6_MedicalSummaryForm**.
2. Resave the file as **LastName_C10_P6_MedicalSummaryMaster**.
3. Follow the format provided in the file that you just opened when completing the medical summary.
4. Open the audio file named **C10_P6_MedicalSummaryAudio** on your electronic storage medium.
5. Listen to the audio file and follow the directions provided to prepare the medical summary.
6. Make a handwritten list of any questions you have as you are completing this project.
7. After completing the medical summary and all instructions from the attorney given in the audio file, resave your work.
8. Submit the medical summary and your handwritten list of questions, if any, to the instructor.

USE MASTER COPIES

Always work from a "master copy" of the medical summary. Additional medical records may be inserted into the master summary at a later time. If you need to create different versions of the summary by sorting by date or provider, do the following:

1. Add new material to the master version of the summary and save it.

2. Sort by date or provider after new material has been added to the master summary file.

3. Save the sorted version as a different name from the master summary file to avoid saving over the master copy.

Project 7   Ethics and Confidentiality regarding Metadata

When documents are created, metadata (or data within data) are embedded or hidden within the document and follow it wherever it goes. **Metadata** are hidden electronic data in a document that can reveal confidential information, such as who created or revised the document, the dates of the revisions, the number of revisions, redlined (deleted) material, tracked changes, or comments made while editing different versions of the document.

The rules of ethics, which govern attorney conduct, prohibit a lawyer from providing confidential client information to third parties. When documents are sent by email to opposing counsel or others outside of your office, confidential information, as described previously, may be inadvertently disclosed through metadata in attachments. Metadata can also be found on CDs/DVDs provided to others. The documents that include metadata are those prepared with word processing programs, spreadsheets, PDFs, and PowerPoint presentations, to name a few. When you merely attach a document to an email and forward it to someone or provide the documents on a CD/DVD, the recipient will be able to find the metadata and may have access to confidential information that is not meant to be seen by that person.

Many states have created ethics opinions on the metadata issue. Most states take the position that lawyers should exercise reasonable care in transmitting electronic documents so that confidential client information is not disclosed to a third party. Some states say that if a lawyer is the recipient of a document that he or she believes contains metadata, the recipient should contact the sender of the information and inform the sender of this fact. Likewise, if a lawyer inadvertently sends a document containing metadata, the sender should contact and advise the recipient of that fact. In that case, some states say the recipient must not search for or look at the metadata. Some states say "sender beware" and allow a recipient to look at metadata. Other states indicate it is unethical for a recipient to search or "mine" documents received for confidential metadata.

At this time no one universal opinion on the use of metadata exists. The best way to avoid disclosing confidential client information is to never send a document attached to an email or provided on a CD/DVD without first removing or "scrubbing" the metadata from the document.

Part A Research Metadata Removal Procedures

1. Go to the following website for the U.S. District Court, District of Georgia, which contains helpful information on the various types of metadata and tips for removing that data from documents: http://lep.emcp.net.gand.uscourts.
2. Print the page addressing metadata from the court's website.
3. Bookmark this page for future reference.
4. Highlight the important points and procedures from the Web page.
5. Discuss with the instructor and the class what you have highlighted and why you think it is important.

Part B Research Metadata Articles on the Internet

1. Search "Help" in the versions of software that you use for information and/ or articles on metadata removal. (For example, Microsoft Office software, WordPerfect, Adobe products, etc.)
2. Summarize in memo format to your instructor the procedures that you found for removing metadata from files you create. Keep this file for a reference on a future job.
3. Save the summary as **LastName_C10_P7B_MetadataRemovalProcedures**.
4. Using the file you created in step 3, follow the steps to identify and remove metadata from that document.
5. Resave the file as **LastName_C10_P7B_MetadataRemovalRemoved**.
6. Open the file you saved in step 5 and determine if the metadata is removed. Compare the properties of the two documents to see how the metadata is not shown on the second version.
7. Discuss with the instructor and the class how the two documents differ.

Now that you have practiced how to find metadata in a document, remember in the future to always check for and remove metadata from documents you attach to emails or save to a disk that will be provided to others. Remember to check with your office administrator, supervisor, or other staff members in your office to learn if the office has a policy and procedure for handling metadata.

Project 8   Tracking Details for Legal Specialty Certification

The areas of law are many and can be quite complex, making it difficult for an attorney to be fully knowledgeable in all areas. Some attorneys may choose to specialize in or concentrate in one or more areas of law. Others may work in many areas of law but pursue legal specialty certification in a particular area of law. Specializing or concentrating in an area of law is not the same as legal specialty certification. A **legal specialty certification** means that the attorney is held to a higher standard of professional and personal conduct and has sufficient experience and reputation to meet certification standards. The attorney must maintain an active trial practice, is required to submit a disclosure of misconduct annually and, at the end of each five-year term after initial certification, must provide proof that the attorney meets the standards for recertification. A specialty certification will help the lawyer market his or her law practice more effectively, assist a potential client with choosing a qualified lawyer, and increase the referrals the lawyer receives from other lawyers both statewide and nationwide. Certification is available in many practice areas such as civil, criminal, family law, elder law, social security, and real estate, to name a few, and the requirements may be different for each area of law. The lawyer is required to demonstrate special training, knowledge, education, and professional competence. A lawyer who is a certified specialist is recognized by an independent professional certifying organization as having an enhanced level of skill and expertise in a particular area of law.

Certification Application Specialty certification is accomplished by completing a detailed application and taking a comprehensive examination. In the application, the attorney must provide details of his/her involvement in contested matters such as trials, depositions, major motions, arbitrations, appeals, and administrative hearings.

Most attorneys do not have the time to keep track of this extensive information, and they may not consider this process until it is brought to their attention. A specialty certification is a feather in an attorney's cap. An attorney works very hard to build a law practice and client base and maintain a good reputation and respect in the legal community. The legal support person can assist the attorney by compiling this information and updating it throughout the year so that it will be available for the next application process.

Gathering Information An attorney usually will not qualify for specialty certification until he or she has been practicing 10 years or more and has a fair amount of trial experience. Data used to complete the applications will be found on the attorney's calendars and from current and closed client files. An attorney may or may not have kept copies of annual paper calendars. Computer calendars are frequently used, so if the attorney has not printed or saved the computer calendars each year, it will be difficult to recreate up to 10, 15, or 20+ years of case information, as required for the applications. Clients' paper files are usually destroyed a certain number of years after being closed, and electronic copies of closed client files may not provide complete information.

For example, Attorney Rasmussen is recognized as a certified civil trial specialist nationally and in his own state. He is licensed to practice law in two states. He has gone through the process of compiling the required information several times in the last 20 years during both initial certification and recertification. Attorney Rasmussen and his assistant spent an entire week preparing the application for initial specialty certification. Fortunately, Attorney Rasmussen has kept a paper calendar for each of the 30 years he has practiced law, so he was able to get a lot of information from the calendars and an office closed-file list. The court system contained some archived case information on its website that was helpful, but it did not contain all the details required by the application. It would have been helpful to Attorney Rasmussen if he had maintained an ongoing list of information from his cases that would be required for specialty certification applications. In addition to specialty certification, an attorney may be nominated by other attorneys for admission to legal organizations that recognize attorneys for their legal experience. Attorney Rasmussen also needed to gather information for application to the American Board of Trial Advocates (ABOTA) in response to being nominated by a peer. His assistant printed the list of requirements and application forms from the organization's website and found he already had most of the information needed because of his previous application for specialty certification.

Gathering the required information is tedious work and can consume a lot of time. As you can see from these examples, it is a good practice to work with the attorney to create a system that works for archiving case information and use it consistently throughout the year so the attorney has all the information needed when it is time to apply for initial certification or recertification.

An attorney cannot rely entirely on memory to produce the many details needed for the application. The following presents a list of steps of how you can assist the attorney with the application process:

- Visit with the attorney and ask if he or she is considering legal specialty certification in the future or if he or she is currently certified.
- Ask if the attorney already has a system in place for recording information that will be needed in the future.
- Suggest to the attorney that you are aware that the application process is tedious and you can assist with the process by tracking details from that point on.
- Determine what information is needed for the application by looking at the website for the certifying organization to see if the application is available there, or request a copy of the application from the organization by phone or email.
- Offer to help the attorney gather information from past cases. When it comes time to make the application, you will be a big hero because you already have the necessary information at your fingertips. It will save money because the attorney will not have to waste precious time looking up information when he or she could be performing billable work for clients. File **C10_P8_LegCertCaseInfoForm** on the Student Data Disc is an example of a form that contains all the criteria needed to apply for certification. Keep one form for each case on which the attorney works.

Part A Your experience working as a floater at your law office has earned you a permanent assignment working as a legal support person for Attorney Kay Burns. Ms. Burns has practiced for a number of years in both civil and criminal law. Over the course of several months, you have gotten to know Ms. Burns and have settled into your new job. You remember learning about legal specialty certification in school and decide to inquire if Ms. Burns has considered this option.

1. Write a short memo to Attorney Burns asking for a time to meet with her and give her a short explanation of why you want to meet.
2. Save your work as **LastName_C10_P8A_CertificationMemo**.
3. Submit the memo to the instructor.

Portfolio

Part B Ms. Burns has read your memo and scheduled a time to meet with you. She tells you during the meeting that she has been so busy that she overlooked thinking about certification but is grateful that you brought it up. She agrees certification is important and is something she should consider. She has a good deal of trial experience and wants to see if she meets the criteria for certification in both the civil and criminal areas. She will get together all the information she has gathered during her years of practice. She asks that you find the criteria to be met in applying for each certification. She schedules a time to meet with you again in four weeks to sort through her documentation and review the criteria.

1. Locate and open the website of the National Board of Trial Advocacy.
2. Find the requirements for both civil and criminal certifications. Bookmark this website.
3. Print the pages listing the certification requirements.
4. Prepare a memo to Ms. Burns that contains the website's address and attach the printed requirements for both civil and criminal certifications.
5. Save your work as **LastName_C10_P8B_CertReqMemo**.

Portfolio

Discuss the Projects

The projects you completed in this chapter have given you exposure to the various types of work you might do as a legal support person. The experience you have gained from these projects will give you the confidence to think critically and creatively as you complete tasks at your future job.

Thinking about this chapter, brainstorm with your classmates a list of critical thinking and common sense tasks you thought about and/or listed while completing the chapter projects. Many of these tasks are difficult to learn from a book. Once you identify these critical thinking and common sense skills, continue to look for ways to apply these skills to other parts of your work. The more you think critically, the easier it becomes.

Write your list on the lines provided.

_____

_____

_____

_____

Capstone

Chapter Objectives

- Work independently to complete projects
- Follow instructions when given
- Apply knowledge from previous chapters to locate official court websites and information needed to complete projects
- Use critical thinking, editing, and proofreading skills to independently prepare documents and letters as instructed
- Determine when additional documents should be prepared to complete a project
- Work collaboratively to create a pleading caption for your local area court
- Proofread a legal description
- Type from dictation and proofread your work
- Prepare task lists and reminder dates
- Evaluate the companion DVD *The Court Is In Session*
- Create a portfolio of your work by following provided instructions
- Outline your career goals and evaluate the lessons presented in the textbook

Before beginning the exercises for this chapter, copy to your storage medium the Chapter 11 folder from the Student Resources disc that accompanies this textbook. Do this for each chapter before starting the chapter's exercises.

This final chapter will require you to apply the skills you learned in Chapters 1 through 10 to a capstone project. This project will test your knowledge and will require you to apply critical thinking skills as well as editing and proofreading skills to a variety of legal documents.

A How-To Guide is not included in this final chapter. Apply your knowledge of the legal office and your skills in critical thinking and analysis to prepare the appropriate information in the documents, even if it is not specifically requested in the instructions. Remember that when you are working at your job, you will not be given every tidbit of information you might need to complete a task. Your employer will expect you to try to locate information on your own and use your critical thinking skills to find what you need to complete the work. A legal support person must also be flexible in using different forms, templates, and office styles to complete work.

While working through the previous chapters in this book, you learned how to:

- Work with information in a variety of situations
- Identify information needed to complete forms
- Perform research to locate information
- Identify conflicting information
- Study and refresh your knowledge of language, spelling, and grammar
- Edit and proofread a variety of legal documents
- Apply critical thinking and reasoning
- Prepare task lists and meet deadlines
- Create, edit, and proofread correspondence and legal documents

In the previous chapters, the project settings included work within a law office as well as the legal department of a corporation. In the following capstone projects, you will assume that you are employed by a temporary service and that you work at different offices throughout the year. As you complete the projects, think about the type of work you are doing and locate necessary attorney details in the background information.

To make these projects applicable to your local area, you are provided with names and street addresses. However, you should apply your local city, state, zip code, and county for all addresses in all projects when the information is required (unless directed otherwise). If a phone number is needed, use the number (555) 555-5555.

New forms are provided; however, forms from previous chapters may be accessed when necessary. As you complete the projects in this final chapter, it may be helpful for you to refer to the work you did in previous chapters to refresh your memory of procedures. General information has been provided to apply to most of the projects in this chapter. Some projects will have additional information that applies only to that particular project. For simplicity's sake, the following projects will address a client and his or her family and the legal troubles they encounter.

In addition to the instructions from the attorney, complete the following tasks in every project whether you are instructed to do so or not:

1. Create a list of tasks you have been directed to complete under the heading of Project # Tasks. Save this list as **LastName_C11_P#_Tasks**.

2. Open the file you just saved in step 1. Under the task list, make a "Reminder Date" heading. Prepare a list of reminder dates.

3. Complete any additional tasks you deem necessary.

4. In the file you used in step 2, make a "Critical Thinking" heading. Under this heading, add any tasks that you know must be done to complete the project but that you can't do right now.

Remember also to apply critical thinking to every project. Complete any additional tasks you think must be done after reading the instructions from the attorney. If you think future tasks or reminders are implied in the instructions but you cannot complete them in this project, add them to your task list.

For example, if you are told in the project to send answers to interrogatories to the client for review and signature, what would you have to remember to do after sending the document to the client? Under the "Critical Thinking" heading, you would add that you would prepare a letter serving the signed document on opposing counsel and prepare a proof of service. You would also add to the reminder list a note to make sure that you get the answers to interrogatories back from the client and then a reminder to serve these documents when they are returned.

You currently work for a temp agency that specializes in providing legal support staff to law firms and legal departments. The work is enjoyable, but you are required to adapt to many situations, office standards, and specific areas of law. The client, Dean Peck, is currently divorced. He was previously married to Joan Peck. They were divorced on May 31, three years ago. They have three children: Sara, age 19; Matt, age 17; and Andrew, age 13. Sara Peck attends college in Minnesota. Matt Peck and Andrew Peck live with their mother.

Figure 11.1 **Background information for Chapter 11 projects.**

Andrew Peck, DOB: March 1, xxxx

Bankruptcy attorney for Dean: Kay Weller, 1414 Willow Road; Attorney I.D. #094XX3

Business attorney for Dean: Kay Weller, 1414 Willow Road; Attorney I.D. #094XX3

Child support referee: Daniel Geller

County attorney for family law: Ann Baker, 130 Oak Avenue; Attorney I.D. #310XX0; phone xxx-555-1111

County attorney for Matt Peck's criminal case: Mary English, 405 N. Fifth Street

Criminal defense attorney for Sara Peck: Bradford S. Delapena, Assistant State Public Defender, P.O. Box 40418, St. Paul, MN 55104

Criminal defense attorney for Matt Peck: Patrick Case, 42 Bermuda Drive; Attorney I.D. #1221XX1

Criminal prosecuting attorney for state of Minnesota: Benjamin Bejar, Rice County Attorney's Office, 218 N.W. Third Street, Faribault, MN 55021

Dana Peck-Gardner, 1049 Clover Lane

Dean Peck: 1907 Center Street (Legal description: Block 2, Lot 15, Reed's Subdivision No. 2, subject to a 6-ft utility easement on the east boundary, city, county, state)

Dr. Mary Drew: 25 Empire Drive

Estate planning attorney for Dean: David Sunn, 903 Washington Court; Attorney I.D. #224XX5

Family law attorney for Dean: Ruth Harvin, 201 Adams Street; Attorney I.D. #123XX2; phone xxx-555-2211

Joan Peck's address: 8110 Johnson Parkway

Joan Peck's family law attorney: Jeanne Just, 87C Royal Road South; Attorney I.D. #796XX1

Jordan Peck, 569 Ridge Lane

Judicial Center: 200 Kennedy Drive

Litigation attorney for Bank: Will Hunt, 61124 Malibu Drive; Attorney I.D. #949XX5

Litigation attorney for Dean: Fred Flint, 835 Rose Street; Attorney I.D. #326XX3

Matt Peck, DOB: January 12, xxxx

Orin Peck, 14035 Ocean Blvd #800, Pismo Beach, CA 93440

Orin Peck's attorney: Jorge Cruz, 21148 Seaport Drive, Suite 102, Pismo Beach, CA 93440

Peck Security Systems: 411 King Drive

Real estate attorney for Dean: Stephen Callen, 145 Byrd Lane; Attorney I.D. #332XX3

Sara Peck, DOB: April 24, xxxx

Work comp attorney for Dean: Frank Flint, 4795 Maple Mountain Road; Attorney I.D. #897XX4

Project 1   Create Local Pleading Caption and Find Local Office Contact Information

You start your day by meeting with the attorney and finding that you will be working on a particular case file most of the day. To get started, complete the following steps to create a pleading caption and locate contact information. Contact information consists of names, addresses, phone numbers, fax numbers, email addresses, and website addresses. Gather as much information as you can for later use.

1. Type what you find for steps a, b, c, and d in a list and save the file as **LastName_C11_P1_LocalInfo**.

   a. Locate the contact information for your local county sheriff.

   b. Locate the contact information for your local county attorney.

   c. Locate the contact information and fee schedule for your local court administrator.

   d. Locate the contact information and fee schedule for your local county recorder or land records office.

2. Create your local pleading caption template.

3. Save the caption as **LastName_C11_P1_CaptionTemplate**.

Project 2   Real Estate

As part of the settlement in his dissolution of marriage action, Dean Peck agreed to pass his interest in the parties' homestead to his wife via a quitclaim deed in return for a payment from his wife of $150,000 for his share of the property.

Read Figure 11.2, which provides instructions from the attorney you are assisting. As noted previously, create a list of the tasks you are asked to complete as well as reminders and critical thinking tasks.

1. Open file **C11_P2_QCD**.

2. Save the document as **LastName_C11_P2_QCD** and use it to prepare a quitclaim deed as instructed by the attorney.

3. Resave the file.

4. Complete any additional tasks and save them along with your task list and reminder dates as **LastName_C11_P2_TaskList**.

5. Save your task list.

6. Submit all files to the instructor.

Figure 11.2 **Project 2 instructions from the attorney.**

From: Attorney Ruth Harvin

Please prepare a quitclaim deed from Dean Peck to Joan Peck. The amount of consideration is $150,000. Get Dean in here to sign the deed, and after that is done, contact Joan's attorney and ask that she send us her trust account check in that amount payable to Dean. After we have the money, do whatever is necessary to record the signed deed with the county and send a copy of the recorded deed to Joan's attorney and to Dean. There are no wells on this Torrens property. Deed tax will be $150. The legal description for that property is: The north 10 acres of the west quarter of the south half of section 18, township 110, range 22 north, located in xxx county, state of xxxx.

Project 3   Corporate, Business, and Employment

Dean Peck used the entire $150,000 from the property settlement in his dissolution of marriage to start his own business, called Peck Security Systems. He is the only shareholder but has two employees who will install security systems. Each employee will need an employment contract.

Review the note in Figure 11.3 and complete the steps to assist the client with employment contracts.

Figure 11.3 **Project 3 instructions from the attorney.**

From: Attorney Kay Weller

Dean Peck is our client. He is starting a new business, which will be known as Peck Security Systems. Please find the appropriate form for organization of a new business and complete it for my review. Dean wants his company to be a limited liability company. He is the sole shareholder.

He will be hiring two employees on March 15, xxxx, and has asked us to draft an employment agreement for each of them. He has given us some preliminary information and will get back to us later with additional terms of employment, so complete as much of the form as you can at this time with the information he provided. Julie Anderson will install and maintain security systems. She will be paid $32,000 per year on a semimonthly basis. Jess Ang will be project manager and will also install and maintain security systems. She will be paid $42,500 per year on a semi-monthly basis. Each will be paid an additional $100 per month for signing a noncompete agreement.

1. Review the instructions from the attorney in Figure 11.3.
2. Open file **C11_P3_EmplAgrmt** from your electronic storage medium.
3. Save it as **LastName_C11_P3_EmplAgrmt_(last name of employee)** for each employee.
4. Open file **C11_P3_ArtOrg**.
5. Save it as **LastName_C11_P3_ArtOrg**.
6. Update each file as needed.
7. Submit all files to the instructor.

Project 4   Estate Planning

Dean Peck's divorce was finalized quite a while ago. His business attorney advised him to update his estate planning documents with his estate planning attorney and make a new will to change the future distribution of his estate.

1. Review the instructions from the attorney in Figure 11.4.
2. Open and review file **C11_P4_ClientInfo**.
3. Open and review file **C11_P4_Will**.
4. Compare the completed will, the client information form, and the instructions from the attorney.
5. Proofread the will for errors in information, spelling, grammar, etc. Make any corrections needed directly in the file.
6. Save the file as **LastName_C11_P4_Will**.

Figure 11.4 Project 4 instructions from the attorney.

From: Attorney David Sunn

Dean Peck was divorced several years ago, but he didn't remember to change his estate planning documents. He has three children and owns a business. We are going to prepare a new will with a trust provision for the benefit of his children. We also need to prepare a durable power of attorney for Dean to sign. I prepared a draft of the will when I met with Dean, but I would like you to double check my work against the information Dean gave me in his client information form. Please proofread the will and correct any errors. I would appreciate it if you would highlight your corrections, so I can see those when I look at the electronic copy of the will again. Also, please prepare a durable power of attorney using the form we usually use. Today is Tuesday, and I told Dean I will email the documents to him on Friday for his review. He made an appointment to sign everything for next week, Wednesday, at 9:30 a.m. Dean is going to keep the original documents but wants extra copies for the executors, himself, his accountant, and his business attorney. Thanks for your help.

7. Open **C11_P4_POA**.

8. Prepare the document following the instructions from the attorney and client.

9. Save the file as **LastName_C11_P4_POA**.

10. Submit all work to the instructor.

Project 5   Probate of Will

The client, Dean Peck, has requested assistance with the probate process for his late father's estate. After retiring from a successful career as an aeronautical engineer, Dean Peck's father, Orin Peck, moved to Pismo Beach, San Luis Obispo County, California. After moving to California, Orin Peck asked his son, Dean, to visit him and help him take care of some personal paperwork, which included meeting with his attorney, Jorge Cruz, to make a new will. Orin Peck rented a condo on the beach and did not own any real property or vehicles in California. Orin owned some personal property and left a $300,000 balance in his savings account. He also had a $500,000 life insurance policy. He did not owe any debts at the time he died. Orin's wife was deceased. Orin has three surviving children and three surviving grandchildren.

A reading of Orin Peck's last will and testament revealed that his personal representative is Dean Peck; Orin's personal property should be sold and the proceeds used to pay for his funeral and any debts he may owe at the time of his death; and the money in his savings account should be distributed to any surviving grandchildren in equal shares. Outside of the will, the insurance company would distribute the proceeds of Orin Peck's life insurance policy to his surviving children in equal shares. After being notified of his father's death, Dean Peck met with his father's attorney and completed some of the documents necessary to properly administer his father's estate.

Read the note from Attorney Jorge Cruz in Figure 11.5 and complete the tasks requested.

1. Review the instructions from the attorney in Figure 11.5.

2. Create a list of tasks you need to complete.

3. Open and review **C11_P5_OrinPeckWill**.

4. Open and print these files:

   • **C11_P5_PetitionProbate**

   • **C11_P5_NoticePetition**

   • **C11_P5_HologWill**

   • **C11_P5_NoticeAction**

5. Compare the completed documents listed ion step 4 with Orin Peck's will, as well as the background information, and instructions from the attorney.

6. Complete the instructions given by the attorney in Figure 11.5.

7. Submit all work to the instructor as directed.

Figure 11.5 **Project 5 instructions from the attorney.**

From: Attorney Jorge Cruz

Orin Peck died on June 11. His son, Dean Peck, will be meeting with me 10 days from now to prepare the documents necessary to probate Orin's estate. At my request, our law clerk intern prepared the following documents:

- Petition for Probate
- Notice of Petition to Administer Estate
- Proof of Holographic Instrument
- Notice of Proposed Action

The law clerk will not be returning to work here because she accepted a permanent position elsewhere. I would like you to print the documents, review Orin Peck's will, and proofread the documents prepared by the intern. Please highlight any errors your find. Write what you think the correct information should be near the error in red ink. The intern did not finish completing the proof of service by mail for the notice of petition to administer estate. Review the file and determine names and mailing information of those who should be served with the notice of petition. Add additional names to the document called "attachment to notice of petition to administer estate—proof of service by mail." Today is Wednesday. Please return all documents to me by 9:00 a.m. on Thursday of next week.

Thanks for your help.

Project 6   Civil Litigation

Part A During Dean Peck's marriage, his wife wanted to start her own business and needed financing, so Dean signed a personal guaranty for her business loan in the amount of $500,000. Dean received a civil lawsuit from his ex-wife's bank for breach of contract stating that his ex-wife has failed to make payments on her business loan for the past six months and owes $150,000. Since Dean signed a personal guaranty for that loan, the bank now expects him to pay for the delinquent payments. Dean also learned from his ex-wife that her business is failing, she will be dissolving her company, and she will have no income to make payments on her business loan. This means that Dean will now be responsible for the entire balance due on her business loan because of the personal guaranty he signed.

Review the instructions provided to you by the client's civil litigation attorney in Figure 11.6.

Figure 11.6 **Project 6A instructions from the attorney.**

> From: Attorney Fred Flint
>
> Dean Peck has been served with a complaint by Local City Bank. We need to send an answer to the complaint. Please use the answer and request for documents forms. Proofread and correct these forms if necessary. I will dictate the specific information for both documents. Please prepare those to be served on the attorney for the bank. File only the answer with the court administrator. Make sure the client receives a copy of all documents.

1. Review the instructions from the attorney in Figure 11.6.
2. Open and listen to the information in file **C11_P6A_AnswerReqDocs**.
3. Using that information, complete both the answer and the request for documents given to you in the following files:
   - **C11_P6A_Answer**
   - **C11_P6A_ReqDocs**
4. Save the answer as **LastName_C11_P6A_Answer**.
5. Save the request for documents as **LastName_C11_P6A_ReqDocs**.
6. Submit all files to the instructor.

Portfolio

Part B Before Dean Peck started his own business, he was employed for many years at SWS, Inc., performing cleaning and equipment maintenance in the factory area. During his employment at SWS, Dean suffered a work injury affecting his right knee and both wrists. The workers' compensation insurer for SWS is denying benefits to Dean. Dean's attorney asks for a report from Dean's doctor seeking a medical opinion. The attorney has dictated a long, rambling letter asking for the doctor's medical opinion relating to the treatment of Mr. Peck's work injuries. The letter is not very organized. It contains repetitive statements and grammatical and other errors. It is your job to transcribe and then edit this letter.

Figure 11.7 **Project 6B instructions from attorney.**

> From: Attorney Fred Flint
>
> Please type the letter I dictated to Dr. Drew. It is a rough draft, and I would appreciate it if you would revise it so it is better organized and grammatically correct. We had better include a current medical authorization for the doctor and give a copy of this letter to Dean. Please let me know if there is anything else you think I should add to this letter.

1. Review the instructions from the attorney in Figure 11.7.
2. Open and listen to the audio file **C11_P6B_DoctorLetter**.
3. Type the letter as it is dictated and save it as **LastName_P6B_DoctorLetter**.
4. Edit the letter to make it clearer, more concise, and better organized. Save your revision as **LastName_P6B_DoctorLetter_Revised**.
5. Make a list of suggestions as to what would make the letter clearer. Add your suggestions to the task list document.
6. Submit the revised letter and the list to the instructor.

Project 7   Bankruptcy

Part A Dean Peck contributes to the support of his three children. He sends his daughter $200 each month to help with her personal expenses while she attends college. He also pays $1,200 each month as child support for his two minor sons. His older son will graduate from high school and turn 18 next year, so Dean hopes to get his child support payment reduced by half at that time. Dean's security business is doing quite well but does not provide enough income to pay the additional obligation of his ex-wife's business loan, for which he has unexpectedly become responsible. Dean will not be able to meet all of his own financial obligations and pay for his ex-wife's business loan as well. Dean has now decided to meet with an attorney to discuss filing for personal bankruptcy protection and for advice on how to save his business. When you arrived at work, you saw an email from Attorney Kay Weller regarding the case and your next task.

Figure 11.8 Project 7A instructions from the attorney.

From: Attorney Kay Weller

I just met with Dean Peck. He needs to file for Chapter 7 bankruptcy. He has partially completed the client information form. I started to fill out the claim petition, schedules, and creditor matrix with the information available. This is only partially complete because I am waiting for Dean to give me more information. I would like you to print all of those documents and proofread the claim petition, schedules, and matrix by comparing them with the client information form and other information in Dean's file and my notes. Please highlight on the printed copy any entry errors that I may have made and write the correct information near the error in red ink so I can review it and make corrections later. Also, add to the task list a list of information that is missing, so I can request that from Dean when we meet in two weeks.

1. Review the instructions from the attorney in Figure 11.8.
2. Open and print the documents in the folder **C11_P7A_Forms**.
3. Compare the information on the client information form with the bankruptcy documents and creditor matrix.
4. Highlight on your printed copies any errors you find in the prepared documents.
5. Write the corrections on the hard copies near where the error appears, using red ink.
6. Submit the documents to the instructor.

Part B Figure 11.9 contains a follow-up email from the attorney.

Figure 11.9 **Project 7B instructions from attorney.**

From: Attorney Kay Weller

I just received a notice from the bankruptcy court regarding Dean Peck. The 341 meeting of creditors has been scheduled for October 14, 2xxx, at 9:30 a.m. in room 23B at the U.S. Courthouse here in town. I started drafting the 341 letter to Dean but got distracted. Would you please finish that letter and return it to me for my signature? Thanks.

1. Review the instructions from the attorney in Figure 11.9.
2. Make a list of the tasks you are asked to complete and save the list as **LastName_C11_P7B_TaskList**.
3. Open the file **C11_P7B_341Ltr** and complete the attorney's instructions.
4. Save it as **LastName_C11_P7B_341Ltr**.
5. Submit the file to the instructor.

Project 8   Criminal

Dean Peck's 17-year-old son, Matt Peck, is a senior in high school. On October 2, xxxx, after attending a high school football game with a group of his friends, someone in the group obtained beer and the group had a party at a cabin on a lake several miles out of town. As Matt was driving the group back to town in his car, he was stopped by the county sheriff for swerving on the road and driving at an inconsistent speed. Matt and his friends were arrested after being given a field sobriety test, which indicated that they had been drinking. Matt's car was confiscated by the sheriff, and the entire group was transported to the sheriff's office. They were all charged with under-age possession and consumption of alcohol. In addition, Matt was charged with driving under the influence, careless driving, and driving without insurance.

You received the following email from Mr. Peck's attorney.

Figure 11.10 Project 8 instructions from the attorney.

From: Attorney Patrick Case

Dean Peck has hired me to represent his son, Matt Peck, who is under 18. Matt was charged with under-age possession and consumption of alcohol, driving under the influence, careless driving, and driving without insurance. Since this is Matt's first offense, I am already negotiating with the prosecutor to work out a plea bargain where Matt will plead guilty to misdemeanor underage possession and consumption. The prosecutor admitted that is all the police can prove, and the balance of the charges will be dismissed after Matt completes 200 hours of community service, or 1 year, whichever occurs first. The first thing I would like you to do is prepare a Certificate of Representation and get that filed with the court. I will finish my draft of the letter to the prosecutor, and I want you to proofread that, put it in proper format, and return it to me for my signature. I will also draft the plea agreement for you to proofread, and we can send that to the prosecutor with the letter. Let me know if I got anything wrong when I was putting these documents together.

Part A

1. Review the instructions from the attorney in Figure 11.10.
2. Make a list of tasks as you complete Parts A, B, and C that you are asked to complete and save them as **LastName_C11_P8A-B-C_TaskList**. Use this file in the other parts of this project.
3. Open file **C11_P8A_CertRep**. It contains a certificate of representation form.
4. Complete the form and save it as **LastName_C11_P8A_CertRep**.
5. Submit the document to the instructor.

Part B

1. Open file **C11_P8B_NegLtr**.
2. Add to the task list you started in Part A.
3. Make revisions and save it as **LastName_C11_P8B_NegLtr**.
4. Submit your work to the instructor.

Part C

1. Open the file **C11_P8C_Plea**.
2. Add to the task list you started in Part A.
3. Make revisions and save it as **LastName_C11_P8C_Plea**.
4. Submit the file to the instructor.

Project 9   Family Law

As part of Dean Peck's divorce 3 years ago, he was ordered to pay child support in the amount of $1,200 per month to his ex-wife for the care of their two minor sons. Dean's older son just turned 18. Dean has met with a family law attorney to discuss decreasing his child support payment and the attorney has sent you an email request.

1. Review the instructions from the attorney in Figure 11.11.
2. Make a list of tasks you are asked to complete and save the document as **LastName_C11_P9_TaskList**.
3. Open and review **C11_P9_ClientInfo**.
4. Open **C11_P9_MotReduceChildSupport** and apply the necessary changes to the file.
5. Save it as **LastName_C11_P9_MotReduceChildSupport**.
6. Open **C11_P9_AffReduceChildSupport** and apply the necessary changes to the file.
7. Save it as **LastName_C11_P9_AffReduceChildSupport**.
8. Submit the file to the instructor.

Figure 11.11 **Project 9 instructions from attorney.**

From: Attorney Ruth Harvin

I met with Dean Peck on Saturday. Dean's older son just turned 18, graduated from high school, has a full-time job, and is moving into his own apartment. In addition, Dean's business has slowed considerably and his gross personal monthly income has decreased by 20% while his personal expenses have stayed the same. He would like me to request that his child support payment be reduced by half since he now has only one minor child. The motion to reduce child support will be heard by child support referee Daniel Geller at 10:00 a.m. at the Judicial Center in Room 3B, 30 days from the date the motion is signed. Please review the information in Dean's file and prepare a motion to reduce child support and a supporting affidavit. There are forms available in our office forms bank. I would like to get this motion filed with the court and sent to his ex-wife and the county attorney on Friday of this week. Since today is Monday, please complete the draft of these documents for my review before noon tomorrow. I will contact Dean to come in to review and sign everything. In the meantime, please prepare the appropriate letters to get this motion served on his ex-wife and the county attorney and filed with the court administrator. I will want to meet with Dean at the courthouse at 9:45 a.m. the day of the hearing. By the way, Dean brought in a copy of his bankruptcy file, so we can also get some information from it.

Project 10   Appeal

Dean Peck's daughter, Sara Peck, is attending her first year of college in Minnesota. Unfortunately, Sara was arrested for possession of methamphetamine. During a probable cause hearing, Sara's attorney made a pretrial motion to dismiss the charges. That motion was granted and the charges against her were dismissed by the judge. The prosecuting attorney for the state of Minnesota appealed that ruling to the Minnesota Court of Appeals. The Court of Appeals agreed with the district court. The state's attorney did not agree with that decision, so he appealed the decision of the Court of Appeals to the Minnesota Supreme Court. The Minnesota Supreme Court reversed the decisions of both lower courts. This allowed the state of Minnesota to continue prosecuting Sara Peck for the original charges against her.

Figure 11.12 **Project 10 instructions from the attorney.**

From: Attorney Benjamin Bejar

Sara Peck was defended by Attorney Bradford Delapena of the local public defender's office on charges of possession of methamphetamine. During a probable cause hearing, Sara's attorney made a pretrial motion to dismiss the charges. That motion was granted and the charges against her were dismissed by the judge. I was the prosecuting attorney for the state of Minnesota. The state has decided to appeal the district court's ruling to the Minnesota Court of Appeals because the state believes the district court judge improperly interpreted the law. The state wants clarification of the legislature's intent when writing a certain law relating to methamphetamine possession. Please prepare a notice of appeal to the Minnesota Court of Appeals. We are appealing from the pretrial order of the district court. You will find the information you need in the case file. After you have prepared the notice of appeal, please return it to me for my review. Thanks.

1. Review instructions from the attorney in Figure 11.12.
2. Make a list of tasks you are asked to complete and save them in a document called **LastName_C11_P10_TaskList**.
3. Open file **C11_P10_StateBriefCoverPage**. Use the information on this document to complete the notice of appeal form.
4. Open file **C11_P10_NoticeOfAppeal** and complete it using the information provided.
5. Save it as **LastName_C11_P10_NoticeOfAppeal**.
6. Submit the completed notice of appeal to the instructor.

Other Projects

The remaining projects are not related to Dean Peck. They will have different scenarios and instructions. However, some projects may use attorney information provided earlier in this chapter.

Project 11   Cut-and-Paste Project From Attorney

In many areas of law, there are procedures that are completed frequently, such as foreclosures, collection work, and quiet title actions to name a few. Most law offices or attorneys will have written instructions or guidelines and forms for those procedures. When changes are made in the laws that affect how the procedures are carried out, the attorney will need to revise the written guidelines. If the office does not have written guidelines, the attorney might create something using pieces of information from various sources and will then ask you to put the information into a usable document. Read the message from an attorney asking you to help update the guidelines of a foreclosure procedure.

Figure 11.13 **Project 11 instructions from the attorney.**

From: Attorney Stephen Callen

I found some motivation late Saturday night and decided to update and edit my guidelines on foreclosure procedure. I found some language I want to include, and I cut sections out of other documents, so there are some loose pieces of paper inserted throughout the document. I also made some handwritten notes here and there for language I want to add to the instructions. I got a little carried away and made quite a mess of the document. My penmanship is terrible and I spilled coffee on it, so some of the ink has smeared. Disregard the purple slash marks on the pages. It is beyond my abilities to make a usable product of this mess. I would appreciate it if you would please key this into a new document following my notes. I know this will be difficult but do the best you can. Just do the first four pages and then we will look it over together. If we decide it is going to take too much time to decipher it, I will just dictate a new document.

1. Review instructions from the attorney in Figure 11.12.
2. Open and print the file **C11_P11_Messy**.
3. Work with only the first four pages of the document you just printed in step #2. Do your best to key a new document.
4. Save it as **LastName_C11_P11_Messy_Revised**.
5. Submit the revised file to the instructor.

Portfolio

Portfolio

Project 12   Prepare a Subpoena in a Civil Case

In addition to being subpoenaed to personally appear for a legal proceeding, a witness may also be asked to produce certain documents. Service of a subpoena must be accompanied by prepayment to the witness for mileage and witness fee. These amounts are governed by state law. The required witness fee for an expert witness (such as a doctor or engineer) might be different from the fee required to be paid to a general fact witness. Mileage rates change often, so double check the current rate when preparing a witness subpoena. Witness fees and mileage rates are published in a state's statutes or the rate may also be published on the subpoena form. After the subpoena has been prepared by the law office or court, it must be served on the witness by personal service or by leaving a copy of the subpoena at the witness's usual place of residence. Service may be made by a law enforcement official or private process server. A witness who fails to obey a subpoena may be found in contempt of court and be subject to penalty by the court.

Figure 11.14 Project 12 instructions from the attorney.

From: Attorney Fred Flint

Thank you for filling in today for my assistant. Please prepare a subpoena in a civil case using the form provided. The case is venued in your local county and state. The case type is personal injury; the court file number is CV-11-ABC1. The plaintiff is Jose Ortiz. My client is the defendant, May Betts. The witness to be served with the subpoena is John Homer, whose address is 123 Jones Road, local city and state. Mr. Homer is being summoned to appear for his deposition on December 1, 20XX, at 10:30 a.m., at my office. The round-trip mileage from the witness's home to the law office is 23 miles. Check our office forms for a civil subpoena form to use. Follow the instructions provided with the subpoena form. After the subpoena is completed and I have signed it, please leave it at the reception desk. The sheriff will pick it up and get it served and return the proof of service to us.

1. Review instructions from the attorney in Figure 11.14.
2. Make a list of tasks you are asked to complete and save them as **LastName_C11_P12_TaskList**.
3. Open **C11_P12_Subpoena**.
4. Complete the form and save it as **LastName_C11_P12_Subpoena**.
5. Submit the file to your instructor.

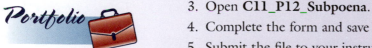
Portfolio

Project 13 Locate an interpreter

Occasionally, a witness will need a language interpreter to assist with giving testimony at a legal proceeding. A document translator may be needed if written materials to be used at the proceeding are written in a language the witness does not understand. The courts maintain a list of interpreters who have met certain requirements and who are allowed to be listed on the court roster. For example, a deaf person will need an American Sign Language (ASL) interpreter. A person whose first language is French will need an interpreter fluent in both French and English. In addition to interpreters who receive work referrals through the court system, there are also independent companies that maintain a national network of people offering interpreting and translating services. A law office might receive marketing materials from these companies on a regular basis. You can also find these services by performing an Internet search.

Figure 11.15 **Project 13 instructions from the attorney.**

From: Attorney Mary Forman

I am taking two new cases in the state of Iowa, in District 5. One of the clients is deaf. The other client is Russian.

Please check the Iowa District 5 official court website for the roster of state court interpreters. Prepare a memo to me with the following information:

- The name, phone number, and qualifications of an ASL-certified interpreter for District 5 who will travel anywhere within the state of Iowa.

- The name, phone number, and qualifications of a noncertified Russian interpreter for District 5 in Iowa.

- List the website's URL address where you found the information, so we can easily locate it again.

Thanks!

1. Review instructions from the attorney in Figure 11.15.
2. Make a list of tasks you are asked to complete and save the list as **LastName_C11_P13_TaskList**.
3. Save your research as **LastName_C11_P13_Interpreter**.
4. Submit your research to your instructor.

Portfolio

Project 14   DVD Review Questions

Read the email in Figure 11.16. It contains instructions for you from an attorney in the office.

Figure 11.16 **Project 14 instructions attorney.**

From: Attorney Benjamin Bejar

Last month, our bar association and local community college were honored by an appearance of several judges from the Minnesota Court of Appeals along with two area attorneys. The judges and attorneys performed a reenactment of a real case that was recently presented to and decided by the Court of Appeals. The case was ultimately appealed to the Minnesota Supreme Court and a law was changed because of this case. The judges and attorneys allowed this presentation to be videotaped for future use as an instructional aid for attorneys and students. I was able to obtain a DVD of the presentation. I am asking all staff, law clerks, paralegals, and attorneys in our office to watch this DVD for various reasons. Your assignment is to watch the DVD and answer the questions I posted in the file **C11_P14_DVDReviewQuestions**. Please respond to the questions directly in the file (adding your answers beneath each question).

1. Review instructions from the attorney in Figure 11.16.
2. Open and read **C11_P14_PeckSynopsis**.
3. Open file **C11_P14_DVDReviewQuestions**.
4. View the DVD *Court Is In Session* and answer the questions posed by the attorney (the DVD is approximately 90 minutes in length).
5. Save your responses as **LastName_C11_P14_ReviewQuestions**.
6. Submit the file to the instructor.

Project 15   Career Goals

Write a short, double-spaced essay describing your career goals and how your experience with the work in this book will help you to meet those goals. List any areas in which you know that you still need practice and note in which areas of legal support you excel. Save your essay as **LastName_C11_P15_CareerGoals**. Submit the file to the instructor, if requested.

Style Guide

You are a recent graduate of a local community college with a legal office degree. Your first professional position is working as a legal support person with Jordan, Leone & Sanchez, PLLP. This is a nation-wide law firm with offices in several states. Some of the attorneys are licensed in more than one state and occasionally travel to work in more than one office. You may be asked to work with attorneys from any of the offices and may have an opportunity to relocate.

Working in the floating position at the office, you learn the procedures for the different types of law practiced by the firm. The firm assigned you a mentor, Joanne Bishop, who spent time helping you understand the office procedures. In addition to working mainly with your supervising attorney, Sharon A. Stensrud, you interact with all the people in the firm, frequently assisting them on various projects.

Jordan, Leone & Sanchez, PLLP, has its main office in Minnesota with branch offices in Detroit, Michigan; Riverside, Illinois; and Golden, Colorado. Below are details such as names, addresses, and phone numbers for each location.

Minnesota Office

Jordan, Leone & Sanchez, PLLP
14937 Fairway Drive
Mankato, MN 56001
Telephone: 507-222-6746
Facsimile: 507-222-6740
Blue Earth County

Minnesota Attorneys

Maria Starzewska, Attorney Identification Number: 0685S6
Amie Roberts, Attorney Identification Number: 00W273
Shamariyah Thompson, Attorney Identification Number: 21G905
Francesca Leone, Attorney Identification Number: 32B641
David L. Nelson, Attorney Identification Number: 007RE96
Jessica Jordan, Attorney Identification Number: 715MY3

Michigan Office

Jordan, Leone & Sanchez, PLLP
200 Agate Lane
Detroit, MI 43203
Telephone: 721-577-0900
Facsimile: 721-577-0905
Wayne County

Michigan Attorneys

Sharon A. Stensrud, Attorney Identification Number: 045X23N
Cynthia McCormick, Attorney Identification Number: 03142V5
Brenda Chin, Attorney Identification Number: 06345T7
James Wong, Attorney Identification Number: 4X37850
Jessica D. Jordan, Attorney Identification Number: 715MY3
Eduardo Sanchez, Attorney Identification Number: 2T4905

Illinois Office

Jordan, Leone & Sanchez, PLLP
1511 Sunflower Lane
Riverside, IL 33211
Telephone: 312-555-1111
Facsimile: 312-555-5123
Cook County

Illinois Attorneys

Jessica D. Jordan, Attorney Identification Number: 715MY3
Brenda Chin, Attorney Identification Number: 06345T7

Colorado Office

Jordan, Leone & Sanchez, PLLP
3966 Bitter Root Concourse
Golden, CO 67203
Telephone: 691-555-9765
Facsimile: 691-555-5230
Douglas County

Colorado Attorneys

Jeremy Smithfield, Attorney Identification Number: 082546

The email format for all offices is:
firstname@jlslaw.emcp.com

Areas of practice at all locations:
- Personal Injury
- Family Law
- Business and Employment Law
- Real Estate
- Criminal
- Appeals
- Estate Planning and Probate
- Bankruptcy

After two years at Jordan, Leone & Sanchez, you have an opportunity to change employment. You like to be involved in community service. While involved in the United Way campaign, you meet the human resources director of Lotton Corporation, who mentions an open position in the legal department. Liking your personality and legal experience, Lotton Corporation offers you a position with an increase of salary and more responsibility. Because this change in employment allows you the opportunity to broaden your skills, you accept the position.

Lotton Corporation is a multi-state corporation specializing in manufacturing of medical devices including artificial joints, prosthetics and necessary supplies. The in-house legal department:
- Sets up business entities necessary for each of the corporation's subsidiaries
- Acquires real estate necessary for expansion of the production and warehouse facilities

- Completes patent and trademark processes
- Creates technical publications related to products
- Creates and manages employment manuals and contracts

The legal department also offers a wide range of legal services to the corporation's hundreds of employees including:

- Estate planning, wills, trusts
- Financial and investment advice
- Real estate services
- Discounted prepaid legal services

The company is located in Texas, which means you will be relocating.

Lotton Corporation
21B Highway 87
Galveston, TX 77658
Telephone: 409-555-7000
Fax: 409-555-7300

Lotton Corporation Attorney
Iris Roma, Attorney Identification Number: 192P67R

Preferred Office Styles

Below are the preferred office styles for both Jordan, Leone & Sanchez, PLLP, and Lotton Corporation. Refer to this section when you have formatting questions while completing exercises and projects.

Letter Format:

- Block letter style.
- Colon after salutation.
- Left justified.
- Set left and right margins to fit letterhead.
- Times New Roman font, 12-point size.
- Set paragraph spacing to 0-point before and after.
- Double space between paragraphs.
- Single space text.
- One space after the period at the end of a sentence.
- Close with "Sincerely," unless otherwise directed.
- Leave 3-4 blank lines after the closing before typing the writer's name.
- Include writer's email address one line below name.

Copy Preferences:

- Courtesy copies to other parties, if instructed
- Enclosures should be itemized in block style and indented .5 inch on all letters

Example of signature block for letters:

Sincerely,

Sharon A. Stensrud
Sharon@jlslaw.emcp.com

SAS:yi (your initials)
Enclosure: (itemized)
      Retainer Agreement
      Medical Authorizations
      Self-addressed return envelope

cc: (if instructed)

Example of correspondence:

Ms. Willa Palmquist
December 9, 20xx
Page 2

If the above-outlined agreement is acceptable to you, sign the atta... acknowledgment of service of process and have your signature not... me in the stamped, self-addressed envelope that I am enclosing.

Sincerely,

Maria Starzewska
Maria@jlslaw.emcp.com

MS:yi
Enclosure:
    Confession of Judgment
    Acknowledgment of Service of Process

cc: Mary Cummins

JORDAN, LEONE & SANCHEZ, PLLP

14937 Fairway Drive
Mankato, MN 56001
P: 507.222.6746
F: 507.222.6740

200 Agate Lane
Detroit, MI 43203
P: 721.577.0900
F: 721.577.0905

1511 Sunflower Lane
Riverside, IL 33211
P: 312.555.1111
F: 312.555.5123

3966 Bitter Root Concourse
Golden, CO 67203
P: 691.555.9756
F: 691.555.5230

Maria Starzewska
Amie Roberts
Shamariyah Thompson
Francesca Leone
David Nelson
Jessica Jordan *
Sharon Stensrud*
Cynthia McCormick
Brenda Chin
James Wong
Eduardo Sanchez
Jeremy Smithfield

*Board Certified as Civil
Trial Specialist by the
National Board of Trial
Advocacy

Reply to: Detroit, MI office
Attorney: Sharon Stensrud
Phone: 721.577.0900
Email:Sharon@jlslaw.com

December 9, 20xx

Ms. Willa Palmquist
611 Seventh Avenue, N.W.
Redmond, IA 45551

Dear Ms. Palmquist:

Re: Smith v. Palmquist
       Our File No.: 9684-4336

This letter follows up our telephone discussion of December 5, 20xx.

I am willing to hold off on further collection activity on this claim, including the report of this matter to the Drivers' License Office, which could result in the suspension of your driving privileges, if you in turn agree to and do in fact do the following:

1. Sign the attached acknowledgment of service of process and confession of judgment.

2. Begin making payments at the rate of $175 per month beginning March 15, 20xx, and continuing on the 15th day of each succeeding month until the entire principal amount owing in the amount of $2,999 (together with any costs or disbursements that may be incurred) has been paid in full together with interest on the unpaid principal amount beginning March 15, 20xx, at the judgment rate of interest which will be approximately six percent per annum.

In the event that you fail to timely make any of the agreed upon installment payments, judgment will be entered against you in the Crow County District Court for the full balance then owing; and the Drivers' License Office will be advised concerning this unpaid judgment, which will most likely result in a suspension of your driving privileges.

Preferences for Court and Non-court Documents

Style for court documents:

- Use local legal style for the venue/caption.
- Set 0-point before and after paragraph spacing.
- Set line spacing to single spacing (shortcut: Ctrl 1) throughout the caption. Enter twice when a double space is needed.
- Use commas after party names.
- Use comma after the word *plaintiff, petitioner, or appellant,* etc.
- Use period after the word *defendant, respondent, or appellee,* etc.
- Double space (shortcut: Ctrl 2) after last line of caption (Defendants).
- Double space all subsequent paragraphs.
- Consider the following when numbering paragraphs:
  - If using Roman numerals, center the numeral on a line alone followed by a period.
  - Double space before and after the numeral.
  - If using Arabic numbers, indent .5 from the left margin, and insert number. Change paragraph indention to first line indent. See example.
- Set to single line spacing at the end of the signature line so that the signer's name is directly under the signature line.
- Adjust spacing throughout to avoid leaving the signature block (signature line, firm name, etc.) on a page by itself, if necessary.

Style for signature block on court documents:

- Use a left block-style signature block starting at the center of the page (do not center).
- Include a date line at the left margin a double space after the last line of the document. Date should always be filled in at the time of signing.

Example of signature block for court documents:

November _____, 20_____

> _____
> Sharon A. Stensrud
> JORDAN, LEONE & SANCHEZ, PLLP
> 200 Agate Lane
> Detroit, MI 43203
> Telephone: 721-577-0900
> Facsimile: 721-577-0905
> Attorney License Number: 045X23N
> ATTORNEY FOR PLAINTIFF

Example of court document:

STATE OF MINNESOTA   IN DISTRICT COURT

COUNTY OF CHIPPEWA   EIGHTH JUDICIAL DISTRICT

                                                          Case Type: Civil-Personal Injury
                                                          Case File No. _____

Jason Neuendorf and Malea Rachel Neuendorf,

      Plaintiffs,

vs.   COMPLAINT

Quentin Pfieffer, as Special Administrator for the
Estate of Wayne Jacks and Alvin Jacks,

      Defendants.

      Plaintiffs, Jason Neuendorf and Malea Rachel Neuendorf, for their causes of action, state and allege:

I.

On or about November 28, 20xx, at or near the intersection of Highway 29 and County Road 13, ...

II.

As a direct and proximate result of the collision, ...

1. Incur losses and expenses for hospitalization and medical treatment;
2. Incur loss of wages, salary and income...

III.

As a direct and proximate result...

IV.

At all times material herein, plaintiffs were and are husband and wife, living and residing together....

      WHEREFORE, plaintiffs, and each of them, demand a judgment against the defendants, and each of them, for a sum in excess of Fifty Thousand and 00/100 Dollars ($50,000.00), together with interest, costs, and disbursements incurred herein.

November _____, 20_____.   _____

                              Jessica D. Jordan
                              JORDAN, LEONE & SANCHEZ, PLLP
                              14937 Fairway Drive
                              Mankato, MN 56001
                              Telephone: 507-222-6746
                              Facsimile: 507-222-6740
                              Attorney License Number: 715MY3
                              ATTORNEY FOR PLAINTIFFS

Style for non-court documents:
- Center title one inch from the top of the page, unless document is a real estate deed or some other document that specifically requires different margins.
- Set one-inch top and side margins on all pages.
- Double space and indent the first line of all paragraphs.
- Format numbered paragraphs using letters or Arabic numbers. See example below.
- Format date and signature block the same as in court document, if signed by an attorney. If signed by a non-attorney, use just a signature line with signer's name below.

Example of non-court document:

LOAN AGREEMENT

THIS AGREEMENT, made and entered into and effective as of this ____ day of _____, 20____, by and among Leopold Lumber Company, Inc., William B. Griffith (individually and as a director and president of Leopold Lumber Company, Inc.), Greg G. Griffith (individually and as a director and vice president of Leopold Lumber Company, Inc.), and Beatrice Griffith (individually and as a director of Leopold Lumber Company, Inc.), (hereinafter cumulatively referred to as "Borrowers") with an office at Pennock, MN 56279, and the Citizens State Bank of Pennock, 701 Main Avenue, Pennock, MN 56279 (hereinafter referred to as "the Bank").

RECITALS

A. Leopold Lumber Company, Inc., is a corporation duly organized and existing under the laws of the State of Minnesota. William B. Griffith, LaTonya Rae Griffith, Greg G. Griffith, and Beatrice Griffith are the sole shareholders and directors of the corporation. William B. Griffith and Greg G. Griffith are also guarantors of the corporation's obligations.

B. Borrowers have from time to time requested the Bank to make various loans and extensions of credit for operating and other purposes. As of August 1, 1992, Borrowers were indebted to the Bank with respect to the following five (5) promissory notes which continue to accrue interest from said date in accordance with their terms:

1. Note No. 282842 (hereinafter referred to as "the Lumberyard Note").
This Note, in the original principal amount of Forty-five Thousand Dollars ($45,000) and dated December 5, 1986, is between Leopold Lumber Company, Inc., and the Bank. It is secured by a Mortgage on the Lumberyard which Mortgage is dated December 5, 1986, and was recorded in the offices of the County Recorder for Kandiyohi County on December 9, 1986, at 4:30 p.m. in Book 891 of Mortgages at page 19-24. The loan matured on December 5, 1991, and has not been extended or renewed. The balance as of October 30, 1992, is Forty Thousand Dollars ($40,000). Borrowers are delinquent in an amount of Forty Thousand Dollars ($40,000). The legal description of the Lumberyard is included in the Mortgage securing the Lumberyard Note, a copy of which is attached as Exhibit A.

2. Note No. 125842 (hereinafter referred to as "the Lumberyard Personal Property Note").
This Note, in the original principal amount of One Hundred Fifty-five Thousand Dollars ($155,000) and dated December 22, 1986, is between Leopold Lumber Company, Inc., and the Bank. It is secured by various personal property of the Borrowers including all inventory, accounts, contract rights, tools, office equipment, machinery, and general intangibles. The Security Agreement is dated June 18, 1984. Appropriate UCC filings (including fixture filings) were made with both the Nicollet County Recorder's Office and the Secretary of State for the State of Minnesota. The security interest in the collateral continues to be valid. In addition, the obligations of the Borrowers under this Note have been further modified by the terms of the Loan Agreement dated February 28, 1987. This Loan matured on December 22, 1991, and has been

in default since then. The balance as of October 30, 1992, is One Hundred Forty-four Thousand Three Hundred Eight and 66/100 Dollars ($144,308.66). Borrowers are delinquent in an amount of One Hundred Forty-four Thousand Three Hundred Eight and 66/100 Dollars ($144,308.66).

3. Note No. 238514 (hereinafter referred to as the "Bowling Alley Note").

This Note, in the original principal amount of Twenty-five Thousand Three Hundred Dollars ($25,300) and dated April 1, 1985, is between William and Greg Griffith and the Bank.

4. Severability.

If one provision of this Agreement is held invalid, that shall not affect any other provision of this Agreement.

IN WITNESS WHEREOF, this Agreement has been duly executed by the undersigned on the date opposite each signature.

LEOPOLD LUMBER COMPANY, INC.

Dated:_____   By:_____

William B. Griffith,
President and Member of the Board of Directors

Dated:_____   By:_____

Beatrice Griffith,
William's Spouse and Member of the Board of Directors of the Leopold Lumber Company, Inc.

CITIZENS STATE BANK OF PENNOCK

Dated:_____   By:_____

Its_____

STATE OF MINNESOTA   )
) ss.
COUNTY OF NICOLLET   )

On this the _____day of _____, 20___, before me the undersigned officer, personally appeared William B. Griffith, Beatrice Griffith, and _____, known to me to be the persons who have signed the foregoing document.

IN WITNESS WHEREOF, I have hereunto set my hand and official seal.

_____
Notary Public

2

How To Deal With Dates In Projects In This Book

In order for the projects in this book to have current dates, figures, examples, student data files, etc., show the date with the year being 20xx. When you complete the exercises and projects, use the current year in which you are completing the project as the document date and when calculating birth dates and other date calculations.

For example, if the current year is 2014 on the Client Information Form, "today's date" would be "current month and day," 2014.

When checking the client's age, use the current year.

- For example, if the form says that the client's birthday is July 1, 1973, verify his age by using the current month, day, and year—2014.
- If the current month and day are before July 1, the client would be 40.
- If the current month and day are July 1or later, the client would be 41.

Practice:

Note: The following date calculation practice is solely for the purpose of determining correct dates for *projects in this textbook*. The process can be applied to real life situations where it is important to verify and use correct dates. Always pay close attention that the dates are true and correct. In the office you would use the true dates of the actual situation.

1. The information below appears on a Client Information Form. Determine the correct year.

   Date and time of accident: Tuesday, July 6, 20__. (two years ago)

   Steps to the correct answer:

   - What is the current year in which you are completing this practice: _____
   - Subtract two years from the current year: _____
   - The result is the year of the accident in this practice: _____

2. The information below appears on a Client Information Form. Determine the year of birth for client Samuelson.

   Date of birth: March 6, _____ (Currently 35 years of age)

   Steps to the correct age:

   - What is the current month and year in which you are completing this practice? _____
   - Subtract 35 years from the current year: _____
   - If the current date is before March 6, how old in client Samuelson today: _____
   - If the current date is after March 6, how old is client Samuelson today:_____

Determining Reminder Dates and Deadlines:

Reminder dates are calculated forward from today's date. Use your personal calendar for the current year or the calendar provided for a project for reference when calculating dates.

You will need to determine reminder dates and deadlines in many instances. When computing time deadlines, ALWAYS review your local rules of court, court orders, agreements, etc., and make a note of any guidelines that apply to the situation, if necessary. When computing due dates for serving documents, do not count the first day from which the time period begins to run; for example, the date a document was served by mail. Time begins to run on the day after a document has been served.

Refer to the certificate of service to determine the date of service. If a response is required to the document you just received and that document was served by mail, some states allow you to add an additional three days to your computation. If the due date for a response falls on a Saturday, Sunday, or legal holiday, or another date on which the court is closed, then the next working day becomes the due date. Include weekends and holidays in your computation. If the time allowed to respond is less than seven days, then exclude weekends and holidays in your computation.

Glossary

You will encounter new vocabulary and terms daily during the course of your career. It would be a good idea to have a notebook handy and keep a list of terms to look up later. If possible, discuss the term with someone else in the office. Find out how to use the term in context with the work that you are doing. Part of being successful means taking the initiative to learn new things and independently read trade-related information or publications—often on your own time. It will help keep your career interesting.

341 meeting A meeting of creditors where the debtor is questioned under oath about his or her financial affairs.

A

abstract of title A document giving evidence of title in the form of a summary of all owners and all transactions since the property began having a recorded history.

acquitted A person is found to be not guilty by a judge or jury.

action in writing The document in which official decisions made by the business are recorded.

action verb A verb that expresses physical or mental action.

addendum A section of an appellate brief that contains an index and copies of the order, judgment, etc., relating to the issues on appeal and offers short excerpts from the record that would be of assistance to the person reading the brief without referencing the appendix.

adjective A word that modifies or describes a noun or pronoun.

admission of service A document used as proof of service when both the petition and the summons are served upon the client's spouse by a process server or sheriff's deputy.

adverb A word that modifies a verb, an adjective, or another adverb.

affiant The person who signs an affidavit.

affidavit A formal sworn statement of fact signed by the affiant (person making the affidavit) and witnessed by a notary public.

affidavit of service A sworn written statement showing proof of service, including the name of the person serving the document (you), the date the document was served, the name of the document served, the method of service, and the name and address where the document was sent.

alternate valuation date The date 6 months after the date of death *or* the date the asset is sold (if earlier).

amicus curiae A Latin word for "friend of the court." A party or organization interested in an issue that files a brief or participates in the argument in a case in which it is not directly involved.

answer A responsive legal document prepared by the defendant or defendant's attorney that admits or denies each allegation or claim made in the complaint and will set out defenses made by the defendant.

answer and counterpetition One of the initial pleadings created by the respondent's attorney that responds to each item in the petition and sets forth what relief the respondent is requesting.

appeal The process of asking a higher court to reverse a verdict, decision, order, final judgment, or other legal ruling of part of all of a previously tried case by a lower court.

appellant The party making the appeal to a higher court to change a judgment made in a lower court.

appellate brief A written argument by either party to the appeal that provides the appellate judges with reasons to rule in favor of the party presenting the brief.

appellate jurisdiction The authority given to higher courts to review and reverse, change, or agree with lower court decisions.

appellee The party responding to an appeal arguing that the ruling of the lower court should stand. Also known as the respondent.

appendix A section of an appellate brief that contains an index and copies of certain documents from the lower court, the notice of appeal, and constitutional challenges.

application for appointment as personal representative A document prepared if the estate is to be administered informally.

application for temporary relief A request to the court asking for an award of temporary custody, temporary child support, temporary spousal maintenance, temporary possession of the home, and other issues as the client's case may dictate.

arbitration A process whereby the parties choose one or more neutral people to listen to both sides of the story and render a decision.

argument Where the attorney cites case law and discusses how the case law supports each party's position on the issues on appeal.

arraignment The accused appears in court to enter a plea of guilty or not guilty.

arrest Taking a person into custody for the purpose of charging him or her with a criminal offense. An arrest is proper and an arrest warrant is issued when a judge has probable cause to believe that the person has engaged in criminal behavior.

article A word that precedes a noun. The most common articles are *a*, *an*, and *the*.

articles of organization The document filed with the state indicating the name and address of the person or persons organizing the business and the business's legal address. This document establishes legal recognition of a limited liability company (LLC). It is known in some states as a certificate of formation.

assets Every form of property owned by a debtor. All assets must be disclosed in the various bankruptcy schedules. An asset may be non-exempt or exempt.

attestation clause A clause at the end of a will in which the witnesses state that the will was signed and witnessed with all the formalities required by law.

automatic stay All lawsuits, foreclosures, garnishments, and collections against the debtor are stopped when the debtor files a bankruptcy petition. Also, all phone calls and letters from creditors to the debtor are stopped if the debtors files for bankruptcy or is represented by an attorney.

average gross monthly amounts Add the gross monthly amounts together for a period of time (e.g., 6 months) and divide by 6 to get the average per month.

B

bail hearing An event that determines if the accused will be released on bail or detained in jail until trial.

bank resolution A statement designating the banking institution for a specific company that conducts financial transactions for the business.

bankruptcy A legal procedure by which individuals and businesses can deal with debt problems.

bankruptcy administrator In some states, another name for a bankruptcy trustee.

bankruptcy code A federal bankruptcy law known as Title 11 of the U.S. Code (11 U.S.C. § 101-1330).

bankruptcy estate All of the debtor's legal and equitable interests in assets and debts at the time of filing bankruptcy.

bankruptcy petition A document filed to open a bankruptcy case. Official forms must be used.

bankruptcy trustee An officer of the court who reviews the debtor's schedules and represents the interest of the creditors; also known in some states as the bankruptcy administrator. The role of the bankruptcy trustee varies under different chapters of bankruptcy. Also known as a U.S. bankruptcy trustee.

basic lender's policy An insurance policy that protects the lender against loss that occurs from a defect in the title for real estate.

basic owner's policy An insurance policy that protects the owner of property against loss that occurs from a defect in the title for real estate.

beneficiary A term used by the Uniform Probate Code to refer to a person who has an interest in a trust. In common usage, *beneficiary* is a generic term that encompasses a person who receives a probate estate by will ("devisee") or intestacy ("heir") as well as one who receives nonprobate assets. Also in common usage, the term *designated beneficiary* means one who receives trust or other nonprobate assets (such as life insurance) by virtue of being designated as beneficiary in a trust, a life insurance policy, or other contract.

bequeath The act of giving an asset by will. (verb)

bequest An asset given by a will. (noun)

beyond a reasonable doubt The level of certainty a juror must have to find a person guilty of a crime.

block-style letter A letter style where all parts of a letter start at the left margin.

bond Insurance that protects the assets of the estate from possible misconduct by a personal representative.

booking An administrative procedure to record the accused person's name, address, telephone number, photograph, fingerprints, and the crime being charged at a police station or other law enforcement facility.

brief printing service A vendor hired to bind, copy, serve, and file the formal appeal brief based on an office's specifications.

business entity A general term for a corporation, limited liability company, institution, or organization.

business law Laws that apply to smaller business entities and cover the various types of organizations a person can use when starting and setting up a new business or changing the structure of an existing business. Also referred to as commercial law.

buzzwords Words or phrases from specialized fields or groups that usually sound important or technical.

bylaws Rules and regulations adopted by a corporation for its internal governance.

C

caption The first section of any written legal pleading (papers) to be filed with the court, which contains the names of the parties involved in the legal situation as well the court name, the title of the case, the number of the case, and the title of the documents (complaint, answer, motion, etc.). Each jurisdiction has its own rules as to the exact format of the caption.

certificate of brief length A document used to indicate the word or line count of a brief as defined in the court's rules.

certificate of formation See articles of organization.

certificate of real estate value A form used in some states to determine the value of the property sold. This value is then used to determine real estate tax values for property taxes to be used to help pay for schools and other concerns.

certificate of representation A document required by the court that lists each party, his or her attorney's names, and all contact information.

certificate of representation A document filed by an attorney with the court indicating the name and contact information for an attorney who represents a party to a lawsuit or indicating pro se party information.

certificate of service Similar to an affidavit of service but not notarized.

certificate of title The actual document that evidences title in Torrens or registered property.

Chapter 7 bankruptcy The most common form of bankruptcy. It gives the debtor a fresh start, as most debts are discharged. It may be filed by individuals, married couples, partnerships, or corporations.

Chapter 9 bankruptcy Reorganization of debt for cities, towns, villages, counties, taxing districts, municipal utilities, and school districts.

Chapter 11 bankruptcy Reorganization of debt for individuals or businesses to pay creditors over time instead of discharging the debts. This has complicated provisions.

Chapter 12 bankruptcy A reorganization plan for family farmers. Debts must fall within certain limits.

Chapter 13 bankruptcy Consolidation of debt and repayment of all or part of the debts over time with no interest charges.

Chapter 15 bankruptcy Deals with cases that cross state borders.

civil lawsuit A legal procedure that covers problems arising between people in the areas of business, contracts, insurance, legal and professional malpractice, estates, domestic relations (family), personal accidents, negligence, and issues that are not criminal in nature.

claimant Another name for plaintiff/petitioner.

client information form A form used to gather personal information about the client.

closing statement A document commonly used in real estate transaction, detailing the fees commissions, insurance, etc., that must take place for a successful transfer of ownership to occur. Also called a settlement statement.

codefendant An additional defendant in a suit.

codicil An addition to a will sometime after the signing of the original will.

collateral (security) Material given by the borrower to guarantee that if the borrower cannot pay, the bank has the right to seize and sell the collateral to covert the amount of the loan.

colloquialisms Informal and sometimes slang expressions that are often specific to a region or specific area.

comma splice When two independent clauses are combined without a coordinating conjunction between them.

common law states A surviving spouse is not automatically entitled to a half interest in all property acquired during the marriage.

community With regard to trusts and estates, two people in a marriage.

community property A form of ownership by a husband and a wife during their marriage that they intend to own together.

community property Property that is acquired by either spouse during the marriage.

community property state Each spouse owns half interest of the marital property and has the right to dispose of his or her half interest in whatever way desired.

comparative form An adjective comparing two nouns.

complaint One of the initial pleadings that requests damages and/or performance by the opposing party. The complaint is the first document to be filed (along with the summons) with the court. It states the factual and legal bases for the claims and must follow statutory requirements as to form.

conditional will A will that goes into effect only when a certain future act or condition happens, not including the testator's death.

confidential domestic relations questionnaire A fact-finding form given to clients to complete.

confidential information form A form required by the court in family law situations where private details are necessary on the forms, such as social security numbers, financial information, bank account numbers, children's names, etc. Private information is provided to the court in this form and should not be included on public documents.

conjunction A word that joins words or groups of words. Common conjunctions are *and, but, for, nor, or, so,* and *yet.*

continuation The process of updating the abstract with any transactions having taken place since the last time the abstract was updated.

contract for deed, land contract, installment sales agreement A contract between a seller and buyer of real property in which the seller provides financing to the buyer of the property for an agree-upon purchase price and interest and the buyer repays the loan in installments. The buyer does not personally get the deed until the final payment is made. Also called a land contract or installment sales agreement.

conveyance (Giving) of the title document is usually require to transfer ownership in the property to another person.

copy typing The act of typing from previously printed or handwritten copy.

corporate law Laws that apply to the governing, finance, mergers, and acquisitions of the big business world and the relationships among corporations, companies, shareholders, boards of directors, and consumers.

corporate minutes A summary of the actions taken by a corporation's board of directors or shareholders, such as information about major purchases by the corporation, hiring/firing, acquisitions, etc.

corporation A separate legal entity from its owners (or shareholders). Owners are not personally liable for losses, debts, or obligations of the business.

counterclaim or cross-action A claim made by the defendant against the plaintiff related to the original complaint.

counteroffer Negotiations between the buyer and the seller before settling on a mutually agreeable price.

court trial A court proceeding at which the judge hears all testimony and makes a final ruling that is binding on the parties.

credit counseling Instruction from a nonprofit agency that individual debtors must attend before filing a bankruptcy petition.

creditor A person or organization to whom the debtor owes money or legal obligation.

creditor matrix A list of the name and address of all creditors to whom the debtor owes money. The matrix must be filed with the bankruptcy petition.

creditors claim period A time period, generally four months after a notice, where creditors file claims against an estate.

criminal lawsuit A lawsuit dealing with crimes against members of the public or state—includes all procedures through charging, trial, and sentencing of the person convicted of the crime.

criminal procedure Legal process for judging if a person has committed a crime or violated laws.

cross-complaint or cross-claim A claim made by an answering party against the plaintiff or against a codefendant by which the answering party states his or her own claim against the other party related to the original complaint.

D

debt Money owed to another. Sometimes called a legal; obligation.

debtor A person or entity who owes money or legal obligations to creditors.

debtor education instruction A program to educate debtors on good personal financial management practices and to counsel them how to avoid debt problems in the future.

decedent A person who has died.

deed An official title document transferring title from one person to another.

defendant The party against whom the lawsuit is started and against whom the complaint is made.

defense attorney The attorney who represents the defendant or accused and protects his or her civil rights.

defense attorney The defendant/respondent's attorney in both civil and criminal actions.

department of commerce An office established within a state to regulate commercial and financial transactions.

deposition An oral examination before trial and during the discovery process in which a witness is placed under oath and asked to answer questions relating to the case at hand.

devise A term used in the Uniform Probate Code as a noun to mean a testamentary disposition of real or personal property and as a verb to mean to dispose of real or personal property.

devisee A person receiving an asset.

devisor A person (decedent) giving an asset.

dischargeable debt Personal liability of the debtor that may be eliminated in bankruptcy.

discovery A fact-finding process that narrows the issues of a lawsuit by discovering information that is not privileged and is relevant to the claim or defense of the parties.

disposable income test Determines if the debtor has enough income left after paying necessary monthly expenses to pay off a portion of unsecured debt.

divorce The legal process of ending a marriage between a man and a woman by a court of law in which grounds or reasons are required.

DNR order Abbreviation meaning "do not resuscitate." That is, do not use mechanical means such as heart support or breathing machines to keep an individual alive.

domicile Where the decedent was living at the time of death.

double jeopardy A law that protects a person acquitted of a crime from being recharged and retried in the future for the same set of facts or circumstances.

down payment Money that is deposited with the seller or the seller's real estate broker when the purchase agreement is signed. Also called earnest money.

durable power of attorney A document that gives decision-making power to another and remains effective even if the maker of the document becomes mentally incompetent or disabled.

E

earnest money See down payment.

easement An official right to use property not belonging to the user. Easements are recorded so that owners and users all have proof of the use of the property.

edit for conciseness Making sure that the document or correspondence communicates clearly and efficiently.

elective share Allows a surviving spouse to claim a portion of the deceased's estate regardless of the will's contents.

employment agreement A document that states the terms of employment, compensation, benefits, and termination of employment.

employment law Laws that govern the relationships between employers and employees.

entity A general term for an organization, to distinguish it from individuals in a lawsuit.

equity state A state in which spouses retain the value of their respective premarital property. Sometimes referred to as a common law state.

estate The property and debt left by a person upon death.

estate administration The process of transferring title of the decedent's assets to heirs.

estate planning A set of tasks intended to manage an individual's assets in the event of incapacitation or death, including the giving of assets to heirs and the settlement of estate taxes.

executor A person responsible for carrying out the directions in a will.

exempt asset Property that a debtor is allowed to retain, free from the claims of creditors who do not have liens on the property.

exemption Property that may legally be excluded from the bankruptcy estate, which the debtor gets to keep after the bankruptcy. Exemptions vary from state to state and are determined by both state and federal statutes. (See also exempt asset, non-exempt asset)

exhibit list A list of documents or evidence a party intends to introduce at trial.

F

face sheet filing (or emergency filing) Often made for the purpose of delaying an eviction or foreclosure or to stop garnishment of wages; a petition filed with incomplete schedules that must be later amended.

fax transmission report A document that shows the fax number of the person served, date and time of the transmission, and the number of pages transmitted.

federal crime A crime that goes beyond state boundaries.

felony A crime serious enough to be punishable by death or incarceration in a state or federal prison for more than 1 year.

FHA-insured loans Financing insured by the government.

fiduciary A person who has been chosen by another to make financial decisions on behalf of that person.

final judgment and decree The final document that resolves all contested issues and terminates the legal proceedings.

final title opinion A title opinion that is created to indicate that all required changes have been made.

findings of fact, conclusions of law, order for judgment, and judgment and decree A document that presents the facts that the judge found to be true and states the conclusions of law that he or she reached regarding those facts. This allows the parties to know how and why the judge reached a decision and whether an appeal is warranted. In a divorce situation, the parties want legal closure, so the judge also includes an order for judgment as well and the final judgment and decree, which is recorded with the county. The divorce is then final.

first-time home buyer loans Financing insured by the government.

fiscal year A period of 12 consecutive months without regard to the calendar year.

formal probate A judicial process required when there are problems with the will that a judge must review, the heirs are not known, the will is missing, there are minor heirs, known heirs do not get along, or problems are expected with the administration of the will. The formal probate process is also required when the estate is insolvent.

front cover The first page of an appellate brief. It indicates the level of the appellate court to which the case is being presented, the court's case number, the case title containing the names of the appellant and respondent, the title of the document, and the contact information for all attorneys involved in the case.

G

grantee The receiver of the deed.

grantor The giver of the deed.

gross pay The total amount of pay earned by an employee before withholding deductions.

grounds The reasons or proof needed to obtain a divorce.

H

handwritten will A will written in the testator's handwriting. Also called a holographic will.

health care directive A document that provides advance instructions regarding care should a person be incapacitated and unable to communicate these decisions directly.

heirs The persons who are entitled by law to inherit the estate if the decedent died without a valid will.

holographic will See handwritten will.

homonyms Words that sound alike and are spelled alike but have different meanings.

homophones Words that sound alike but are spelled differently and have different meanings.

I

idioms Words, phrases, or expressions whose meanings cannot be taken literally.

impartial jury A panel of people selected to serve on a jury who have no prior knowledge of the situation and no preconceived opinions as to the guilt or innocence of the accused. They are selected by the attorneys involved in a case from a random group of citizens.

income The sum of all the forms of earnings received within a certain period.

informal probate A nonjudicial process conducted by a judge, registrar, or other designated person.

informational statement A document that gives the court an idea of the issues involved and when the parties believe they can have certain pretrial tasks completed, such as discovery requests and responses, mediation, and when the parties believe they can be ready for trial.

inheritance law A law that governs the rights of a decedent's survivors to inherit property.

initial pleadings The summon or the petition.

insolvent An estate that has more debts that it does assets.

insurable title A title that can be insured by a title company and is reasonably free from risk of litigation because of possible defects

interested persons All those who are named in the will.

interjection A word used to express emotion. Common interjections are *oh, ah, well, hey,* and *wow.*

interrogatories Written questions used during the discovery process from one party to the other in order to obtain more information about the positions or claims of the parties to a lawsuit.

intervenor An outside party who has some right or interest in a case that already exists between other parties.

intestate Referring to a person who has died without a will.

inventory A document in the probate process that lists all probate assets with their fair market value on the date of death.

irregular verbs Changing the spelling of the verb of the present tense.

irrevocable trust A trust that cannot be changed once it has been created.

issues on appeal The appeal is restricted to the issues addressed or ruled upon in the lower court. No new issues can be brought up in an appeal if they were not addressed in the lower court.

J

joint tenancy A type of ownership in which the decedent owned property with a spouse or other person. Upon the death of one owner, title passes entirely to the other person. The other person is said to have rights of survivorship.

joint tenancy Occurs when two or more people hold title to real estate jointly with equal rights to enjoy the property during their lives.

joint will A will that distributes the property of two or more people, usually a married couple. A joint will is one that two people make together, each leaving all of his or her property and assets to the other. Also called a mutual will.

jurat clause Certification on an affidavit declaring when, where, and before whom it was sworn.

jurisdiction The authority given by law to a court to try cases and rule on legal matters within a particular geographic area and/or over certain types of legal cases.

jury trial A court proceeding that includes a panel of jurors who are chosen by both sides.

L

land sales contract See real estate installment sales contract.

last will and testament An old-fashioned term meaning the same thing as *will*.

lawsuit A legal action brought between two private parties in a court of law.

legal newspaper A newspaper that has been designated by the county to publish legal notices. Legal notices are not to be published in any other newspaper in the county.

legal pleadings The summons and complaint in a lawsuit.

legal specialty certification Certificate verifying that the attorney is held to a higher standard of professional and personal conduct and has sufficient experience and reputation to meet certification standards.

letters of general administration A document giving authority to the personal representative to gather the decedent's assets and pay the expenses of the estate when he or she has died without a will.

letters testamentary A document giving authority to the personal representative to gather the decedent's assets and pay the expenses of the estate when a person dies with a will.

lien The legal claim of one person upon the property of another person to secure the payment of a debt or the satisfaction of an obligation.

limited liability company (LLC) The owners are not generally personally liable for the business's debts and losses.

limited liability partnership (LLP) Usually used by professional groups (such as doctors and lawyers) when the law or rules of ethics do not allow them to use a different business type. Owners of an LLP are not personally liable for the negligence of other partners but do remain liable for their own negligence and for the debts and losses of the business.

linking verb Connects the subject with a word or words in the predicate.

liquidation A sale of property with the proceeds used for the benefit of creditors.

listing agreement A contract that describes the services to be rendered by the real estate agent, describes the property for sale, and sates the terms of payment.

litigant A participant in a lawsuit.

litigation The process of bringing and pursuing a lawsuit to enforce a right.

living will A written health care directive outlining an individual's wishes that is addressed to health care providers concerning health care decisions.

M

marital termination agreement An agreement made by the divorcing spouses regarding the division of property, custody and parenting time, child support, and alimony/maintenance.

marketable title Real estate title that a reasonable purchaser could find no discoverable defects (such as tax liens, mechanic's liens, mortgages, or unpaid assessments).

means test A section of the bankruptcy code that determines under which chapter of the code a debtor may file a petition; determines if a debtor can repay some part of the debt.

mechanic (as in mechanic's lien) A person who has done work on the property, such as a carpenter, plumber, and other construction workers, and wants to be paid before the property is sold to another owner.

mediation An informal, voluntary process in which a mediator, trained in facilitation and negotiation techniques, helps the parties reach a mutually acceptable conclusion outside of court.

medical or health care power of attorney A document that gives an agent the power to make health care decisions.

medical provider An institution or individual who has rendered health care of any type to persons involved in litigation at any time during their lives.

medical record summary An itemized listing of each date of treatment, the treatment facility or doctor, and the type of treatment received by an individual. Also called a résumé.

meeting of creditors A meeting at which the debtor is questioned under oath by the trustee about assets and liabilities. Also called a 341 meeting.

members and board of governors The governing body in a limited liability company.

metadata Hidden electronic data in a document that can reveal confidential information, such as who created or revised the document, the dates of the revisions, the number of revisions, and redlined (deleted) material, tracked changes, or comments made while editing different versions of the document.

minute/record book An official book containing permanent and detailed records of the resolutions adopted at the official meetings of the business as well as all organizational documents.

misdemeanor A lesser crime punishable by fine, county jail time of less than 1 year, probation, or community service.

mortgage The document that pledges property to the lender to secure the payment of a debt.

mortgagee The bank that take the mortgage document (and title to property) as security for lending money to the mortgagor.

mortgagor The person borrowing money and pledging property as security.

motion A written request to the court.

motion for temporary relief A document that allows the court to consider an award of temporary custody, temporary child support, temporary spousal maintenance, temporary possession of the home, and other issues as the client's case may dictate.

motion in limine A pretrial motion requesting that information which might be prejudicial not be allowed to be heard in a case. Also called a motion to suppress evidence.

multiple listing service (MLS) A marketing database set up by a group of cooperating real estate brokers. This service provides accurate and structured data about properties for sale. It also is a mechanism for listing brokers to offer compensation to buyer brokers who bring a buyer for their listed property.

N

net pay The amount of pay an employee takes home after deductions are made from gross pay.

no-asset case No assets are available to satisfy unsecured claims.

no-fault dissolution of marriage A legal process for terminating a marriage in any way by annulment, usually on a no-fault basis.

no-fault divorce system A system of law whereby the dissolution of a marriage does not require an allegation or proof of fault of either party to be shown.

noncompetition agreement A document that restricts the employee's work activities after termination of employment with the company. It protects the company's trade secrets, client lists and other confidential matters.

non-court documents The documents that do not have court captions and in general, are not signed by an attorney. Examples include promissory notes, leases, and contracts.

non-dischargeable debt A debt that cannot be eliminated in bankruptcy. The debt remains legally enforceable.

non-exempt asset Property of a debtor that can be liquidated to satisfy claims of creditors.

non-probate assets Real property owned with a spouse or another person with joint tenants with rights of survivorship (or with a spouse as "tenants by the entirety" in some states.

notice of appeal A written notice to the lower court and all parties and attorneys involved in a case that the losing party wishes to have a higher court review the decision made in the lower court.

notice of commencement of case A notice sent by the court to the debtor and creditor after the bankruptcy petition is filed. It lists the time of the 341 meeting and deadlines.

noun A word that names a person, place, thing, or idea.

O

objective case pronoun A word used when it is the direct or indirect object of a verb, the object of a preposition, or the object of an infinitive.

omnibus hearing Determines the admissibility of testimony and evidence seized at the time of arrest.

operating agreement A document that outlines how a business will function.

oral argument An attorney's opportunity to orally summarize his or her part of the case in a limited time.

oral will A will spoken at the time of imminent death that is recognized only in certain states.

order A command of a court or judge, normally made or entered in writing, that determines some point or directs some step in the proceedings.

P

paid time off (PTO) Includes vacation time, sick days, personal leave days, holidays, regular working hours, and overtime hours.

partnership Formed by multiple owners who have chosen not to be set up as a formal corporation or limited liability company. The owners are personally liable for any losses, debts, or judgments against the partnership.

performance Specific actions to be taken by a party, such as completing items required in a contract.

perpetual calendar Fourteen 1-year calendars with a table to show which calendar to use for a particular year.

personal property Movable property, which may or may not have a title.

personal representative In the Uniform Probate Code, personal representative is a generic term to replace the masculine and feminine names for one designated in a will ("executor" and "executrix" or "testator" and "testatrix") and one not named in a will ("administrator" and "administratix"). Unfortunately, the term "personal representative" is also sometimes used to include other fiduciary positions such as Guardian or Conservator.

petition A written request to the court asking for an order of the court. Petitions include writs, orders to show cause, modifications of previous orders, continuances, request to dismiss a case, reduction of bail in criminal matters, decrees for distribution of an estate, appointment of a guardian, and family law matters.

petition for appointment as personal representative A document that is filed with the court to initiate a formal probate proceeding.

petitioner Party who starts the dissolution of marriage, as opposed to plaintiff in states that require proof of fault. Another name for petitioner/claimant.

plaintiff The person or entity making a complaint or accusing another party of committing a crime.

plaintiff's attorney The attorney for the person bringing the complaint in a civil action.

plea The defendant's answer to a charge (guilty, not guilty).

plea agreement The negotiated disposition of a case where a defendant may plead guilty to lesser charges or plead guilty to some of the charges if other charges are dropped.

positive form An adjective comparing one person or thing.

possession A right that often accompanies ownership but is not necessarily sufficient to prove it.

possessive case pronoun Used when the pronoun shows ownership.

pre-bankruptcy counseling Used to determine the debtor's financial status prior to filing the bankruptcy petition.

preliminary hearing A hearing at which the prosecutor must present enough evidence to convince the judge that a crime has been committed.

preliminary title opinion A title opinion that states the current condition of the title.

preposition A word that shows the relationship between its object—a noun or a pronoun—and another word in a sentence. Common prepositions include *after*, *around*, *at*, *behind*, *beside*, *off*, *through*, *until*, *upon*, and *with*.

preresiduary gift Assets or money given to heirs or beneficiaries as stated in the will and distributed after all debts of the estate are paid but before the payment of residuary bequests.

presentence investigation A report prepared by a probation department to assist in sentencing. It may contain details about prior convictions and arrests, work history, and family circumstances.

priority The order in which certain liens and encumbrances must be paid.

pro se A person who represents himself without the assistance of an attorney is acting pro se.

pro se representation Advocating on one's own behalf.

probable cause Reasonable belief that a crime was committed and that the accused person committed the crime.

probate A legal process needed for the orderly transfer of possession and/or title to the decedent's property to the decedent's heirs.

probate assets Property titled in the decedent's name alone, without a "payable on death" or other beneficiary designation.

probate deed A deed executed by the executor (personal representative) of an estate when the executor conveys the real estate owned by the decedent.

process server Anyone who delivers legal pleadings to the appropriate parties. This person could be a law enforcement officer or private party not involved in the lawsuit who is at least 18 years of age.

promissory note A contract stating that a person or entity owes money to another person or entity. May be secured or unsecured.

pronoun A word used in place of a noun.

proof of service A document that shows name of the person serving a document, the date the document was served, the method of service, and the names and address to which the document was sent.

prosecuting attorney This attorney represents the plaintiff. Also called district attorney or U.S. attorney.

prosecutor The person (attorney) appointed by the government to prosecute all criminal offenses.

public defender or court-appointed attorney An attorney appointed by the court if defendant cannot afford to pay a private attorney.

purchase agreement A legal, binding agreement between the buyer and seller setting out price and terms of sale. Also called a real estate contract, bid, binder, or offer to purchase.

Q

quitclaim deed A deed that transfers or "quit" any interest a person may have in property.

R

reaffirm Allows a debtor to continue to make payments on debts if the debtor wishes to keep the property, or the property can be sold at fair market value.

reaffirmation agreement An agreement to continue paying a dischargeable debt, such as an auto loan, after the bankruptcy in order to keep property that might otherwise be repossessed. The creditor may repossess or sue if the debtor does not continue to pay the debt.

real estate agent An individual who is licensed to negotiate and arrange real property sales and works under the authority and supervision of a real estate broker. Also called a real estate professional.

real estate broker A person who is licensed and authorized to hire and supervise real estate agents and manage a brokerage business.

real estate closing The meeting that is the final step in executing or finishing a real estate transaction. Also called a settlement.

real estate closing in escrow A closing process in which a third party takes over the duty of holding the money, the signed deed, and arranges for the title transfer.

real estate installment sales contract An agreement between the seller and buyer indicating the purchase price and method of payment made directly to the seller, as well as other rights and duties. Also called a land sales contract or a contract for deed.

real estate legal description The official description of property written by the county recorder in a county to indicate the official location of the property.

real property Land and anything attached to it, such as a building. Also called real estate.

realtor See real estate broker.

reciprocal will A mirror image of a will made by another person—usually a spouse.

recording The process of recording written documents pertaining to real estate in the public record, which is generally the courthouse of the county in which real estate is located.

redact (verb) The process of editing a document to remove confidential references or offensive material.

redundancies Repetitive words or phrases that do not add useful meaning to a sentence.

regular verb Adding *ed* to the present tense of a verb.

request for documents and things A document used during the discovery process requesting the other party to produce copies of items such as photographs, maps, statements, and so on.

request for inspection of property A document used during the discovery requesting an inspection of property to verify certain claims.

request for medical reports A document used during the discovery process requesting copies of medical information to support a claim of injury or lost wages.

requests for admission A request made during the discovery process that relates to the pending action only and asks that the truth of certain matters regarding statements, opinions of fact, or the genuineness of documents be either admitted or denied by the opposing party.

residuary bequests A bequest that gives money or assets to heirs after the debts are paid and preresiduary gifts are distributed.

resolution A formal business decision made by a company.

respondent Party who responds to the documents served in a dissolution of marriage as opposed to defendant in states that require proof of fault. Another name for defendant.

response In some cases the answer may also be called a response.

responsive document A document that responds to other discovery requests, answering questions or providing things.

responsive pleading Any court document that is created in response to another document.

revocable trust A trust that can be changed after the trust is created.

rider A document that is attached to an existing document stating additional terms or condition relating to the existing document.

rules of appellate procedure Specific rules and procedures to be followed during the appeal and the deadlines for performing certain actions.

Rules of Court A book used as reference for details and rules that maintains fairness in the administration of cases and controls expenses and unnecessary delay in proceedings.

Rules of Evidence A book used as reference for details and rules that maintains fairness in the administration of cases and controls expenses and unnecessary delay in proceedings.

run-on sentence A term used to describe what happens when two sentences are run together without punctuation between them.

S

sanction A penalty or punishment attached to a court order or law so that it is followed.

schedules Detailed lists of the debtor's assets, liabilities, and financial information. Bankruptcy schedules A through J are official forms.

secretary of state The office in some states that is responsible for the administering the election laws, the Uniform Commercial Code records, and business filings.

secured debt Debt secured by collateral or lien, such as a home mortgage, lien against a vehicle, security interest, Uniform Commercial Code (UCC) filing, or tax lien. A secured claim must be perfected to be treated as such in the bankruptcy action.

secured promissory note A promissory note in which the lender is lending money based upon cash flow as well as other assets that could be sold to cover the amount of the debt.

secured property A tangible asset such as a home or vehicles included in secured debt.

sentence A group of words that contains a subject and a predicate. The subject is a noun or pronoun, and the predicate is the main verb phrase. The sentence is a complete thought.

sentence fragment A group of words that may contain a subject and a verb and may be punctuated like a complete sentence, but do *not* contain a complete thought.

sentencing The penalty ordered by the court.

settlement statement See closing statement.

simple will A will that leaves an entire estate to one or more named beneficiaries. No portion of the estate is left in trust.

sole ownership The ownership by an individual or entity legally capable of holding title.

sole proprietorship The business and its owner are considered one and the same and there is usually only one owner. If the business is sued or defaults on a debt, the owner is fully responsible for any losses, debts, or judgments against the business.

speedy trial A defendant's constitutional right to be tried for alleged crimes within a reasonable time after being arrested. Most states have laws that set forth the time by which a trial must take place after charges are filed.

state crime An action or lack of action that breaks the criminal laws of a state.

statement of intention A statement concerning plans for dealing with debts secured by property of the bankruptcy estate. This is an official form.

statutory will A will that contains standard terms provided by state law.

stay of execution A temporary delay in the carrying out of an order (execution) based on certain conditions.

stipulation An informal, voluntary process in which a mediator, trained in facilitation and negotiation techniques, helps the parties reach a mutually acceptable conclusion.

subjective case pronoun Used when the pronoun is the subject of a sentence or the subject of a verb in an independent or dependant clause.

subpoena A legal document ordering a person to appear as a witness.

substitute service Leaving the documents with an adult resident of the defendant's home or with a designated agent or person authorized to accept service on a business.

successor The person who officially takes over or fills in for another after death.

summons A document that notifies the defendant of a lawsuit and includes instructions about the length of time within which the defendant must respond.

superlative form An adjective comparing three or more nouns.

supervised The formal probate process whereby the court must approve distributions to heirs.

T

table of authorities A categorized outline of all legal cases, statutes, and precedents upon which the brief writer relies to support the parties' arguments to the court and lists the page numbers on which each case, etc., appears in the brief.

table of contents A section in a brief that outlines each element of the brief and lists the page numbers on which each element is found.

tax identification numbers A set of numbers that are used to identify a business.

tenancy in common Two or more persons who hold title to real estate jointly with equal rights to enjoy the property during their lives.

tenants by entirety Ownership in real estate under the fictional assumption that husband and wife are one person for legal persons.

testate Referring to a person who has died leaving behind a valid will.

testator Historically, a man making a will. Modern legal writers use it to refer to either a man or a woman making a will.

testatrix An obsolete word meaning a woman making a will.

title The legal right to own, possess, use, control, enjoy, and dispose of real estate.

title company A firm that verifies ownership of real property, often done in connection with a conveyance of real property from buyer to seller.

title opinion An attorney's professional judgment of the owner's rights to the property following a title search by the attorney.

title policy an insurance policy that protects the owner of property or the lender against loss that occurs from a defect in the title for real estate.

title search A search of the public records to determine the status of a title, including any encumbrances, liens, mortgages, and future interests affecting the property.

Torrens or registered property A system for land titles under which a court directs the issuance of a certificate of title upon application by the landowner.

transcription The process of typing a written text from an audiotape, video, DVD, or digital recording.

trial by judge An examination of the evidence by which a judge makes all decision. Also known as a bench trial or court trial.

trial by jury An examination of the evidence in a lawsuit by a panel of impartial citizens chosen by the parties to hear the evidence. The jury makes decisions which are then applied by the judge.

trust A legal entity that holds assets for the benefit for another.

trustee A person who holds legal title to property and has broad powers over its maintenance and investment.

trustee deed A deed executed by a person serving as a trustee; for example, a trustee deed is often used by a trustee in bankruptcy to sell real property of the debtor.

trustor A trust maker, grantor, donor, or settlor.

U

Uniform Probate Code (UPC) A standard comprehensive set of laws, adopted in whole or in part by various states, that regulate the administration of estates, including wills and trusts.

unsecured debt Debts for which credit was given without security or collateral.

unsecured promissory note A promissory note in which the lender is lending money based solely upon the signer's cash flow.

unsupervised Describes a personal representative who does not need court approval for distributions before closing the estate.

V

VA-guaranteed loan A loan that is financially insured by the government.

venue A geographic location that is the proper or most convenient location for trial of a case.

verb A word that expresses action or a state of being.

W

warranty deed The most secure type of deed from the buyer's perspective.

will A document spelling out what is to be done with person's assets after he or she has died.

witness list A list of people a party intends to call to testify at trial.

wordy phrases A word phrase that can typically be replaced with a one-word alternative.